Scientists of the Mind

Scientists of the Mind

Intellectual Founders of Modern Psychology

CLARENCE J. KARIER

University of Illinois Press

URBANA AND CHICAGO

This book is printed on acid-free paper.

Library of Congress Cataloging in Publication Data

Karier, Clarence J.
  Scientists of the mind.

  Includes index.
  1. Psychologists—History—Addresses, essays, lectures.
  2. Psychology—Addresses, essays, lectures.   I. Title.
BF81.K34   1986   150'.9   85–996
ISBN 0–252–01182–1 (alk. paper)

Illustrations by Nancy B. Karier

Dedicated to

Fred
Kathy
Tom
and
Nan

Preface

This book had its origins in seminars I held at the University of Rochester during the 1960s and at the University of Illinois in the early 1970s. The subject was the nature of human nature. Students came to those seminars from history, philosophy, psychology, education, literature, and guidance and counseling, as well as religious studies. What emerged was an intellectually rich, exciting dialogue about human nature.

As we intensively searched the writings of such notable Western thinkers as Sigmund Freud, Karl Marx, Fyodor Dostoyevski, Franz Kafka, Albert Camus, Martin Buber, Jean-Paul Sartre, William James, John B. Watson, and John Dewey, among many others, for clues as to how each defined human nature, we became more critically aware of the role that the discipline of psychology had come to play in defining what the modern person considered his or her own nature to be. We also became more conscious of many of the hidden religious and philosophical assumptions that lay at the heart of the discipline of psychology itself. Thus, we became increasingly sensitive to the delicate relationship that existed between what we perceived to be psychological assumptions about human nature and our own philosophical and religious commitments. Out of these thoughtful seminar exchanges arose the basic conceptualization of this book.

The idea that the psychological society today exists coterminously with the theological society, and that the former developed from the latter, began to crystallize during our discussions. More and more we realized that just as every religious movement in the past had defined human nature in a particularly distinctive way, so too did virtually every psychological movement. Lastly, out of these seminars came the realization that a critical biographical approach to key leaders of psychology in its formative years might help shed light on some of the philosophical and religious assumptions implicitly operating within various modern schools of psychology.

I am, therefore, first and foremost indebted to the many students who participated in such fruitful dialogue, in and around those seminars, over the years; I thank them for their many critical insights which helped me shape this book. I acknowledge as well the faculty members of both institutions who contributed to that ongoing dialogue. I am very much aware that many of these individuals—students and faculty—would not wholly agree with the final outcome; yet, if we remain true to our beliefs, that is as it should be. I, of course, accept full responsibility for the book's limitations.

Dean William Fullagar of the University of Rochester and Deans J. Myron Atkin and Joe Burnett of the University of Illinois provided the administrative support which made possible the development of this work; they have my sincere thanks. In doing research for this manuscript I have incurred the debt of Peter Sola, Stephen Yulish, Lauren Weisberg, Spiro Rasis, Stuart McAninch, and Geoffrey Lasky. I also am most grateful to Chris Shea and Gini Hennen for generously sharing their archival research with me.

In writing this manuscript I was most encouraged by the supportive comments of Merle Curti on both the James and Hall chapters. I also found very helpful the many incisive suggestions I received on the various chapters read by Ann Keppel, Jim Anderson, Paul Violas, Ralph Page, Philip Steedman, Tim O'Hanlon, Tim Reagan, Mary Leach, Marion Metzow, Terry Denny, Charles Burgess, and Merle Borrowman. Harry Broudy provided a particularly insightful reaction to the Freud chapter, as did Tom Hastings and Bob Stake. I am indebted as well to Steve Tozer, not only for critically reading portions of the manuscript, but for providing expert translations from the German when needed. To Judy Mogilka I owe a significant debt, both for her research assistance and her thoughtful editorial comments on the final manuscript. And I greatly appreciate the work Barbara Franklin and Ruth Burnham did in typing the manuscript.

I acknowledge here the Spencer Foundation, the University

of Illinois Research Board, and the University of Illinois College of Education for providing the research funding that allowed me to develop this book. For permission to reproduce previously published material, I recognize the editors and publishers of the *Psychoanalytic Review*, the *Journal of Aesthetic Education*, the *Journal of Libertarian Studies*, and the *Journal of the History of Ideas*, as well as Pergamon Press and the Aberdeen University Press. I also am grateful for permission to use portions of materials drawn from the University of Chicago Archives, the Clark University, the Alan Mason Chesney Medical Archives of the Johns Hopkins Medical Institutions, and the General Education Board Archives.

Lastly, I wish to thank my daughter, Nancy, for the artwork in the book; and my wife, Norma, for her splendid support, advice, and encouragement, without which this work would not have been possible.

Introduction

Shortly after the beginning of this century, Hermann Ebbinghaus remarked that psychology "has a long past, but a short history."[1] What Ebbinghaus probably had in mind was that, although psychology had a long past as a significant component of philosophy and religion, it was not until 1879, when Wilhelm Wundt established the first experimental psychological laboratory in Leipzig, that psychology came to be expressly regarded as a distinct discipline. In America, a similar development occurred around 1890 when William James published his influential two-volume work *The Principles of Psychology*. The twenty-year period from 1890 until 1910, when James died, represents the formative years for the establishment of psychology as a separate academic discipline in America. During this period psychology departments at many major American universities emerged as separate units from the parent discipline of philosophy. This was also the period when many of the field's major professional societies and journals came into existence. By 1920 various discrete schools of psychology were fairly well established in both America and Europe—notably, behaviorism in America and psychoanalysis in Europe.

Significant portions of psychology's "long past" had roots that, for the West, were deeply embedded in Judeo-Christian moral philosophy and theology. The important questions, as posed by a present-day critic of Western psychology, Thomas S. Szasz—How does man live? and How ought man to live?[2]—were still considered to be answerable within the domains of philosophy and religion for much of the nineteenth century, as they had been for previous ages. If we search the past for what today might be termed "psychological knowledge," that is, knowledge concerning the human condition, invariably we must turn to philosophy texts, church sermons, theological tracts, rabbinical discourses and/or biblical commentaries, as well as literary works of the period.[3] Such sources contain much of the record of how Western civilization came to conceive of human nature, as well as of the good life toward which the individual ought to aspire. That body of work also contains ideas about how men and women learn and how they ought to interpret their day-to-day living experiences.

The Judeo-Christian civilization of the West evolved out of a number of theologically based beliefs which permeated the generally accepted assumptions about the human condition. These beliefs about human nature were often rationalized from the crucial belief in the existence of a personal God, which was the keystone of the Judeo-Christian arch of civilization in its broadest cosmological form. In general, that theistic perspective of the cosmos which came to dominate the early Middle Ages maintained itself not only through the stormy challenges of Aristotelian naturalism of the twelfth and thirteenth centuries and the humanistic naturalist criticism of the Renaissance, but it managed to survive the trauma of the Protestant Reformation as well as the birth of capitalism itself. In short, while the religious beliefs of the West were changing, the basic cosmology around which Judeo-Christian theological society functioned remained well intact throughout the seventeenth and eighteenth centuries.

God appeared to be alive and well in much of colonial America. Despite the threatening secular winds of the Enlightenment, the theological society, with its moral demand system of the Ten Commandments, remained the code by which many people in America attempted to live. As such, it was a well-developed social system which not only presumed the existence of God but embodied both the rational and emotional guidelines for much human activity, and thereby provided the framework for a comprehensive way of life.

The growing secularization of the West ultimately proved to be the greatest threat to that way of life. While the secular beliefs of eighteenth-century Enlightenment leaders had their impact, and the secular beliefs of nineteenth-century scientific thinkers also took their toll, it was not until the twentieth century that another, more comprehensive, fully secularized view of life emerged. Within such a worldview the theological society would be severely challenged, and alternative, competing ways of life would be fully established. Over the past three centuries of American history, the theological society has responded repeatedly to the dangers of this growing secularization through periodic evangelical reawakenings, passionately and emotionally recalling the faithful back to the ways of God. An example of such reawakening, which occurred shortly before the outbreak of the American Revolution, was the "Great Awakening" initiated by Jonathan Edwards, the last of the Puritan divines.

The theological society as reflected in colonial America was, for the most part, well in place when Edwards's voice was heard thundering across the New England landscape, calling his parishioners' attention to the painful consequences awaiting "sinners in the hands of an angry God."[4] As images of spiders and beastly devils danced across the minds of his congregation, their heightened consciousness caused some to surrender themselves to "ecstasies that left them writhing on the floor of the meeting-house, or found them clasped in the arms of their neighbors' wives or daughters."[5] Joseph Hawley, Sr., was so moved to despondency as to cut his own throat.[6] These extreme, bizarre events in Northampton were ignited by the passionate flames that seared the conscience of New England during the Great Awakening. Such was the evangelical rebirth which from time to time would reawaken theological men and women to the will of their God. For Edwards, these events were moments in the "History of Redemption," the history of God's will at work in the world.

Jonathan Edwards was far more than a skillful preacher who could readily drive his congregation into an emotional frenzy. He was also the last of the great Puritan divines whose theological views perhaps best symbolized the meanings embedded in theology's conception of human nature and the social order. As Edwards charted the relationship of God to the individual, he explicitly answered the questions, How does man live? and How ought man to live? The moral demand system of his theological man, coupled with keen psychological insight into the human soul, reverberates throughout Edwards's work. While he was undoubtedly one of America's leading theologians, he was also one of its leading purveyors of psychological knowledge, as much a physician to the natural psyche as to the spiritual soul. To Edwards, each was simply a component of a unified human condition.

Edwards repeatedly and forcefully preached against the Arminian heresy, in which he sensed a dangerous challenge to his theological worldview. The Arminian heresy, like the Pelagian heresy of St. Augustine's time, assumed far too much human freedom in controlling one's own destiny. The suggestion that men and women might achieve salvation through their own efforts worried Edwards more than anything else, and led him to conjure up some of his most vivid pictures of eternal damnation. He both rationally and intuitively sensed that the road from fifth-century Pelagian heresy to eighteenth-century Arminianism and Deism would eventually threaten his own theological worldview: the secularization of culture with a scientifically based, rather than a theologically based, explanation for all human phenomena. More than most, Edwards clearly sensed this danger, not because he hated the scientific thinking of his day, but rather because he personally was attracted to it. He understood John Locke and Isaac Newton well, and many of his most poignant theological arguments adopted an inductivist methodology. Like a moth to a flame, so was Edwards attracted to science. Ironically, he was to die of a self-injected small-pox vaccination that went awry.

Even though eighteenth-century Enlightenment philosophers tended to secularize the Christian virtues of faith and hope in terms of science and progress, the greatest impact of their ideas, which swirled around Edwards, had not yet materialized. A century later, Auguste Comte, in his development of the law of human progress, as expressed in *Positive Philosophy*,[7] suggested a view of humanity evolving through three stages of progress: "the Theological, or fictitious; the Metaphysical, or abstract; and the Scientific, or positive."[8] Comte prophesied that the twentieth century would be one of science, in which not only physical nature would be forced to lay open its secrets, but human nature itself would become scientifically comprehensible. Thus, a science of the individual and society would provide the positive knowledge necessary to create those institutions which could lead human beings out of the bondage of "theological fiction" and "metaphysical egotism."

In the broadest sense, the eighteenth-century idea of progress found expression in nineteenth-century German idealism, French positivism, and English Darwinism. While Comte wrote about a positive "science of humanity," Charles Darwin directed his efforts to "scientifically" describing *The Origin of the Species* and *The Descent of Man*, and Karl Marx wrote of a scientific view of humanity that might break the chains of illusion which

4

still bound humanity in a theological society. Dostoyevski, by contrast, argued that although "science" might provide us with bread, it could not provide us with purpose—hence the debilitation of humankind. The masses, he suggested, crave the security of absolute belief—they love their chains. As his Grand Inquisitor noted, "There are three powers, only three powers that can conquer and capture the conscience of these impotent rebels forever, for their own happiness—those forces are miracle, mystery and authority."[9] Such was his disclaimer as to the possibility of science ever achieving humankind's liberation. The thinking of the Grand Inquisitor was to reappear in the shimmering half-light of the twisted corridors of twentieth-century false consciousness, all too often in the name of the science of psychology. As the twentieth century wore on, some continued to look to science as the panacea for all that ailed humanity, while others saw it as the instrument by which new and more effective chains might be forged.

Even before Marx and Dostoyevski were lowered into their graves, Herbert Spencer had embraced the ruthlessly competitive spirit of an emerging industrial capitalism by rationalizing the plight of the poor as indicative of a "Natural Law"—the survival of the fittest. As America became the land of "social Darwinism," survival of the fittest came to justify virtually any privation. The rattling chains of this social Darwinian doctrine eventually could be heard in the corporate board rooms, the soup kitchens, and the breadlines that all came to mark distinctively the urban landscape of twentieth-century American industrial capitalism.

Neither the biological sciences nor the social sciences were, it seems, immaculately conceived. Friedrich Nietzsche observed, most perceptively, that "over the whole of English Darwinism there hovers something of the odor of humble people in need and in straits."[10] There is considerable evidence to suggest that both Alfred Wallace and Darwin derived their important metaphoric thesis of survival of the fittest by reading Thomas Malthus's essay "The Principle of Population as It Affects the Future Improvement of Society" (1778).[11] In that essay, Malthus himself rationalized the plight of the poor by raising the "principles" of scarcity, struggle, and survival to the level of self-governing natural laws. It is important to note that the "principle" of survival of the fittest seems to have been derived initially from observing the suffering, diseased poor in the growing slums of England's new urban industrial centers, not from observing life in the laboratory or on the deck of the *Beagle*. Although this metaphoric "principle" was used by Darwin to explain the biological evolution of different species, the metaphor came home to roost in social Darwinism, as it was propounded by Herbert Spencer and William Graham Sumner, and subsequently countered by Lester Frank Ward. Perry Miller once remarked that America of the twentieth century has never fully made up its mind as to the veracity of this metaphor, as exemplified by Sumner and challenged by Ward. In many ways, these contradictory views can readily be discerned as operational in American political-social history throughout the century.

Darwinian evolutionary theory in the latter half of the nineteenth century heavily influenced the Western, and in particular the American, view of the social order since it reinforced the belief that the spirit of capitalism was, so to speak, in tune with nature itself. However, Darwin's theories helped rationalize more than just economic and social views—they changed humankind's view of itself. Both Aristotle and Darwin, as biologists, profoundly shaped Western consciousness. The Aristotelian classifications of physical, biological, and mental reality, which managed to withstand the wear and tear of centuries of dialogue and discourse, had fallen on hard times by the latter half of the nineteenth century. Aristotle had perceived the mind as possessing faculties that functioned as total expressions of the human organism; by the end of the nineteenth century, these faculties were understood by many to be discrete muscles in need of exercise. This nineteenth-century version of faculty psychology would have been rejected by Aristotle himself. Nevertheless, the overarching conception of human nature—held by most Western theorists prior to Darwin—invariably carried Aristotelian assumptions concerning human life as being fundamentally distinct from animal life, a distinctness predicated on the human faculty of reason.

The attack on faculty psychology, which began in the closing decades of the nineteenth century and was fully developed in the twentieth century, was undergirded by a new psychology which had embraced Darwin's view of humans as propounded in *The Origin of the Species* and *The Descent of Man*. New conceptions of mind and of "reason" were being proposed, and with them came a new conception of human nature and the place of human beings within nature itself. As the secure world of Aristotelian psychology, which had been effectively integrated into Christian cosmology by St. Thomas Aquinas and others, began to be called into question, so too was the Judeo-Christian creationist metaphor for the origin of the species. The arguments about the theory of evolution, which continue throughout the twentieth century, were at heart fundamental arguments involving key elements of culture. The older philosophical and theological metaphors with respect to human nature, its origins, and its place in the universe, were called into question by an increasingly potent, secular scientific conception.

By the end of the nineteenth century, debates about evolution could be heard resounding from lecture halls, pulpits, and newsrooms across America. The flames of impassioned beliefs were fanned by the winds of progress, as a technological growth unprecedented in the known history of humanity seemed capable of sweeping aside any obstacle. Under these circumstances, some thought of utopian futures, others talked of the transvaluation of culture, and still others mistook the end of the century for the end of the world. Henry Adams nostalgically sensed the depth of change that was occurring, and created his own metaphors of "the Virgin" and "the Dynamo" to symbolically describe the lost, theological "other"-wordly view and the rise of "this" world's new scientific secularism. It is clear that a new, "scientific" view of human nature and culture was assuming a commanding lead over the previously dominant theological worldview.

The term "science" itself became increasingly confused. Earlier in the nineteenth century it was often used to describe any body of organized knowledge—for example, the science of theology. Some continued to use the term in this older sense throughout the century, while others restricted the term exclusively to that process by which certain knowledge might be validated by a rigorous experimental test. To others, science meant simply a method of problem solving, while still others used the term to encompass virtually all practical, useful knowledge. With the "miracles" of technological progress vividly present in their daily consciousness, the terms "science" and "technology" for many became not only linked but virtually synonymous.

An increasing respect for the term "science" has characterized the secular mind in the twentieth century and was perhaps nowhere better reflected than in the theme of the 1933 Chicago World's Fair, fittingly titled "The Century of Progress" and subtitled "Science Explores: Technology Executes: Mankind Conforms."[12] In effect, "science" came to be a sanctifying term; in which redemption was to be found (contrary to the theological orientation, which held that only God and his grace promised redemption).

7

According to the secular mind, men and women would be redeemed from their pain and suffering through the efforts of science. The pain of guilt from sin, suffered at the hands of God in the older theological society, was, in a variety of ways, transformed in the secular psychological society of the twentieth century into the pain and suffering of an anxiety neurosis. Certainly, Sigmund Freud and others saw science as offering, at best, only a limited redemption; the secular scientific mind, while it embraced science, often scaled down its redemptive expectations. As such a sci-entifically minded figure, Freud wrote, "No, our science is no illusion. But an illusion it would be to suppose that what science cannot give us we can get elsewhere."[13]

Marx and Freud both sought to "free men" or "redeem them" from the chains of their illusions. While Marx, the "scientific" social theorist, sought to uncover the "conditions which required illusions" within the nature of society, Freud, the psychologist, sought to uncover the need for illusions within human nature. Marx called these illusions "false consciousness"; Freud called them "rationalization." Both men were caught up in their own history, participating in the Westerner's struggle to achieve a humanistic worldly explanation of life's meaning. While Marx found the problem resting in social relations, and thus more amenable to reordering, Freud found the problem embedded in human nature itself, and therefore much more intractable. Both men stood at the dawn of the secular society. Although each conceived of "science" differently, they both still looked to some kind of secular materialistic science for answers as to how we actually live, as well as how we ought to live.

From the very inception of the secular psychological society, fundamental, unresolved philosophical and religious questions remained. Any reconciliation between science and religion in the twentieth century seemed destined to provide, at best, only an uneasy truce. As the "scientific" study of human institutions progressed, the social sciences developed into the disciplines of political science, economics, education, sociology, and anthro-pology, while the "scientific" study of human nature itself emerged, in part, as a "scientific" psychology. Within each area of inquiry, similar patterns of professionalization and a growing accumulation of expert scientific knowledge occurred. The tension between science and religion has been reflected in each of these disciplines in different ways throughout the twentieth century.

8

The psychological society thus emerged in this century as part of the nineteenth-century quest for a "scientific" redefinition of human nature. For some people, the psychological society replaced the theological society, while others remained committed to the older, theological worldview. From the perspective of the latter, the former was often viewed antagonistically. Nevertheless, the two societies have managed to coexist to the present. They are different in fundamental ways but are similar in certain respects. A central difference is that on one account "man is the measure of all things," while on the other "God is the measure." They are similar, however, in that they are concerned with answering many of the same questions, and thus they sometimes make similar sorts of assumptions about human nature. A particular psychology might start from the assumption that human nature is beastly, while a selected theological view might assume it to be "sinful." So, too, another psychology might assume human nature to be "good," just as some religious sects also assume human nature to be "good." Thus we find the grounds upon which the peaceful coexistence of both worldviews is sometimes adjudicated. When pressed to the level of fundamental cosmological beliefs, however, the differences reappear.

Writing in the midst of the psychological society in the early 1960s, Abraham H. Maslow, as a psychologist, sought to describe two significant psychological movements, embodying very different conceptions of human nature which had played central roles in the creation of modern American society. To Maslow, the first half of the century had been dominated by the development of psychoanalysis and behaviorism, each with distinctly different assumptions about human nature. The latter half of the century, he argued, would see the rise of a "third-force" psychology, which would come to dominate the field. This "third-force" psychology would help people to seek out and create authentic values, which would aid them in determining both how they live and how they ought to live. Within this "third-force" psychology Maslow included such diverse theorists as Carl Jung, Alfred Adler, Otto Rank, Herbert Marcuse, Thomas Szasz, N. O. Brown, Gardner Murphy, Kurt Lewin, Gordon Allport, and Carl Rogers.[14]

In Maslow's psychological opinion, it was clear that humankind suffered from a "value-illness," a lack of belief which might find its cure in the "third-force" psychology. As he analyzed it,

Historically, we are in a value interregnum in which all externally given value systems have proven to be failures (political, economic, religious, etc.) e.g., nothing is worth dying for. What man needs but doesn't have, he seeks for unceasingly, and he becomes dangerously ready to jump at *any* hope, good or bad. The cure for this disease is obvious. We need a validated, usable system of human values that we can believe in and devote ourselves to (be willing to die for), because they are true rather than because we are exhorted to "believe and have faith." Such an empirically based Weltanschauung seems now to be a real possibility, at least in theoretical outline.[15]

The function of psychological therapy was to help the individual clarify and develop his or her own values. Maslow went so far as to assert that, "Indeed, I think it possible that we may soon even *define* therapy as a search for values, because ultimately the search for identity, is, in essence, the search for one's own intrinsic, authentic values."[16] With Maslow the psychological person had come of age, and was now prepared to attempt to answer the questions, How does man live? and How ought man to live? In search of the answers to these questions, both the body and the mind were turned on to "peak experiences." A whole new lexicon of therapeutic practices flowered, including reality therapy, encounter groups, T-groups, sensitivity training, bioenergetics, primal scream therapy, Rolfing, Gestalt therapy, expanded-consciousness movement, nude encounter, Rogerian marathon, Synanon, transactional analysis, est, human growth sessions, and human potential workshops. Names such as Carl Rogers, Fritz Perls, Wilhelm Reich, Ida Rolf, and Alan Watts became familiar to those who sought healing in the psychological society.

Even as Maslow was preaching the doctrine of his psychology of "being," some seven million Americans each year were undergoing some sort of therapy.[17] Some estimates suggest that 80 percent of the adult population reflected some symptoms of mental illness, and that perhaps one in four adults was actually impaired.[18] The therapeutic cults and practices which emerged in this environment were equally as diverse as the religious cults and practices that had existed in the theological society. Just as the religious mystic in the theological society invariably condemned the voice of "reason," so too in the secular psychological society do we find Fritz Perls, in *Gestalt Therapy Verbatim*, condemning "reason" as one's guide: "Each time you ask the question *why*, you diminish in stature. You bother yourself with false, unnecessary information. You only feed the computer, the intellect. And the intellect is the whore of intelligence. It's a drag on your life."[19] Only feeling, apparently, can get us in touch with our true selves, with the true course of our own psychological awakening.

The quest for some form of spiritual awakening and redemption was not to be denied the secular soul in the psychological society, as newer and higher levels of consciousness were sought. Both legal and illegal drugs became part of the diet of millions of Americans as they learned to "cope" and "enjoy" life. In the midst of all this, Maslow sensed the "frustrated idealism" implicit in the reaching and groping of many who sought psychological healing. They were seeking a new way, he said, "a religious surrogate." Maslow believed that his "third-force" psychology was but a transition psychology on the road to a still higher force. He sensed the need of many for a "still higher Fourth Psychology which would be transpersonal, transhuman, centered on the cosmos rather than on human needs and interest."[20]

As Martin Gross so aptly notes, "Maslow was an accurate prophet."[21] Soon a variety of modified oriental "guru systems" captured the consciousness of large numbers of idealistic, striving young people. While millions sought escape, if not healing, in transcendental meditation, others subjected themselves to mind manipulation and mind control in the form of Synanon and Moonie cults, searching for the meaning and purpose of life. In its most extreme form, this was demonstrated in the mass suicide of the Jim Jones cult in the jungles of Guyana. These quasi-religious cults still capture in many ways the "frustrated idealism" which Maslow accurately sensed just beneath the surface of many youths' frantic search for new experiences. The manipulation of mind and control of being in these cults are clearly as effective as any practiced by the older religious cults of the theological society. As the twentieth century wears on, more and more people will find a home immersed completely within the psychological society; others will attempt to maintain a theological worldview; and still others will straddle both worlds with considerable difficulty.

American consciousness during the latter half of this century is being profoundly influenced by the development of the psychological society. The secularization, as well as the psychologicalization, of the traditional Judeo-Christian belief system has proceeded with impressive speed. This is perhaps best reflected in the Roman Catholic cleric's worry over the psychological effectiveness of the confessional, and in the Protestant minister's reference to modern America as a "sick" society. In Jonathan Edwards's world, sin was real and conversion experience was the work of God. Because people suffered guilt and anxiety for transgressing the laws of God, confession was essential for genuine reconciliation with God. It was decidedly not a way of "getting in touch with one's self" or "communicating with one's fellows." The function of the cleric was to save souls, and with that saving function came physical as well as mental healing. Christ, as both God and man, was a healer of bodies as well as of souls. Theologians such as Edwards, with their firm belief in the traditional God, were always careful to emphasize that it was God's grace and God's will that "healed and helped," rather than human effort. Redemption was God's doing—human beings could not save themselves. The ontological belief in the oneness and authenticity of God found in the First Commandment was the cornerstone of the theological society. Belief in God was justified as descriptive of reality, and not because it might somehow be psychologically "helpful" in ordering one's personal life. The First Commandment was, after all, the "first" commandment.

William James's *The Varieties of Religious Experience* was (and is) a landmark work and a great classic of American letters. In it, James rationalized his belief in God, not on the traditional ontological grounds, but rather on therapeutic grounds. He was taking the vital step millions of his countrymen would soon take into the therapeutic society of the twentieth century. For him, belief in God was justifiable if such belief was therapeutically helpful. The God, or the "more," which he embraced in *The Varieties of Religious Experience* was just such a therapeutic God, and his justification for that belief was to be reiterated throughout the therapeutic institutions of the psychological society, as well as in some of the major liberal schools of theology for which a "modern" approach to the justification of belief was propounded.

While James developed the crucial rationale for religious belief within the psychological society, he was also a key transition figure between the theological society and the emerging psychological society. In the past, we turned to theologians for discourse on psychological knowledge. In the dawning decade of the twentieth century, however, William James, the philosopher-psychologist, could be heard discoursing on religious experience and, in the end, justifying belief on therapeutic grounds.

The two worlds symbolized by Edwards and Maslow appear both different and strangely similar. Each world sets interpretive guidelines, not only on how people lived, but also on how they ought to live. One spoke of sin, the other of sickness; one spoke of the soul, the other of the unconscious. Both had rational as well as antirational schools. Both defined human nature from distinct perspectives which, in turn, set guidelines for the cultivation of a variety of competing movements in both worlds. In the theological world, a variety of religious beliefs, rituals, and practices emerged to assuage guilt and reduce the anxiety of having sinned against God. So, too, in the psychological society therapeutic ritual practices emerged, again concerned with relieving anxiety from the guilt of modern secular living.

Confession is good for the soul in whichever society we live. Both the theological and the psychological societies have cultivated their own unique versions of confession, in public as well as private settings. Werner Erhard's attack therapy (est), which reduces the individual identity to a quivering mass of anxiety before beginning its indoctrination process, does not seem so far removed from what Edwards was doing to his congregation as he harangued them about their sinfulness and the consequences that were to flow from the "hands of an angry God." Here, too, we are reminded that the reward-and-punishment psychology of John B. Watson's behaviorism was never far removed from the Baptist rewards and punishments of his childhood. While we can perhaps best understand the differences and similarities between the theological and psychological worldviews by focusing on two historical figures, such as Edwards and Maslow, these two worldviews can also be observed today by contrasting the activities taking place in a psychiatric clinic with those taking place in a Fundamentalist church. Both exist coterminously, often operating side-by-side despite their inherently different premises. When they carry on overlapping functions, the results are usually severe social tension and conflict, as evidenced by the periodic controversy that erupts in our schools, courts, hospitals, families, churches, and synagogues over the interpretation of human behavior. It makes a difference whether unacceptable behavior is interpreted as evil or as sick. As such, it hardly seems coincidental that during the most recent religious reawakening, the insanity plea as a legal maneuver has once again come under fire.

This book is not a critical analysis of either theological society or psychological society, nor is it an analysis of Edwards's or Maslow's historic worldviews. Rather, it is a biographical analysis of selected individuals who played key roles in creating the major movements of the psychological society during its critical, formative period from 1890 to 1910. In this sense, the book is not a definitive history of psychology, which would be expected to take into account the institutional development of the field. Although this study is limited to select leaders during this early period, it must be recognized that there was, in fact, a second generation of leaders who became prominent in America after 1910. Such individuals as Wilhelm Reich, Erich Fromm, Jean Piaget, Harry Stack Sullivan, Adolf Meyer, William Alanson White, Lewis Terman, Karen Horney, Philip Rieff, Gardner Murphy, and a host of others, were not only significant ideational shapers of the field but institution builders as well. The history they created, and the institutions they fostered, clearly warrant separate treatment and thus are not dealt with here.

It is important for the reader to recognize that this book is not about the fruit of the psychological society, nor even about its full flowering, but rather about the "roots" of that society. While these roots often have relevance today, and in many respects may challenge the most strongly held assumptions about our society, the central focus of this work is not on these kinds of developments. Rather, it is on the lives of significant early shapers of the field. This is done under the assumption that a critical examination of their lives might reveal some of the social dimensions and personal dynamics from which these significant thinkers generated their ideas.

I begin with William James, as there is little doubt that he can be identified appropriately as the father of American psychology. James was broadly educated, at home in both European and American circles. As a young man he participated in the "Metaphysical Club" at Harvard, with such fellow students as Charles S. Peirce, Chauncey Wright, and Oliver Wendell Holmes. In a context of swirling debates, James learned about evolution, science, religion, and the meaning Peirce ascribed to pragmatic philosophy. As a would-be artist who eventually became a scientist, James maintained a respectful but critical eye for both the theological world of his past and the newer secular scientific world of his future. He suffered a neurasthenic breakdown; on the road to recovery, he walked the darker caverns of the human mind, thereby exploring much of the depth of the human condition. By training, experience, and temperament he was fit to become a leader of the developing psychological society.

In an age when the human sciences were still very young and had yet to find a place in our consciousness as creditable explanations for human phenomena, James warned his peers that psychology, as a science, must inevitably have its limitations. "Science," he argued, "must be constantly reminded that her purposes are not the only purposes, and that the order of uniform causation which she has use for, and is therefore right in postulating, may be enveloped in a wider order, on which she has no claims at all."[22] James was acutely aware of the limitation of the human science of his day and firmly believed that if and when the Galileo and Lavoisier of psychology would arrive, "the necessities of the case will make them 'metaphysical.' "[23] Although psychology sought to become "scientific" by divorcing itself from philosophy during his era of leadership, James always assumed that psychology could never really escape the larger questions of human purposes, goals, and values which ultimately linked it to both philosophy and religion. For James, the issues of religion and philosophy were interlaced with the issues of a scientific psychology.

James profoundly influenced the development of American psychology through his many publications and lectures. However, he was much more than a speaker and a writer—he was a broadminded, gifted teacher who probably made as large an impact on the field through his students as through his written work. Some teachers are open to and accepting of competing and strange, even bizarre, ideas because they have a rather easygoing view of life; others may be broadminded because, having explored both the light and dark sides of the human condition, they have returned holding only tentatively to "truths." The latter teacher often reflects a lively respect and appreciation for the importance of the search for truth, as opposed to its possession. William James was such a teacher. He would resonate well with Albert Einstein's quotation from Gotthold Lessing: "It is open to every man to choose the direction of his strivings; and also, every man may draw comfort from Lessing's fine saying, that the search for truth is more precious than its possession."[24] For James, all the truths of psychology had not yet been attained. He was always at home with competing views of human nature and reality. His was an open-ended universe, an unfinished world in which new truths were yet to be discovered.

These points of view were nurtured by James in his students as they set forth to create their own conceptions of human nature in the psychological society: George Herbert Mead, one of the founders of social psychology in America; Edward L. Thorndike, a leader in educational psychology; and G. Stanley Hall, instrumental in founding child psychology and adolescent psychology. Even John B. Watson, the founder of behaviorism in America, had his own ideas nurtured by a major professor, James Angell, who was fresh from James's Harvard seminar. It is not hard to find the roots of Thorndike's connectionism in James's discussion of "Habit"; nor is it difficult to find elements of Mead's subjective "I" in James's "stream of consciousness," or Hall's propensity to seek out the "life force" in *Volk* beliefs and practices in James's curious interests in psychical research.[25] Each student drew differing views of human nature and social life from James, and each held different assumptions about God as well as about human beings. They also differed with respect to the "good life" toward which each thought humankind "ought" to move. Some, such as Thorndike and Hall, reflected the ethnic and sexist stereotypes of their teacher as well as their times. In his own way, each of these men generated a new movement in American psychology, yet each responded differently to the winds of history which swirled about them. All of them came from rural or small-town environments, and all ended up as urban dwellers. They reflected the estrangement, if not the alienation, which was in part derived from this rural-to-urban passage. Their society was changing radically, and they were attempting to change with it.

While James's conception of the individual and the social order remained grounded in the classical liberal tradition, Mead forged ahead to help create the new ideology which came to undergird the American liberal reform state of the first half of the twentieth century. He was influenced by James's individualism, especially in recognizing the importance of the subjective "I." He was equally influenced by Josiah Royce's quest for community. As the son of a minister who taught homiletics at the Theological Seminary at Oberlin College, Mead conceptualized his ministerial calling in terms of the secular world. His early student days reflected just how many of his most important ideas about the social self, as well as liberal reform, had their origins in his youth. Henry Castle's interactions with Mead during those years were as crucial to the development of Mead's thoughts as his later interactions with John Dewey were for their mature applications. The flow of religious fervor from the older missionary goal to that of the new liberal reform spirit, generated in the context of the Bismarckian state, is very clear.

James and his students all embraced an evolutionary position, yet each spawned a different conception of psychology. Mead heavily influenced social science leaders with his social behaviorism; Thorndike influenced educational thought and practice with his connectionism; and Hall infused into the field some strange notions of child and adolescent psychology. John B. Watson, although not a James student, influenced psychologists and media advertisers with his behaviorism. "By their fruits you should know them," James would say of his students and followers, and their fruits tended most often to be primarily behaviorial in nature. In many ways this behavioral emphasis in American psychology is but a larger reflection of the American antimetaphysical, practical consciousness, which nurtured the pragmatism of James, Peirce, and Dewey, and also the connectionism of Thorndike and the behaviorism of Watson and B. F. Skinner. Ultimately, the roots of American psychology are not to be found in the laboratories so much as in the American's practical consciousness, which sets high store in what "works" and has little patience with any accompanying abstract metaphysical reasoning.

James was at home in Europe as well as in America. He personally stood between a religiously oriented theological society and a scientifically oriented psychological one. His psychology was heavily laden with contradictory assumptions. While he appeared to look down the path toward behavioral psychology, he never seemed satisfied with what he saw there—the subjective side of human experience was far too complicated to permit such a simplistic reduction. Although some European phenomenologists thought they saw James creating an American phenomenological psychology, James himself defied any satisfactory classification. What is clear, however, is that both James and Hall were open to a variety of interpretations of the human experience. It is not surprising, then, that Hall invited both Freud and Jung to America for the first time, to lecture at Clark University on the psychoanalytic movement.

Religion was a significant factor in the lives of the major

shapers of distinctive psychological movements, as were their own personal psychological problems. For Freud, religion and personal psychological factors combined to form his view of "religion as an obsessional neurosis." Psychoanalysis developed out of much that he learned about himself as he searched for a cure to his own obsessional neurosis. Freud's "Rome" phobia was the key with which he poetically unlocked the door to his own unconscious. In the depths of his own "dark, steamy, pulsating" unconscious, he believed he had found the very process whereby evil was transformed into sickness, and the place where the theological society was transformed into the psychological society.

Freud's fascination with Moses can be seen as a metaphorical expression of his own mission in the world.[26] Just as the old rabbinical scribes sought the Messiah at the gates of Rome, so too did Freud wait at the gates of Rome until he was ready to create the movement of psychoanalysis. He was the Moses, the lawgiver, the giver of new life, meant not for Jews alone but for Gentiles as well. As the founder of the psychoanalytic movement, Freud thought he saw the way through the thicket of religious illusions. To complete the aesthetic picture, it was necessary in his last major work, *Moses and Monotheism*, to make Moses an Egyptian, for just as it was Moses the "Egyptian" who led the children of Israel out of bondage, so too would Freud the Jew lead humanity—Christians and Jews alike—out of the bondage of their religious illusions.

Although Freud had many followers, all of whom deviated in some respect from his teaching, none could match his poetic genius. While Alfred Adler constructed his individual psychology out of his own feelings of inferiority, he did not attain the depths of analysis that Freud had. It was very important for Freud that psychoanalysis not be viewed as "Jewish psychology," even though many of its major tenets were derived from Freud's own Jewish experience. For Freud, the role Jung was expected to play was crucial in applying psychoanalysis to the gentile world. As the son of a Protestant minister and an adopted son of the psychoanalytic movement, Jung was supposed to spearhead a breakthrough to the Gentile's consciousness, and thus propel Freud's movement toward its universal goals. This, of course, is not what happened. Jung had his own psychological and religious problems. His "father problem" often reappeared in his relationship with Freud, as his wife, Emma, surmised. Nevertheless, Jung's "Father-Freud" problem was often interpreted by Freud himself as anti-Semitic.

Jung's own mystical beliefs found expression in a gnosticism which called on people to listen to their inner voice and, in the name of individuation, to learn to accept the violence of the age as an expression of a new, more evolved barbaric future. His philosophy was adopted by Hermann Hesse when he underwent Jungian therapy. Hesse expressed that philosophy in his book *Demian*, which proved to be extremely popular among the youth of his day. In it, the reader was reminded that some children were marked as were the children of Cain, destined to carry out the murderous violence of a new emerging order. Jung's philosophy of gnosticism, which was at the core of his psychological beliefs, fit well with the German *Volkish* beliefs that fueled the flames of national socialism. His philosophy, though ancient in its mystical symbolization, fit the age in which he moved. In such a crisis-ridden period of history, the outline of the social consequences of key beliefs can often be clearly seen in their more stark reality. Fundamental ideas about human life are seldom socially neutral—we cannot escape the consequences of our ideas, nor can we escape the responsibility of having chosen them. In this respect, Jung was not an innocent bystander of his age, but rather a participatory actor of his time. In that measure, he was to some degree responsible for helping to create the historic tenor, if not the events, which ultimately occurred.

In adopting the basic premises of Freudian, Adlerian, or Jungian psychology while under therapeutic analysis, the person involved also adopts a particular philosophy of life. Margaret Naumberg's application of her own "Freudian-Jungian" worldview to education, and later to the field of art therapy, clearly carried with it her ideological commitments as components of her unique philosophy of life.

The examination of psychoanalytic thought ends with Otto Rank, who drank deeply from Arthur Schopenhauer's cup of despair, and who, in the end, announced that all was illusion. He ultimately came to believe that what the individual needed to survive in the strangely alienated twentieth-century world of faceless urban dwellers was a new and better set of illusions. Rank's beliefs were very different from eighteenth-century Enlightenment ideals and the dream of rational progress, as well as those of Marx, who asked about the conditions of a society which required illusions, and Freud, who in the end sought at least partial freedom from that ancient crippler of human consciousness by attempting to understand it. More than anyone else, in preaching the need for illusions to the thousands of social workers who passed through Jesse Taft's Philadelphia School of Social Work, Rank signified the birth of a new and different worldview—and, most clearly, the end of the Enlightenment.

Maslow was correct when he said that the two major movements of psychology which had come to dominate the American Psychological Society were behaviorism and psychoanalysis. However, in the commercial-minded America of the early twentieth century, Watson's behaviorism took the lead. It is interesting to note that both movements were founded by individuals who suffered from phobias: Watson feared the dark and Freud had a phobic inability to travel to Rome. Both men grew up in highly conflicting, strident, transitional social environments, which tended to rub raw the basic values of their culture. Freud came from a small rural town, of eastern European parentage. He was one of that first generation of his faith who came to breathe the emancipated air of scientific secularism. He successfully crossed over from the relatively closed world of eastern European Jewry to become a leader in the modern Western, scientifically oriented secular world of Vienna. No matter how successful he became, however, he always maintained his personal identity as a Jew. Watson, the white Baptist, grew to manhood in the racially strident, religiously gripping, small-town rural society of Greenville, South Carolina. He found success in such urban centers as Chicago, Baltimore, and New York, yet maintained his central identity, not as a Southern Baptist, but as a landed Southern "macho gentleman." Both men tied their personal problems to their early childhood experiences, in which each came into personal contact with the "other side": a Catholic nurse to whom Freud would trace his difficulty, just as Watson found his problem rooted in his early childhood experience with a black nurse. Both, it seems, were brought face to face with the divided worlds of their cultural milieu at tender ages. In many ways they were responding to the social milieu that nurtured them, the consequences of which were two very different ways of representing human nature and social reality.

All historical work is written from a particular perspective which invariably shapes both the structural design as well as the color and texture of the picture created. While I inevitably have been influenced to some extent by both the theological and the psychological society, and while I consider the questions each raises to be important, this book is written from the perspective of a nonbeliever, from a position of critical disbelief with respect to the basic assumptions of both the theological society and the psychological society. The reader is thus forewarned.

Saint Augustine once said, "I believe so that I can understand." Psychologically speaking, that was a useful phrase. To fully understand another person, our critical judgment of that person's beliefs must be suspended at least long enough to consider those beliefs, and to treat them as if they were true. In so doing, we invariably run the risk of coming to accept a portion of those beliefs and, as a consequence, never being quite the same again. I take it that this risk is an inevitable price of human understanding, and I hope that in researching and writing each chapter I have suspended my critical judgment long enough so that the individual treated has been correctly and fairly understood and then appropriately described. Last, it is hoped that my critical judgments, which usually emerge most forcefully toward the end of each chapter, reasonably follow more from the preponderance of evidence than from my own particular belief system, which inevitably influences them.

Although I continue to entertain a critical disbelief in the basic assumptions of both the theological and the psychological societies, I do hold positive beliefs with respect to the rationality of life and the human quest for meaning. How people live, and how they ought to live, are important questions whether we answer them by our thought or our actions. Indeed, in a certain sense, these questions are answered even if we choose to ignore them. Almost a century has passed since William James worried about the problem of a human science in the new society. In many ways he was most prophetic. He was perhaps most insightful when he postulated an open-ended universe, along with the clear recognition that if and when the Galileo of psychology arrived, he or she would be a metaphysician. It is clear that wherever we look in the human sciences of the twentieth century, we find the field riddled with unexamined philosophical and religious assumptions about human nature and the "good" society. From my perspective, the human sciences ought to be more scientific. Such "sciences" might then, at least, be somewhat more circumspect in their philosophical and religious claims.

My perspective in writing this book is as a humanist who believes that we do not yet know the answers to many of the important questions raised here. My assumptions are rooted in that humanistic past which accepts the view that men and women are not only inheritors but ongoing participant-creators of their past, their present, and their future. In this sense, the thought of the fifteenth-century humanist Giovanni Pico della Mirandola appears particularly illustrative: "Neither heavenly nor earthly, neither mortal nor immortal have we made thee. Thou, like a judge appointed for being honorable, art the molder and maker of thyself; thou mayest sculpt thyself into whatever shape thou dost prefer."

With that said, we begin our examination of these scientists of the mind by joining Henry James, Jr., at the freshly dug grave of his religiously oriented father.

Notes

1. Quoted in A. R. Luria, *The Making of Mind: A Personal Account of Soviet Psychology: A. R. Luria*, Michael Cole and Sheila Cole, eds. (Cambridge, Mass.: Harvard University Press, 1979), p. 1.

2. Thomas S. Szasz, *The Myth of Mental Illness* (New York: Harper and Row, 1974), p. 9.

3. For example, while Scottish realism dominated much of the academic philosophical thought of nineteenth-century America, it is in the texts on moral philosophy that we find not only Aristotelian notions of faculty psychology and modified Lockean assumptions casting the human mind in a quasi-religious perspective, but also the basic elements of what many in the twentieth century regard as secular, scientific psychological knowledge. The "laws of effect" as espoused by Edward L. Thorndike under the mantle of twentieth-century scientific educational psychology, while far removed in time, are not all that different in substance from Francis Wayland's popular nineteenth-century text *The Elements of Moral Science* (New York: Cooke and Co., 1835). On page 64, we read: "The sensibility of conscience, as a source of *pleasure or of pain*, is strengthened by use, and weakened by disuse." See also Francis Wayland, *Elements of Intellectual Philosophy* (New York: Sheldon and Co., 1854), p. 9, which "treats of the faculties of the human mind, and of the laws by which they are governed."

4. Vergilius Ferm, ed., *Puritan Sage: Collected Writings of Jonathan Edwards* (New York: Library Publishers, 1953), pp. 365–78.

5. Perry Miller, *Jonathan Edwards* (Toronto: William Sloane Associates, 1949), p. 318.

6. Ibid., pp. 103, 140.

7. Harriet Martineau, trans., *The Positive Philosophy of Auguste Comte* (New York: William Gowans, 1868).

8. Ibid., p. 25.

9. Fyodor Dostoevsky, *Notes from Underground and The Grand Inquisitor* (New York: E. P. Dutton and Co., 1960), pp. 129–30.

10. Quoted in Clarence J. Karier, "Science, Racism, and the Oppression of the Poor," *Review of Education* 3 (Sept./Oct. 1977): 337.

11. See ibid.; see also Richard Hofstadter, *Social Darwinism in American Thought* (New York: George Braziller, 1959).

12. Lewis Mumford, *The Myth of the Machine* (New York: Harcourt Brace Jovanovich, 1970), p. 213.

13. Sigmund Freud, *The Future of an Illusion* (New York: Anchor Books, 1964), p. 92.

14. Abraham H. Maslow, *Toward a Psychology of Being* (New York: D. Van Nostrand Co., 1962), p. vi.

15. Ibid., p. 192 (original emphasis).

16. Ibid., pp. 166–67 (original emphasis).

17. Martin L. Gross, *The Psychological Society* (New York: Random House, 1978), p. 8.

18. Ibid., p. 6.

19. Quoted in ibid., p. 294.

20. Quoted in ibid., p. 310.

21. Ibid.

22. Quoted in part in Perry Miller, *Jonathan Edwards*, p. 234.

23. Quoted in Clarence J. Karier, *Man, Society, and Education* (Glenview, Ill.: Scott, Foresman and Company, 1967), p. 150.

24. Quoted in Karier, *Man, Society, and Education*, p. x.

25. It is doubtful that Hall would have agreed with this assessment; see chap. 5.

26. For a perceptive analysis of Freud's mission in the world, see Erich Fromm, *Sigmund Freud's Mission* (New York: Harper and Brothers Co., 1959).

1

WILLIAM JAMES [1842–1910]

Religion and the Rise of the Therapeutic Society

On a clear, crisp December day in 1882, Henry James, Jr., stood by his father's graveside in Cambridge, Massachusetts, and read aloud his brother William's touching farewell letter, which had arrived too late to reach their father before his death. Henry was certain that "somewhere out of the depths of the still, bright winter air," their father heard the message.[1] That letter, while recounting William's indebtedness and esteem for his father, and promising to take care of his literary effects, ended on a note of doubt as to the existence of an afterlife: "As for the other side, and Mother, and our all possibly meeting, I *can't* say anything. More than ever at this moment do I feel that if that *were* true, all would be solved and justified. And it comes strangely over me in bidding you good-bye how a life is but a day and expresses mainly but a single note. It is so much like the act of bidding an ordinary good-night. Good-night, my sacred old Father! If I don't see you again—Farewell! a blessed farewell!"[2]

A few days later William wrote his brother Henry: "As life closes, all a man has done seems like one cry or sentence. Father's cry was the single one that religion is real. The thing is so to 'voice' it that other ears shall hear,—no easy task, but a worthy one, which in some shape I shall attempt."[3] William James kept his word. Twelve years later he was to remark, "Religion is the great interest of my life,"[4] and within a decade he would complete that great classic of American letters, *The Varieties of Religious Experience.*

James was quite perceptive when he noted that in many lives a dominant thread may be discerned around which other threads are woven to form the unique fabric of one's life history. For William James that thread was captured in a single word: "freedom." Throughout his life James struggled to be free: sometimes against a universe without meaning, which for James meant a universe without God, and at other times against the idea of a universe predetermined by an almighty God. Standing amid the contested beliefs of much of the Christian society's theological explanations of human experience, he sensitively responded to the many important personal issues relevant to both the past and the emerging future.

As a young scientist, James was painfully aware of the declining credibility of God within the scientific laboratories of his day; as a young son of a devoted follower of Swedenborgian mysticism, he was very conscious of the importance of beliefs about God within one's personal life. Through these troubled waters, James charted a career from would-be artist, biologist, physiologist, and psychologist, to philosopher. In that process, he turned away from the faith of his father—a man to whom he was deeply attached.

James's struggle for freedom can be viewed not only as an intellectual struggle against a predetermined universe, but also as a personal struggle to free himself from a father he loved and respected, and one who powerfully influenced the course of his life. Again and again, at every turning point in his life, the shadow of Henry James, Sr., appeared: from the depths of despair during an emotional breakdown, to the choice of a career in science, as well as to the selection of a mate. Charles S. Peirce, who knew James well, recognized this influence throughout *The Varieties of Religious Experience.* An astute observer, he realized that James had not been able to break clear of his father, even after the latter's death. James's struggle for freedom, which he translated into a variety of intellectual propositions as well as courses of action, remained a lifelong struggle fraught with tension and pain. Early in life, neurasthenic symptoms appeared and persisted throughout his life. James's promethean struggle earned him the title of "individualist"[5] at the same time it earned him a life of psychological pain and physical suffering.

In many ways, James's education, life experiences, and personal psychological problems were unique to him and his family situation while in other ways they were not. The struggle with his father, albeit often symbolic, carried with it a more universalized significance. Furthermore, although the James family rejected the business world, they accepted, in their day-to-day living, its class status and values, which they tended to project upon the universe. More importantly, the unique educational and personal experiences of William James so sensitized him to the nature of the psychological problems of the secularized mind, that much of his probing analysis, as well as his tentative solutions, remain highly relevant for many modern thinkers. Wherever we seem to look in twentieth-century therapeutic psychology, we regularly see people coming back with Jamesian solutions. By the mid-twentieth century, large numbers of James's countrymen came to hold many of his views on psychology, philosophy, religion, and the nature of social reality.

Along with Peirce and John Dewey, James is rightfully recognized as one of the founders of American pragmatic philosophy. Yet, as the teacher of George Herbert Mead, Edward L. Thorndike, and G. Stanley Hall, and as the author of the leading work in psychology during the closing decade of the nineteenth century, he clearly earned the title "father of American psychology." Living and working in a time when the field of psychology was just beginning to separate from philosophy into a distinct discipline, James helped shape that development, incorporating his pragmatic philosophy into his psychology.

James popularized his psychology not only with his book *Psychology, the Briefer Course*, which was aimed directly at teachers, but also through his many public lectures. Merle Curti notes, "It has been estimated that nine-tenths of the teachers who studied any psychology at all in the years between 1890 and 1910 read James."[6] While his popularity among his contemporaries was attributed to his style of writing and lecturing, as well as to his breadth of view, a significant measure of the strength of his following derived from his willingness to seek out and address the critical issues of his day. He probed his own consciousness in search of freedom within a meaningful universe; yet neither his pathological states nor his religious experience could blunt his curiosity.

27

The cosmic questions of life were personally important to James. Intellectually, he sketched out the shadowy perimeters of a new ideology that for many would undergird a new society, a new worldview—indeed, a new way of life. James stood among the mourners at the graveside of the older Christian society and read its eulogy. However, he also served as midwife to the birth of the new society—the therapeutic society. It is in his role as a pivotal historic figure—a man who, while looking over his shoulder at the older Christian-oriented culture, struggled to fashion the intellectual basis for the emerging secular culture— that we begin to sense James's profound significance for the modern age.

In the older, God-centered universe, the theologian or the cleric would help individuals analyze the psychological dimensions of their human experiences, whereas in the newer, man-centered universe, the psychiatrist or the psychologist is more often called upon to analyze and probe the dimensions of that same experience. In the older culture, some of the very best psychological insights into the human condition could be found among the writings of theologians. For example, the works of the greatest Puritan theologian Jonathan Edwards literally glisten with such psychological insights. With the modern world quite beyond his perceptual field, Edwards expounded on the psychological dimensions of man in a God-centered universe in his "Sinners in the Hands of an Angry God," and he defined human nature in *The Great Christian Doctrine of Original Sin Defended*. His was a total weltanschauung, encapsulating human nature, society, human destiny, and purpose. Edwards's system was based on the belief that the First Commandment was, of necessity, the foundation of all reality. Only in such a world could sin be defined, guilt assuaged, and sinners redeemed or punished in hellfire, according to the wishes of an omnipotent God. Although religions would vary in their particular perceptions of human nature and its relationship to the Deity, the primary assumption underlying all of Judeo-Christian culture was, and still is, the First Commandment.

By the time James published *The Varieties of Religious Experience* in 1902, Friedrich Nietzsche, in *Gay Science* (1882), had already declared, "God is dead. God remains dead. And we have killed him."[7] With both Nietzsche and James we pass from a culture with God at its center to a culture with man at its center. This fundamental shift in Western thought initiated a corresponding shift in the ideological structure of the social system. As the universe became increasingly anthropomorphized, the "self" for many became an object of exclusive fascination and exploration, the sole touchstone of reality. For some, this exploration ultimately ended in narcissistic contemplation. Western society underwent a transformation of the basis for personal and collective values: the soul became the psyche, while the transcendent character of the soul reappeared as the unconscious mind. Salvation was now a matter of survival, sin became a sickness, and such religious rituals as confession, designed to alleviate guilt and atone for sin, were replaced by individual and group psychotherapeutic interventions, designed to alleviate the guilt of anxiety neuroses.

These, then, were the signs of an emerging therapeutic society, a society born in the closing decade of the nineteenth century and nourished in the secular world of the twentieth century. In this chapter we will analyze the way in which William James, as one of the first secular theologians of this new therapeutic society, conceptualized the fundamental ideas that came to underpin that society. We will consider as well the social and economic contexts in which James's ideas were generated and, to a limited extent, the practical historic role he played in helping to bring this new society into existence.

The peculiar life experience of William James fitted him for the role he eventually played as the "father of American psychology." Not only was a considerable share of his thought and action profoundly shaped by his own father, particularly in terms of religious experience, but it is also clear that Henry James, Sr., was himself rebelling against his own father and his religion. James's grandfather, William James, Sr., of Albany, New York, had come to America a penniless immigrant yet bequeathed a family estate worth nearly three million dollars. In part, he amassed that fortune because of his austere, frugal, Calvinistic way of life. Henry James, Sr., reflecting on his own rebellious years, commented late in life on the severity of his early home life and the total lack of what he called "a spontaneous religious culture." He struggled against both the strict Calvinistic faith in which he had been reared and the style of life dominated by the Calvinistic principle of stewardship. His father had interpreted such actions as not only frivolous but extravagant, and created a will that discriminated against his wayward son. Shortly after his father's death, Henry James, Sr., along with other members of the family, successfully contested the will, and thus he received a steady income to ensure his family's independent wealth.

In revolting against his own father's piety and frugality, Henry James, Sr., created a way of life for himself and his family that maintained the personal values of the entrepreneur without necessitating the actual conduct of business activities. Henry, Jr., once remarked that his grandfather's heirs for two generations were never in a single case "guilty of a stroke of business."[8] Their life was not like that of the older rich, who built into their reason for being a sense of noblesse oblige; rather, it resembled the Greek conception of leisure in which one's time and energy were dedicated to cultivating the arts and sciences for the fulfillment and development of the self. For William James, Jr., this self would be nourished in the community of intellectual leaders of western Europe and America.

Although the affluent, cultured, classical Greek community had been sustained by slave labor and the Euro-American community was sustained by the somewhat different wage-labor system of an emerging industrial capitalism, each system was effectively rationalized. Just as Aristotle had justified slavery as a natural given, so did many within the modern social-economic community rationalize as natural both wage labor and all the exchange values between work and property that it entailed. Even though the James family rejected the business activities of the entrepreneur, because they could afford to do so, they did not reject the basic economic values which sustained those activities. In reality, they were very much members of the bourgeoisie. Once having achieved economic independence, however, they turned away from the world of business and found their reason for existence in the development of the individual self and the spiritual fulfillment of that self in an aesthetic culture and in religious experience. The life-style Henry James, Sr., cultivated included travel, study, and personal dialogue with intellectual leaders. In response to a question as to his occupation, Henry remarked, "Say I'm a philosopher, say I'm a seeker for truth, say I'm a lover of my kind, say I'm an author of books if you like; or best of all, just say I'm a Student."[9] He remained a student throughout his life, as did his two oldest sons, William and Henry, Jr.

Before launching onto this kind of life, Henry, Sr., attempted a final reconciliation with his late father's faith. He entered Princeton College, the last home of Jonathan Edwards, to study for the Presbyterian ministry. He quickly became disenchanted with the intellectual climate of Princeton, which he found to be self-righteous and permeated with "pharistic pride." Unable to withstand its peculiar austerity, Henry dropped out of Princeton and traveled to Europe. Upon returning to America he married a friend's sister, Mary Walsh. Their firstborn, William, was only three months old when he received Ralph Waldo Emerson's formal blessing and was little more than a year old when he experienced the first of what would become virtually uncountable transatlantic voyages.

The young William grew to manhood, equally at home in England, Germany, France, and America. He learned foreign languages by living in the countries in which the languages were spoken, just as he assimilated many of the major ideas of his day by direct discourse with their authors. Men such as Henry David Thoreau, Ralph Waldo Emerson, Horace Greeley, Nathaniel Hawthorne, Thomas Carlyle, and John Stuart Mill were but a sampling of the many illustrious visitors in the James household during those formative years. Throughout, Henry, Sr., kept a watchful eye on the education of his children, changing their schools and tutors almost at whim—so much so that late in life William attributed his own lack of discipline, as well as his tendency to be an intellectual dilettante, to those early educational experiences. Nevertheless, William was afforded opportunities to learn that few youngsters would ever have. From his experiences with Louis Agassiz on a Brazilian trip, to his extensive work and observations in the psychological laboratories at the German University, James's formal training was as unique as were his personal family experiences.

William James was little more than two years old when his father, still in revolt against his own dead father, had a mystical experience that led to his adoption of the Swedish mystic faith of Emanuel Swedenborg. Henry, Sr., recounted the experience, which occurred in Windsor, England, in 1844, as follows:

> One day, however, towards the close of May, having eaten a comfortable dinner, I remained sitting at the table after the family had dispersed, idly gazing at the embers in the grate, thinking of nothing, and feeling only the exhilaration incident to a good digestion, when suddenly—in a lightning-flash as it were—"fear came upon me, and trembling, which made all my bones to shake." To all appearance it was a perfectly insane and abject terror, without ostensible cause,

and only to be accounted for, to my perplexed imagination, by some damned shape squatting invisible to me within the precincts of the room, and raying out from his fetid personality influences fatal to life. The thing had not lasted ten seconds before I felt myself a wreck; that is, reduced from a state of firm, vigorous, joyful manhood to one of almost helpless infancy. The only self-control I was capable of exerting was to keep my seat. I felt the greatest desire to run incontinently to the foot of the stairs and shout for help to my wife,—to run to the roadside even, and appeal to the public to protect me; but by an immense effort I controlled these frenzied impulses, and determined not to budge from my chair till I had recovered my lost self-possession. This purpose I held to for a good long hour, as I reckoned time, beat upon meanwhile by an ever-growing tempest of doubt, anxiety, and despair, with absolutely no relief from any truth I had ever encountered save a most pale and distant glimmer of the divine existence, when I resolved to abandon the vain struggle, and communicate without more ado what seemed my sudden burden of inmost, implacable unrest to my wife.

Now, to make a long story short, this ghastly condition of mine continued with me, with gradually lengthening intervals of relief, for two years, and even longer.[10]

Henry, Sr., came to believe that this experience was what Swedenborg called a *vastation*, a new birth, in which the force of God entered his soul and gradually dispelled the darkness of "doubt, anxiety and despair." While suffering through his recovery period, he followed his physician's advice and took water-cure treatments, which he found of little help. During this time he reflected a deeply alienated state in which he longed for an escape from consciousness. *"The curse of mankind, that which keeps our manhood so little and so depraved, is its sense of selfhood, and the absurd, abominable opinionativeness it engenders. How sweet it would be to find oneself no longer man, but one of those innocent and ignorant sheep pasturing upon that placid hillside, and drinking in eternal dew and freshness from Nature's lavish bosom!"*[11] Although many romantics sought a return to the innocence of the original Garden of Eden, most mystics came to learn that only through the hell of fear and trembling would the worldly self be so shattered that the spiritual light of God could be admitted into the soul. Under such a conversion experience Henry, Sr., became a lifelong follower of Swedenborg, at long last "free" of his father's Calvinism.

If the father had experienced difficulty freeing himself from the faith of his own father, son William had an even more difficult time. Living a leisured life, Henry, Sr., had both the time and the inclination to pay careful attention to the education of his firstborn son. That, and the fact that he remained permissive, untyrannical, and very much loved and respected, made it even more difficult for William to break with his father. As Gay Wilson Allen, a biographer of William James, puts it: "Henry James Sr., perhaps unintentionally, restrained his children by indulgence: he appeared to give them complete freedom of choice, but somehow their knowledge of his wishes and opinions did more to curb them than overt opposition. It was difficult to rebel against a father who seemed so untyrannical."[12]

Whether intentional or not, it is clear that Henry, Sr., closely monitored the education of his two oldest sons. As he remarked, "I have had a firm grip upon the coat tails of my Willy and Harry who both vituperate me beyond measure because I won't let them go. The coats are a very staunch material."[13] Under such a firm grip, William James's career development and independent adulthood were delayed. Interested in becoming a painter, William persuaded his father to move the family back to Newport in 1860 so that he could study with William Hunt. His father, however, thought painting to be an unwise career choice and preferred that William choose a career in science. Within the year, William gave up painting and entered Lawrence Scientific School to study under Charles W. Eliot. Only two years earlier, Henry, Sr., had hesitated to enter William in the school because he could not find adequate housing for the entire family, and he could not bear the thought of prolonged separation from his oldest son.

While his sister Alice suffered from a mental illness and had her first breakdown in 1868 at the age of nineteen, so too did William James enjoy relatively good mental health until his nineteenth year, when he exchanged his career plan in painting for a scientific career.[14] Interestingly, it was about this time that he began to develop physical disabilities and increasing symptoms of a neurasthenic condition that would remain with him, intermittently, for the rest of his life. By 1869 he had completed his formal training in the sciences, receiving a degree in medicine. The following year he suffered an emotional breakdown, and it was not until two years later that he began to show signs of overcoming his semi-invalid state.

By 1873 James had accepted an instructor position at Harvard.

Both his success as a teacher and the personal independence such a position provided proved therapeutic for the young man. So fragile was his condition, however, that he required the next year to recuperate in Europe before returning in 1875 to teach. Gradually, his successful teaching career at Harvard led to greater degrees of independence and corresponding degrees of better health, although he never did manage to completely shed his father's influence. For example, in 1876, at age 34, he was told that his father had just met William's future wife.[15] It was up to William to meet, court, and marry the young lady, which he dutifully did some two years later. Having played such a significant role in choosing not only his son's career but his wife, it is not surprising that the persona of Henry James, Sr., is inextricably woven into William's various psychological states as well as his formal psychological, philosophical, and religious views.

Like his father, who took two years to overcome the emotional effects of his "vastation," William James needed time to recover from his emotional breakdown. And, like his father, he ascribed a religious quality to his experience.

Whilst in this state of philosophic pessimism and general depression of spirits about my prospects, I went one evening into a dressing-room in the twilight to procure some article that was there; when suddenly there fell upon me without any warning, just as if it came out of the darkness, a horrible fear of my own existence. Simultaneously there arose in my mind the image of an epileptic patient whom I had seen in the asylum, a black-haired youth with greenish skin, entirely idiotic, who used to sit all day on one of the benches, or rather shelves against the wall, with his knees drawn up against his chin, and the coarse grey undershirt, which was his only garment, drawn over them inclosing his entire figure. He sat there like a sort of sculptured Egyptian cat or Peruvian mummy, moving nothing but his black eyes and looking absolutely nonhuman. This image and my fear entered into a species of combination with each other. *That shape am I,* I felt, potentially. Nothing that I possess can defend me against that fate, if the hour for it should strike for me as it struck for him. There was such a horror of him, and such a perception of my own merely momentary discrepancy from him, that it was as if something hitherto solid within my breast gave way entirely, and I became a mass of quivering fear. After this the universe was changed for me altogether.

I awoke morning after morning with a horrible dread at the pit of my stomach, and with a sense of the insecurity of life that I never knew before, and that I have never felt since. It was like a revelation; and although the immediate feelings passed away, the experience has made me sympathetic with the morbid feelings of others ever since. It gradually faded, but for months I was unable to go out into the dark alone.

In general I dreaded to be left alone. I remember wondering how other people could live, how I myself had ever lived, so unconscious of that pit of insecurity beneath the surface of life. My mother in particular, a very cheerful person, seemed to me a perfect paradox in her unconsciousness of danger, which you may well believe I was very careful not to disturb by revelations of my own state of mind. I have always thought that this experience of melancholia of mine had a religious bearing."[16]

James went on to interpret this experience in terms of fear—fear of a universe without God, which for him was a universe without meaning: "I mean that the fear was so invasive and powerful that if I had not clung to scripture-texts like 'The eternal God is my refuge,' etc., 'Come unto me, all ye that labor and are heavy-laden,' etc., 'I am the resurrection and the life,' etc., I think I should have grown really insane."[17] Reflexive prayer for James had a therapeutic value. In analyzing his own situation, he cited his father's experience as another "case of fear equally sudden" in which the confident self is laid to ruin. As he put it, "Here is the real core of the religious problem: Help! help! No prophet can claim to bring a final message unless he says things that will have a sound of reality in the ears of victims such as these."[18]

Unlike his father, who found "help" in his struggle to be free of the stern Calvinistic God of his father by losing himself in the kinder, more loving God of Swedenborgia, William could not find "help" in such a God; in effect, such a God could only hinder his conceptual struggle to be free of the faith of his father. Deeply troubled, on the brink of insanity, James found his God, his "help," psychologically, and survived the double threat of insanity as well as suicide.[19] This experience convinced him that something "more" existed as a cosmic force in the universe, evolving toward an undeterminable end. The God that James discovered was a therapeutically useful God.

James's God, which he described as the "more," was never

absolute, predetermining, or personally loving. Instead, his God was more of a force, always partial in the making, pluralistically and pragmatically working through the individual subliminal self helping to wrest meaning out of a universe that otherwise appeared to be nihilistic. Having looked into the stark void of being and nothingness, and having come back in fear and trembling, James knew he could not survive in such a universe alone. Something more had to exist for him to maintain his sanity. In thus perceiving the void, he found not the traditional God but one whose existence filled James's own psychological need.

The road from a God-centered universe to a human-centered universe was not without its twists and turns. The particular pragmatic turn that James took in the justification of his faith was not unlike that which other Americans would take throughout the twentieth century. For many, the death of God did not come easily. Nietzsche had earlier sensed these difficulties when he said: "What did we do when we unchained this earth from its sun? Whither is it moving now? Whither are we moving now? Away from all suns? Are we not plunging continually? Backward, sideward, forward, in all directions? Is there any up or down left? Are we not straying as through an infinite nothing? Do we not feel the breath of empty space? Has it not become colder? Is not night and more night coming on all the while? Must not lanterns be lit in the morning?"[20]

In the human-centered universe of the future, lanterns would have to be lit while the churches themselves would become tombs, indeed "sepulchres of God." Observing the state of awareness of Western consciousness in the closing decade of the nineteenth century, Nietzsche knew that for many the sun had not yet set. As he put it: "This tremendous event is still on its way, still wandering—it has not yet reached the ears of man. Lightning and thunder require time, the light of the stars requires time, deeds require time even after they are done, before they can be seen and heard. This deed is still more distant from them than the most distant stars—*and yet they have done it themselves.*"[21] Nietzsche appreciated the importance of God for this civilization. He also believed that when the sounds of this deed reach the ears of humankind, we will either suffer disaster or become like gods: "What festivals of atonement, what sacred games shall we have to invent? Is not the greatness of this deed too great for us? Must not we ourselves become gods simply to seem worthy of it? There has never been a greater deed; and whoever will be born after us—for the sake of this deed he will be part of a higher history than all history hitherto."[22] Thus to fulfill our truly human character, to become recognized creators of human values, is to become superhuman. "Beyond good and evil" is the creator, the superhuman.

This transformation of Western thought from a God-centered universe to a human-centered universe took place within the intellectual parameters of a pervasive romanticism, with its corollary emphasis on individualism. The focus of the problem was set in terms of strong-willed people with God-like characters.[23] The vast ocean between American and Europe hardly proved a barrier to the diffusion of this thought. Thus Nietzsche read James's "beloved Master,"[24] Ralph Waldo Emerson, and proclaimed him "the richest in ideas of this century."[25] Emerson's own answer to the problem was a kind of pantheism which found "God" and "Man" in nature. As James interpreted Emerson: " 'Other world! there is no other world.' All God's life opens into the individual particular, and here and now, or nowhere, is reality. 'The present hour is the decisive hour, and every day is doomsday.' "[26] He found "his [Emerson's] life was one long conversation with the invisible divine, expressing itself through individuals and particulars:—'So nigh is grandeur to our dust, so near is God to man!' "[27] All three men thus were acutely sensitive to the larger issues buffeting Western civilization, and all three, each in his own way, sensed the declining possibility for belief in the faith of their fathers.

While James found it difficult to maintain his sanity in a godless universe, and therefore found it pragmatically necessary to believe in a therapeutic God, Nietzsche found his way out by placing his faith in the emerging superhuman. In *The Varieties of Religious Experience*, James considered Nietzsche's critical perspective of the saint and concluded that while much of what Nietzsche described was "sickly enough," he had correctly expressed the clash between the world of the "strong man" and that of the morbidity of the saint's "gentleness and self-severity."[28] James asserted that the saint was "entirely adapted" to a "millenial society" which in fact did not yet exist. The difference between these two types of people, he further argued, came down to this: "Shall the seen world or the unseen world be our chief sphere of adaptation? and must our means of adaptation in this seen world be aggressiveness or nonresistance?"[29] While he believed that both worlds must be "taken account of," James also thought that it was a mistake to talk of an "ideal man" when the corresponding ideal society had not yet been achieved. Using Herbert Spencer as his guide, he argued the utility of sainthood to balance the aggressiveness of a world of thieves: "Economically, the saintly group of qualities is indispensable to the world's welfare."[30] The way out of this problem for James was the pragmatic method; in a sense, he would judge the "cash" value of sainthood. Thus, rejecting Nietzsche's superhuman solution, James continued to pursue the issue by considering the utility of mysticism, ultimately exploring what he himself believed.

While many have recognized in *The Varieties of Religious Experience* James's personal apology to his father, which it is in some respects, the book is also a classic of American letters for at least two additional reasons. In this work James explores human nature[31] insightfully and subtly employs the pragmatic test to all kinds of broad-ranging human experiences. More importantly, the work itself is a historical benchmark in that it signals a turning point in American civilization from the earlier God-centered culture of the previous centuries toward the new human-centered culture of the twentieth century. James's Gifford lectures were written at the turn of the century when Darwinian naturalism had cut deeply into traditional religious beliefs. For many of the troubled faithful, these lectures, given by a man of science espousing a pluralistic doctrine of "live and let live," and justifying virtually any religious experience on the basis of therapeutic utility, were a welcome relief. Small wonder the lectures were so well received.

In many respects, *The Varieties of Religious Experience* culminated James's life-long struggle for freedom. From the depths of depression he wrote in his diary on April 30, 1879: "I think that yesterday was a crisis in my life. I finished the first part of Renouvier's second *Essais* and see no reason why his definition of free will—'the sustaining of a thought *because I choose to* when I might have other thoughts'—need be the definition of an illusion. At any rate, I will assume for the present—until next year—that it is no illusion. My first act of free will shall be to believe in free will."[32] His personal struggle to be free thus found its way into virtually every aspect of his thought. What was repressed in his relationship with his father reappeared, not only in his reaction against a God that predetermined his universe, but also against any form of knowledge, scientific or otherwise, that might suggest such a universe. James's pragmatism—or as he later called it, radical empiricism—was fundamentally premised on an open-ended universe, placing a premium on action and de-emphasizing the contemplation of metaphysical truths. This he felt maximized his freedom. Gradually regaining his health, James wrote: "I may perhaps return to metaphysic study and skepticism without danger to my powers of action. For the present, then, remember: Care little for speculation / Much for the *form* of my action."[33] Action, not metaphysics or contemplative study, was his touchstone.

This line of thought also appealed to Benito Mussolini in his study of pragmatism. As he wrote: "The pragmatism of William James was of great use to me in my political career. James taught me that an action should be judged rather by its results than by its doctrinary basis. I learnt of James that faith in action, that ardent will to live and fight, to which Fascism owes a great part of its success."[34] While it is clear that Mussolini could have found justification for his actions elsewhere, and that James's individualism could hardly be compatible with the state facism of Mussolini, it is also apparent that Mussolini had correctly tapped into a significant element of James's thought.[35] Early in his career, Mussolini came into contact with some of James's most enthusiastic Italian disciples through his association with the Leonardo group, while writing articles for *La Voce*.[36] Of this group, Giovanni Papini most excited James. In that young man he found the "tone of feeling, well fitted to rally devotees and to make of pragmatism a new militant form of religious or quasi-religious philosophy."[37]

James sensed that what he and others like Papini were witnessing was the dawn of a new "quasi-religous philosophy." Writing to F. C. S. Schiller, James said: "It is queer to be assisting at the éclosion of a great new mental epoch, life, religion, and philosophy in one—I wish I didn't have to lecture, so that I might bear some part of the burden of writing it all out, as we must do, pushing it into all sorts of details."[38] In Papini's work, James saw his own thoughts writ large. He told Schiller: "Papini is a jewel! To think of that little Dago putting himself ahead of every one of us (even of you, with his *Uomo-Dio*) at a single stride. And what a writer! and what fecundity!"[39] Commenting specifically on the young Italian's article "From Man to God," James enthusiastically defended Papini's discussion of "man the creator."[40] He also espoused Papini's characterization of pragmatism as "a collection of attitudes and methods, and its chief characteristic is its armed neutrality in the midst of doctrines. It is like a corridor in a hotel, from which a hundred doors open into a hundred chambers [where a hundred different doctrines may be espoused in separate rooms while] . . . the corridor belongs to all and all must pass there. Pragmatism, in short, is a great corridor-theory."[41] No doubt, it was the action in the corridor, free of the doctrinaire thought in the rooms, that Mussolini found so appealing.

The traditional notion of metaphysics, with all its doctrinaire basis of truth, divorced from the world of action, ultimately pointed to "God," not man, as the measure of all things. The older metaphysics could be his undoing. James realized the hazards to his emotional well-being, yet like a moth around a lighted candle he continued to flirt with metaphysics for the rest of his life. *The Varieties of Religious Experience*, written late in life, was originally planned to consist of two volumes: the first, which he completed, being a description of the varieties of religious experience; the second, which was never really finished, dealing with metaphysics. In the twilight of his life, James gave the Hibbert lectures at Manchester College (1908), and tried to make clear what he meant by a *pluralistic universe*. The older notion of God as an absolute had eroded, and with it all the traditional views of metaphysics. His radical empiricism projected the universe as ever-forming, indeterminate, and pluralistic, one in which all human beings participated in some related fashion. Almost in Emersonian fashion he asserted: "We are indeed internal parts of God and not external creations, on any possible reading of the panpsychic system. Yet because God is not the absolute, but is himself a part when the system is conceived pluralistically, his function can be taken as not wholly dissimilar to those of the other smaller parts—as similar to our functions consequently."[42]

James constructed what he called his "faith-ladder" out of such phrases as "might be true," "may be true," "fit to be true," "must be true," "held for true."[43] He knew that such a ladder did not rest on logical grounds: "Not one step in this process is logical, yet it is the way in which monists and pluralists alike espouse and hold fast to their visions. It is life exceeding logic, it is the practical reason for which the theoretic reason finds arguments after the conclusion is once there."[44] James's pluralistic universe rested on the practical grounds of experience and, ultimately, on his own psychological experience.[45] The ontological argument upon which the First Commandment rests thus could be pragmatically dismissed. For James, the nature of truth, God, humankind, and the universe had taken on vastly new and different meanings.

In *The Varieties of Religious Experience,* James worked his way through a labyrinth of over-beliefs. He repeatedly adopted an agnostic position, falling back from the unseen to the seen world. He argued that yes, there just might be something "more" out there, but while we can't be sure, we can pragmatically judge its effects on the seen world. The religious life could have a salutary effect.

> Summing up in the broadest possible way the characteristics of the religious life, as we have found them, it includes the following beliefs:—
> 1. That the visible world is part of a more spiritual universe from which it draws its chief significance;
> 2. That union or harmonious relation with that higher universe is our true end;
> 3. That prayer or inner communion with the spirit thereof—be that spirit "God" or "law"—is a process wherein work is really done, and spiritual energy flows in and produces effects, psychological or material, within the phenomenal world.
> Religion includes also the following psychological characteristics:—
> 4. A new zest which adds itself like a gift to life, and takes the form either of lyrical enchantment or of appeal to earnestness and heroism.
> 5. An assurance of safety and a temper of peace, and, in relation to others, a preponderance of loving affections.[46]

Repeatedly, James came back to the therapeutic function of religious experience as necessarily individual. The sick soul required one kind of "deliverance" and the "healthy minded another." All kinds of religious experience, morbid as well as pathological, were to be tolerated if in the end they proved useful to the individual's well-being. Religious faith thus was justified on the basis of its therapeutic value. For James, bourgeois individualism had reached its extreme. The realm of science, which dealt with public, impersonal collective experience stated in terms of rationally understood abstract laws, was indifferent to that more complete reality which was always individual: "In spite of the appeal which this impersonality of the scientific attitude makes to a certain magnanimity of temper, I believe it to be shallow, and I can now state my reason in comparatively few words. That reason is that, so long as we deal with the cosmic and the general, we deal only with the symbols of reality, but *as soon as we deal with private and personal phenomena as such, we deal with realities in the completest sense of the term.*"[47]

James's sense of reality was ultimately nominalistic and individualistic.[48] Within the individual he believed there existed a need for deliverance that would be fulfilled by religion. The initial part of that process was a feeling of *"something wrong about us,"* while the next part suggested that *"we are saved from the wrongness* by making proper connection with the higher powers."[49] This process, which Jonathan Edwards called "conversion" and James's father called "vastation," James called "deliverance"—the experience that kept him from going "to pieces in the wreck."[50] To James, the " 'more' with which in religious experience we feel ourselves connected is on its *hither* side the subconscious continuation of our conscious life."[51] The spiritual experience was thus working in the subconscious mind, and all of this was set in a pluralistic model of consciousness. He concluded:

> The whole drift of my education goes to persuade me that the world of our present consciousness is only one out of many worlds in consciousness that exist, and that those other worlds must contain experiences which have a meaning for our life also; and that although in the main their experiences and those of this world keep discrete, yet the two become continuous at certain points, and higher energies filter in. By being faithful in my poor measure to this over-belief, I seem to myself to keep more sane and true.[52]

These thoughts were, and still are, reiterated in thousands of sermons as well as religious and/or psychological counseling sessions during the twentieth century. Down through the long corridors of religious seminaries, mental hospitals, and clinics, this Jamesian solution, with a life almost its own, echoes and re-echoes. Religion has always had its healing function, but for many in the secular city of the twentieth century, "healing" increasingly is its sole legitimate function. As the First Commandment has lost its ontological dimension, and the very idea of God has come to be justified by what such a belief achieves for us therapeutically, survival and sanity logically have displaced salvation as sin has become sickness. In *The Varieties of Religious Experience,* James moved away from labeling what Jonathan Edwards had called the experience of the "sinful soul" toward labeling essentially the same experience as that of the "sick soul." While Edwards had analyzed the guilt of the sinful soul, James analyzed the anxiety of the sick soul, employing the therapeutic yardstick of mental health as the very justification for faith.

As in the past, when fierce, passionate arguments and debates were heard on the "nature of redemption," so too in the secular city of the twentieth century the nature of "mental health" became the critical issue. Conceptually, James had begun to outline the emerging, therapeutically oriented society of the future that would justify virtually any "over-belief." Ten years after his death, a former student, G. Stanley Hall, sensed the social consequences of James's ideological leadership. In a letter to Dr. Joseph Jastrow, Hall said,

> I have been amazed to note among my own friends in whom I never suspected anything of the sort, a great and growing disposition to believe that their friends killed in the war are somehow in *rapport* with them. I am also surprised to see how many people are of late resorting to the Ouija board, and I am scandalized by Southard's apology for this sort of thing. The "medium-mad" Bostonians, even Southard, who says he sees no harm in it, all point to James and say with him that there is a germ of truth in all the bosh and dross. It is James who laid the foundations of all this credulity that is springing up among more or less intellectual people all over the country. He is the coadjutor and the John the Baptist of Lodge-ism, though I would not for the world be quoted. The first thing I shall look for in your book is whether you have had the courage and insight to deal with James' responsibility in this matter as it ought to be dealt with. I don't know but I am too much of a coward to do it as it should be done.[53]

While it does seem a bit unfair to ascribe to James the responsibility for all the "over-beliefs" of the "medium-mad" Bostonians, it seems reasonable to recognize that the road James took was essentially the same one many others would take in the twentieth century. Saying this, however, should not detract from the fact that James also had played a historically important role, not only in consciously blueprinting the route that road would take, but also in building a significant part of it. As the teacher of some of the most important leaders in psychology in the twentieth century, his influence was undoubtedly substantial. However, he also was important in lending his name to support the credibility of the field of psychical research. As president of the British Society for Psychical Research, and as author of articles reporting his investigation of spiritualistic mediums, James lent his active support to the movement. He was intrigued by spiritualism and mental telepathy, as well as by the "mind-cure movement."

As the traditional Christian ontological view of God in the universe weakened, many clergy consciously began to shift their role from one of helping people save their souls for the next world, to helping them survive psychologically in this world. James welcomed this development and defended those within the movement against attacks from both the traditional clergy and the organized medical profession. In discussing his reaction to Freud's visit to America, James criticized Freud's attack on religious therapists: "A newspaper report of the congress said that Freud had condemned American religious therapy (which has such extensive results) as very 'dangerous' because so unscientific. Bah!"[54] Repeatedly, he came to the support of the Emmanuel Movement, which emphasized the psychological healing ministry within the Episcopal church.[55]

James was not only a theoretical conceptualizer of the therapeutic society but also an active historical actor, helping to shape its development. Late in life (1909), as an executive committee member of the National Committee for Mental Hygiene, he wrote to John D. Rockefeller and "begged" him for a million dollars to support the efforts of the National Committee for Mental Hygiene. Sending along a copy of Clifford W. Beers's *A Mind that Found Itself*, James tried to interest Rockefeller in broadly supporting the emerging mental health movement. As he put it, "if I myself, by Heaven's grace, should ever be able to leave any money for public use it should be for 'Insanity' exclusively."[56] Shortly thereafter, the foundations under Rockefeller's influence began to pour millions of dollars into the mental hygiene movement, into the development and construction of psychopathic hospitals, and into the training of psychiatrists, psychologists, and mental health workers in a variety of institutions across the country.[57] In this and other ways, James was actively involved in the practical work of creating the institutional framework through which the therapeutic society came into existence.

While James had conceptualized some of the key parameters of twentieth-century therapeutic society, as well as played a significant role in helping to build such a society institutionally, his philosophy of pluralism was fundamentally grounded on a nineteenth-century, classical liberal conception of individualism, which itself implicitly accepted a laissez-faire political economy. Just as his personal relationship with his father helps to explain how certain doors of consciousness were opened for him to see the relationship of religious ideology to personal philosophy as well as psychology, so too does the broader economic and cultural milieu in which he was reared also help to explain his social perspective. Important here is the way in which his peculiar consciousness transactionally emerged from his social and cultural milieu.

The James family was very much a part of that complicated bourgeois romantic movement of the nineteenth century, which found purpose and meaning in life by exploring the alienated self while rebelling against the Philistine life of business.[58] Romanticism was, as many have noted, a bourgeois protest movement, and the James family clearly reflected dimensions of that protest. Ultimately, the meaning of life was to be found not in collective abstractions or social institutions, but in the exploration of the individual soul. That soul, although fragmented, detached, and alienated, was prepared for "deliverance," a religious experience. As earlier noted, even though the James family clearly rejected a money culture as their way of life, their life of leisure economically depended on that culture. While, from time to time, they optimistically dreamed of utopian futures, their life, and that of most of the idealistic bourgeoisie, remained one of fundamental contradiction. The individualism of James, as an independent, separate, responsible, competitive free agent, was nurtured in the larger communal crucible of an emerging laissez-faire capitalistic economy.

The market economy of Thomas Malthus and others literally depended on the construction of this kind of individualism. As Max Weber, R. H. Tawney, and Karl Marx had noted, significant relationships exist between religion and the economic order. The feudal economy of the medieval world necessitated a conception of the individual that was vastly different from the Protestant individualism of a capitalist economy. Much of the individualism of James was classical liberal, premised on a conception of a laissez-faire capitalist social order. However, as the political economy moved from the predominantly laissez-faire capitalism of the nineteenth century to that of a state-monitored monopoly capitalism of the twentieth century, there occurred a corresponding necessity for a reconstructed conception of individualism. Thus, the crisis in late-nineteenth-century religious beliefs could be viewed as related to changes in the political economy. A new economy requiring a new individualism would ultimately require a new faith.

The revolt of the bourgeoisie against crass materialism— finding solace in the spiritual self—carried with it the potential for undercutting the very ideological value structure that fundamentally sustained that order. This is what periodically has occurred when the sons and daughters of the affluent-idealistic bourgeoisie have carried their protest against the materialism of their age over into an attack on the personal values sustaining that order economically. Although some of James's students, such as Hall and Gertrude Stein, began to explore such a route, James's own individualism definitely stopped short of such exploration. From the turn of the century on, many children of the bourgeoisie critically tested those values in both urban and rural bohemian communes. Another James student, George Herbert Mead, along with John Dewey and others, attempted to reconceptualize the meaning of individualism in the context of a broader reconstruction of liberalism itself. In this respect, when Dewey called for a reconstruction of liberalism in *Individualism Old and New* (1928), he recognized the extent to which the corporate order of society now required a new kind of individualism.

James's individualism throughout remained unreconstructed, premised largely on a tacit acceptance of the economic order. Merle Curti is probably correct in *The Social Ideas of American Educators* when he points to the economic affluence of the James family as a partial factor in the fashioning of James's individualism, as well as his reluctance to engage in serious institutional criticism. While Mead and others attempted to reconstruct the older meaning of individualism in the context of a limited degree of social criticism, others, such as Edward L. Thorndike, followed James's tacit acceptance of the economic order and constructed their psychology on the basis of a presumed idealized meritocratic order.

William James was the teacher of Edward L. Thorndike, who in turn became one of the leading educational psychologists in the first three decades of the twentieth century. Although in many ways the broad introspective psychology of James was very different from Thorndike's, in certain key respects their social views were remarkably similar. James, very much like his student Thorndike, accepted the economic order as given and extolled the virtues of competition, genius, strong leadership, and expressed belief in the fundamentally unmalleable nature of intellectual ability. Both men thought in terms of the noble obligation of the "college bred" to become the new "aristocracy"[59] and to meritocratically lead the "white trash,"[60] which they believed existed in significant numbers in their society.

While from time to time James would reflect Emerson's romantic indulgence of the common man by periodically sitting "at the feet of the familiar, the low,"[61] he also fundamentally believed with Emerson that: "The young adventurer finds that the relations of society, the position of classes, irk and sting him, and he lends himself to each malignant party that assails what is eminent. He will one day know that this is not removable, but a distinction in the nature of things; that neither the caucus, nor the newspaper, nor the congress, nor the mob, nor the guillotine, nor fire, nor all together: can avail to outlaw, cut out, burn or destroy the offense of superiority in persons."[62] He was opposed to those revolutionaries who would take law and order into their own hands. The Haymarket riot, he believed, was the "work of a lot of pathological Germans and Poles."[63]

James's democracy was not egalitarian but, like Thorndike's, aristocratic: the "college bred" were meritocratically chosen to lead. Thorndike had insisted that "the argument for democracy is not that it gives power to all men without distinction, but that it gives greater freedom for ability and character to attain power."[64] Like Thorndike, James worried about from whom the masses "shall take their cue." "In our democracy, where everything else is so shifting, we alumni and alumnae of the colleges are the only permanent presence that corresponds to the aristocracy in older countries. We have continuous traditions, as they have; our motto, too, is noblesse oblige; and, unlike them, we stand for ideal interests solely, for we have no corporate selfishness and wield no powers of corruption. We ought to have our own class-consciousness. '*Les Intellectuals*'!"[65] The pragmatically best possible society for James was a meritocratically organized society where "Les Intellectuals," romanticized as having "no corporate selfishness," ruled.

Along with Thorndike, James believed that some races are inherently more instinctive, and hence ultimately less educable:

> when we survey the human race, we actually do find that those which are most instinctive at the outset are those which, on the whole, are least educated in the end. An un-tutored Italian is, to a great extent, a man of the world; he has instinctive perceptions, tendencies to behavior, reactions, in a word, upon his environment, which the untutored German wholly lacks. If the latter be not drilled, he is apt to be a thoroughly loutish personage; but, on the other hand, the mere absence in his brain of definite innate tendencies enables him to advance by the development, through education, of his purely reasoned thinking, into complex regions of con-sciousness that the Italian may probably never approach.[66]

A similar "psychological" explanation for racial stereotyping can be found in Thorndike's work on *Individuality*, published a year after James's death.[67]

If for James the Italian instinctively learned the ways of the world quicker than the German, but in the end could not match the inherent superiority of the educated German, so too did James find "an identical difference between men as a whole and women as a whole."[68] Because of a fundamental instinctual difference, girls mature faster than boys and are therefore set in their thoughts earlier; boys develop later and have greater flexibility of mind. As a consequence, "the masculine brain deals with new and complex matter indirectly by means of these, in a manner which the feminine method of direct intuition, admirably and rapidly as it performs within its limits, can vainly hope to cope with."[69] James thus grounded his sexual and racial stereotying on presumed instinctual psychological differences, which he believed were empirically verifiable. Shortly after his mentor's death, Thorndike published *Educational Psychology: Briefer Course*, which, like James's *Psychology: The Briefer Course*, was directly aimed at practicing schoolteachers. Thorndike argued that male superiority instinctually was based on "original nature" and was linked to occupations: "No one will doubt that men are more possessed by the instinct to fight, to be the winner in games and serious contests, than are women; nor that women are more possessed than men by the instinct to nurse, to care for and fuss over others, to relieve, comfort and console."[70] Clearly, both men had absorbed the racial and sexist attitudes of their day and, in turn, justified them on the basis of the new empirically oriented psychology. In so helping teachers to conceptualize their curriculum, they put the force of the emerging field of psychology behind the racist and sexist thinkers of their day.

Although James would periodically decry the "bitch goddess SUCCESS"[71] and condemn with equal ferocity the materialism of his age, his own individualism was fundamentally laced with entrepreneurial values. Private property was grounded in the psychological instinct for "acquisitiveness."[72] Thus firmly grounding the taproot of capitalism in nature, he proceeded to repeatedly romanticize the competitive life of that system by extolling the virtues of poverty, as well as the life of the workingmen who required so little to survive.[73] He also reflected the new nationalism of his age by romanticizing the selfless dedication of the soldier in his service to the state.[74]

Although the personal values of James's individualism were clearly laissez-faire-classical-liberal, in his emerging views of state power one could sense some beginning steps toward various facets of the new liberalism which Herbert Croly, George Herbert Mead, Charles Horton Cooley, and John Dewey would develop later. Curti appropriately criticizes James for not seriously questioning the economic institutions of his day; yet James could not have ventured very far down that path without completely jeopardizing his own personal philosophy of individualism, which apparently he was not prepared to reconstruct. Implicit in his individualism was a general acceptance of the political economy as given; the social consequences of his psychology were equally clear.

> Habit is thus the enormous fly-wheel of society, its most precious conservative agent. It alone is what keeps us all within the bounds of ordinance, and saves the children of fortune from the envious uprisings of the poor. It alone prevents the hardest and most repulsive walks of life from being deserted by those brought up to tread therein. It keeps the fisherman and the deck-hand at sea through the winter; it holds the miner in his darkness, and nails the countryman to his log cabin and his lonely farm through all the months of snow; it protects us from invasion by the natives of the desert and the frozen zone. It dooms us all to fight out the

battle of life upon the lines of our nurture or our early choice, and to make the best of a pursuit that disagrees, because there is no other for which we are fitted, and it is too late to begin again. It keeps different social strata from mixing. Already at the age of twenty-five you see the professional mannerism settling down on the young commercial traveller, on the young doctor, on the young minister, on the young counsellor-at-law. You see the little lines of cleavage running through the character, the tricks of thought, the prejudices, the ways of the "shop," in a word, from which the man can by-and-by no more escape than his coat-sleeve can suddenly fall into a new set of folds. On the whole, it is best he should not escape. It is well for the world that in most of us, by the age of thirty, the character has set like plaster, and will never soften again.[75]

The shift in the American political economy from nineteenth-century laissez-faire capitalism to a liberal state-monitored twentieth-century monopoly capitalism involved not only a change in attitude toward the legitimacy of state action but required a new view of individualism as well. James's individualism, as earlier noted, was very much part of the older classical liberal tradition. His analysis of the function of habit as an integral part of his individualism clearly reflected the social function of habit in preserving the competitive nature of the political economy. Thus any serious reconstruction of individualism had to take into account not only the changed social-economic order but also the very function of habit itself. It was precisely at this point in the new liberal social behavioral analysis of Mead's, Cooley's, and Dewey's concept of the social "self" that an emphasis on cooperation, rather than competition, appeared. In a fundamental way they were reconstructing James's individualism.

The Jamesian view of the individual not only required a distinctive psychology, but it also included a particular view of the social order as well as education. Thus when James spoke to teachers, he called upon them to capitalize on the instinct for rivalry among their students, because "the feeling of rivalry lies at the very basis of our being, all social improvement being largely due to it."[76] The teacher ought to encourage competition by cultivating the students' instinctive sense for ownership, which begins in the "second year of life." As he noted, "In education, the instinct of ownership is fundamental, and can be appealed to in many ways."[77] Private property, competition, and acquisitiveness are all inherent in human nature, James argued, and must be appealed to in shaping the educational context in which the proper laws of habit are formed to stabilize and preserve the political economy. His "tough-minded" educational values were not far afield from those Thorndike was "stamping-in." To be sure, James maintained a broader view. Nevertheless, when it came to economic order, the two men shared a common perspective.

James's pluralistic, ideal vision of society and life ultimately was based on competitive individualism cast in a "free market-place" where, assumedly, the "cash value" of all items might be ascertained—that cash value to be measured in individual, Darwinian, survival terms. Religion itself, thus viewed as a reflection of men's ideal aims, was but a workable segment of his individualism. Ironically, James, the antagonist of the competitive self-seeking character of business life, most thoroughly embraced those values operationally, both in his philosophy of individualism and in his educational beliefs. Faith, in the new therapeutic society, was to be treated always as a "hypothesis" without any "authoritative pretensions." "Meanwhile the freest competition of the various faiths with one another and their openest application to life by their several champions, are the most favorable conditions under which the survival of the fittest can proceed."[78]

With Malthus and Darwin thus standing in the shadows, the ultimate test of survival would be the "help" each over-belief provided individuals in their quest for psychological survival. All this was to be accomplished without ever seriously touching the political and economic institutions of the day. For James, the pragmatic justification of faith turned into the therapeutic use of faith; even the concept of God was pragmatically useful. As the twentieth century unfolded and these beliefs became commonplace, therapeutic society became for many a secular religion where "help" was, as James said it must be, the sole criterion of one's religious beliefs.

James's own religious beliefs were constructed out of his own personal struggle for freedom and his own psychological need for help. In the midst of that struggle, standing on what he believed was the very brink of insanity, he found the religious exercise of repetitive prayer therapeutically useful, as he did the personal discovery that something "more" existed. In his over-beliefs the "more" was something which somehow gave strength, "indeterminate, partial but yet something which one could invest in and rely on for help." An abstract description to be sure, but one that is not far afield from his perceptions of his own father, living or dead. James grounded his faith on his psychological need to overcome the influence of an overzealous father he could not bring himself to hate. In many ways his God appears as God, the Father—his father. Whether it was or not matters little from a Jamesian point of view. The important point is that it worked, helping him to integrate his life and proceed to an extremely successful career in psychology and philosophy. Clearly, it also helped him to avoid both a very painful break with his father and conceptually coming to grips with himself and his world. At critical points in his life, the therapeutic road he chose to follow helped him to escape from the world of critical consciousness: "care little for speculation / Much for the form of my action." With this therapeutic principle buried deep in his psyche, it was but a short step to romanticizing the virtues of poverty, tortuous work, and martial values, while criticizing the materialism and "bitch goddess of *SUCCESS*!" so characteristic of his own class.

It would have been just as painful for James to own up to the social injustices of his age as it would have been to break with his father. In the first case he creatively substituted a romanticized, benign view of poverty, tortuous work, etc., which effectively insulated him from the painful reality of social injustice, while in the latter case he created a benign view of the "more," which allowed him the freedom he so desperately sought and which thereby insulated him from the painful consequences of breaking with a loving but all-pervasive father. In both cases, the therapeutic principle based on individual survival served as a narcotic to effectively deaden the pain of reality in a world where values were human creations. James's life experiences were part of the bourgeoisie's nineteenth- and twentieth-century privatized romantic experiences, which sought authenticity and "deliverance" in the individual self rather than in the social order. In its larger ramification, the therapeutic principle served as an escape, cultivating a false consciousness in the name of healing while tolerating enormous social injustice in exchange for social stability.

Heinrich Heine and Karl Marx spoke of religion in the nineteenth century as a spiritual opium of the proletariat, one that promised solace and comfort in the social justice of an afterlife.[79] In the secular city of the twentieth century, with its declining belief in life after death, James and others appeared to cultivate a therapeutic opiate not so much for proletarians as for the bourgeoisie. Early in the nineteenth century, Marx noted this narcotic characteristic of religion: "Religious suffering is at the same time an expression of real suffering and a protest against real suffering. Religion is the sight of the oppressed creature, the sentiment of a heartless world, and the soul of soulless conditions. It is the opium of the people. . . . The abolition of religion, as the illusory happiness of men, is a demand for their real happiness. The call to abandon their illusions about their condition is a call to abandon a condition which requires illusions."[80] William James never answered that call. He did, however, cultivate illusions.

If we believe, along with Marx, Nietzsche, Dewey, and others, that we are the creators of human values, then the transformation of religion into the secular psychological society of the twentieth century, where any therapeutic belief is acceptable as long as it works, needs to be critically examined. Equally important is the fact that this Jamesian faith, which pragmatically emphasizes healing, survival, and adjustment, can and often is used to cultivate a false consciousness which, in effect, produces a "social amnesia,"[81] a new opiate, capable of sustaining the social order just as well as did any traditional religion in the past.

Notes

1. Quoted in Gay Wilson Allen, *William James: A Biography* (New York: Viking Press, 1967), p. 257.

2. Ibid., p. 255.

3. Quoted in F. O. Matthiessen, *The James Family* (New York: Alfred A. Knopf, 1947), p. 133.

4. Ibid., p. 138.

5. See Merle Curti, *The Social Ideas of American Educators* (Paterson, N.J.: Littlefield, Adams, and Co., 1961), p. 429.

6. Ibid., p. 443.

7. Walter Kaufmann, *The Portable Nietzsche* (New York: Viking Press, 1954), p. 95.

8. Quoted in part by Allen, *William James*, p. 7.

9. Ibid., p. 27.

10. Quoted in Matthiessen, *James Family*, p. 161.

11. Ibid., p. 162.

12. Allen, *William James*, p. 64.

13. Ibid.

14. For a very interesting analysis of his sister Alice's breakdown

at age nineteen in relation to his own, see Jean Strouse, *Alice James: A Biography* (Boston: Houghton Mifflin Co., 1980), pp. 117–31.

15. Allen, *William James*, p. 214.

16. William James, *The Varieties of Religious Experience: A Study in Human Nature* (New York: Collier Books, 1961), pp. 138–39. While the case in *Varieties* is reported as that of a "Frenchman," late in life William James admitted his identity to his son Henry. His son also thought that the experience occurred sometime in the spring of 1870. See Allen, *William James*, p. 165. For a similar analysis of William James's personal identity problem in relation to his father, see Cushing Strout, "William James and the Twice-Born Sick Soul," *Daedalus* 97 (Summer 1968): 1062–82. Strout very effectively uses Erik H. Erikson's ego-identity model to analyze James's relationship with his father.

17. James, *Varieties of Religious Experience*, p. 139.

18. Ibid.

19. Henry James, *The Letters of William James*, 2 vols. (Boston: Atlantic Monthly Press, 1920), 1:148.

20. Kaufmann, *Portable Nietzsche*, p. 95.

21. Ibid., p. 96.

22. Ibid.

23. It is interesting to note that James, Emerson, and Nietzsche each wrote about leadership characteristics of strong-willed people. For example, see Emerson's "Napoleon: Or, the Man of the World," Nietzsche's *The Will to Power*, and James's "Great Men and Their Environments." To be sure, each interpretation is different, but what is common here is the view of the social order from an individualistic rather than a collectivistic eye.

24. William James, *Memories and Studies* (New York: Longmans, Green and Co., 1911), p. 34.

25. Nietzsche once said, "Emerson, I have never felt so much at home in a book, so much in my own house as,—I ought not to praise it; it is too close to me." He also wrote of Emerson: "The author as yet the richest in ideas of this century has been an American." Quoted in Stephen Donadio, *Nietzsche, Henry James, and the Artistic Will* (New York: Oxford University Press, 1978), p. 41.

26. James, *Memories and Studies*, p. 31.

27. Ibid., p. 33.

28. James, *Varieties of Religious Experience*, p. 295.

29. Ibid.

30. Ibid., p. 297.

31. The book is appropriately subtitled "A Study in Human Nature."

32. Ralph Barton Perry, *The Thought and Character of William James, Briefer Version* (Cambridge, Mass.: Harvard University Press, 1967), p. 121.

33. Allen, *William James*, p. 163. Prof. Charles Burgess has called

to my attention the nineteenth-century dictionary definition of "empiricism": "the practice or profession of quacks who consulted their own personal experiences." If we then consider the older definition of radical as "getting-to-the-root of," together with James's possible nineteenth-century use of the term, we get a much clearer picture of what he meant by "radical empiricism." It was getting to the root of one's own personal experience. Thus, his "radical empiricism" was truly introspective.

34. Andre Revesz, "Fascism's Indelible Mark on History," *Sunday Times*, Apr. 11, 1926, p. 15.

35. As Ralph Barton Perry put it, "Mussolini has a right to cite James, even if it be an afterthought." Perry, *The Thought and Character of William James*, 2 vols. (Boston: Little, Brown and Co., 1935), 2:578.

36. Ibid., p. 577. See also Giovanni Gullace, "The Pragmatist Movement in Italy," *Journal of the History of Ideas* 23(Jan.-Mar. 1962): 91–105.

37. Perry, *Thought and Character of William James*, 2:571.

38. James, *Letters of William James*, 2:246.

39. Ibid., pp. 245–46.

40. William James, "G. Papini and the Pragmatist Movement in Italy," *Journal of Philosophy* 3(June 21, 1906): 340.

41. Ibid., p. 339.

42. William James, *A Pluralistic Universe* (Cambridge, Mass.: Harvard University Press, 1977), pp. 143–44.

43. Ibid., p. 148.

44. Ibid.

45. For an excellent critique of this argument, as well as James's conception of truth and fact in relation to his discussion of a belief in God, see Bertrand Russell, *Philosophical Essays* (New York: Simon and Schuster, 1966), pp. 112–30.

46. James, *Varieties of Religious Experience*, p. 377.

47. Ibid., p. 386.

48. For a discussion of the nominalism inherent in James's thought, see Clarence J. Karier, *Man, Society, and Education* (Glenview, Ill.: Scott, Foresman and Co., 1967), pp. 123–26.

49. James, *Varieties of Religious Experience*, p. 393.

50. Ibid., p. 394.

51. Ibid., p. 396.

52. Ibid., p. 401.

53. Letter from G. Stanley Hall to Dr. Joseph Jastrow, Feb. 9, 1920, Hall Collection, Clark University Archives, box 25, folder no. 2. I am indebted to Chris Shea for first calling my attention to this letter.

54. Quoted in Allen, *William James*, p. 467.

55. For example, see Raymond J. Cunningham, "The Emmanuel Movement: A Variety of American Religious Experience," *American*

Quarterly, 14(1962): 48–63; Robert P. Casey, "Religion and Psychoanalysis," *Psychiatry* 6(1943): 291–99; Lois W. Banner, "Religious Benevolence as Social Control: A Critique of an Interpretation," *Journal of American History* 60(1973): 23–41. See also "Mental Healing and the Emmanuel Movement," *Psychological Clinic* 2(1908–9).

56. Letter from James to Rockefeller, June 2, 1909, Rockefeller Foundation Archives, record group 1.1, ser. 200, box 32, folder 363. I am indebted to Chris Shea for first calling this letter to my attention.

57. For a history of the use of Rockefeller money in support of this movement, see Christine Mary Shea, "The Ideology of Mental Health and the Emergence of the Therapeutic Liberal State: The American Mental Hygiene Movement, 1900–1930," Ph.D. dissertation, University of Illinois at Urbana-Champaign, 1980. For a history of some of these developments, see also Barbara Sicherman, "The Quest for Mental Health in America, 1880–1917," Ph.D. dissertation, Columbia University, 1967.

58. See Ernst Fischer, *The Necessity of Art* (Baltimore: Penguin Books, 1971), pp. 49–115.

59. James, *Memories and Studies*, pp. 318–19.

60. Merle Curti, *Social Ideas of American Educators*, p. 441.

61. Ralph Waldo Emerson, *The Complete Writings of Ralph Waldo Emerson* (New York: Wm. H. Wise and Co., 1929), p. 35.

62. Quoted in Karier, *Man, Society, and Education*, p. 56.

63. James, *Letters of William James*, 1:252.

64. Edward L. Thorndike, "Intelligence and Its Uses," *Harpers* 140 (Dec. 1919–May 1920): 235. See also Edward L. Thorndike, "The Psychology of the Half-Educated Man," *Harpers* 140(Apr. 1920): 666–70.

65. James, *Memories and Studies*, pp. 318–19.

66. William James, *The Principles of Psychology*, 2 vols. (New York: Dover Publications, 1950), 2:368.

67. See Edward L. Thorndike, *Individuality* (Boston: Houghton Mifflin Co., 1911), pp. 33–39.

68. James, *Principles of Psychology*, 2:368.

69. Ibid., p. 369.

70. Edward L. Thorndike, *Educational Psychology: Briefer Course* (New York: Teachers College, Columbia University, 1914), pp. 350–51. See also Clarence Karier, *Shaping the American Educational State* (New York: Free Press, 1975), pp. 235–37.

71. Quoted in Curti, *Social Ideas of American Educators*, p. 457.

72. See James, *Principles of Psychology*, 2:422–25. See also James, *Varieties of Religious Experience*, p. 252.

73. See James, *Varieties of Religious Experience*, pp. 252, 291–92. See also Curti, *Social Ideas of American Educators*, pp. 434–35.

74. See James, "The Moral Equivalent of War," in *Memories and Studies*, pp. 265–96. In many ways James's glorification of the idea of service to the state is not far afield from the kind of state service G. Stanley Hall dreamed of.

75. James, *Principles of Psychology*, 1:121.

76. William James, *Talks to Teachers* (New York: W. W. Norton and Co., 1958), p. 50.

77. Ibid., p. 52.

78. William James, *The Will to Believe* (New York: Dover Publications, 1956), p. xii.

79. See Jeffrey L. Sammons, *Heinrich Heine* (Princeton, N.J.: Princeton University Press, 1979), p. 262.

80. Karl Marx, *Selected Writings in Sociology and Social Philosophy*, T. B. Bottomore, trans. and ed. (New York: McGraw Hill Co., 1969), pp. 26–27.

81. See, for example, Russell Jacoby, *Social Amnesia: A Critique of Conformist Psychology from Adler to Laing* (Boston: Beacon Press, 1975).

2

GEORGE HERBERT MEAD [1863–1931]

In Search of Self
in a Moral Universe

Erik Erikson has called attention to the critical role of adolescence in an individual's life cycle. During this important transitional period, the individual puts aside the things of childhood and assumes the characteristics of an adult, possibly undergoing an identity crisis in the process. The outcome of such a crisis usually has significance only for the individual, but it sometimes may have significance for the broader culture as well. As certain individuals, destined by their peculiar personal characteristics and historic circumstances to become leaders of the culture, undergo the Sturm und Drang of adolescence, it is often possible to perceive the sources for what eventually may be their unique contributions to that culture. Erikson states:

> In some young people, in some classes, at some periods in history, this crisis will be minimal; in other people, classes, and periods, the crisis will be clearly marked off as a critical period, a kind of "second birth," apt to be aggravated either by widespread neuroticisms or by pervasive ideological unrest.

Portions of this chapter originally appeared in the *Journal of the History of Ideas* 45(1), Jan.-Mar. 1984, and are reprinted here by permission of Journal of the History of Ideas, Inc.

Some young individuals will succumb to this crisis in all manner of neurotic, psychotic, or delinquent behavior; others will resolve it through participation in ideological movements passionately concerned with religion or politics, nature or art. Still others, although suffering and deviating dangerously through what appears to be a prolonged adolescence, eventually come to contribute an original bit to an emerging style of life: the very danger which they have sensed has forced them to mobilize capacities to see and say, to dream and plan, to design and construct, in new ways.[1]

Erikson also has observed that the identity crisis for those who "dream and plan, to design and construct, in new ways," often occurs in young adults who are circumstantially locked into life courses that are incompatible with their personal inclinations. He found this to be the case in *Young Man Luther* (1958), as well as with George Bernard Shaw, who "broke loose," to use Shaw's term, at the age of twenty.[2]

Comparable circumstances prevailed in the early years of two of America's leading psychologists: William James and George Herbert Mead. Both men underwent severe emotional crises involving their religious faith, just as they were making critical career decisions which, symbolically at least, meant breaking away from parental controls. In James's case, his father appears to have played the role of "significant other"; in Mead's case, his mother's role was critical. Both men, born and bred in the bourgeoisie, were highly creative as well as sensitive to the declining credibility of Christian dogma in an emerging scientific world.

Equally at home in the intellectual life on either side of the Atlantic, each man in his own way wrestled with the romantic presuppositions that permeated nineteenth-century literature, art, and philosophy.[3] Although both rejected romanticism, they themselves were absorbed in the romantic's problem of an individual's isolation from culture as well as self-estrangement from God, nature, and community. These men painfully turned away from the tradition-oriented religious culture of their youth and faced the future by attempting to fashion a new faith in a scientific psychology. Under such circumstances, both were cognizant of the therapeutic value to be found in religious faith. Long before James declared in *The Varieties of Religious Experiences* that any faith, to be successful, must first satisfy the individual's anguished cry for "help," George Herbert Mead, in the midst of his own religious crisis, said: "Because I felt the necessity of help out of myself, I could not continue any longer with such a flagrant distance between ideal and action and so I tried and succeeded in getting help outside myself. Of course I have not changed very materially my views. Except that I believe it is philosophical to pray. I do not know that there is any God. But in someway I get help. It may not reach beyond my own sensibility but still it gives me help and I need it so much that I cannot afford to drop it."[4] Mead, like James, had traveled far enough down the secular road to have found it "philosophical to pray."

The religious crisis each man experienced in his youth was an identity crisis that involved the anguished stripping away of an older belief system and the corresponding destruction of the self thereby entailed. Also included was the creation of a new self-concept within the broader construction of a faith system based more on philosophical and psychological tenets than on traditional religious beliefs.[5] In this process, both men struggled with the problem of the relationship of the inner and outer worlds, the individual and the community, and the subjective and objective self in an evolutionary world, where the ultimate faith in healing was to be found in science.

William James was instrumental in popularizing pragmatism as a philosophical basis for the emerging field of American psychology. His conception of human nature, though broad enough, remained substantially based on an unreconstructed classical liberal conception of human nature, derived from an earlier political economy. James's student, George Herbert Mead, along with John Dewey, Charles Horton Cooley, and others, founded the field of social psychology and did the creative work in reconstructing American liberalism. More than anyone else, Mead reconceptualized the classical liberal view of the individual into that of the new liberal "social self." His reformulations eventually came to permeate the conceptual assumptions upon which most American social scientists tend to function in the twentieth century.

Dewey and Mead were both significant leaders in the reconstruction of American liberalism; in many respects, their ideas were almost identical. From 1891, when Mead first began working with Dewey at the University of Michigan, until Mead's death in 1931, while at the University of Chicago, they were dialogically engaged in shaping and refining the basic tenets of the new liberal philosophy and psychology. To Mead, his friend

Dewey was "the Philosopher of America,"[6] while to Dewey, his friend Mead's "mind was deeply original—in my contacts and my judgment the most original mind in the America of the last generation."[7]

Much of Mead's creative contribution to new liberal thought was a function of his particular personal characteristics and tensions, as well as the specific historic setting in which he interacted. To a considerable extent, his basic assumptions with regard to mind, self, and community had taken effective shape, at least in a nascent form, before he joined Dewey at Ann Arbor in 1891. Given these circumstances, I focus here on the early adult years of his life, analyzing his personal world in relation to his social environment, looking for clues as to how—and suggesting reasons why—Mead came to be one of the key architects of the new liberal faith. Lastly, I examine critically some traditional Christian assumptions underlying that faith developed by Mead, and suggest possible linkages with the problematic present.

George Herbert Mead was born in South Hadley, Massachusetts, in 1863, to Elizabeth Storrs (Billings) Mead and Hiram Mead, D.D., from Cornwall, Vermont. When George was seven years old the family moved to Oberlin, Ohio, where his father assumed the chair in homiletics at the Theological Seminary of Oberlin College. In 1879, at age sixteen, Mead entered Oberlin College, where he met two young people from Hawaii, Henry and Helen Castle, who would profoundly affect the course of his life. Henry and Helen Castle were the son and daughter of American missionaries Samuel and Mary Castle. The close friendship which they struck up at Oberlin bound the three young people together for life. Henry became Mead's closest friend, someone with whom he carried on youthful dialogues, to whom he confided his personal thoughts, and with whom he elaborated his views concerning the world. Together they interacted with the world at Oberlin, then at Harvard, and later at the Universities of Leipzig and Berlin. These student days not only shaped the intellectual life of Mead, but in a very real sense helped to establish the future direction of his life.

While the tragic death of Henry Castle in 1895 closed, in one sense, a significant chapter in Mead's life, in another sense that chapter would never really remain closed.[8] Mead's marriage to Henry's sister, Helen, as well as his close association with the Castle family, were significant reminders of things past. As if to seal that past, symbolically at least, George and Helen privately printed for family and friends the *Henry Northrup Castle: Letters* (London, 1902). Sixteen years of Castle's friendship had had a profound effect on Mead's life and thinking.

It was no accident that Mead's identity crisis revolved around religious issues. His best friend's father was a missionary, and his own father was a clergyman who taught homiletics. His mother had been educated in the Seminary at Ipswich, Massachusetts (1849–51) and later taught in a boarding school for young ladies at Andover, Massachusetts (1852–58), under the direction of her sister, who was married to Professor B. B. Edwards of Andover Theological Seminary, until her marriage to Dr. Hiram Mead in 1859. Clearly, Elizabeth Mead was a most unusual woman. George was seven when she received an M.A. from Oberlin College; after his father's death in 1881, his mother taught at Oberlin College, then at Abbott Academy at Andover, and from 1893–1901 served as president of Mt. Holyoke College. The later years of her life found her writing reports for the U.S. Commissioner of Education on women's education in England, and receiving an L.H.D. from Smith College. Mead therefore found himself struggling to break away from a role-model father who was an expert in the art of preaching and a strong-willed, very able mother who was equally steeped in the religious tradition.

For Mead, freedom from parental control, religious commitment, career, and the strange outer world's relationship with an evolving inner self-identity, were all intertwined in his Oberlin years. Upon receiving word of Henry Castle's untimely death, Mead wrote to his wife, Helen, reflecting on the Oberlin years and his relationship with her brother:

> Of course this has brought up those days or rather years of Oberlin life to me so that I have lived them over almost day by day. That was the romantic period—the *Sturm und Drang* period of my life when the outside world and the world of thought had the purple hues of distance—and this life was inseparably connected with Henry—Between that and Ann Arbor lies a period of groping. With a feeling for the reality of the world in the scientific statement and then when I came to know John [Dewey] I found the possibility of asserting the reality and living in it. But more of this has the rich coloring—the fullness of interest which belongs to Henry's and my valiant attacks upon the giants of unreason and prejudice in Oberlin days—We could get no further there,

because we had no art but that of denying but we *felt* there was a positive basis for the denial and this gave those years a real romance—Henry is a larger part of my Oberlin life than all the rest put together, his friendship was more education than what beside the place afforded.[9]

Mead's personal philosophy of life emerged, intimately related to Henry Castle's, as together they attacked those "giants of unreason and prejudice." His most creative years extended from the Oberlin period, when "the outside world and the world of thought reflected the purple hues of distance," to his Ann Arbor years and his collaboration with Dewey. Castle had embodied the romantic component in which their joint denial of crucial Christian tenets was based on what they *felt* was positive; Dewey reflected the scientific, practical side that addressed Mead's rationality. Castle had appealed to Mead's subjective, creative side; Dewey appealed to his more objective, rational side. Castle represented the youthful period of creating a new vision of the world; Dewey represented the more mature period of applying that vision through scientific social engineering.

Throughout his life Mead struggled with this split between the subjective and objective sides of his personality. There remained for Mead an inner and an outer world, an emotional and a cognitive experience, an inner and an outer self—or, as he would finally refer to them, an "I" and a "Me." Mead's greatest contribution to the field of social psychology rests in his penetrating analysis of the "social self." This professional interest, through which he eventually contributed so much, undoubtedly grew out of his Sturm und Drang experiences, some of which provided the ground from which his creative thinking emanated. These experiences also provided the problem that remained with him throughout his life: the integration of the subjective and objective sides of his "self."

Oberlin College, in its earlier days, had achieved notoriety for its courageous stand on the issue of black emancipation, as well as for the evangelical preaching of Charles G. Finney. By the time Mead and Castle enrolled there as students, however, the school had come under the direction of the more moderately conservative evangelist James H. Fairchild. President Fairchild taught a philosophy course at Oberlin which attempted to retain Christian doctrine and avoid science and evolutionary thought. Mead and Castle began a running attack against the ideas of

Fairchild, calling him one of those "giants of unreason and prejudice."[10]

During this time Mead's father passed away. While there is no evidence of a confrontation with either parent on religious issues, it is clear, as Mead's letters suggest, that his evolving position was at odds with their religious beliefs. On a number of occasions during his later crisis years, Mead berated himself for not being completely forthright and truthful about his religious views while at Oberlin. Some of his most heartrending, tormented letters questioning his religious faith were written in the period 1883–85, two years after his father's death, and after his mother had left Oberlin for a teaching position at Andover. By then Mead also had finished his work at Oberlin and was financially and socially independent. The more difficult task of breaking away psychologically still lay ahead, however.

Free from the direct influence of his late father, and from the immediate supervision of his mother, Mead wrote Castle of the emotional appeal of Christianity: "I can't tell you old boy what temptations of the most insidious and perplexing kind I have had to resist to keep from becoming a Christian with no reference to my reason but out of deference to my sensibilities which seem to be clamoring for Christianity."[11] Cognitively, he could not justify his faith; sentimentally, he could.

> It was not for naught that I was brought up in a Christian family fed with the conceptions of Christianity steeped in the reverence of Christianity. Today I could with more pleasure offer the most unreasonable prayers give myself up to the most unreasoning faith than anything I know of almost. I could find a companionship in a supposed intercourse with God which I know (excuse the expression) would [be] but a satisfaction of a sentiment that yearns for some support outside of itself that creates ideals that its imagination lends reality to because they are impossible and mostly because my life is such a contradiction so full of undesirable motives so teeming in fickle inconstant aims and attempts, so un-reasonable in its action that there would be an infinite pleasure in feeling (not believing save in Hume's sense) that it was all unfolded before some being who would appreciate and give support.[12]

Brought up thoroughly steeped in the Christian faith, Mead yearned to break free of the sentimental chains that bound him. Yet, in the end, he doubted that he wanted freedom if it meant a world without ideals, values, and moral purpose. The therapeutic function of prayer was not enough. "I am not surprised that men gain satisfaction in prayer, nothing is so credulous as human nature when it gets outside of the little circumference of its own immediate perceptions."[13] His faith could no longer stand the purview of reason and ultimately rested on sentiment: "I sift my beliefs upon this subject to their bottom realities I find them sentiments. I am plagued with sentiments now a days. I wish I could become pure intellect but that is another sentiment."[14] Tormented, Mead offered his friend a bit of advice: "My dear fellow never if you can help it get into a situation when duties too much for you are laid upon you and you try to find strength in sentiment for if you do it will end in suicide I can trust myself but I could not trust you."[15]

To be free of his parents' faith involved Mead not only in making a nonreligious career choice, but, more importantly, in carrying on a struggle with his "self": "I'm miserable, too much reason and too little strength to be a Christian, and too little reason and too much sentiment to be a philosopher. But from this time on (hear you the latest determination) I shall throw overboard all sentiment that I can and bend me to my work."[16] If he was ever to become a philosopher, Mead believed he would have to "throw overboard" the sentiment that controlled him, along with those "giants of unreason and prejudice" that bound him to Christianity. His lifelong problem of separating the subjective from the objective, sentiment from rationality, carried far more meaning than what might appear to some as a mere academic problem. His problem involved his association with Christianity, parents, early life, and career choice. Given Mead's view of sentiment, it is little wonder that in his later years his professional writing was not only limited in quantity but devoid of feeling as well. He was, after all, attempting to write as a "philosopher," not as a "theologian."

Mead's struggle to carve out his own unique identity, moving away from dogmatic Christianity and toward a kind of secular agnostic humanism, was not an easy one, and he sometimes vacillated. He felt a need to justify his leading prayer meetings in Oberlin and Berlin Heights: "I continue praying and reading the bible daily the latter mainly for my mother's sake. I do not get much help from it. Prayer does not seem very logical but enough so to make me feel that I ought to try it a good while before giving it up. I feel that I do get considerable help from it in striving to live up to my ideal and that justifies it."[17] The significant role of Mead's mother in his identity crisis is clear: "My Mother lives in me. Her happiness is bound up in me. I sometimes wonder if it is not my duty to profess Christianity just for the infinite satisfaction it would give her. It would do no harm and how perfectly happy she would be. . . . But I cannot do it."[18] His mother, his family experiences, his own personal sentiments pulled Mead toward the ministry: "If I only could get a strong character some settled beliefs I could find more pleasure in the ministry than anywhere in the world."[19] A few days later he remarked: "the spirit of a minister is strong in me and I come fairly by it."[20] However, he still complained that he was "wallowing in the depths of agnosticism," which cut deeply into the faith of his childhood: "I tell you that agnosticism is a most dangerous tool to handle especially by one who believes in realities. I would as soon call in the Ohio river to undermine the foundations of a woodshed and expect my house to stand as to call in agnosticism to remove difficulties and expect to find my faith's foundations still secure."[21]

With his faith fundamentally eroded, we cannot help but sense Mead's personal dilemma: "I have been praying and reading the Bible. For I do most thoroughly believe if I do anything that there ought to be some communion between maker and creature, and where should such communion be found but in prayer. To be sure I do not know that there is a God and more fundamentally still I do not even believe in the intuitions."[22] Yet there was some movement toward a kind of resolution to his many-faceted problem: "But if I can pursue religion as I do other matters I can find surety enough and perhaps coming years will bring a confidence in the intuitions which I do not now possess. But beyond a determination to do the right as I see it—to follow what light I can get I am utterly at sea."[23] Attracted by Immanuel Kant's philosophical idealism, and the partial solution that a career in philosophy could provide, Mead was certain of one thing—he was not interested in following in his father's footsteps: "And yet as I look at it now there is hardly any position I would not rather occupy than that of a dogmatic theologian." He feared that his feelings might get the best of him and he might lapse into his Christian faith: "this is my great danger that I will swallow Christianity whole because it will give me peace and not as the world giveth."[24]

66

Mead clearly felt the need for Christianity, even though he could not believe in its basic tenets:

> And yet nothing can meet the wants of mankind as Christianity, and why not have a little deception if need be? I should like to go right into revival work here because I see the position of the town in a spurious infidelity, and without God and without hope in the world. I am torn this way and that, and the outcome I cannot conceive. I need the strength of religion in my work here, that is need not only the confidence in right action but all the consoling power which I know to be in the belief in Christ.[25]

While reiterating an awareness of the therapeutic power of Christianity, he could not allow himself to succumb to such mystical beliefs: "But as certain as I enter as a Christian I see before me a mystical belief in faith which I do not want to descend to."[26] He chastised himself for not being completely candid with himself and others about his real beliefs, his real lack of faith while at Oberlin. To have done so would have relegated him to direct confrontation with his dying father and his mother who "lived in him." Once Oberlin was behind him, he was able to be more candid as he struggled to find his own purpose and meaning in life.

Gradually, Mead became certain that his path was philosophy rather than theology. His mission was to be in the world where he knew evil did exist and souls had to be saved: "speculation keeps [me] out of the strength and consolation I am hungering for. It keeps me out of direct work for men's souls which I want to enter."[27] Mead's new purpose in life was to battle the world's evil forces. The heart of a significant liberal reformer was taking shape: "I have no doubt that now the most reasonable system of the universe can be formed to myself without a God. But notwithstanding all this I cannot go out into the world and not work for men, the spirit of a minister is strong in me and I come fairly by it. I want to fight a valiant personal hand to hand fight with evil in the world."[28] At this point he had reached a fork in the road. One path would return him to the Christian ministry, while the other would lead him to a career in philosophy: "The other course lies in the line of metaphysics. I can give myself up to thought and literature and conscientiously try to find the truth as I see I am most likely to find it or find that I can't find it."[29]

As Mead's belief in God faded, he came more and more to appreciate the therapeutic value of such a belief. His mentor, William James, had had a similar experience, although Mead felt a calling to preach a moral gospel in a world devoid of the necessity of believing in God, whereas James did not. Mead wrote: "The moral realities of the world are powerful enough to stimulate me and Christianity lays the strongest hold upon and uses to the greatest advantage these realities and so I shall adapt myself to these realities just as I should have advised the Barbarians of the middle ages to kneel in prayer to saints and the Virgin Mary because they were what they could appreciate."[30] He cast his future career in terms of "popularizing metaphysics among the common people"[31]—a metaphysics that was to be Christian yet devoid of the need to believe in God.

The spirit of this evolving liberal reformer was conceived in the Christian demand to save souls from sin. Mead's work in philosophy would permit him to engage existing evil in battle. People were somehow free, yet they often chose to sin: "Upon the subject of the freedom of the will I am not so much troubled for of this I am confident. That under even that philosophy there is something that answers to sin. I cannot conceive exactly what it is but that there is something I am certain."[32] Mead's mission, his calling in life, would be that of a secular philosopher translating the moral capital of traditional Christianity into a new kind of secular humanism to "save souls" in this world. "Now in working for others the best way to meet them will be to keep to the old nomenclature, at least. At present the motives are strong enough upon this side to keep me at work and I trust will remain so. After all, old boy, we know that the only good thing to work for is humanity unless there is a God who is greater than all and commands our services in the same way."[33]

In closing a long personal letter to Henry Castle, Mead reiterated his friend's importance in helping him develop his perspective on life: "I would to God that I could see you and talk with you my dear boy. You are a very David to me. I have been appreciating your friendship more and more lately. May we soon meet in Germany or somewhere. Well goodbye old fellow and don't forget me for I love you better than a brother."[34] By the time Castle joined Mead at Harvard in 1886, Mead's identity crisis was about over and his mission was clear. He now had to equip himself for the many battles that lay ahead.

While Castle studied law at Harvard (1886–89), Mead worked in philosophy with William James, Josiah Royce, George Herbert Palmer, and others. During this period, he studied Greek, German, Latin, and Sanskrit languages while concentrating his reading in moral philosophy on Plato, Aristotle, Kant, Hegel, Spinoza, and Schopenhauer. Royce had just finished *The Religious Aspects of Philosophy* (1885), in which he began his own lifelong struggle to answer the question, In what sense can modern man be a Christian? Royce cultivated an idealistic view of reality in which the ancient problem of the one and the many, the individual and the community, was resolved in what he defined as loyalty to the ultimate redeemer, the "Blessed Community." For a young man who was then cutting away from his traditional moorings and suffering the pangs of alienation, this voice, calling for commitment to life's cause or purpose within a "Blessed Community" wherein the sins of self-assertion and disloyalty could be redeemed, appeared attractive. Many years later, reflecting on Royce's influence, Mead said: "I received an impression from him of freedom of mind, and of dominance of thought in the universe, of a clear unclouded landscape of spiritual reality where we sat like gods together—but not careless of mankind—and it was a vision that followed me for many years."[35] His understanding of Royce's vision may have faded with the years, and his belief that we are eventually redeemed by pragmatically using scientific intelligence can be traced more clearly to James and Dewey, yet Mead's assumptions about the "self" in a moral community carry the lasting mark of Royce's influence. Whatever that exact influence, Mead's honors thesis returned to his old personal problem: "How Large a Share Has the Subject in the Object World?"

In the spring of 1888, Mead graduated magna cum laude and was awarded a $250 scholarship for the following year. Shortly thereafter, he was elected to membership in the Philosophical Club. During these years, he also developed an avid interest in the theater and the symphony. By the summer of 1888, Henry Castle had returned to Hawaii and Mead lived with the James family in their summer home at the foot of the White Mountains in New Hampshire. To earn living expenses, Mead cared for one of the younger James boys and taught him arithmetic and U.S. history. In his spare time he had the opportunity to discuss metaphysics with William James. During his stay in the James's household, Mead also was introduced to the field of psychical research. He met Mr. Hodgson, of the Society of Psychical Research, and was impressed. In a letter to Henry Castle he said: "I have tried some thought transference, hypnotism and learned a great deal of the phenomena so that I respect the study of them thoroughly. It is a branch of psychological study which has the keen interest of the marvelous."[36]

Increasingly, Mead gained James's respect, confidence, and support. He wrote Castle about how well things were going with James, and reminded his friend how they were going to "carry out our plan" in the world. This plan, however, had to be delayed, for Mead now felt the need for further work at a German university. With James's support, he received a two-year traveling scholarship, enabling him to work toward a Ph.D. at the University of Berlin. There Mead worked with Dilthey and Zeller, and read Plato, Fichte, Schelling, Kant, Hegel, Schopenhauer, and Lotze. He also became acquainted with Wundt's work at Leipzig, as well as with Helmholtz's and Stumph's work at Berlin.

During part of the time that Mead was studying at Berlin, Henry Castle was at Leipzig, where he met and married Frida Steckner. When Frida was killed later in a carriage accident in Hawaii, Mead wrote to console his friend:

> The world is a lonely place, I know that we are walking along the bank of the largest and deepest stream of life and satisfactory life—that in nature and society God expresses himself if he could only be read but it doesn't belong to our day to read him and every time I attempt to make the spring into the current I feel as if I tried to step into the fourth dimension of space. We have to deny ourselves great emotions and great upliftings, but not the satisfactoriness of thinking and acting that is above the pettiness and low desires and filth of narrow egotisms. I have a growing faith that we can live calmly and greatly—that is a life that looks before and after—if not gloriously and deeply. My dear Henry don't lose courage don't lose confidence in yourself."[37]

Mead also described how he thought of Frida as part of their overall plan, and the role she might have played in their reform efforts. The Oberlin dream of carrying philosophy into the world against the forces of ignorance, vice, and evil now adopted a more specific concrete character: "My vague plan now is that I go to the University of Minnesota as a teacher—and you to Minneapolis as lawyer and that we finally get control of the

Minneapolis Tribune." From this position, Mead believed they could influence the city government and launch their social reforms, to be drawn from the best in European city management:

> But the immediate necessity is that we should have a clear conception of what forms socialism is taking in life in European lands especially of the organisms of municipal life— how cities sweep their streets manage their gas works and street cars—their Turnvereins their houses of prostitution, their poor their minor criminals their police etc. etc. that one may come with ideas to the American work. Now Henry you must come and at least get such a share in these subjects and hold of the social political literature that you can go right on when we are back.[38]

Mead told his friend: "I am more and more convinced that we can do some work worth doing in America. I know we are needed there and that we can see some results even in our own days." He predicted a reaction to the old order "soon and with it a new order of life in many ways—there will be ever greater inclination to apply reason to the every day life, and one can do everything so rapidly in America so far as construction is concerned, that a rational city could spring up like a mushroom in a night, that we could fight anyway on the side of reason or righteousness as we might like to call it."[39]

Combining their personal need for a calling in the world, their growing interest in the social and political problems of rapidly growing American cities, their sensitivity to the many social reforms instituted by Bismarck and others to ameliorate the dreadful social and economic conditions of the lower classes and stave off revolution, Mead and Castle molded their thinking toward a new kind of socialism, indeed, a new liberalism. Writing to his parents from Leipzig in 1889, Castle reported: "I am reading political economy and philosophy, and have begun my study of Christianity."[40] He thought the greatest danger from social revolution lay with the wage-labor class, who might take the reins of power into their own hands, posing a fundamental threat to civilization itself. It had to be avoided and it could be avoided, or so he thought, by ameliorating the social conditions generated by extreme inequality through the institution of practical, intelligent social reforms, undertaken by the state: "The social question—the labor question—is the most pressing problem, and the most imminent danger of our times, and to deal with it, to ameliorate social conditions, to elevate the working class, and moderate the extremes of social inequality, is the essential task of civilization in this century."[41]

The practical instrument for resolving this problem necessitated a new view of the state and its proper uses. Rejecting the classical liberal theory that a government is best which governs least, Castle wrote: "There cannot be much social progress as long as the notion of government prevails which has been so general in the United States—that the government, namely, is a necessary evil, the only object of which is to guarantee the individual security in the exercise of his private rights, which, having done it, ought to do nothing more, but *laissez faire*, and let every one go to heaven or the devil, as he sees fit, or in his own way." He went on, endorsing the new liberal conception of the state: "[the] state is rather the guardian of social as distinguished from private interest, and as such the patron of art and science, the general educator, the promoter of morality, and the organizer or reorganizer of society."[42]

Castle believed that the state would have to assume the social role the church had formerly played:

> The Church once held this position, but its stubborn conservatism, its unprogressiveness, its misguided and misdirected zeal, have put it to a forced abdication. It has fallen utterly out of sympathy with the complex life and social aims of the present world, and some other agency must take up the work of civilization thus laid down. There is no other to do this except the government. This is peculiarly to be regretted, because there are many reasons why the Church could handle the matter better.[43]

This second generation of American missionaries represented by Castle and Mead had found their peculiar mission and purpose: "This world cannot be left to go to the dogs while the 60,000 American ministers are saving souls for the next. Of course, from the point of view of Christianity, which makes *that* the object of life, such an expenditure of energy is justified; but from the point of view of science, which makes the end of action, not salvation in heaven, but the leading a rich, full, and worthy life on earth, it is all misdirected, though of course not utterly useless, effort."[44]

The Leipzig-Berlin years for both young men were important ones in which they rationalized their new liberal philosophy. The reform program they envisaged would start first with the city government, where they believed they could confront cor-ruption directly.[45] Once successful at the city level, they would move up the ladder to state and national politics. Mead saw the issue not as local control versus federal control, but where it would be best to start:

> if the reform starts in the city, we remove the machine in large degree, educate the public politically and start at the point where the new social duties and functions which our government can take on should make their entrance and upon pure city government no impure central government could rest. We may as well meet this worst element at once—if we can purify there we can throughout if we can't there we can't anywhere. If we can give American institutions the new blood of the social ideal it can come in only at this unit of our political life, and from this starting point it will necessarily spread.[46]

Rejecting the classical liberalism of the past, Mead continued: "We go on the principle now that the government should do as little as possible in order that as little as possible may be badly done, but it should do as much as possible in order that it may become vitally necessary that it be well done—but I am convinced that it should start with the city where the problem is as simple as possible, where it can flow naturally from American institutions and where everybody recognizes the necessity of change."

This new liberal philosophy was modeled to a significant degree after the German state, which from 1870 onward effectively regulated the flame of social rebellion through industrial com-pensation laws, social security pensions, and a variety of progressive social welfare legislation.[47] Whether we examine the Wisconsin progressive movement, or read Castle's letters from Leipzig or Mead's from Berlin, the German influence is clearly marked. The new compulsory liberal state beginning to take shape in America was rooted in the German experience of many reform-minded Americans. As Mead saw it, writing from Berlin,

> Our government in ideas and methods belongs to the past—our constitution with its checks and guards against the usur-pations of a king—the utter lack of all that is fresh or pro-gressive in our law making—that no one at least who sees America from the point of comparison with Europe sees her where he can sum up her activities into an understandable picture—can doubt that new blood must be infused into the governmental structure and that unless we utterly forsake

the evident line of progress of the rest of the world this change must come in the government doing vastly more than it does now.[48]

As late as October 1890, Mead still spoke of Minneapolis as the target city for carrying out their reform plans. Repeatedly, he reminded Castle that they must become knowledgeable concerning the operations of city government; they must get a strong "hold upon the socialistic literature and the position of socialism here in Europe. We must go back full and with such a hold upon the sources that we can keep full."[49] He argued that what they needed was a practical program for an American city:

> I imagine that two men alone could make no small impression in a city if they had decent election laws and good vigorous ideas—it will be a new thing ideas—not reform for itself not trying to make the city do the work it has to do decently and pull the government out of the saloons but giving her so much to do that she must do it well. It will be an enormous onslaught upon the American idea, but the ground is ready for nothing can be worse than the cities as they are.[50]

The Minneapolis plan never materialized. The following summer, Mead was asked by John Dewey to replace Professor Tufts, who was leaving the University of Michigan to help develop the new University of Chicago. Dewey asked Mead to teach one course in physical psychology, one course in the history of philosophy, a half-course on Kant, and another half-course on evolution. Mead was delighted with his teaching responsibilities, except for the course on physical psychology: "the drudgery will be the Phys. Psy. for I shan't have much opportunity for original work and to use it for pedagogical purposes is hard."[51] His reservations were well-founded. While his reputation as a successful teacher became legend, especially later at Chicago, students who took his physical psychology course at Michigan had little to say that was favorable.[52]

Henry Castle returned to Hawaii to become editor and owner of the two major newspapers on the Islands. From that vantage point, he became involved in the revolution that overthrew the native rule of Queen Liliuokalani. Castle wrote to Mead that the real basis of the revolution was easy to explain:

> It sprang simply from a universal feeling that native misrule was not to be borne any longer; that palace corruption, royal usurpation, and legislative stupidity had abridged the rights

of freemen, and played fast and loose with every moral and material interest long enough. The point had been reached where manhood and self-respect were directly involved. The situation could not be ignored. We would have been curs if we had not resisted. For fifty years white men had quietly submitted to aboriginal rule. Can the world present a parallel? In that time they had built up a national prosperity, and created a civilization. It is quite true that these 30 or 40 millions were at stake, but so was every political and moral and social interest. We could not have been quiescent without surrendering every gain which civilization has made here in the last seventy years.[53]

Here was the racism implicit in the "white man's burden" which so easily rationalizes the victim of oppression as the oppressor in the name of progress and liberal reform. Here, also, was a direct application of the new liberal reform politics, which in the name of clean and better government would deprive the populace of their political influence. Although the battle against aboriginal rule in Hawaii was different in many respects from the battle against ward-boss rule in Chicago, New York, or San Francisco, the structure of its argument, as well as its outcome, were essentially the same.

Shortly after the Hawaiian revolution, Henry Castle died. With his death, a significant chapter in the life of George Herbert Mead closed. However, a new chapter had already opened in the form of his association with John Dewey—first at Michigan and then at Chicago.

Working with Dewey from 1894 to 1904 at Chicago, Mead gradually refined and completed his conception of psychology. Even though Dewey left Chicago for Columbia University in 1904, the close intellectual alliance between the two continued unabated until Mead's death in 1931. Dewey's instrumentalism and Mead's social psychology evolved out of their searching dialogue. Mead constructed the psychology that furnished a basis for Dewey's instrumentalism, while Dewey generated the practical philosophy that steadied Mead's psychology. Dewey often expressed his indebtedness to Mead, and regarded Mead's contribution to philosophy as providing for an evolutionary conception of nature and man which made man neither a pawn of the universal forces of nature nor a victim of individual subjectivism: "His identification of the process of evolution with that of continuous reconstruction by which nature and man (as a part of nature that has become conscious) solve the problem of the relations of the universal and the individual, the regular and the novel—this identification is his own outstanding contribution to philosophy."[54]

Although Mead had been influenced by his reading of Aristotle, he rejected Aristotle's conception of human nature as fixed, instead viewing it as emerging within a social context. In the course of this evolution, individuals became human when they began to think reflectively—when, in a social context, they advanced from gestures to a language that could be internalized symbolically. In contrast to Freud, who saw the original development of culture as the loss of some portion of our happiness in order to attain security, Mead saw the development of culture as the origin of intelligence which increased our chances for happiness. Indeed, while there was continuity between the mind of a human and that of an animal, there remained a qualitative difference in our ability to reflectively symbolize the past, present, and future, and to direct our actions accordingly. To Mead, stimulus-response psychology explained how animals and humans learn certain habitual kinds of behavior, but it failed to adequately explain symbolically generated purposive behavior. In his view, mind, self, and society were functionally related in a transactional, continuous, and emerging process.

At birth, children are physiological organisms with undifferentiated tendencies to act. Through verbal gestures within a social context they learn the meaning of the group's symbols. Once they learn language, children can internalize conversation and thus become thinking beings. Through various social activities, they learn to symbolically assume the role of the other, and there gradually emerges a conception of self in which they see themselves as others see them. As this occurs, a "generalized other" develops that includes society's values, attitudes, and beliefs, which are then internalized within the individual in the form of the "me." This is substantially a picture of the "organization man." The other side to the self—the "I"—is unlike either the "generalized other" or the "me"; it represents the novel, creative, impulsive side of the self that repeatedly surprises the "me." The "I's" behavior is never completely predictable.[55]

In keeping with his mentor, William James, Mead's social behaviorism rejected the notion of complete determinism. He suggested that the ability of the self to introduce novel behavior into the social group forever confounds attempts to predict individual behavior, as well as to completely standardize group control. The group undergoes continuous change as individuals change within the group. To Mead, social institutions were basically made up of neither "I's" nor "me's" but of whole individuals with emerging selves behaving cooperatively to achieve greater freedom. This socialized individualism assumes that freedom is gained through active participation in society and not by an escape from society. Alienation from society, in Mead's context, only dehumanizes the individual.

Although Mead did a great deal of creative work in analyzing the self in an increasingly alienated society, his major focus was not so much on the "self," nor on the society, but on their transactional relationship. In that arena he found intelligence at work and the possibility that science, as a kind of creative questioning intelligence, might prove to be the real redeemer of humanity. All this was possible within a moral community. Mead's writings are laced with moral questions which emerged as he translated key assumptions drawn from his Christian background. [56]

> It is that the intelligible order of the world implies a determined moral order—and for a moral order we may substitute a social order, for morality has to do with the relations of intelligent beings with each other—and that this determined moral or social order is a world as it should be and will be. . . . Whatever the conception of this moral order, definite or vague, it always has implied that the process of the universe in which we live in a real sense is akin to and favorable to the most admirable order in human society. [57]

An implicit moral ideal exists in every society and reflects living reality as it becomes a functional part of institutional life. Insofar as some ideals are not functionally alive, they are usually kept alive only by the activities of some cult.

> The cult value of the institution is legitimate only when the social order for which it stands is hopelessly ideal. In so far as it approaches realization, its functional value must supersede its ideal value in our conduct.
>
> It is to this task that a scientifically trained intelligence must insistently devote itself, that of stating, just as far as possible, our institutions, our social habits and customs, in terms of what they are to do, in terms of their functions. [58]

Our inherited values "possess and control us," while the values we "discover and invent" help us to "possess and control the world." [59]

Mead developed a pragmatic, functionalist theory of value in which the appeal was not to fixed codes external to the individual, but rather to the "actual problem" out of which the functional values might be wrought. If "the intelligible order of the world implies a moral or social order, i.e., a world as it should be and may be," what form, then, does this take if we apply scientific method to social conduct?

> Scientific method has no vision, given in the mount, of a perfected order of society, but it does carry with it the assumption that the intelligence which exhibits itself in the solution of problems in natural science is of the same character as that which we apply or should apply in dealing with our social and moral problems; . . . Not only is man as an animal and as an inquirer into nature at home in the world, but the society of men is equally a part of the order of the universe. What is called for in the perfection of this society is the same intelligence which he uses in becoming more completely a part of his physical environment and so controlling that environment.[60]

Mead's functionalist theory of value was premised upon the necessity of social control so as to perfect society. The older Judeo-Christian moral system pictured the individual as a pilgrim and stranger on this earth, seeking an abiding city of God in another world. Mead, however, pictured his scientific humanism as "a great secular adventure" where society got ahead, "not by fastening its vision upon a clearly outlined distant goal, but by bringing about the immediate adjustment of itself to its surroundings, which the immediate problem demands."[61] Through the process of interaction within the problematic situation, both the individual and society are changed. A human being cannot see great distances into the future but does have a mind and can test for solutions in the present problematic world: "He does not know what the solution will be, but he does know the method of the solution. We, none of us, know where we are going, but we do know that we are on the way."[62]

Rejecting the Christian dualism of his youth, Mead embraced a functionalist theory of value in his mature years, with the reformist faith of a missionary carrying forth the social gospel of scientific redemption. His was a neo-Enlightenment faith, perhaps no better expressed than in the conclusion to his essay on "Scientific Method and Moral Sciences":

The order of the universe that we live in *is* the moral order. It has become the moral order by becoming the self-conscious method of the members of a human society. We are not pilgrims and strangers. We are at home in our own world, but it is not ours by inheritance but by conquest. The world that comes to us from the past possesses and controls us. We possess and control the world that we discover and invent. And this is the world of the moral order. It is a splendid adventure if we can rise to it.[63]

Although Mead saw himself as thoroughly endorsing a humanist faith—and if he had lived longer would have endorsed Dewey's *Common Faith*—it is clear that he never completely broke with certain key assumptions derived from his Christian background. The first of these involved the desirability of the common "brotherhood of man." T. V. Smith has suggested that this was one of Mead's supreme values— "the sharing of experience is the greatest good"[64]—an assumption which Mead seems to have carried over from his Christian past yet which appears to have remained largely unexamined. Mead saw the private as subjective and disintegrative, and much of Christianity perpetuated as a cult because of the incompleteness of the "organization of society." He thought scientific intelligence might help to build a society in which the ideal values embedded in Christianity as cult values might ultimately become the functional values of society. God had died for Mead, just as He had for Nietzsche. For Nietzsche, however, Christian brotherhood was a fraudulent conception. By contrast, Mead retained his Christian faith in fellowship. According to Smith,

> It is so uncharacteristic of Mead's cautious curiosity to make a cause of what really is not uncontestably good that it arouses the suspicion that he but carried on uncritically in this regard the Christian tradition. Would a Mohammedan thinker, not to mention a classic Greek mind, of Mead's acumen have assumed that all human experience implies enlargement and intensification of community without limit? If not, it is certainly a high tribute to the strength of the Christian leaven that it could so raise the threshold of even Mead's tough mind as to bring curiosity to its knees before the sacred altar of brotherhood.[65]

Mead's functionally moral community was not far removed from the Christian ideal that also appears to have underwritten

Josiah Royce's "Blessed Community." Fundamental to Mead's ethics was the Christian secularized doctrine of enlightened self-interest, not far removed from the Golden Rule. The danger was that this rule would be preached from the pulpit as, indeed, his father might have preached it, and so depended on its cult value rather than on its functional value to survive. Mead argued that it must be recognized as a functioning part of the moral structure of community life itself: "The most grandiose of these community ideals is that which lies behind the structure of what was called Christendom, and found its historic expression in the Sermon on the Mount, in the parable of the Good Samaritan, and in the Golden Rule. These affirm that the interests of all men are so identical, that the man who acts in the interest of his neighbors will act in his own interest."[66]

The social psychology of Mead, which described the process of the emergence of "self," taking the role of the other and the idea of the generalized other, made possible the functional expression rather than the cultist acceptance of the Golden Rule. Smith suggests as much when he asks, "has not Mead implemented the Golden Rule so thoroughly by his social psychology that it is no longer a prescription at all but now a description of how we do inevitably act?"[67] As we pass from cult to function, or prescription to description, or "ought" to "is," we move from moral choice to moral inevitability. There is slippage here between a prescriptive and a descriptive view of the world, and it is found in the precise nature of the transactional relationship between the individual and his or her social environment. In summing up Mead's faith, Smith says, *"Man can if he will; and he will if he knows; but he can know only through the concrete technique called science."*[68] Thus, Mead's social psychology, at least with respect to unexamined assumptions about fellowship, the nature of the Golden Rule, and the perfectability of society, rested in some abbreviated form on the moral capital of the past. For many of us in modern-day society, this capital long since has been spent.

A powerful ambivalence toward the personality's subjective and objective sides permeated Mead's work. At times the "I" and the "me" were treated as approximately equal. Yet, more often Mead avoided treating the "I" and all the subjective emotional elements that accompanied it. He regarded the "private," the "mystic," the "sentimental," and the "emotional" as personal phenomena which some day, perhaps through better social institutions, might be controlled. Recall that throughout his crisis years, Mead had regarded his own attachment to Christianity as emotional, whereas his growing interest in philosophy was associated with rational intelligence. "I" and "me" were clearly in evidence in those early years. Mead's reluctance to commit his social behaviorism to an environmental determinism may have been due to his personal psychological makeup, or perhaps to his lingering Christian values. For whatever reason, it remains to his credit that his social behaviorism did not eliminate the "I" and thus produce a social psychology such as Mao Tse Tung's, which utilized the group to scientifically control and predict the "me" and eradicate, as far as possible, the "I."

Some years after studying the effectiveness of Mao's social behaviorism for the United States Air Force, Robert Jay Lifton, following in the footsteps of Erik Erikson, wrote the "Protean Man." Since World War II, he argues, the individual has been undergoing what appears to be a continuous identity crisis where the inner and outer worlds remain unconnected and every kind of faith and loyalty exist as tentative propositions of the passing present. Lifton attributes this phenomenon to two things: "The first is the worldwide sense of what I have called *historical* (or *psychohistorical*) *dislocation*, the break in the sense of connection which men have long felt with the vital and nourishing symbols of their cultural traditions—symbols revolving around family, idea-systems, religions, and the life cycle in general. . . . The second large historical tendency is the flooding of imagery produced by the extraordinary flow of postmodern cultural influences over mass-communication networks."[69]

Lifton argues that we are in an era in which a new kind of person is being produced, one with relatively weak loyalties, who is nonideological and has the ability to survive in a world of rapid change without too much psyche damage. In the alienated consciousness of the modern individual, Lifton thinks he sees the historical event that marked this break in consciousness, namely, World War II. A number of other psychiatrists and sociologists also have tried to describe what is happening to the modern individual. Some speak of anomie, others of identity diffusion. David Reisman writes about the other-directed person, and Erikson focuses on the identity crisis. They all deal with the same growing phenomenon of the alienated person in post–World War II society.

Earlier in the century, Mead sensitively analyzed a similar

phenomenon in the alienated self—involving the cult value of religion in modern society. More than most, he understood the interrelationship of religion, self, and community. His analysis of cults as working in terms of the increasing reification of ideal values in a functionally alienating social system helps to explain, in part at least, the quest for cult worship, as evidenced in the modern-day experiences with Jim Jones, Synanon, the Moonies, and many others. In retrospect, however, that phenomenon appeared in Mead's time as a gentle stream bounded by tradition, whereas in the post–World War II period, it became a raging torrent sweeping away many cherished values. Thus, the condition of the alienated self subsequently appears today more desperate than it was in Mead's own lifetime. Although this phenomenon of alienation surfaced earlier, at the turn of the century, in European culture, and in a somewhat abbreviated fashion in America's Greenwich Village in the early 1900s, its major American groundswell appeared after World War II.

Mead did yeoman's work in analyzing the modern alienated self. He insightfully described the ontological, essentially ahistorical nature of such a person. The ontological nature of the thoroughly alienated person is essentially ahistorical. For such a person the world is no longer made up of pasts, presents, and futures, but rather only of significant presents. Mead's analysis of history very well describes the ahistorical sense of reality of many twentieth-century thinkers. For Mead, there was only one reality and that was the present. Mead's view of the past as "that conditioning phase of the passing present which enables us to determine conduct with reference to the future which is also arising in the present"[70] was similar to Dewey's later view of history. For Mead, the past was dead and had meaning only as meaning was ascribed to it from the present context. In this sense, he felt that we actually constructed our history from the present to the past while creating the illusion that it was created from the past to the present. (For instance, the historical perspectives of Hegel, Marx, Comte, and Freud were all interpretations of the past derived from the present perspective of their individual lives.) Mead asserted that "every great social movement has flashed back its light to discover a new past"[71] and that there are as many possible pasts as there are futures since "the novelty of every future demands a novel past."[72] He summarized his conception of history as follows: "The long and short of it is that the only reality of the past open to our reflective research is the implication of the present, that the only reason for research into the past is the present problem of understanding a problematic world, and the only test of the truth of what we have discovered is our ability to so state the past that we can continue the conduct whose inhibition has set the problem to us."[73] In essence, the thoroughly alienated person exists in a problematic present without a history, other than that which can be generated from the world today.

Along with Dewey, Mead also was involved in actually formulating new liberal reforms. Active in both city and school politics in Chicago he served as chairman of the Chicago City Club in 1912 and later retired as its president in 1920. Mead worked with Dewey at his laboratory school, served as trustee of Jane Addam's Settlement House, edited *The Elementary School Teacher*, and became deeply involved in the vocational educational movement. The considerable influence he exercised in practical reform politics as well as education in effect carried through on his youthful dreams. However, his greatest impact was clearly within the fields of sociology, social psychology, and the social sciences in general. He helped to originate the functionalist theory of value and has been hailed, along with C. H. Cooley, as the cofounder of social psychology. Mead's ideas on human nature were carried into educational thought by Dewey, into the mental hygiene movement by Adolph Meyer, into therapeutic psychology by Harry Stack Sullivan,[74] and into social science theory by Talcott Parsons, Kingsley Davis, Robert K. Merton, and others. Many social scientists of the twentieth-century who think in terms of social psychology, moral values, community, communication, and transactional relationships, do so in terms Mead had previously laid out.

Interestingly, in a world of publish or perish, George Herbert Mead would have perished. In forty years of academic work he failed to publish a single book. He was first and foremost a teacher, creating and re-creating ideas with his students, leaving little time for publication of those ideas. Compared to the massive publication lists of Hall, Thorndike, or Dewey, Mead's few articles appear sparse indeed. Consequently, his influence on American thought must not be gauged by his publications, but rather by the many influential people who, either formally or informally, were his students. The fact that Mead was at the University of Chicago, one of the leading institutions in the field of sociology during the first half of the twentieth century, no doubt contributed to his influence. As students from the new fields of sociology and social psychology flocked to his philosophy course, it became clear that he had something significant to offer. After his death in 1931, dedicated students compiled his notes and articles into some four volumes: *Movement of Thought in the Nineteenth Century; Mind, Self and Society; The Philosophy of the Present;* and *The Philosophy of the Act.*

Mead's preference for teaching over publication may have been due to the subjective versus objective split that appeared in his thinking as well as his writing. His professional writing is best characterized as highly rationalized and devoid of emotion, while his personal correspondence is heavily laced with evidence of the poetic. In defining freedom as the "expression of the whole self," Mead wrote: "but in freedom the personality as a whole passes into the act. Compulsion disintegrates the individual into his different elements; hence there are degrees of freedom in proportion to the extent to which the individual becomes organized as a whole. It is not often that the whole of us goes into any act so that we face the situation as an entire personality."[75]

In an earlier age, freedom had been defined in terms of a capacity to act or refrain from acting. Now, in the alienated world of modern men and women, freedom is being defined more often in Mead's terms of "getting one's act together" as a "whole person." For Mead, this was no easy task; in fact, it would be safe to suggest that he was not often free. He was the philosopher of the alienated self par excellence, always seeking ways to overcome that alienation, always in search of self in a moral universe. In 1901 he wrote to his wife:

> The world is strange and it gets stranger as I get older. The infinitisimal shifts of a day or an hour make the things that had the solidity of the everlasting hills and the dull grey of the unquestioned commonplace become like dreams and opalescent as the Hawaiian Sea. The iridescence of youth and its imagination is unstable and lacks the assurance which makes real poetry of life. There is always the dualism of the untried world which is not yet one's own that the youth cannot surmount. He must be romantic. But to be at home in one's world and yet be able to see it shift and change and feel the movement with no question of its reality and therefore no discount upon its appreciation. It's a process of going into one's self and finding the world there. As one grows older he gets deeper and nearer the creator. But for all emotion,

reflection from one's other self is necessary even if that self has to be built up. The Lord in his great mercy grant that we may continue to be the other selves to each other's experience.[76]

Later in life Mead seems to have overcome his alienation, to have found his way through that labyrinth of emotional self-analysis by discovery and invention of the moral universe: "We are not pilgrims and strangers. We are at home in our own world, but it is not ours by inheritance but by conquest. The world that comes to us from the past possesses and controls us. We possess and control the world that we discover and invent. And this is the world of the moral order. It is a splendid adventure if we can rise to it."[77]

Notes

1. Erik H. Erikson, *Young Man Luther* (New York: W. W. Norton and Co., 1962), pp. 14–15.

2. Erik H. Erikson, "The Problem of Ego Identity," *Psychological Issues* 1(1959): 102–10.

3. For example, see Morris Peckham, *Beyond the Tragic Vision* (New York: George Braziller, 1962); Lionel Trilling, *Sincerity and Authenticity* (Cambridge, Mass.: Harvard University Press, 1971). See also Peter Berger, " 'Sincerity' and 'Authenticity' in Modern Science," *Public Interest* 31(Spring 1973): 81–90.

4. Letter from Mead to Henry Castle, Oberlin, Ohio, Mar. 5, 1883, George Herbert Mead Papers, University of Chicago Archives.

5. Throughout this chapter I use the terms "self" and "identity" virtually interchangeably, as Erikson does in his essay on "The Problem of Ego Identity," p. 147.

6. See George Herbert Mead, "The Philosophies of Royce, James, and Dewey in Their American Setting," *International Journal of Ethics* 40(Jan. 1930): p. 231.

7. Quoted in Clarence J. Karier, *Man, Society, and Education* (Glenview, Ill.: Scott, Foresman and Co., 1967), p. 166.

8. In 1891, when Mead ended his student life and joined Dewey at the University of Michigan, he married Helen Castle. Henry Castle had earlier returned to Hawaii with his new wife, Frida Steckner, from Leipzig. Shortly thereafter, he became editor and owner of the two principal newspapers on the Islands, the *Pacific Commercial Advertiser*, and the *Hawaiian Gazette*. Frida died in a carriage accident shortly after the birth of their first child, and by 1892 Henry had married Mabel Wing. The following year he testified in Washington before the Hawaiian

Commission, which was investigating American involvement in the revolution that overthrew Queen Liliuokalani. By 1894 Henry returned to Leipzig with his daughter from his first marriage, to visit grandparents and to study. Late that year he received word of a pending counterrevolt by Hawaiian royalists, and immediately booked passage to Hawaii for himself and his daughter aboard the steamship *Elbe*. On the night of January 30, 1895, that ship collided with another vessel in the North Sea and sank.

9. Letter to Helen Mead from Mead, Jan. 31, 1895.

10. For a further analysis of this argument in the context of Oberlin College, see John Barnard, *From Evangelicalism to Progressivism at Oberlin College 1860–1917* (Columbus: Ohio State University Press, 1969).

11. Letter to Henry Castle from Mead, Berlin Heights, Nov. 15, 1883, p. 2.

12. Ibid., pp. 2–3.

13. Ibid., p. 3.

14. Ibid., p. 4.

15. Ibid.

16. Ibid., p. 3.

17. Letter to Henry Castle from Mead, near St. Paul, Minn., Apr. 23, 1884.

18. Letter to Henry Castle from Mead, Mar. 30, 1885.

19. Letter to Henry Castle from Mead, Mar. 7, 1884, p. 4.

20. Letter to Henry Castle from Mead, Oberlin, Ohio, Mar. 16, 1884, p. 5.

21. Letter to Henry Castle from Mead, Mar. 7, 1884, pp. 1–2.

22. Letter to Henry Castle from Mead, Berlin Heights, Feb. 23 (corrected from Feb. 25), 1884, p. 1.

23. Ibid.

24. Ibid.

25. Ibid., pp. 1–2.

26. Ibid., p. 4.

27. Ibid.

28. Letter to Henry Castle from Mead, Oberlin, Ohio, Mar. 16, 1884, p. 5.

29. Ibid.

30. Ibid., p. 2.

31. Ibid., p. 6.

32. Letter to Henry Castle from Mead, Berlin Heights, Feb. 23, 1884, p. 5.

33. Ibid.

34. Ibid.

35. Quoted in T. V. Smith, "The Religious Bearings of a Secular Mind: George Herbert Mead," *Journal of Religion* 12(Apr. 1932): 201.

For many insights involving the moral thrust of Mead's mature thought and its religious bearing, I am indebted to the work of T. V. Smith.

36. Letter to Henry Castle from Mead, Tamworth Iron Works, N.H., July 18, 1888, p. 4.

37. Letter (incomplete) to Henry Castle from Mead, Berlin, Germany, Aug. 1, 1890, p. 3.

38. Ibid., p. 1.

39. Letter (incomplete) to Henry Castle from Mead, 1890, pp. 3–4.

40. Letter to his father and mother from Castle, Leipzig, Germany, Sun., Apr. 7, 1889, p. 614, in George and Helen Mead, eds., *Henry Northrup Castle: Letters* (privately printed for the Castle family and friends, London, 1902), CT275, C35A3, Rare Books, University of Chicago Archives.

41. Ibid.

42. Ibid.

43. Ibid., pp. 614–15.

44. Ibid., p. 615.

45. Throughout American progressivism there existed a social gospel bent on city reform. See Henry F. May, *Protestant Churches and Industrial America* (New York: Harper and Brothers Co., 1949). See also Aaron Ignatius Abell, *The Urban Impact on American Protestantism 1865–1900* (London: Archon, 1962).

46. Letters to Henry Castle from Mead, Berlin, Germany, Oct. 19, 1890, p. 3.

47. Mead was impressed with the German trains running on time and, more importantly, with the way they were managed so that laborers could afford to live out of town. Writing from Berlin (Oct. 31, 1890, p. 3) to Castle, he said: "The government managing railroads can make it an inducement to the laborers to live out of town and come in to work. In Halle, my sister's *waschfrau* comes in and goes out as often as she wishes for 30 pf. a week. Very suggestive bit of city politics."

48. Letter to Henry Castle from Mead, Berlin, Germany, Oct. 19, 1890, p. 4.

49. Letter to Henry Castle from Mead, Oct. 21, 1890, p. 1.

50. Ibid., p. 2.

51. Letter to Henry Castle from Mead, Schierke in Hartz, July 22, 1891, p. 1.

52. See Corliss Lamont, ed., *Dialogue on John Dewey* (New York: Horizon Press, 1954), pp. 19–20. See also "The Department of Psychology," *The University of Michigan: An Encyclopedia Survey*, W. B. Shaw Pillsbury, ed., 2 vols. (Ann Arbor: University of Michigan Press, 1940), 2: 709–10.

53. Letter to Helen and George Mead from Castle, Honolulu, Mar. 1, 1893, in *Henry Northrup Castle: Letters*.

54. Quoted in Karier, *Man, Society, and Education*, pp. 166–67.

55. In direct contrast to Watson and Skinner, Mead assumed that

an important part of human behavior would remain unpredictable. See Anselm Strauss, ed., "The Process of Mind in Nature," *George Herbert Mead on Social Psychology* (Chicago: Phoenix Books, 1964), p. 105.

56. See Smith, "Religious Bearings of a Secular Mind."

57. George Herbert Mead, "Scientific Method and the Moral Sciences," *International Journal of Ethics*, 33(Apr. 1923): 229–30.

58. Ibid., p. 243.

59. Ibid., p. 247.

60. Ibid., p. 245.

61. Ibid., p. 247.

62. Ibid.

63. Ibid.

64. Smith, "Religious Bearings of a Secular Mind," p. 211.

65. Ibid., p. 212.

66. Mead, "Scientific Method and the Moral Sciences," p. 239.

67. Smith, "Religious Bearings of a Secular Mind," p. 213.

68. Ibid.

69. Robert Jay Lifton, *History and Human Survival* (New York: Random House, 1970), p. 318.

70. Quoted in Strauss, *George Herbert Mead on Social Psychology*, p. xxv.

71. Ibid., p. 321.

72. Ibid., p. xxv.

73. Ibid., p. 324.

74. For Dewey, see Anselm Strauss, *The Social Psychology of George Herbert Mead* (Chicago: University of Chicago Press, 1959). For Meyer, see Christine Mary Shea, "The Ideology of Mental Health and the Emergence of the Therapeutic Liberal State: The American Mental Hygiene Movement, 1900–1930," Ph.D. dissertation, University of Illinois at Urbana-Champaign, 1980. Sullivan traced his own thinking from the social psychology of Mead. See Ernest Becker, *The Birth and Death of Meaning* (New York: Free Press of Glencoe, 1962), p. 48.

75. George Herbert Mead, *The Philosophy of the Act*, Charles W. Morris, ed. (Chicago: University of Chicago Press, 1938), p. 663.

76. Letter to Helen Mead from Mead, June 12, 1901, pp. 1–2.

77. Mead, "Scientific Method and the Moral Sciences," p. 247.

3

EDWARD L. THORNDIKE [1874–1949]

Toward a Science
of Psychology

In one of his rare ventures into fictional writing, Edward L. Thorndike, America's most influential educational psychologist, wrote a very revealing morality play, *The Miracle*. In it he assumed the character of Dr. Richard Cabot, who, discoursing with a traditional clergyman, said:

> My God is all the good in all men. My God is the mother's courage in childbirth; the laborer doing an honest job; the citizen counting his own advantage less than the common weal; the little child, brave, just, and happy in his play; the father toiling to educate his children—all the good in all men. Your God is in heaven; my God is on earth. Your God made us; but we ourselves make my God. He is as great and wise and good as we choose to make him.
>
> My God does not hear prayers. Work for him.[1]

This God would play a most significant role throughout his adult life.

Thorndike was the son of a strong-willed, determined, Puritan woman, Abbie Ladd Thorndike, and an itinerant Methodist minister, Edward Robert Thorndike, who preached the gospel of Christ throughout Massachusetts. Reared in a controlled religious environment, his family instilled in him a respect for practical disciplined values for living, while he developed a general disinterest in music and theater and only a limited interest in books.[2] His background thus established the moral capital on which he drew throughout his professional career. However, by the time Thorndike graduated from Wesleyan and moved on to Harvard to continue his education with William James, he had begun to break away from the traditional faith of his father and mother. His new naturalistic faith was intimately tied to his career as an educational psychologist. He was convinced, as he stood in the dawning secular light of the twentieth century, that the "scientific" psychologist was destined to displace the traditional philosopher and theologian. His faith was to be a faith in empirical science. Unlike his father, he would preach the gospel of positivistic science, one that included not only a careful empirical description of what "is," but also a highly selective, relatively unexamined set of assumptions about what "ought" to be. Embedded in those assumptions were the ethical and ideological values that marked much of his work. Merle Curti notes that, "Despite Thorndike's predominant interest in applying the scientific method to education, his statement of general aims was determined by ethics. To make men 'want the right things, and to make them better able so to control all the forces of nature and themselves that they can satisfy these wants' is the basic doctrine of his educational philosophy."[3]

The "right" thing to do, according to Thorndike, "is the thing which a man who could foresee all the consequences of all acts, and who considered fairly the welfare of all men, would in that case choose."[4] This would be the role of empirical science. The purpose of education, then, was not only to help us see the truth but to help us want the right things. From Thorndike's perspective, "the aims of education as a whole are identical with those of morality."[5] He believed that science could be employed as an instrument to shape better human beings and ultimately a better social order. By "better" he did not necessarily mean a significantly different social system; rather, it was a matter of bringing our wants into line with the realities dictated by "truth." Hence, the more knowledge we have of the "truth," the better off we will be. Such knowledge leads to the satisfaction of human wants and, more importantly, "predisposes men against unsatisfiable wants—to know what the world really is prevents us from wanting what it cannot give. It leads to the satisfaction of all good wants—knowledge is power." The aim of education,

Thorndike continued, should be "to cultivate good will to men and the higher or impersonal or unselfish pleasures, and to get rid of irrational wants—wants not fitted to the world in which we live."[6] The irrational wants cultivated by organized religions would thus fade away in the light of scientific knowledge.

Thorndike espoused that branch of Enlightenment thinking that, from Helvétius to Comte, conceived of the progress in scientific knowledge not in terms of freeing men from an oppressive system, but rather in terms of binding them to a more orderly system. He was very much a part of that positivistic tradition usually appearing on the conservative side of the social-economic ledger. In this chapter I will analyze Thorndike's major educational ideas and practices and consider the moral assumptions upon which many of his ideas were based, the social implication these ideas seemed to contain, as well as the impact his work had for educational thought and practice in the twentieth century.

In 1898, when William James introduced the term *pragmatism* to popular audiences at the University of California, his student Edward L. Thorndike (1874–1949) was completing his epoch-making dissertation, "Animal Intelligence: An Experimental Study of Associative Processes in Animals." It was quickly recognized as a landmark work in experimental psychology, and Thorndike's career sky-rocketed. Within a few years he was a full professor at Columbia University, with major interests in human learning and educational psychology. For almost half a century Thorndike held sway at Columbia, during which time he taught thousands of teachers and administrators, and published 50 books and 450 monographs and articles. His massive three-volume work entitled *Educational Psychology* (1913) set the tone for almost the next two decades. From his pen flowed a prodigious number of educational maxims, psychological laws, textbooks and scales of achievement for elementary, secondary, and college courses in varied fields, dictionaries for children in elementary and secondary schools, and teacher manuals. Because he wrote so many of the texts and tests used in elementary and secondary schools, his impact on American educational practice was both immediate and pervasive.

In 1901, in collaboration with Robert Woodworth, Thorndike published his now-famous paper on the transfer of training, in which he attempted to empirically refute the claims made by the exponents of the traditional doctrine of formal discipline. At a time when attacks on the classical languages were increasing at a feverish rate, the findings of Thorndike and Woodworth were received with great enthusiasm. Down through the years, the classicists had argued that the study of Greek and Latin was to be valued not so much for its specific content as for its power to develop the faculty of reasoning. The experiment of Woodworth and Thorndike appeared to demonstrate that specific ability did not transfer beyond the learning environment, except in those cases where the new conditions under which the ability was to be utilized were identical or closely identical to the original conditions under which the ability was learned.[7] Thorndike concluded that school subjects are to be valued for their specific content and not for any generalized disciplinary powers.[8] For the next thirty years, the battle would rage with relentless fury, until Greek was eliminated from the public school curriculum and Latin was reduced to an elective course. Not only the disciplinary value of studying these languages was lost, but also the intellectual stimulation of engaging many of the West's most profound thinkers. Although many factors contributed to the demise of the classics in American education, Thorndike's timely arguments were of major importance.[9]

The elimination of the classics from American public schools meant, in the end, the elimination of the aim of classical education itself—to teach the "best that was thought and said in the past" and to ensure the development of independent thinkers, well equipped with all the necessary intellectual tools for formulating their own critical judgments. As this aim disappeared from the educator's rhetoric, it was replaced with discussions about individual differences and meeting individual needs in the name of social efficiency.

Throughout its history, the classical ideal existed as an elitist's educational achievement, never effectively translated into a system of mass schooling. What remains today of that classical system is to be found largely among America's elite prep schools. What eventually displaced it in America's public schools was a meritocratic system with an elitist principle as a cornerstone. That system required an intensive concern for individual differences, the measurement of those differences, and the development of educational experiences to ensure differential treatment. While the classical ideal had emphasized the education of the well-rounded individual for leadership, the new educational ideal emphasized a differential curriculum which presumed to prepare people for a variety of career roles. Designed mainly for the rapidly growing high school, the new education would prepare some people for the factory, some for the office, and others for college. In the name of individual differences, an educational tracking system was born, all in the name of social efficiency.

While John Dewey, George Herbert Mead, and others wrote and spoke of a new individualism arising out of the ruins of the older laissez-faire competitive system, and from time to time had their names evoked to support a given educational reform, the direct effect of their work on education in its broadest context was quite different. Dewey and Mead created a philosophy of new liberalism which tended to satisfy the ideological needs of the professional class, especially the social scientist; men like Thorndike, Lewis Terman, and others worked more directly with teachers to structure and develop the mainstream of thinking and practice in American public education. Although these two views never seemed to rest too comfortably with each other, in the end they both included the primary notion of a meritocratic society, namely, that somehow the meritorious must be allowed to lead. Questions about the role of the expert, the meaning of democracy, and the idea of freedom were crucial, however. In this regard, Dewey and Thorndike held significantly different opinions. For example, the role of the expert in Dewey's *The Public and Its Problems* is vastly different from the role of the expert in Thorndike's "The Psychology of the Half-Educated Man." In the former case, Dewey attempted to dissolve the role of the expert in an idealistically fluid community; in the latter case, Thorndike recommended outright public subservience to the expert: "Outside that field [our own expertise] the intelligent procedure for most of us is to refuse to think, spending our energy rather in finding the expert in the case and learning from him."[10] The differences between Thorndike and Dewey are very much a result of Mead's and Dewey's reconstruction of liberalism, and with it a new view of individualism. Thorndike's position on individualism remained similar in many respects to that of his mentor, William James. In the end it was the James-Thorndike brand of individualism that came to dominate much public school thought and practice in the twentieth century.

In certain striking respects, Thorndike modeled his professional career after that of his former teacher. Just as James's two-volume work on *The Principles of Psychology* (1890) dominated the field for two decades, so did Thorndike's three-volume work on educational psychology (1913). Both men found it necessary to condense these volumes into a single work—Thorndike called his *Educational Psychology: Briefer Course* (1914)—for teachers. Thorndike also used James's earlier work as the basis for his own thought. For example, moving from the James-Lange theory of bonds, Thorndike constructed his own theory of connectionism,[11] which gradually came to include various "laws of learning" based on a physiological conception of the nervous system. Thorndike's psychology, too, was replete with the conventional wisdom of the period, including the stereotyping of women and ethnic groups as well as races. Reminiscent of James's tendency to romanticize the condition of the worker, we find Thorndike suggesting, "Probably three out of four chauffeurs would really much rather drive a car than live as the King of England does."[12] His psychology also justified the competitive spirit of capitalism; although he did not suggest, as James had, that private property was an instinctive characteristic of human nature, he did find the "mastery and submissive" characteristic of the human species among their original endowment. While both men from time to time uttered certain criticisms of the social economic system, by and large they both not only accepted that system as given, but embraced many of the personal values that made it work. Again, even though he found certain educational problems with it, he, like his mentor, recognized the need for the "instinct of rivalry." Both men accepted the social class system and looked to the elite for leadership. Although it should be clear that James held a far broader view of reality, tolerating and incorporating many more subjective experiences within his psychology, much of Thorndike's empirical psychology is in line with James's. The spirit of capitalism is writ large across the value system of both men. Perhaps for this reason, more than any other, Thorndike's work proved to be so popular among practical-minded educators as well as philanthropic foundations.

In more ways than one, Edward Thorndike was a man of the hour, spearheading the Zeitgeist of his time. This Zeitgeist saw science as an instrument to organize the public school on the model of a business establishment.[13] George P. Strayer, a leader of the efficiency movement in education, stated: "all our investigations with respect to the classification and progress of children in the elementary schools, in high schools, and in higher education are based upon Professor Thorndike's contribution to the psychology of individual differences."[14]

In 1904 Thorndike published his *Introduction to the Theory of Mental and Social Measurements*, which made him a leader in the test and measurement movement. Many years later he chaired the Committee on Classification of Personnel of the United States Army, and for the first time group intelligence tests were introduced into American culture on a massive scale. In the post–World War I era, Thorndike's influence led to the use of various tests in business and industry, as well as in education. By serving on the National Research Council, he helped to develop the popular National Intelligence Test used in elementary schools. By 1926 he published *The Measurement of Intelligence*, dealing with the well-known C A V D test. Throughout the 1920s and 1930s, Thorndike stood at the center of the storm raging over the meaning of intelligence as well as the nature-nurture argument. His response to both problems was consistent with his psychological conception of the individual.

As an evolutionist, Thorndike believed that "amongst the minds of animals that of man leads, not as a demigod from another planet, but as a king from the same race."[15] Because human minds were continuous with the minds of animals, the study of animal learning could provide a simplified key for understanding human intelligence. Such study led in part to his theory of *connectionism*, which "as conceived by Thorndike can be defined in rather simple terms. In all species of animals, including man, certain neurobiological connections of such a nature that the application of a given stimulus tends to elicit a particular type of response (S-R bonds) are found to exist. Some of these connections have already been established in the normal animal at the time of birth; others which he is potentially capable of forming, are acquired as a result of post-natal experiences."[16] Connections are "stamped in" by way of the law of *exercise* and the law of *effect*. The former implies that repetitions strengthen connections; the latter, that rewards also strengthen connections, while punishment weakens them. Later research by Thorndike and others seemed to indicate that punishment did not effectively weaken those connections, however.[17]

With the law of effect stripped of punishment, Thorndike evolved a theory of reinforcement, which B. F. Skinner eventually would develop more fully. Thorndike was, however, no Skinnerian, or even a Watsonian behaviorist. He disagreed with Watson as to the origin of differences among individuals. Both men were determinists, although Watson attributed individual differences to environment and Thorndike attributed them to heredity. As Joncich notes, "Thorndike early concluded that heredity is the major reason for human variation in intellect and character, that no other factor is more significant than innate and inherited inequalities in the capacity to learn."[18]

Throughout his life, Thorndike assumed a positive correlation between intellect, character, and wealth, and usually assumed that each was determined primarily by heredity. In this view we find something of the older Puritan doctrine of predestination of the elect. The God of nature had showered some people with the grace of intelligence, which somehow not only made them wiser but also morally better and richer. These were the elect who, in a really good society, would rule. Thorndike believed this could be proven quantitatively. These visible saints were not, however, just the pure products of natural evolution, somehow inevitably destined for sainthood, but also the products of what goodness had been achieved by people changing themselves. As Thorndike said: "original nature has achieved what goodness the world knows as a state achieves order, by killing, confining or reforming some of its elements. It progresses, not by *laissez faire*, but by changing the environment in which it operates and by renewedly changing itself in each generation." Man makes himself "civilized, rational and humane," to suit himself. "His nature is not right in his own eyes. Only one thing in it, indeed, is unreservedly good, the power to make it better. This power, the power of learning or modification in favor of the satisfying, the capacity represented by the law of effect, is the essential principle of reason and right in the world."[19] The power of God is thus in the world of the secular minister of science. According to Thorndike, "we ourselves make my God. He is as great and wise and good as we choose to make him. My God does not hear prayers. Work for him."[20]

Putting aside the traditional religious garb of his father, Thorndike donned what he believed to be the robe of the scientist: objective quantitative measurement. The major thrust of his thought and influence followed these lines. "Whatever exists at all exists in some amount,"[21] he asserted early in his career, and he spent the rest of his life trying to measure what existed. Curti correctly notes: "His influence in establishing and popularizing the fact-finding, statistical, and experimental technique in education has been immeasurable. Taking over the methods of the physical and natural sciences, and using the more quantitative devices of such pioneers as Pearson, Galton, Cattell, Rice, and Boas, Thorndike, together with Judd, revolutionized American educational technique."[22] Advising teachers to think in terms of measurable behavioral objectives,[23] and to conceive of learning as a stamping-in process, Thorndike went on to suggest that the new science of psychology might quantitatively determine not only the best methods to be used but the best objectives of education as well.[24] His unbounded faith in a quantitative science of education led him to define not only what is, but what ought to be, unrestrained by the fact that what he thought ought to be actually was predetermined by his personal values. Strangely enough, when Thorndike reported his experimental work with animal behavior, he tended to be quite circumspect; when he dealt with complex human social systems, however, he tended to speculate freely.[25] Many of his professional colleagues warned him that he moved too freely beyond his data. Curti observes: "One must question to what extent his social opinions are truly related, scientifically, to his experimental work, and to what extent they are determined by his own unconscious participation in the prejudices of our own time."[26]

For Thorndike, the role of the secular minister preaching a gospel of secularized Methodist values and that of a scientist constantly testing for truth, repeatedly came into conflict. The latter role usually was sacrificed at precisely those points where Thorndike's personal values were at stake. His attitudes toward the sexes, races, and lower classes bring this problem into sharper focus.

Thorndike believed that men were more variable, and thus we might find more genius among the male rather than the female of the species. He argued that while, in general, women may be as intelligent as men, and can usually profit from similar kinds of education, the variability factor accounts for the disproportionate number of men doing graduate work. Women, he believed, were instinctively different from men, which should be taken into account in the educational guidance and tracking of women toward their occupational destinies. While men were possessed of the instinct to fight and compete, women (or so he thought) were possessed of the instinct to nurse, to care for and fuss over others, to relieve, comfort, pet, coddle, console, and do for others.[27] Thus, men and women ought to receive a partially differentiated curriculum, which would channel women into those occupations appropriate to their nature, such as nursing, teaching, and medicine, while men would be channeled into the more competitive world of statesmanship, philosophy, and scientific research.[28] Just as the social inferiority of immigrants and blacks was embedded in the curricular content and practices of the school, so too was the inferior status of women.[29] Thorndike clearly played a significant role in establishing that content and encouraging those practices.

As an elitist, Thorndike supported the emergence of those characteristics in American education. He believed that progress depended not on the extension of culture to the masses, but rather on the education of the gifted elite. Repeatedly, he argued against the upward extension of the compulsory education law on the grounds that such attempts at further education of the mentally unfit were doomed to failure. His emphasis on individual differences and objective classification of students led to the logical conclusion of segregating, for educational purposes, the superior intellects, whom he believed to be of higher moral character and good will.

> But, in the long run, it has paid the "masses" to be ruled by intelligence. Furthermore, the natural processes which give power to men of ability to gain it and keep it are not, in their results, unmoral. Such men are, by and large, of superior intelligence, and consequently of somewhat superior justice and good will. They act, in the long run, not against the interests of the world, but for it. What is true in science and government seems to hold good in general for manufacturing, trade, art, law, education, and religion. It seems entirely safe to predict that the world will get better treatment by trusting its fortunes to its 95- or 99-percentile intelligences than it would get by itself. The argument for democracy is not that it gives power to all men without distinction, but that it gives greater freedom for ability and character to attain power.[30]

Thorndike was quite sure that "to him that hath a superior intellect is given also on the average a superior character." His own white middle-class values seemed obvious when he suggested that his scientific observations indicated that "the abler persons in the world in the long run are the more clean, decent, just, and kind."[31] He saw a positive correlation between moneymaking, intelligence, and moral character. In many ways, Thorndike was a twentieth-century example of the traditional spirit of capitalism which, from Benjamin Franklin to William Graham Sumner, equated virtue with wealth. The difference, however, was that he equated it "scientifically."

People were not, he believed, solely a product of their environment; moral and intellectual differences existed due to ancestry. Because "mental and moral inheritance from near ancestry is a fact," Thorndike was also sure that "racial differences in original nature are not mere myths."[32] He objectively tested black and white children and found that even though there was considerable overlap between the two races, the white pupils were demonstrably superior in scholarship. This, he concluded, was attributable to original nature, since "the differences in the environment do not seem at all adequate to account for the superiority of the whites."[33] Thorndike believed in the genetic superiority of whites over blacks, just as he firmly believed that the good society was ultimately a society ruled by the talented, morally righteous, and wealthy.

As a son of the Enlightenment, Thorndike believed in the progress of humanity through the manipulation and reform of social institutions. He carried the idea of social melioration and the perfectibility of humankind to one of its possible conclusions, eugenics, a movement he supported throughout his professional career. As he grew older, however, he tended to place greater emphasis on heredity and increasingly less on the importance of an improved environment. In his last major work he argued for the legal sterilization of those with low intelligence and morals, as well as those he called "dull or vicious epileptics and for certain sorts of dull and vicious sex perverts." He concluded: "By selective breeding supported by a suitable environment we can have a world in which all men will equal the top ten percent of present men. One sure service of the able and good is to beget and rear offspring. One sure service (about the only one) which the inferior and vicious can perform is to prevent their genes from survival."[34]

Thorndike included in his twenty-point program for social progress such advice as: society should practice scientific "eugenics"; "the able and good should acquire power"; and "quality is better than equality."[35] Interestingly, some thirty-three years earlier, Thorndike had attacked Lester Frank Ward's *Applied So-*

ciology for ignoring the Galton thesis which made ancestry so significant. Ward's egalitarianism, Thorndike surmised, was nothing more than a "defense of intellectual communism."[36] Throughout his life, Thorndike held fast to a conception of human nature which saw the individual as the product of biologic evolution, with some higher and others lower on the genetic scale. His massive studies of individual differences confirmed, for him and for others, that social and economic classes were largely caused by differences in inherited intelligence. Thorndike's original view of human nature was confirmed by the statistical charts of a lifetime of work. Humans could progress if they recognized the pernicious nature of Ward's egalitarianism and proceeded to practice eugenics to ensure the mental and moral best.

One of Thorndike's last major research projects was to develop a "G" scale for judging the value (goodness) of American cities and a "P" scale for judging the personal qualities of their inhabitants. He studied over 310 municipalities, compiling a list of more than three hundred criteria by which each city might be evaluated. "Among the three hundred items or features or traits there are thirty-seven, all or nearly all of which all reasonable persons will regard as significant for the goodness of life for good people in a city."[37] Of the thirty-seven criteria used, over twenty items deal with public and private value of property, size of income and expenditures, as well as the number of people who possess such items as automobiles, radios, and telephones. The "all reasonable persons" upon which he based his study were, it seems, highly materialistic, upper-middle-class people who valued their *Better Homes and Gardens*, *National Geographic*, and *Good Housekeeping* magazines.[38] Under the circumstances, it should come as no surprise that the ten cities rating the highest on the "G" scale were Pasadena, Montclair, Cleveland Heights, Berkeley, Brookline, Evanston, Oak Park, Glendale, Santa Barbara, and White Plains.[39] Thorndike found that the more black families a city contained, the lower the "G" and "P" ratings.[40] Thus, the cities with the least "goodness" were in the South: Augusta, Columbus, Meridian, High Point, Charleston, Savannah, and Durham.[41]

The important thing to do to improve a city, Thorndike argued, was to get "good" people to join the community and, most of all, to get "good" people who knew how to earn money— the more money the better.

Cities are made better than others in this country primarily and chiefly by getting able and good people as residents—people who, for example, are intelligent, read books, do not contract syphilis, or commit murder, or allow others to do so, own their own homes, have telephones, and support doctors, nurses, dentists and teachers rather than lawyers and domestic servants. The second important cause of welfare is income. Good people, rich or poor, earning much or earning little, are a good thing for a city, but the more they have and earn the better. They and their incomes account for at least three-fourths, and probably more, of the differences of American cities in the goodness of life for good people.[42]

Since "good" cities are largely made up of high-income "good" people, the logical question to ask is how might the community manage to get more good people. Thorndike's answer: "The surest way to have good people is to breed them."[43] In the end, it was always a matter of sterilization of the unfit and breeding of the best.[44]

It should not go unnoticed that Thorndike found church memberships inversely related to his rating of the general goodness of life. He asked, "What are the churches doing with their prestige and power if they are neither helping the health and education and recreation of a community nor improving the personal qualities of its residents?" His response: "Unless the better communities under-report their church membership or the worse communities over-report theirs, we must suspect that the churches are clubs of estimable people and maintainers of traditional rites and ceremonies rather than powerful forces for human betterment."[45] Perhaps his own lifetime of success also had helped him to reach the conclusion that the work of the scientist, rather than that of the clergy, was a more powerful force for human betterment. From this perspective, he had chosen the right path.

Edward Thorndike objectified, standardized, and typed both the individual and society. He played a significant role, indirectly at least, in the "scientific management" movement in business, and directly in the efficiency movement in education. Through his many disciples, and his textbooks, tests, achievement scales, and teachers' manuals, he had a profound impact on American education. Perhaps more than any other single individual, he helped to structure American education in the twentieth century. Through his efforts, and the work of others, American school administrators, teachers, and curriculum experts learned how to regard their students objectively and quantitatively. The question of this standardization of the educational frontier enhanced social mobility or decreased it, and questions concerning the merits of the value system on which the standards were based proved to be embarrassing for many educators by the mid-twentieth century. As more and more people involved in education came to reject the possibility of a value-free science of education, a value-free science of testing, and a value-free system of public schooling, they, in turn, began to see the extent to which significant bias against racial and ethnic minorities, women, and the lower social-economic classes had been institutionalized in American education. Much of this institutionalized bias can be traced directly to the work of professional educators like Thorndike who embraced what they thought was an objective science of education and confused what is with what they thought ought to be.

The vast influence Thorndike exercised over American education may be accounted for in part by his own values, which were those of white middle-class America. At least as important, however, is the fact that his empirical findings were essentially what business-minded Americans wanted to hear. His positive correlations of wealth, morality, intelligence, and social power could ruffle no one on the upper end of the power structure. Nor, indeed, would a well-washed, growing, middle-class America be upset to learn that science substantiated the notion that "the abler persons in the world in the long run are the more clean, decent, just and kind." The conservative social values of Thorndike were clearly and fundamentally compatible with a business-minded, conservative, middle-class, racist-oriented America.

In the early years of this century, Max Weber, in a brilliant series of essays, called attention to the intimate relationship between the Protestant ethic and the spirit of capitalism. He discussed how, when Protestant views with respect to work, thrift, predestination, calling, elect, asceticism, and divine grace become secularized, they seemed to fit into and become part of the ideological structure of capitalism. Weber further explained how the work of John Wesley and Methodism contributed so much to the utilitarian ethic of the capitalistic system. Sometime after Friedrich Nietzsche announced to the world that "God is dead and we have killed him," Thorndike, the young son of a Methodist minister, no longer accepting the faith of his father, set forth to preach a new gospel of scientific education and psychology. Implicit in many of the most important doctrines he espoused were values drawn from the Methodist moral capital of his past. While the God of his father may have died, the values and ethics of his father were very much alive for him, as was the spirit of capitalism. As he put it: "My God does not hear prayers. Work for him." Edward L. Thorndike did.

Notes

1. In Geraldine Joncich, *The Sane Positivist: A Biography of Edward L. Thorndike* (Middletown, Conn.: Wesleyan University Press, 1968), p. 64. "The Miracle, A Play in Three Acts" was written "about 1920" but never published, according to archival sources cited by Joncich.

2. See ibid., p. 29.

3. Merle Curti, *The Social Ideas of American Educators* (Paterson, N.J.: Littlefield, Adams and Co., 1961), p. 464.

4. Edward L. Thorndike, *Education* (New York: Macmillan Co., 1912), p. 29.

5. Ibid.

6. Ibid., pp. 12, 13.

7. See Edward L. Thorndike and Robert S. Woodworth, "The Influence of Improvement in One Mental Function upon the Efficiency of Other Functions," *Psychological Review* 8(1901): 247–61, 384–95, 553–64.

8. Charles H. Judd, at the University of Chicago, found a different alternative to Thorndike's explanation. He argued that when a subject is taught for "generalizations," these generalizations transfer; various experiments have since confirmed Judd's hypothesis. See Charles H. Judd et al., *Education as Cultivation of Higher Mental Processes* (New York: Macmillan Co., 1936). If we push Thorndike's thesis to its logical extreme, the formal school might best return to an apprenticeship system. For a critical appraisal of Thorndike's theory that only identical elements transfer, see Pedro T. Orata, *The Theory of Identical Elements* (Columbus: Ohio State University Press, 1928).

9. Whether the ready acceptance of Thorndike's work on this subject was due to the evidence he presented, or because he found what the culture wanted, is indeed a moot question. See Walter B. Kolesnik, *Mental Discipline in Modern Education* (Madison: University of Wisconsin Press, 1958).

10. See Edward L. Thorndike, "The Psychology of the Half-Educated Man," *Harper* 140(Apr. 1920): 670.

11. See Edward L. Thorndike, *Educational Psychology*, 3 vols. (New York: Mason-Henry Press, 1913), 1:150–54.

12. Edward L. Thorndike, "The Psychology of Labor," *Harpers* 144(May 1922): 800.

13. For one aspect of this development, see Raymond E. Callahan,

Education and the Cult of Efficiency (Chicago: University of Chicago Press, 1962).

14. Quoted in Curti, *Social Ideas of American Educators*, p. 483.

15. Edward L. Thorndike, "The Evolution of the Human Intellect," *Popular Science Monthly* 60(Nov. 1901): 65.

16. Florence L. Goodenough, "Edward Lee Thorndike, 1874–1949," *American Journal of Psychology* 63(1950): 292.

17. Thorndike's connectionist view of human learning accounts for his persistent attitude that intelligence must not be viewed as general but as specific kinds of behavior. He attributed the quantitative speed of making these connections to heredity.

18. Geraldine M. Joncich, ed., *Psychology and the Science of Education: Selected Writings of Edward L. Thorndike*, Classics in Education, no. 12 (New York: Bureau of Publications, Teachers College, Columbia University, 1962), p. 21.

19. Thorndike, *Educational Psychology*, 1:281, 282.

20. Joncich, *Sane Positivist*, p. 64.

21. National Society for the Study of Education, *Seventeenth Yearbook* (Bloomington, Ill., 1918), part 2, p. 16.

22. Curti, *Social Ideas of American Educators*, p. 460.

23. See Edward L. Thorndike, "The Contributions of Psychology to Education," *Journal of Educational Psychology* 1(Jan. 1910): 5–6.

24. In 1903 he admitted that the aim and goal of education was determined "not by facts but by ideals." It was not long, however, before he asserted that ideals and values were proper subjects of scientific investigation and control. See Robert Woodworth, "Edward Lee Thorndike (1874–1949)," *National Academy of Science* 27(1952): 217.

25. I am indebted to Geoffrey Lasky for first calling my attention to this phenomenon in Thorndike's work.

26. Curti, *Social Ideas of American Educators*, p. 498.

27. See Edward L. Thorndike, *Educational Psychology: Briefer Course* (New York: Teachers College, Columbia University, 1914), pp. 340–51. This book was designed specifically for teachers.

28. See Edward L. Thorndike, *Individuality* (Boston: Houghton Mifflin Co., 1911), pp. 30–34.

29. See Clarence J. Karier, *Shaping the American Educational State* (New York: Free Press, 1975), chaps. 6, 7.

30. Edward L. Thorndike, "Intelligence and Its Uses," *Harpers* 140(Dec. 1919-May 1920): 235.

31. Ibid., pp. 233, 235.

32. Thorndike, *Individuality*, pp. 40, 36.

33. Ibid., pp. 37–38.

34. Edward L. Thorndike, *Human Nature and the Social Order* (New York: Macmillan Co., 1940), pp. 455, 957. Readers here should be cautioned that if they are seeking a clear understanding of Thorndike's ideas on sterilization and eugenics, they ought to use this edition, not

the edited and abridged version by Geraldine Joncich Clifford (Cambridge, Mass.: M.I.T. Press, 1969). The latter work omits many of Thorndike's more significant and revealing statements on the subject. The above quote from p. 455, for example, does not appear in the latter work.

35. Ibid., pp. 957–62.

36. Edward L. Thorndike, "A Sociologist's Theory of Education," *Bookman* 24(1906–7): 294. See also Edward L. Thorndike, "Scientific Books," *Science* 24(Sept. 1906): 299–301.

37. Edward L. Thorndike, *Your City* (New York: Harcourt, Brace and Co., 1939), p. 22.

38. Ibid., pp. 29–31.

39. See *Science News Letter* 35(May 6, 1939): 284–85.

40. Thorndike, *Your City*, p. 77.

41. *Science News Letter*, p. 285.

42. Thorndike, *Your City*, p. 67.

43. Edward L. Thorndike, *144 Smaller Cities* (New York: Harcourt, Brace and Co., 1940), p. 91.

44. This position can also be found among his earlier works; see, for example, Edward L. Thorndike, "Eugenics: With Special Reference to Intellect and Character," *Popular Science Monthly* 83(Aug. 1913): 125–38.

45. "Best Cities Distinguished by Dentists, Not Clergymen," *Science News Letter*, p. 284. It should be noted that Thorndike's finding—the prevalence of dentists over clergymen in the upper-class suburban communities—comes as no surprise. Lower-class people seldom can afford the luxury of dental care, whereas upper-middle-class people can. Furthermore, church attendance had been dropping off among the white upper-middle-class population during the 1930s.

4

JOHN B. WATSON [1878–1958]

The Image Maker

At the height of his career in psychology, John B. Watson, the founder of behaviorism, was accused by Adolf Meyer, psychiatrist-in-chief at Johns Hopkins Hospital, of creating a substitute dogma for the Baptist faith of his childhood. The accusation arose out of an exchange over a paper Watson had given at Johns Hopkins entitled, "What is Mental Disease?" In it Watson attempted to apply the behaviorist "paradigm of conditioned reflexes" to the entire field of mental disease. Meyer took issue with Watson not at the point where he introduced his method of conditioning as a possible tool in psychotherapy, but rather at the point where Watson propounded his method to the exclusion of all others.

Meyer insightfully sensed that at the root of Watson's dogmatic behaviorism lay a psychological need for a substitute faith.

> Your application of the concept of conditioned reflexes is acceptable enough as far as it attempts to make fairly clear what the term may be made to mean; but to use it as you do as a formulation with the character of a dogma of exclusive salvation is a mere evasion of a psychophobic character, reminding me very much of the tone of the traditional "atheist" or the evolutionist à la Clevenger: it overexploits a special term from a neutral territory to make any possible reference to the old gods unnecessary, but it is not capable

of any tolerance such as would give a simple and natural formulation to the main points which force themselves upon the physician.[1]

Meyer went on to point out that the faith Watson propounded was *"hopelessly* narrow," and he characterized the paper as just one more of those "half-cocked pioneer schemes" which created more confusion than clarity in the field. Not only had Watson stepped into areas in which he simply was uninformed, but he had made no attempt to become informed. He could, Meyer said, at least ask questions.

Meyer perceptively sensed other problems as well. "Behaviorism," as Watson was developing it, "physiologizes the data of experience" by too easily translating the data of "preliminary surveys" into the special jargon of physiology.[2] It ought to prove its case not on the grounds of another discipline, which might lend it an aura of scientific respectability, but rather on the basis of its own experimental evidence and data. Meyer repeatedly invited Watson to prove his assertions by working on three or four real cases of neurasthenia. Finally, he asked Watson not to publish his material, or he would be forced to publicly refute Watson's ideas: "I have not the conviction that you have given any consideration to our problem, and I feel that it is not wise or fair to throw a doctrine of purism and exclusive salvation on the physician while you still continue as editor of the Psychological Review and the Psychological Bulletin, hoisting all kinds of Psychology on the public. I naturally do not assume any attitude of censorship; but I feel that this publication would lead to discussions on my part which had better remain unpublished."[3] Watson responded that he would "publish the article in the *Journal of Philosophy, Psychology and Scientific Methods* and . . . leave the matter in the hands of our colleagues." In "all humbleness" he would deny "knowing anything about the psychiatric end of neurasthenia;" however, he did claim that "in the past three years I have done a large amount of work [in the] psychopathology of everyday life." From his own study he believed he had found the same mechanism that was at work in Meyer's patients: "I have run across the same mechanism that my inference leads me to think that you find in your admissions to the Clinic. While this does not meet your very proper suggestions that I examine a few cases of neurasthenia, I think it does give even me, laboratory theorizer as I am, the right to make the suggestions I have made in my paper."[4]

While there is no evidence that Watson had done any significant work on the psychopathology of everyday life, as he suggested, there is evidence to indicate that he had read Freud's work by that title and that he had had a nervous breakdown in which his lifelong fear of the dark played a central role. It is highly likely that his reference to "work" in this context was work done trying to understand his own problems. Earlier, he had arrived at the conclusion that his phobia was a consequence of a conditioning process that a black nurse inflicted on him in early childhood. Such was the mechanism Watson believed he had found at work in his own case, and "by inference" in Meyer's clinical admissions' cases. Lastly, Watson reminded Meyer that he was "not trying to butt in on your preserves. I have a theory of psychology which I am trying to develop into a system. I tentatively try it out first in one field and then in another. This is my sole interest."[5]

At first, Meyer seemed to interpret this latter statement as a weakening of Watson's dogmatic stance. In replying he said, "I should not have the slightest objection to any of your formulations as long as you feel inclined to avoid a dogma of exclusive salvation."[6] Meyer seemed pacified. It proved to be short-lived, however, for in a sharply worded letter dated the next day, Meyer denied Watson's claim to fairness and humility, as well as the validity of Watson's claim to the tentativeness with which he was employing his methodology. While Watson asserted that Meyer and others who used the term "mental" were, in fact, employing a useless term which he, Watson, could not understand, Meyer responded by suggesting that Watson had not even taken the first step of inquiry by raising questions.[7] With respect to Watson's suggestion that Meyer might be afraid of encroachment on his preserves, Meyer quickly pointed out that it was he, Meyer, who had extended the "hospitality of our clinic" to Watson, and he hoped that Watson might avail himself of that liberality and hospitality to learn more about real, serious, actual cases of mental illness. Meyer saw in Watson a distasteful intolerance, based not on a scientific quest for hard evidence, but rather on a compulsive need to eliminate whole spheres of life interests as a consequence of his Baptist upbringing. Watson had developed and was using the conditioned reflex in a dogmatic fashion, much as his earlier Baptist mentors might have used their faith. Meyer pointed out: "My forefathers have been free of the dogma of exclusive salvation since 1521; and I never had any need of eliminating a whole sphere of life interests as you did when you shed the Baptist shell. That is probably why I am much more tolerant in what I formulate as critical common sense; and I certainly do not see why we should spoil that which is most likely to help physicians in the task of formulating what lies between the complaint and needs of the patient and the final scientific solution."[8]

Meyer seemed to understand Watson better than Watson appeared at times to understand himself. In many ways his behaviorism *was* an outgrowth of his Baptist background. It was not, however, a direct, one-to-one relationship, but rather a dialectical consequence of his personal interaction with the psychosocial milieu of his family and the larger Greenville, South Carolina, community where he grew to young manhood. Watson's life experiences fall into three rather distinct, but continuous phases. His early, formative years were spent in Greenville, where he was born, grew up, went to college, and lived until his mother's death in 1900. The second phase involved the development of his professional career at the University of Chicago (1900–1908) and then at Johns Hopkins University (1909–20), where he became the leader of the Behaviorist Movement in the developing field of professional psychology. The third phase of his life, from 1920 to 1946, while he still continued to popularize his views on psychology, was primarily preoccupied with Madison Avenue advertising.

In this chapter I consider selected biographical aspects of Watson's life that seem to shed some light on the way his behavioristic views evolved through each phase of his life. Then I review both the psychology he was attempting to create and the social values he propounded along with that psychology. Lastly, I critically consider the impact these ideas have had on American culture, not only from the position of Watson as a leader who influenced that culture, but, more importantly, from the position of Watson as a reflection of that culture.

Meyer's rather intense argument with Watson over his "dogma of exclusive salvation" did not stand in the way of their continuing professional relationship, at least on the surface. Meyer and his staff at the Phipps Psychiatric Clinic helped Watson critically review his new manuscript, *Psychology from the Standpoint of a Behaviorist*, before its 1919 publication. Watson clearly believed that their relationship was on a solid footing, so much so that in 1920, when details of his scandalous marriage became public knowledge, it was Meyer in whom he confided and from whom he sought advice.[9] In a letter dated August 18, Watson told Meyer that he would like to place the whole matter of the breakup of his marriage before Meyer, as head of the clinic, Professor Lovejoy, of the education department, and Dean Willoughby, of the medical school. Watson evidently trusted these men. Meyer advised Watson to take the matter directly to President Goodnow. Eleven days later, after discussing the problem with Lovejoy and Willoughby, Meyer wrote to Goodnow that he believed Watson had disgraced himself, the university, and science. He advised the president: "Without clean cut and outspoken principles in these matters we could not run a co-educational institution nor could we deserve a position of honour and responsibility before any kind of public nor even before ourselves."[10] The next day Goodnow called Watson into his office and compelled him to resign on the spot. Meyer thus played a key role in forcing Watson's resignation from Johns Hopkins and, in effect, in Watson's leaving the academic side of psychology.

As Watson packed his bags for New York and a new career, leaving behind a broken marriage and his two children, he no doubt was cognizant that his friends had not come to his aid; yet he never seemed to be aware of the direct role Adolf Meyer had played in his dismissal.[11] Whatever the final motive for his actions, Meyer must have felt that the loss of Watson to the profession of psychology was not debilitating. He never had liked Watson's dogmatic stance or his eagerness to venture into areas in which he was so uninformed.

Watson was a rebel as well as a conformist. In some respects, his rebelliousness was directed against the sacred icons of the field of psychology and the social mores of the community. The latter made Meyer even more uncomfortable than the former. Much of Watson's rebelliousness, however, was held in check by his compulsive need to succeed—a need that often was translated into docile homage toward those who occupied authoritative positions.[12] In this way he appeared as a conformist, although he saw himself as a rugged individualist, a "self-made" man. It was a rather strange self-image for a behaviorist; nevertheless, it was central to Watson's self-concept. He believed he knew how the game of life was to be played, and he played it accordingly. He had gone far in his academic career through what he believed were his own efforts, and he had no reason to suspect that he might not go even further in the business career that lay ahead.

While in the academic world, Watson had come to relish the fame of the "scientist" and the respect American society accorded to the university man; in the world of business, he would come to relish instead the comforts and other symbols of success that wealth could purchase. The new life upon which he embarked, as well as the old one he left behind, was far removed from his early beginnings in Greenville.

John B. Watson was born in 1878, the fourth child of Pickens and Emma Roe Watson. For the next twenty-two years, he grew to manhood in a psychically stormy, intensely religious, highly racist, socially strident environment. From the beginning it appeared that Emma Roe had married beneath her social station; nevertheless, her efforts made the marriage work. The young family settled on a small farm six miles from Greenville. Although they were dirt poor, forever facing survival crises, Emma's strong will held the family together and kept up the appearance, at least to the outside world, of a clean, decent family managing in true Christian piety. As did so many other white poor at the time, the Watson family rationalized their economic plight by believing they had lost their wealth in the Civil War.[13] In spite of economic hardships, Emma managed to squeeze out enough money to afford a black nurse for the children, thus maintaining some degree of respectability, always an important item in the Watson household. Locked in between a decaying Southern aristocracy of "social betters" and a race of black "inferiors," the white poor who sought and craved respectability often found at least the trappings of it in their church activities.

Watson's mother was "insufferably religious." She took an active role in the Reedy River Baptist Church and became one of the "principal lay organizers for the Baptists in the whole of South Carolina."[14] In keeping with her proselytizing zeal, Emma named her youngest son John Broadus Watson, after John Albert Broadus, "one of the founding ministers of the Southern Baptist Theological Seminary which had been located in Greenville up until a few months before Watson's birth in January, 1878." John was made to vow to his mother that he would become a minister— "slated," as he put it, at an early age.[15] Emma tied her family closely to the church, strictly adhering to the fundamentalist prohibition against drinking, smoking, or dancing. Cleanliness was always next to godliness, and Emma never ceased to keep her family next to God.

Watson's personal life profoundly shaped the values he expressed through the scientific behaviorism he ultimately came to develop. Although there is no record of the toilet training he underwent as a child, we might reasonably suspect that it was not without some kind of trauma. As a child development expert, and in his own family, he stubbornly advocated training children in eliminative functions at the age of *two to three weeks*, without any empirical or experimental evidence to justify his recommendations.[16] The origin of this rather strange notion, as well as the compulsive way he held to it, is more likely to be found in his own childhood experience than in any "scientifically" derived laboratory process.

The compulsive attitude Watson held toward his work, his frequent depressions, and his fear of the dark, which afflicted him throughout his adult life, were consequences of his early years. In 1903, as a graduate student at the University of Chicago, he suffered his first nervous breakdown, after which his phobia came to dominate his life. He believed that his black nurse had conditioned him to fear the dark. Later, as a professional psychologist studying child development, he became most interested in the conditioning and deconditioning of such fears. He attempted to decondition himself on a number of occasions, but to no avail. His phobia seemed to involve more than the fairly common practice of Southern mothers and black nurses telling bogeyman stories to control a child's behavior. In Watson's case, it was more than a straightforward conditioning process, especially if we consider the role his white, fundamentalist Baptist mother played standing immediately behind his black nurse.

Baptist leaders would periodically meet in the Watson home to discuss church affairs. Emma's husband, Pickens, much to his displeasure, was inducted as a deacon in the church. The moral structure of their home, encompassing the emotionally circumscribed will of God, seemed all-pervasive. However, there always was an emotional release during the church services and the repeated witnessing for Christ—the experience of being born again into a purer, truer Christian life. Public confession was but one part of this highly ecstatic experience, which at times seemed to pervade the entire congregation.[17] John thus grew to manhood in an intense, psychically charged, moralistically laced family and community.

In such an environment there often exists a considerable difference between the outer appearance, the superficial shell of moral strictures, and the behind-the-scenes reality of sinful transgressions. There are those who remain blind to the sinful side of life, those who see it but do not care to face it, and those who thrive on the intrigue of a life based on a double standard of morality. There are also a few rebellious souls who seek to flaunt their sinfulness in a community that lives on the appearances of "virtue." Such was the role Pickens Watson gradually came to play in the Watson household and the Reedy River Baptist Church community.

Early in his marriage, Pickens was recognized as a stable, loyal family man and a deacon in the church. John had fairly pleasant memories of his father teaching him how to care for animals and use practical manual tools: "At nine years of age I was handling tools, half-soling shoes, and milking cows. At 12 I was a pretty fair carpenter. This manual skill has never lost its charm, and in the Summers of 1909 and 1910 I built a ten-room house from blue prints."[18] These were the years when he was close to his father. He grew to like animals, often preferring them to humans. He loved the land, and within his mind's eye, the idyllic life was always to be found on the family farm. He wandered the countryside, enjoying the sense of freedom it gave him. Much of this wandering provided an escape from Sunday school, to his mother's consternation, and also served as an escape from a family situation that was becoming increasingly intolerable.

Pickens Watson was a handsome man. He took to having affairs with a number of women who found him attractive, and he also began drinking bourbon. At first, all this was done on the sly; however, his increased swearing became noticed publicly. While Watson's mother remained a pious, religious pillar of the community, his father became known as a womanizer and the town drunk. When Pickens finally decided to leave his family and live with two Indian squaws on the edge of Greenville, John, only thirteen years old, was significantly affected. He came to believe that his father, who had taught him many things, had not only deserted his family but in a real sense betrayed his youngest son. John's role model had abandoned him at a crucial point in his life, and he never forgave his father for it. David Cohen relates: "Years later, in the 1920s, when Pickens was in New York he got in touch with his now famous son. But John refused to see the old man even though Pickens was by then well over eighty. He rejected his father as his father had rejected him, though he did send him a little money so that Pickens could buy some clothes. Watson felt the loss of his father, and of his teacher in carpentry, very keenly."[19]

John was the spitting image of his father, and Emma Watson unfortunately saw many of the same traits her husband possessed in her spirited young son. Unlike his older brother, Edward, who had turned to religion (a middle brother, Thomas, had passed away), John needed careful watching. He seemed destined to be particularly attractive to the opposite sex, and his rebellious spirit would likely get him into trouble. By fifteen he had taken to mocking his teachers in school, and he had been arrested twice, once for " 'nigger' fighting" and once for discharging a firearm within the city limits.[20] His mother paid especially close attention to him until he was twenty-two—some might say too close. While in one sense young John loved the attention, for it seemed to fill the void of a drunken father who had deserted him, in another sense he hated it, for it forged the psychological chains that bound him to his mother for the rest of his life. As an adolescent and a young adult, John could not break away from her, and his attachment may have set in motion his fears of homosexuality, expressed in his later work. Cohen suggests that "Watson . . . was tremendously afraid of homosexuality. He knew how close he had been to his mother. Emma had a considerable hold over him and that hold did not pass till she died."[21] Watson later overcame this fear, temporarily at least, through his machismo depersonalization of women as sexual objects, as well as by his frequent extramarital conquests. He clearly had something to prove—or disprove.

Watson's difficulty in freeing himself from the psychic influence of a strong-willed, extremely religious, overprotective mother accounts for much of the rather strange, if not bizarre, recommendations he repeatedly made with respect to child rearing. More than anything else, he knew the powerful influence of a mother's "love." In later years he would shock the world by warning mothers to "stop loving their children to death." His aim was to produce an independent, free individual, one who was emotionally detached from mother, father, sister, or brother. Such was the image of the rugged individualist, the self-made man, that Watson cultivated for himself. He pictured himself as someone who could struggle against all odds, face all kinds of crises, and, mostly through his own efforts, pick himself up and redirect the course of his life. He had learned in adolescence how to deal with authority, how to handle emotional attachment, and, indeed, how to survive the pain of estrangement. He had learned how to effectively blank out and repress much of his painful inner emotions. Gradually, he anesthetized his inner soul, until it was like a desert that could nurture life only on the fringes of experience. With this kind of personality, all life, all reality, would be seen as structurally simple and one-dimensional. By the time Watson reached adulthood, his one-sided perspective on life was well in place. The emotional wounds of his childhood had been cauterized, leaving only tough scar tissue, resistant to any penetration by the existential world into which he moved.

At age fifteen, Watson applied to Furman University and was admitted. At the time, Furman was a small Baptist school whose goal was to prepare young men for the Baptist ministry. Why a rebellious young man with a police record, who showed little inclination toward formal schooling and religion, would decide to attend such a school—and why he would be admitted— remain unanswered questions. Perhaps the influence of his mother and her church connections are the best explanations. Once enrolled, Watson studied the Bible, the classics, William James's psychology, and physiology. He also became attracted to pretty girls, and they to him. Before finishing Furman University, he managed at least one affair, which he successfully kept from the public eye.[22]

Watson's general attitude toward his schoolwork was much the same as his attitude toward the social mores of the community. He saw behind the veil of "academic" appearances at Furman University as easily as he had seen behind the veil of "religious" appearances at the Reedy River Church. What his personality helped him construe to be reality was crucial. The formal educational experience Watson received at Furman was ultimately regarded as artificial, impractical, and unrelated to real life. Later in life, he would advocate dropping the veil of appearances with respect to the sexual mores of college students, in addition to making the curriculum more practical—one designed to train rather than educate. Since his views of education were narrowed accordingly, it is not surprising that he regarded his own university education as not much more than an academic game which he, of course, had learned to play with considerable success.

His idea of education as mere training is a kind of reductionism which obscured, indeed prevented, him from ever academically coming to appreciate the meaning of a liberal education. Symptomatic of his attitude, Watson only managed to pass the final examination in Greek and Latin in his senior year by getting high on cocaine. From two in the afternoon until the next day, when he took the exam, he crammed intensively while drinking a quart of Coca-Cola syrup. In some of his other subjects, he pointed out, he successfully managed to manipulate the professors into writing "my exam papers for me."[23] Much of education, he had come to believe, was really just a game.

Watson felt that he excelled in philosophy and psychology. He seems to have developed some interest in the area with an eccentric professor, Gordon B. Moore, who had studied at the University of Chicago. His decision to go into psychology was spurred on by a negative happening, not by thoughtful choice. Moore announced, before receiving final papers from his civics class, that any student who handed a paper in backwards would be flunked. Watson, as an honor student, had learned how to play academic games, but he still had a bit of the rebel in him. He handed his paper in backwards and was flunked. As a result, he stayed on for an A.M. rather than an A.B. degree. This incident, he said, made him resolve then and there that "I'd make him [Moore] seek me out for research some day."[24] In the year before he died, Moore did, indeed, seek out Watson at Johns Hopkins. It is revealing that Watson's drive to prove himself in his field was motivated in part by this kind of superficial impetus.

Without hesitation, Watson universalized his college experience. Blinded to any possible serious notion of a liberal education, he concluded that college ought to be simply a place where vocational careers and relevant practices of daily living were taught.

> This failure of college to mean anything to me in the way of an education gave me most of my slants against college. Those years made me bitter, made me feel that college only weakens the vocational slants and leads to softness and laziness and a prolongation of infancy with a killing of all vocational bents. Only with the years have I reached a point of view to the effect that, until college becomes a place where daily living can be taught, we must look tolerantly upon college as a place for boys and girls to be penned up in until they reach majority—then let the world sift them out.[25]

Watson's relatively vacuous views on education remained with him throughout his adult life. He blamed the college, not for failing to give him a liberal education, but rather for failing to teach him how to live. More specifically, college failed to give him the courage, or the strength of character, he most needed to confront his mother directly and "break away." Graduation came and went and he was still, for all intents and purposes, tied to his mother and to the Greenville environment.

Shortly after his graduation, Watson's mother took ill; under such circumstances, he had that much more reason to stay close to her. He taught school at "Batesburg Institute" in Greenville, which turned out to be Watson's own contrived name for a one-room school where he earned twenty-five dollars a month and free room and board.[26] He worked with twenty pupils of different ages and a cage of white rats, which he managed to train to the delight of the children. At the age of twenty-two, however, Watson was still not a free man. He joined the church to please his mother, and she died on July 3, 1900, with the satisfaction of knowing that her most rebellious son was safely tucked away in the Baptist fold.

The sod had not yet settled on Emma Watson's grave when John applied to both Princeton University and the University of Chicago to do graduate work. The president of Furman wrote letters of recommendation for him to both institutions, and Watson corresponded with Mark Baldwin at Princeton. He decided against Princeton because of the required reading knowledge of Greek and Latin—even though he had passed his final exam in Greek with the highest score in his class, he had been under the influence of cocaine, and he knew he could not pass an entrance exam without serious study. From Watson's point of view, Chicago would be the easier of the two. Besides, Moore had worked with Dewey there, and Watson thought he might have some interest in philosophy.

As the young Watson boarded the train for Chicago, he most likely looked back at Greenville with mixed feelings—the usual nostalgia as well as a sigh of relief. Although the direct influence of his mother had ended, her indirect influence remained. The personality and values he had developed in reaction to her and the environment in which he was reared would never leave him and would have a significant impact on the peculiar professional course his life would take.

With fifty dollars in his pocket, Watson stepped off the train in Chicago and into a whole new world. This would be his home for the next eight years. Upon arriving at the university, he met

John Dewey, James Angell, and John Manly, his brother Edward's brother-in-law. Almost immediately, Watson felt he had made the right choice. Angell had just completed his Ph.D. thesis with William James and was beginning his professional career, and he impressed Watson with his "erudition, quickness of thought, and facility with words."[27] Somewhat later, Watson met H. H. Donaldson, who taught him neurology, and Jacques Loeb, who instructed him in biology and physiology. He took philosophy courses from Mead, Tufts, and Dewey, which by his own admission had little effect on him: "God knows I took enough philosophy to know something about it. But it wouldn't take hold." Of his two courses with Dewey, Watson later remarked: "I never knew what he was talking about then, and, unfortunately for me, I still don't know." As for Mead's effect on him: "I didn't understand him in the classroom."[28] Watson liked Mead as a person, however, largely because he took an interest in his laboratory rat research. Failing to "flower" in philosophy, and impressed with Angell's "erudition," Watson thus heeded the latter's advice to work in animal psychology.

His childhood education fortuitously equipped Watson for the task before him. His father had taught him the carpenter's skills he now needed to build his own laboratory equipment, and his pleasurable childhood experiences with animals also served him well. Recall that he had successfully trained a cage of rats at his "Batesburg Institute." Watson liked animals and identified with them, probably because their lives seemed much less complicated than human lives. While the field of animal physiology had existed for a considerable time, the field of animal learning was just beginning to get underway. By 1899, Edward L. Thorndike had published his thesis on *Animal Intelligence*, and by 1901, Albion Small had published his study of rats and their behavior in puzzle boxes. During the spring term of 1901, Watson completed his work in philosophy, without distinction, and began to devote extended time to his animal research.

Watson approached his work in the laboratory in an increasingly compulsive manner. He knew that his road to success lay in the laboratory, and by November 1901, he had built enough apparatus and raised enough rats to begin his experiments. Throughout the winter, spring, and summer, Watson worked intensely with his rats, teaching them how to run complex mazes and work their way through problem boxes. He repeatedly projected human qualities and characteristics onto them by describing them as his "bright intelligent little fellows," often "playful" but sometimes the "picture of discouragement." The more he worked with them, the more he came to believe that their maze learning was most likely comparable to human learning.

Watson believed that it was possible not only to learn everything about rat behavior through a system of rewards and punishments, but also to extend this same process up the evolutionary scale and thereby understand all human behavior and patterns of learning. To him, human beings were animals, more so than anyone really cared to believe. This being the case, then the dominant practice of introspective psychology, with which Watson always had felt uncomfortable, might also be proven inadequate and possibly could be replaced with a much simpler stimulus-and-response variety of psychology. Such ideas, and their possible implications, sent nervous shock waves through his own psyche, and they would prove even more shocking to others. Uncharacteristically, Watson exercised caution:

> At Chicago, I first began a tentative formulation of my later point of view. I never wanted to use human subjects. I hated to serve as a subject. I didn't like the stuffy, artificial instructions given to subjects. I always was uncomfortable and acted unnaturally. With animals I was at home. I felt that, in studying them, I was keeping close to biology with my feet on the ground. More and more the thought presented itself: Can't I find out by watching their behavior everything that the other students are finding out by using O's? As I have said elsewhere, I broached this to my colleagues, as early as 1904, but received little encouragement.[29]

When Watson observed his rats in their cages, he was watching far more than just rats. To be sure, he was studying a lower form of life, but by reducing the learning process to its barest common denominator, he believed he was studying all human behavior. For Watson, that common denominator vis-à-vis rats and humans was the motivational concept of reward and punishment, which eventually would be developed into a stimulus-and-response psychology. In his mind there was an obvious association between the idea of reward and punishment, which he drew from his Baptist past, and the stimulus-and-response psychology he was developing in the laboratory. As his rats ran their mazes, they seemed to cast shadows; from Watson's perspective, those shadows often appeared to take the form of interacting human beings. Conceiving of human beings as animals, as little more than soulless, physiological, reactive mechanisms, could have profound, long-range consequences for both humans and the whole field of psychology. Could Watson dare express this idea in a frank way to Angell and his associates? Cohen suggests that at the time Watson was too ambitious to take such a chance—he needed Angell's support and could not risk an open confrontation.[30]

Watson escaped from such dilemmas by spending considerable time in the laboratory on his thesis research. His personal life was in a bit of a shambles, as Miss Vida Sutton, with whom he was enamoured, had rejected him for another lover. Such a blow to the machismo self-image he had cultivated in his Furman days only increased his determination to make his thesis something special. Ultimately, his research would pit Watson against virtually all of his colleagues, including Angell, his advisor. However, his thesis had to be written in such a way that, for the time being, it would have Angell's and the committee's support, yet in the long run could serve as the basis for the coming behaviorist revolution Watson would lead. He sensed that he was developing not only a thesis but a total perspective on life, one which would influence him for the rest of his life. Watson's own philosophy thus undergirded his thesis; it was a philosophy that denied everything his mother had held sacred.

On a number of occasions, Watson defined happiness as an "escape from one's self," and in his work he found that escape. He labored longer and slept less. Gradually, however, his obsessive work habits failed to satisfy his need to escape. Unable to sleep, Watson took to walking eight to ten miles at three o'clock in the morning to overcome his anxiety. In the fall of 1902, he suffered a breakdown, or as he described it, "a typical Angst." As therapy, he took a vacation with some friends, the Van Pelts, in Norwood, Michigan. The change of environment and the long walks in the country had a soothing effect, yet for those three weeks he could sleep "only with a light turned on."[31] Psychically, at least, this had the effect of warding off the evil spirits of his childhood, which now seemed all-encompassing and vividly present. Although Watson's fear of the dark persisted throughout his life, within a month he had recovered from his depression, at least to the point that he could resume his work. Retrospectively, he viewed this process of overcoming his depression as "one of my best experiences in my university course. It taught me to watch my step and in a way prepared me to accept a large part of Freud, when I first began to get really acquainted with him around 1910."[32]

Exactly how much of Freud's work Watson ever came to understand or accept remains difficult to determine. While Freud's discussion of the Oedipus complex indeed might have been applicable to Watson's personal problem, Watson did not, at the time of his breakdown, know of Freud's work. By 1902, Freud had just overcome his "Rome" phobia and published both *The Interpretation of Dreams* and *The Psychopathology of Everyday Life*, much of which, drawn from his own self-analysis, helped form the substantive content of his movement (see chap. 6). Both Freud and Watson suffered from phobias and both came to form major movements in psychology; both accounted for their phobias through the respective psychologies they developed.[33] Thus, Freud's problem stemmed from his early childhood oedipal experiences with his Catholic nurse and his Jewish mother; Watson's problems stemmed from his early childhood experience with a black nurse and a Baptist mother. By the time Watson discovered Freud, around 1910, Freud already had developed his method of "free association," while Watson was convinced that the "conditioned reflex" was the most important concept for understanding all animal and human learning. Agreeing with Freud that sex was very important and that it should be demystified, Watson disagreed with Freud's conception of human nature as involving both a conscious and an unconscious mind and a highly developed symbol system. To Watson, mother love was important; however, he explained it not as an oedipal complex, but rather as an oedipal habit developed by direct sense experience. Ultimately, he came to believe that just as we learn to feel with our senses, we also learn to think with our body muscles rather than with our minds. Although psychoanalysis remained the nemesis of behaviorism, Watson always felt that he could adequately explain what Freud was talking about through a liberal use of the conditioned reflex concept.

Watson's escape to Michigan had not cured him of his depression, but it did help him overcome it to the point that his phobia did not disable him and he could now control the depressions that would return from time to time. About thirty years later, in one of his last, unpublished essays, entitled "Why I Don't Commit Suicide," Watson advised those who were brooding over taking their own life to "run away for a week, a month or a year. There is no psychological medicine so potent in all the wide world as a *new environment.*"[34] He had developed a series of behavioral techniques that made him immune to suicide. It is significant, of course, that whether he was defining happiness or dealing with depression, his mode of operation was invariably one of escape. In both his personal and his intellectual lives, Watson had developed a sharply ingrained habit of blanking out troublesome emotional states and competing cognitive thought. A good example of the latter can be found in his encounters with John Dewey.

About four years before Watson arrived at Chicago, Dewey had published his classic essay on "The Reflex Arc Concept in Psychology" in the *Psychological Review.* In that 1896 essay, Dewey persuasively argued that the reflex arc concept was inadequately conceived. Logically, it would be more correct to conceive of a stimulus as part of a cycle rather than an arc, and thus to look for the meaning of the stimulus in terms of the "entire organic situation." If Watson had taken Dewey's essay seriously, he would have had considerable logical difficulty in arriving at his own position of denying the functional existence of mind.[35] Watson did not have this problem because, although he took courses from both Mead and Dewey, he pleaded ignorance of what they taught. If Watson was honest in this plea, and there is no reason to suspect that he was not, then the extent to which he could block out, and thereby deny, the competing intellectual experiences of others is striking. This is precisely what Adolf Meyer on another occasion reacted to as the "dogma of exclusive salvation." As a prophet of a new gospel, Watson had created the necessary personal and intellectual blinders to render as insignificant the counter-experiences of others.

Returning to his laboratory work, Watson ensured Angell's support and approval by involving his advisor in writing his thesis. We are reminded of Watson's earlier claim, that at Furman he managed to get his professors to write his exams for him. Whatever the case, Watson acknowledged his indebtedness to Angell: "Indeed, he worked daily with me on every sentence I wrote on my thesis, 'Animal Education.' He taught me rhetoric as well as psychology, and, if he failed me on logic, it was not his fault."[36] While Donaldson and Loeb helped him with neurological physiology, Angell monitored his thesis line for line.

What was Watson's thesis, and what was he trying to prove? A physiologist named Flechsig, in his own work on higher and lower mammalian brains, had argued that a decreasing degree of certain kinds of medullation occurs down the mammalian scale until the level of the rodent, where such medullation finally disappears. Flechsig suggested that this medullation involved centers of association necessary to the psychical life of the mammals. Watson quoted him to the effect that, "It is in these centers of association that psychical activity finds the elements of all our intellectual life. In these centers is the substratum of all human experience, knowledge, language, sentiments, and morals."[37] While Flechsig denied that these centers were present in rats, Watson wanted his study, and Small's earlier work, to prove that in certain respects rats learn as easily as higher mammals, such as dogs, cats, and monkeys. Consequently, Watson contended that "Flechsig has assumed for the associative processes of the higher mammals a neural mechanism more complicated than is necessary."[38] He went on to argue that if rodents as low on the scale as rats could learn definite associations without these centers of association, then it appeared the centers were not the "indispensable condition in the formation of such associations."

Basing his experimental work on Small's study, but improving on it considerably, Watson went on to show that the rat learned more quickly at an earlier age, before medullation had developed. In the rat, at least, medullation of the cortices had little to do with the learning that took place. Watson attempted to demonstrate not only that associative learning took place in rats as well as in higher species, but that such learning happened before medullation of the cortices had occurred in both the rat and other species. He found it relatively easy to show that learning did occur in rats, thus refuting Flechsig's notions of higher mammals as fundamentally different from lower forms with respect to associative learning patterns. Watson went on to suggest that the learning stages or plateaus he found in rats were also to be found in humans, and he further speculated that learning also occurred in the human infant before medullation was complete. Watson and the members of his committee came to believe that he had proved Flechsig wrong on a number of counts. He had seemingly confirmed not only what Small had found—namely, that rats are capable of associative learning—but that much learning occurred before medullation. The exact function of medullation remained unknown, however.

If Watson had stopped with his rats, his thesis would have been sound. He chose, however, to include a shadow thesis of implicit assumptions and unproven analogies that went far beyond any of the experimental data he presented. He repeatedly drew unsubstantiated analogies between human beings and rats. While Watson himself carried out the necessary associative learning experiments on his rats, he relied on other sources for detailed information on the physiology of human brains and human learning. Such reliance on physiological data at first glance may seem impressive, but his reasoning was still mostly by analogy, sometimes strained to the breaking point: human learning was assumed to be like that of rat learning, just as human medullation of the cortex was assumed to be like that of rat medullation of the cortex; the stages of human learning were assumed to follow the stages of animal learning because of Watson's implicit assumption that such learning was the same for all species. Watson concluded his thesis by denying Flechsig's correlations and replacing them with his own.

> If any analogy can be entertained between man and the rat, it seems to me that we need not make any such correlations as Flechsig. Why not assume that at some point in the development of the nervous system of man there exists a period comparable to the twenty-four-day period in the rat. At this age the individual will be teachable; he will not have the ready ability to handle difficult situations that his father has; the psychical life of the child lacks the rich and varied experiences that have come to the parent with age. Corresponding to this stage in the psychical life we should have on the neural side a condition in the medullation process similar to the one found in the rat at twenty-four days; certain nerve tracts, which must be the pathway of nervous impulses would still be unmedullated. Why one tract should become medullated sooner than another we can at present answer in the case of the man no better than in the case of the rat.[39]

On a number of occasions Watson made unproven as well as unwarranted analogies between rat and human learning. Nowhere in his thesis is this more striking than in the conclusion of Part 1, "An Experimental Study on the Psychical Development of the White Rat," when he said: "From the twelfth to the twenty-third day is a gradual but rapid increase in the complexity of the memory processes until at the latter age psychical maturity is reached. Development after this age is analogous to the development that takes place in a child of ten years as he gradually becomes more and more mature."[40] Here Watson gives no indication of ever having studied the learning development of a ten-year-old child, nor does he give any basis for his claim—it is simply unfounded.

Watson projected onto human learning and development that which he had discovered about rat learning and development. Mentally this was easy to do, for repeatedly throughout his thesis Watson attributed human qualities and characteristics to the rats he was studying.[41] Under such circumstances, analogies between humans and rats came easily. Watson simply ignored the obviously complex gulf which, in the minds of most people, exists between a rat and a human being. Instead he came to believe that both learned in the same way. For Watson, the human being was just another animal, more complex to be sure, but nevertheless an animal, all of whose learning processes were essentially the same. At an early point in his career Watson embraced the proposition that all human learning involved the same process as animal learning, a proposition that undergirded many of the analogies he invoked in his thesis. It was an unproven assumption then, and it remained so throughout Watson's later career when he developed his "scientific" behaviorism.

Watson's thesis expressed his own developing philosophy of life, which meant a denial of his Baptist roots and adoption of the mantle of science. Agreeing to stay on at Chicago and teach in the department, he decided it was time to share his ideas with Angell as to what direction the field of psychology ought to take. Angell curtly rejected Watson's ideas as essentially "ignorant" and advised him to stick to animal psychology.[42] Always sensitive to hostile criticism by those in positions of authority, Watson returned to his laboratory work and two major areas of future professional inquiry. First, he needed to learn more about what mechanism the rat actually used in its associative learning; and second, he needed to undertake experimental laboratory work with children. The latter would be delayed until his move to Johns Hopkins; the former began immediately. To develop his laboratory skills further, Watson spent the summer of 1904 at the Johns Hopkins Medical School studying surgical techniques. While there, he met Mark Baldwin who earlier, at Princeton, had been impressed with his application for doctoral study. The two got along very well that summer. In the fall, Watson returned to Chicago, an eager young professor who would help Angell develop psychology as a separate department, now that they had lost Dewey to Columbia.

Angell became more involved with the affairs of the department and less with Watson's research, and Watson took the opportunity to extend his experimentation. First, he taught his rats to run the maze as before. Then he blinded them, and was surprised to find that they could still run the maze. After he cut off their whiskers and destroyed their capacity to smell, taste, and hear, they could still run the maze. Not until he confused the rats' "kinesthetic sensations" did they seem sufficiently impaired so as to prevent them from running the maze. The rat, Watson concluded, through a process of reward and punishment, learned with its body muscles. He surmised that human beings might, too, but such a claim could not be pronounced at least until he was free of the direct influence of his mentor and close friend, James Angell.[43] An opportunity for professional freedom was rapidly approaching, thanks to Mark Baldwin at Johns Hopkins, who was attempting to create a new position for Watson—a professorship and an endowed chair. Angell supported the move. Angell's relationship with Watson was always something more than just one of academic advisor. Angell was also Watson's personal friend and a counselor for his private life as well.

Recall that during the second year of graduate work, shortly before his breakdown, Watson had fallen in love with, and been rejected by, Miss Vida Sutton. Late that following year, he became interested in Mary Ickes, and they were married secretly on December 26, 1903. In January, Mary's brother Harold became suspicious of Watson, prompting him to refuse to further finance Mary's college career; he sent her to stay with an aunt in Altoona. No sooner had Mary left town than Vida Sutton returned to tell Watson that she had made a mistake and loved him after all. Watson told her of his secret marriage to Mary; regardless, they resumed their relationship, which continued until a mutual breakup in August 1904. Watson then sent for Mary and publicly married her on October 1, 1904. Their first child, John, was born later that year. Watson told Mary of his most recent relationship with Vida Sutton, getting their public marriage off to an extremely rocky start. About three years later, shortly after their second child, Polly, was born, Watson resumed contact with Vida Sutton. Mary's suspicions sent her to her brother, who hired a detective to keep Watson under surveillance. After some time, "Mary and her brother went to Judson the president [of the University of Chicago] and took up the matter with him. They wanted me fired and her brother wanted her to get a divorce."[44]

President Judson and James Angell investigated the case, and Angell counseled John and Mary to continue their marriage, at least for the sake of the children. His argument proved persuasive. In the midst of this crisis, an offer came from Johns Hopkins. Watson now had the opportunity to make a third start of a faltering marriage in a new environment, while at the same time advancing his career and gaining the professional independence he felt he needed to speak his own mind. Watson felt very close to Angell, yet he wanted his freedom. Watson wrote Edward Titchener: "Angell and Donaldson have been like parents to me and I am sure that they will live in my memory as long as I live. My first debt is to them. It is an intellectual, social and moral debt."[45]

If the private life of John Watson did not flourish during his Chicago years, his professional life certainly did. During those years he took up his summer study of the noddy and sooty terns in the Tortugas for the Carnegie Institute, while continuing his laboratory work during the winter and teaching department courses as needed. He became acquainted with introspective psychologist Edward Titchener, of Cornell, and with Robert Yerkes, of Harvard, and was nationally recognized himself as an expert on animal behavior. When Mark Baldwin hired him to develop his laboratory work at Johns Hopkins, he sought to test the waters of his new professional freedom. The opportunity came in November of 1908, when he was invited by Yerkes to give a seminar at Harvard. In three days of almost continuous conversation with Yerkes and his students, Watson laid out his views on psychology. Yerkes was so upset that he wrote to Titchener, asking "him to guide Watson into being a proper psychologist rather than a 'behaviour man.' "[46] Watson immediately sensed this reaction and realized that he must be a bit more cautious in his relationship with Yerkes. Neither was he completely sure of Baldwin, who was still chair of his department.

By the end of the year the situation changed. Baldwin was caught frequenting a Negro brothel in Baltimore and was summarily fired by the university. On his way out, he appointed Watson editor of the *Psychological Review*. Ironically, only twelve years later Watson would leave the same way because of transgressions against the social mores of the academic community. In the meantime, Watson at last felt free to pursue his work: "The whole tenor of my life was changed. I tasted freedom in work without supervision."[47]

We can never be sure whether it was freedom or courage Watson sought. He did, however, begin to make his views public, first in a *Harpers* article on the "New Science of Animal Behavior," and later at Columbia University, when he began a series of lectures on February 24, 1913, entitled "Psychology as the Behaviorist Views It." There were now sleepless nights and periods of depression and illness, when the lights were kept on to ward off the demons of childhood.[48] Watson felt that the time had come to face the issues squarely. He argued that the main goal of psychology ought to be the "prediction and control of behavior," free of the introspective psychology of Wundt, James, or Titchener. The behaviorist should reject all notions of consciousness, believing that all human and animal learning can be objectively explained in terms of a unitary response system.

> Psychology as the behaviorist views it is a purely objective experimental branch of natural science. Its theoretical goal is the prediction and control of behavior. Introspection forms no essential part of its methods, nor is the scientific value of its data dependent upon the readiness with which they lend themselves to interpretation in terms of consciousness. The behaviorist, in his efforts to get a unitary scheme of animal response, recognizes no dividing line between man and brute. The behavior of man, with all of its refinement and complexity, forms only a part of the behaviorist's total scheme of investigation.[49]

Watson's behaviorist movement was underway. By the time he wrote *Psychology from the Standpoint of a Behaviorist* (1919), his school of behaviorism was well established and had attracted a cadre of young believers. Watson forcefully argued against any notions of introspection, consciousness, soul, mind, or any kind of hereditary determinants such as instincts. In place of the usual instincts, he postulated only three primitive reactions: fear, rage, and love, each of which could readily be shaped through the process of stimulus and response. All behavior, he insisted, might be explained by this process.

Watson went back and re-read Darwin's *The Descent of Man*, where he found support for his initial beliefs: "As man possesses the same senses with the lower animals, his fundamental intuitions must be the same."[50] Watson, however, went further. Having made the quantum leap between the animal and human kingdoms, he quickly proceeded to deny soul, mind, consciousness, or any unique status for man or his mental or spiritual experiences. Angell's mentor, William James, not long before had completed his lectures on the *Varieties of Religious Experience*; Watson, a student of Angell, now was denying the validity of any such experience. He felt free enough to publicly express what he had assumed in his doctoral dissertation some ten years earlier: rats learn not so much with their brain as with their muscles and their kinesthetic sensations; and so, too, must human beings. Watson coupled his reductionism with an appeal for all psychologists to become as "objective" as the behavioral psychologist had while working in the laboratory. His message was attractive to many young psychologists, in part because it was clear, simple, and striking. Also, the younger generation had become disenchanted with introspective psychology and was looking for a change. Watson's message was even more effective because of his charismatic presentations at public gatherings.

The approach Watson took to those in authority was one of ambivalence, and his relationship to Titchener, the leader of introspective psychology, was no different. He befriended Titchener while professionally attacking him.[51] Titchener was generous but critical of Watson's behaviorist movement: "The first impression is that of their unhistorical character; and the second is that of their logical irrelevance to psychology as ordinarily understood." While he appreciated the experimental laboratory techniques of the behaviorists, Titchener found their logic flawed: "The actual experimental work that the behaviorists turn out is good enough; but the general logic of their position is ridiculously crude." His major criticism of Watson was that he seemed to want to replace a science with a technology. Watson was, in fact, trying to change the meaning of "science" for psychology. For him, the traditional psychological knowledge gained through introspection was worthless. Titchener sensed this shallow, one-dimensional view of reality when he wrote to Yerkes that "Watson is the kind of man, I think, who should never trust himself to write on general questions, but should stick to his concrete work. He has no historical knowledge, and no power of continuous thinking in the realm of concepts."[52]

After Titchener published his critique of Watson's behaviorism, Angell suggested that he should have been tougher on his (Angell's) former student. Watson's problem was a lack of historical knowledge: "Indeed, I think if Watson had ever had my historical courses, which were developed after he graduated, he could hardly have fallen into some of the pits which have entrapped him." While his personal friendship with Watson prohibited any public criticism, Angell wanted Titchener to know how he felt: "My own position has been rendered rather difficult by virtue of my personal attachment. Of course I am wholly impatient of his position on this issue which seems to me scientifically unsound and philosophically essentially illiterate. Meantime for much of his actual work I have very high regard, as I have for him personally. I shall therefore be glad to see him properly spanked, even tho I cannot publicly join in the censuring."[53]

Interestingly, Angell apparently failed to recognize that the dissertation, which he had supervised most carefully, was the very cornerstone of Watson's later work. He apparently also had forgotten the time when, shortly after Watson finished his thesis, he had attempted to discuss his own broader views of psychology, only to be curtly dismissed by Angell and advised to stick to his animal laboratory work. Although a decade had passed and his memory might have blurred, the basis for many of Watson's current claims could be traced to his thesis work under Angell. In many ways, at Johns Hopkins, Watson was just carrying through on the work he had begun at Chicago. To complete his analogy, Watson needed a human development laboratory, and his opportunity to begin one was rapidly materializing.

Recognized as a leader in his field, and having been newly elected as president of the American Psychological Association, Watson was invited by Adolph Meyer to create a research laboratory at Johns Hopkins for the study of child development. Since his Chicago experience, Watson had dreamed of such a laboratory, where humans would replace rats. While the problem of how far a researcher could go with human subjects would be troublesome, much could still be done. From 1915 through 1920, with the exception of his World War I years, Watson worked with children in his child development laboratory.

The problem of supplying human subjects for experimental purposes has been a difficult problem throughout the twentieth century. For the most part, subjects have come from those categories of citizens who, in some way or for some reason, have been declassed of their normal citizenship rights and who, therefore, have less than adequate powers to protect themselves—that is, orphans, mental patients, prisoners, and certain members of the armed forces. From these classes, America has drawn most of its human experimental subjects. In Watson's case, orphans often met his need.

Just as he had studied rats in their cages, Watson now studied babies in their cribs, watching them, measuring them, and recording their every apparent development. What original reactions might children in their earliest days possess? Interestingly enough, they possessed the same basic reactions he could see among his rats: fear, rage, and love. While some babies were dropped into an assistant's arms or lowered into water to see if fear or rage might ensue, others were placed in dark rooms to determine whether fear of the dark was an inherent trait. Watson concluded that such fear was a conditioned reflex, not one of the primitive reactions. Although he never managed to decondition himself, he remained certain that all learning, including training the emotions, could be explained by way of the conditioning process.[54]

To demonstrate how a fear might be conditioned in a baby, Watson and his graduate assistant, Rosalie Rayner, financed by the American Association for the Advancement of Science, set out to condition an eleven-month-old orphan baby who was still nursing. The subject was given the experimental name Albert B., probably after Watson's namesake, John Albert Broadus, the great leader of the Southern Baptist ministry. The name was highly appropriate, given the fact that the older "religious" traditions functioned on reward and punishment, just as the newer "scientific" behaviorism also would. Watson was trying to show how his own fear of the dark had developed. In many ways, the Albert B. experiment symbolized for Watson the passing from a "religious" tradition into a "scientific" one, as well as the painful revenants of his own childhood. To what extent his own childhood experiences and psychological problems entered into his readiness to inflict pain on a defenseless child remains an open question.[55] In any event, he and Rosalie did not hesitate to carry out the experiment.

Albert B. was given a small white rat to touch. During a number of such rather pleasant experiences, the baby exhibited no fear of the rat. After he had gotten used to touching the animal, a new stimulus was added: as the child reached for the rat, Watson would hit a long steel bar with a hammer, sending a shocking noise through the room. At first Albert B. merely jerked, falling forward and burying his head in the mattress. After repeated attempts to touch the rat brought on the same shocking sounds, "the infant jumped violently, fell forward and began to whimper."[56] The process was repeated intermittently, enough times so that eventually Albert B. would break down and cry, desperately trying to crawl away, whenever he saw the rat. Watson and Rosalie had successfully conditioned the child to fear rats. Proceeding further, Watson conditioned Albert B. to fear rabbits, dogs, fur coats, and Santa Claus masks. However, before he and Rosalie could "decondition" the child, or experiment any further, Albert B. was adopted and moved away from Baltimore. Little Albert was destined to go through life with a strange set of fears he would never understand. Watson and Rosalie appeared to make light of the problem, suggesting that some day, when Albert B. was twenty years old and underwent psychoanalysis to overcome his fear of sealskin coats, his analyst might convince him that his phobia was caused when "at 3 years of age [he] attempted to play with the pubic hair of [his] mother and was scolded violently for it."[57]

John Watson and Rosalie Rayner seemed to have the necessary personality traits to do this kind of experimentation in the interest of "science" without flinching a moral muscle. They would not hesitate in the years ahead to experiment on their own children. By contrast, Mary Cover Jones, a friend of Rosalie's and one of Watson's last laboratory graduate assistants, did have some personal reservations: "I could not have played the role of creating a fear in a child, no matter how important the theoretical implications."[58] She would work with Watson only in attempting to decondition children of their fears, regardless of how the fears might have been instilled.[59]

While Watson discovered things about fears, he also discovered things about rage and love as primitive reactions. Most of what Freud was talking about in terms of "sex," Watson now translated into "love," which for him was simply a sensual reaction that could be accounted for through conditioning. For Watson, the Oedipus complex became an oedipal habit; and mother love, as well as love of mother, were mere consequences of physical stimulation.[60] He concluded that his black nurse had conditioned him to fear the dark, and he now understood as well why he was so closely attached to his mother. At this point, Watson forcefully advised mothers against too much physical contact with their children.

Watson turned to assembling his behaviorist platform, *Psychology from the Standpoint of a Behaviorist* (1919). The book, like his dissertation, contained considerable physiological information about the brain and the central nervous system. Much of this data and information, while helpful in creating the image of a scientific perspective, nevertheless remained unconnected with the peculiar content of the behavioral psychology he was attempting to develop, a considerable share of which was drawn from his own personal problems.[61] Meyer's earlier criticism—that Watson was physiologizing experience—was, it seems, on the mark. Nevertheless, his behaviorist platform was well received. The book had hardly been published, however, when Watson's personal life once again began to fall apart, and Meyer was forced to recommend his dismissal from Johns Hopkins.

Watson resembled his father in more than just appearances. Indeed, Emma's fears for her son were not so ill-founded. Like his father, he became heavily attached to bourbon; and like his father, he freely transgressed his marriage vows. Throughout his married life, Watson had affairs with many women, a fact to which his wife almost had become accustomed. However, when John took up with Rosalie, Mary decided that she had had enough.[62] She needed advice, but could not turn to her brother, Harold, who had advised her twelve years earlier to end her marriage. Instead, she turned to another brother, John, in New York. He told her to obtain evidence of her husband's unfaithfulness and hire a good lawyer.[63]

Mary Watson invited Rosalie and her parents to dinner. It was clear that Rosalie came from a very distinguished and prominent Baltimore family. It was also evident that Rosalie's parents did not know about their daughter's affair. The Rayners returned the Watson's dinner invitation, and it was during this second dinner party that Mary managed to slip into Rosalie's room, where she found fourteen incriminating love letters from John. Mary took the letters and rejoined the dinner party without revealing what she knew. Later, her brother photocopied the letters and advised her to take immediate action. Upon returning to Baltimore, Mary confronted John, Rosalie, and the Rayner family with the evidence. Still trying to save her marriage, she talked Rosalie's father into pressuring his daughter to take an extended trip to Europe. Rosalie refused. Watson, now more interested in saving his job than his marriage, tried to talk Mary into an extended trip and then a quiet divorce. Mary also refused.

The Watsons separated in April 1920, and by summer, news of the scandal was sweeping the academic community. At some point, Mary attempted to get her husband back by returning the original letters to him; at approximately the same time, and unknown to her, John Ickes was trying to sell the photocopies to the Rayners, with the expectation that they would be willing to pay a price to protect their daughter's good name. His attempt at blackmail failed, and a few of the letters somehow were passed on to the president of the university.[64]

At Meyer's insistence, President Goodnow forced Watson's immediate resignation. Before the year was out, John and Mary Watson were divorced; shortly thereafter he married Rosalie Rayner. In the interim, Watson left Baltimore for New York City, where he lived with William Thomas, a friend who had been dismissed earlier from the University of Chicago for sexual indiscretions. It was Thomas who introduced Watson to Stanley Resor, the owner and president of the J. Walter Thompson advertising firm. Resor took a liking to Watson and offered him a job with his agency.

The former academician turned his full attention to cultivating a career in advertising and rearing a new family. Resor was so impressed with his flamboyance that, not long after his apprenticeship, Watson was elevated to the vice presidency of the firm. His career in advertising skyrocketed, due in part to his personality. Also, the field of advertising was expanding at an unparalleled rate, serving the new mass consumer market created by the combined influences of assembly-line production techniques and the corollary extension of easy credit. Watson rode the crest of this great wave in advertising, and by 1930 he was salaried at nearly $70,000.[65] Unlike many others, he successfully played the stock market through the 1929 crash. Within a decade, this charismatic, flamboyant individual had reached the top in his second career. He now could dress as he wanted, in handmade suits and shirts and shoes imported from England. He also could afford quite easily the bourbon he consumed daily. And at last he was in a position to fulfill a childhood dream—he purchased a farm in Westport, Connecticut. Rosalie was a social hit in New York circles as well as in the growing suburban setting of Westport. Happily married, she gave birth to two sons, Billy and Jimmy.

Watson's business success was due to timing, his own personality, and the personal and professional psychology he had to offer. Always a compulsive worker with a strong drive for success and a quick eye for making the best of an opportunity with little introspection and few ethical inhibitions, Watson's perspective on reality remained ethically relativistic, reductionist, one-dimensional, and simplistic. His brand of behaviorism, with its emphasis on the prediction and control of human behavior, flowed freely from these views of life and led to his success on Madison Avenue. Morally insensitive and intellectually vacuous, he readily functioned in a flexible manner, according to the circumstances and demands of the marketplace. Little was lost as Watson moved from the laboratory to the business world: "I began to learn that it can be just as thrilling to watch the growth of a sales curve of a new product as to watch the learning curve of animals or men."[66] Whether it was rats running the laboratory mazes or humans forced to run the mazes of twentieth-century life, his principles of prediction and control applied equally well. The consumer-animal now became Watson's experimental object of study: "No matter what it is, like the good naturalist you are, you must never lose sight of your experimental animal—the consumer."[67]

As a behaviorist, Watson remained interested in what seemed to move people en masse. During World War I, he had helped to evaluate the effectiveness of V.D. films for the government.[68] That study had led him to suggest future behavioral studies of human sexuality and also had sharpened his opinions on how to use film as a medium to predict, control, and shape human behavior. Watson clearly brought a considerable repertoire of experience to his advertising job.

Stanley Resor enjoyed the aura of respectability that a university man such as Watson brought to a business often held in low repute. J. Walter Thompson Co. had a history of breaking new ground in the advertising field. In the closing decades of the nineteenth century, this religious advertising firm broadened its base by specializing in national magazines.[69] This was the company that brought the Rock of Gibraltar to modern consciousness, and Watson became the first full-time, professional psychologist the company employed.

During his year of apprenticeship, Watson conducted door-to-door surveys of consumers' boot needs along the Mississippi Valley; he sold Yuban coffee in Pittsburgh, Cleveland, and Erie; and he spent a summer clerking in Macy's in New York City. At Macy's, Watson noted that people, like his rats, always reached for those items within proximity. Certain items sold better when displayed at the store entrance or at the cash register. Yuban, which J. Walter Thompson was advertising, was moved to a counter next to the cash register, and sales increased. As Cohen notes, "the ethology of the supermarket was born."[70]

Watson also introduced a number of innovative devices to check consumer reaction, including free samples in exchange for filling out questionnaires. He was influential in helping to change the image of life insurance salesmen and their product from that of harbingers of death to bearers of "life." As he moved deeper into the business, each success rapidly led to another. While at times Watson worked to get the producers of products like Pebeco toothpaste to change its taste to better suit consumer tastes, more often he sought ways to train the consumer to buy the product as it was. He was one of the first people to be successful in radio advertising. On April 11, 1923, for example, American radio listeners heard the following announcement: "Our next speaker is Dr. John B. Watson, Editor of the *Journal of Experimental Psychology* and formerly Professor of Psychology at Johns Hopkins University, who will talk on 'Glands—The Mysteries of the Human Body.' This talk is given through the courtesy of Lehn and Fink, Inc., makers of Pebeco Tooth Paste."[71] For the next ten minutes he delivered a practical, straightforward lecture on the function of glands in the body, focusing in the end on mouth care. Posing as the "scientific" expert, Watson carefully arranged for the actual Pebeco toothpaste pitch to be made by another announcer, after he had completed his talk, so as not to reduce public credibility of his expert status. Along with the sales pitch came an offer of free samples and a booklet on mouth care for those who wrote letters commenting on the program. One hundred thirty-three people responded. This radio program was then co-ordinated with magazine and newspaper ads entitled, "Another set of glands now in the public eye," also sponsored by Pebeco toothpaste. The coordinated campaign also was most effective.

In his work on advertising campaigns for cigarettes, Watson conducted a series of experiments to test blindfolded smokers' tastes. He concluded that people could not identify their preferred cigarettes by taste alone—they bought certain cigarettes not because of inherent differences in the product but because of satisfying images they had learned to associate with their particular brand. This was not the "image" of introspective psychology; rather, it was a behaviorist image that was predictable and controllable.[72]

Given the proper sights and sounds, people could be made to brush with Pebeco toothpaste or "walk a mile" for a Camel. In the past, medicine men sold their wares under false pretenses, claiming that their products were something other than what they were; people, at worst, only mistakenly bought a product that was not what it was claimed to be. The modern-day image maker, however, sells products by managing the psychosocial images surrounding them, so that the consumer not only buys an image rather than a product, but more importantly, the consumer is psychologically reinforced to be satisfied with the purchased image. In a growing consumer-oriented society, the significance of image making for quick and huge profits was obvious. Twentieth-century America was rapidly moving from a basically producer-oriented culture to a consumer-oriented one. Included in that new worldview was a series of new images to readily exploit the consumers' primary reactions: fear, rage, and love. Watson, one of the first of a large army of image makers, helped to usher in that worldview.

Watson directly helped to shape the consciousness of American life by attempting to manage American consumer needs. In the older, producer-oriented world, the sight and smell of sweat were accepted "givens"; in the new white-collar, middle-class, consumer-oriented culture, the attitude toward the sight and smell of sweat changed. The cosmetic industry became more important, symbolizing the man and woman of the new age. Again, Watson was in on the ground floor. In 1921 he was the sales advisor for the Odorono Company, one of the early deodorant manufacturers. By 1925, he had organized the Ponds Cold and Vanishing Cream advertising campaign, using the testimonials of the Queens of Spain and Romania to sell the product.[73] That same year, Watson directed a campaign for Johnson and Johnson, persuading mothers to use its baby powder after every bath and every diaper change. Mothers were made to feel guilty if they failed to do so. Shortly thereafter, Watson directed a campaign for Lux soap, and by 1928 he also had directed the Maxwell House coffee campaign, which ultimately helped to institute the "coffee break" in American offices, factories, and homes.

From his work in the animal laboratory, the child development laboratory, and his own familial laboratory, Watson knew that the primitive reactions of animals and humans were fear, rage, and love. He believed that the closer he could align the image of a product with one or all of these basic reactions, the more successful would be the advertising campaign. For Watson, "love" was sensual, sexual pleasure, a basic, most powerful reactor. In 1924, when he spoke to the United Dressmakers of America, he cautioned against the fashion trend toward long skirts. Consult the consuming public, he urged, and you will reverse such a trend. In machismo fashion, speaking for the male consumer, Watson said: "We men like short skirts and wonder why we should not be allowed to gaze in admiration at something we want to see."[74] He knew what the virile American male wanted, and that was sexual pleasure. The image he created around any given product thus exploited the sexual desires of both men and women whenever possible.

The other "primitive reactions" of fear and rage were also exploited. When his ad for the Scott Paper Company appeared, featuring a surgical team at work, with the caption, "And the trouble began with harsh toilet tissue,"[75] it was not difficult to tell which "primitive reaction" he was exploiting. Watson believed that people in crowded public trains and street cars suffered the same kind of rage his rats did in a crowded maze. His ads for the Pennsylvania Railroad thus featured roomy, uncongested passenger cars and spacious dining cars.

Over and over again, Watson worked on woman's self-image, playing heavily on her roles as mother, wife, and sweetheart. With equal deliberation, he worked on man's self-image as the machismo, rugged individual, always a successful producer, provider, and lover. Throughout, the themes of both being loved and getting more love were apparent. Watson's advertising did not just exploit the primitive reactions in isolation; rather, it also used these reactions, wherever possible, in combination. As Watson said: "Can't the position be taken that every piece of good copy must be some kind of combination of these factors?"[76] However he conceptualized his activities, he was highly successful. Sales rose noticeably. While in the professional field of psychology, Watson had reached only limited numbers of people; now, in the field of advertising, he was reaching millions: "The university psychologist deals with a few individuals, the *advertiser* with millions. The scientific approach is equally applicable in both fields."[77]

Throughout his sixteen years of university work, Watson had nurtured the image of "science" and of being "scientific." During his twenty-six years in the business world, he polished that image. It was terribly important to him that he be considered an expert, a scientific behaviorist whose specialty was child development and human behavior. As he moved onto the lecture circuit and gave institute-type advice, he became much in demand at sales conferences and executive business conventions. Watson's message was for the successful salesman: he must always know his own strengths and capitalize on them; he must know his consumer; and most of all, he should be well liked. The message was one that might have been picked up in a Dale Carnegie course on how to be "successful." The more Watson spoke, the more he reminded the astute observer of Willie Loman, in Arthur Miller's *Death of a Salesman*.[78]

Watson's popularity was not limited to sales conferences and quick business courses on how to succeed. He was asked to write articles for such magazines as *McCalls, Cosmopolitan, Ladies Home Journal*, and *Good Housekeeping*, for which he received fees ranging from $750 to as much as $1,500. Watson, the expert on human behavior and child development, was free to express his thoughts on a variety of topics ranging from women's suffrage, family problems, the future of marriage, and child rearing. In all of these articles, he reflected his macho, sexist values as he attempted to shape the male-female image along his preferred lines.[79]

It should come as no surprise that Watson reacted strongly against the suffragettes of his day. He argued that these women protested only because they were not sexually satisfied. He claimed to have studied them over a long period of time, "making careful observations," and then, as "any other scientist," he put two and two together and concluded that:

> When a woman is a militant suffragist the chances are, shall we say, a hundred to one that her sex life is not well adjusted? Marriage as such brings adjustment in only approximately 20 per cent of all cases, so poorly have men and women been taught about sex. Among the 20 per cent who find adjustment I find no militant women, I find no women shouting about their rights to some fanciful career that men—the brutes— have robbed them of. They work—they work like a man (than which nothing better can be said about work)—they often quietly achieve careers. Most of the terrible women one must meet, women with the blatant views and voices, women who have to be noticed, who shoulder one about, who can't take life quietly, belong to this large percentage of women who have never made a sex adjustment.[80]

Watson then asserted that most biographies confirmed his belief that women's militancy "passes as soon as the woman, by the trial-and-error process, finds sex adjustment. Then they cease to hunt for freedom, they lose themselves in their work. Surely the only freedom worth striving for is complete engrossment in activity, be that activity writing a play, washing infant's clothes or losing oneself in the sway of passion."

Here, again, Watson expressed not only his own male chauvinist values, but also his view of happiness in terms of escape and loss of self. He solved all of his anxiety problems by such a method, and his advice to the world was to do likewise. Watson proceeded in this essay to suggest that the great weakness in women was not to be found in their physical strength but mostly in their training. Women ought to be trained from infancy in habits of manipulation, he argued. While in the past, family work was a full-time occupation, in the modern world, many would find in it a "shady spot that causes them to lie down and rest." However, as some women attempted to rear families and cultivate a professional career, they were faced with almost insurmountable barriers. Thus, they ought to be trained for their life work, just as men were. Some twenty-five years earlier, when Watson "scientifically" studied his caged rats in Chicago, it was possible to sense the shadow of a human figure in his work; conversely, in his discussion of human life and the varied aspects of the human condition, it was just as easy to detect the shadow of the rat.

> The behavioristic moral—and we must have morals— is: Women do not like to work (neither do men). There is no natural "instinct" to work. Biologically speaking the hungry animal reaches up and pulls down a banana, reaches out and grasps his female (or vice versa); his hunger adjusted, he rests and sleeps. Work habits are the result of civilization and competition. If you want your children to have careers, be they boys or girls, teach them from infancy habits of manipulation, skillful technique, endurance. Work must become "first nature"—"second nature" is not enough. And along with it teach them (or have them taught if you are a Puritan) what to expect in the realm of sex.[81]

Watson's values with respect to women, men, and marriage, nurtured over his lifetime, were perhaps nowhere better expressed than in a 1929 essay in *Cosmopolitan*, entitled "Men Won't Marry Fifty Years from Now." In it Watson lamented the fact that women have difficulty maintaining their sex appeal in and out of marriage. Most women, he insisted, are "over the hill" at thirty and know full well their "hunting is over at forty." This is especially true for women who mistakenly take their doctor's advice and have children while in their twenties. One child is bad enough, but two or three will only put a marriage in jeopardy. Watson also argued that ten years of married life and three children would turn any once-attractive young girl of thirty into a "dumb drab," a sexually unattractive bore: "Any woman who has a child before thirty takes a considerable chance with her married happiness. My advice to a woman who wants to stay married is not to have a child before thirty, even if her husband takes a sledge hammer to her."[82] Stay physically fit, he warned, at least until thirty; thereafter, a woman might as well have children because her sexually attractive days are over. By contrast, he surmised that men were just coming into their prime between thirty and forty-five years of age. In general, men take better care of themselves and stay trim, while their mates become "fat, waddling and fatuous." Women "let down in dress, in care of the body, in psychological care"; and worst of all, approximately 80 percent of these women fail to be sexually satisfied in their marriages, becoming "huntresses" for other women's husbands. Watson perhaps was feeling the pressure of these "huntresses": "So the married man today who possibly is trying a little harder to stay married with an eye blind to the charm of women other than his wife is doubly hunted—hunted by the 20,000,000-odd married women who are not successfully married, hunted by a large percentage of the 1,250,000 flappers who reach the age of eighteen every year."[83]

Given all these problems, Watson concluded that marriage was clearly an institution that was passing out of existence: "We are all too sophisticated to go on believing that there is anything mystical in a man and woman living together—and we do not want helpmates any longer, we want playmates. But as soon as we turn a playmate into a helpmate, we lose a playmate."[84] Since marriage as an institution failed to solve the dilemma of how to keep a playmate readily handy, it seemed clear to him that marriage as an institution was about to go under. After all, Watson asked, who decreed that one should have only one mate? In this "age of science," "the behaviorists who believe in the objective reexamination of millions of age-old social customs and habits are also asking why [marriage is so important]."[85] While most of the sexual problems of the world were curable with practical training in sexual performance (Watson surely would have been delighted with the current popularity of sex manuals), marriage as an institution presented an unresolvable problem. Watson could not imagine what might take its place; he only knew that the present-day family was doomed. And about that Watson had no regrets.

Just how "scientific" were Watson's behavioristic critiques of sex, marriage, family, women's and men's social roles, and appropriate child-rearing practices? Repeatedly, we confront his sweeping recommendations for social reform, which were not drawn from scientific empirical study or even, for that matter, from reflective study; rather, they came from Watson's personal life experiences, including his own psychological difficulties. The problems he encountered while growing up in Greenville were evident in his *Cosmopolitan* article, when he insisted that children should be brought up by someone other than their parents: children would be "happier and better brought up anyway if kept away from parents and brought up by trained persons." Watson's own unhappy childhood and his difficulties in breaking away from the influence of his own mother were reflected in his analysis: "One of the things that every psychiatrist meets is the fact that the son gets conditioned on the mother. The mother is not happy with her husband and turns to her son after the first few years have passed. A strong attachment grows up. This continues throughout youth and adolescence, and it is often difficult for the son to break this attachment and find happiness with another woman."[86] Watson's fear of mother love was extreme, if not bizarre. Before the National Conference on Character Education, he repeatedly warned against the killing effect of mother love. In the name of the "bringing up of youngsters and the making them as independent of people," Watson proposed that "I should never let a mother handle her child longer than three weeks, and I should never let a nurse stay longer than three weeks."[87]

Even though he was no longer affiliated with a university or clinic, Watson maintained his image as a professional psychologist. By 1924 he had published *Behaviorism*, and in 1928 he published *Psychological Care of Infant and Child*. In *Behaviorism*, Watson dropped the heavy use of physiological information, which tended to dominate his earlier work. Much of that information often appeared as unnecessary window dressing, since he had not related it very convincingly to behaviorist doctrine. That doctrine now stood free, clear, and crisp. Watson denied any "evidence of the inheritance of traits." In its place he found "unlearned beginnings of emotional reactions," which he described as "fear, rage and love," each of which he reduced to a simple animal behavior. He was so convinced that all learning could be described by some form of conditioned response that he adopted a completely environmentalist position: "Give me a dozen healthy infants, well-formed, and my own specified world to bring them up in and I'll guarantee to take any one at random and train him to become any type of specialist I might select—doctor, lawyer, artist, merchant-chief and, yes, even beggarman and thief, regardless of his talents, penchants, tendencies, abilities, vocations, and race of his ancestors."[88]

To Watson, human life could be reduced to pliable bits of protoplasm, which he, as a potter, could shape into whatever his heart desired. In a dialogue with American educator Will Durant, Watson said: "Now in dealing with this bit of human material—finding that I can train it to develop in any direction, finding, too, that I can reduce it from a state of maturity to idiocy and then gradually repair the damage—do I need to appeal to any extraneous force? No; I want no God; I want no mind; I want no spiritual force. I want only the ability to handle my clay as the potter handles his clay."[89]

Although Watson often seemed to slip rather easily into an environmentalist-determinist position, where he was the potter, at other times he advocated a self-determinist position. While it is clear how the potter could shape the pot, and even how the pot might in some ways influence the potter, just how the pot might shape itself would remain a mystery. There was always an unresolved contradiction between the freedom implicit in the rugged individualism he preached and the determinism of his behavioral science. Watson did have a messianic vision, however, and in it lay his solution to the problem of freedom and determinism. Behaviorism, he argued, "ought to make men and women eager to rearrange their own lives, and especially eager to prepare themselves to bring up their own children in a healthy way. I wish I could picture for you what a rich and wonderful individual we could make of every healthy child if only we could let it shape itself properly and then provide for it a universe in which it could exercise that organization."[90] He seemed forever oblivious to the contradiction inherent in the phrase, to "make of every healthy child if only we could let it shape itself properly."

The meaning of the word "freedom" took on new and different

connotations in Watson's messianic vision of a brave new world. He suggested that "the universe will change if you bring up your children, not in the freedom of the libertine, but in behavioristic freedom—a freedom which we cannot even picture in words, so little do we know of it."[91] What, then, does behavioristic freedom look like? As freedom becomes control, the notion of freedom to be wrong disappears; all that remains is freedom to be right. Watson's one-dimensional view of personality and of science led him straight to a one-dimensional view of social reality. His brand of behavioral psychology led him to espouse a totalitarian social order in which no one ran afoul of group standards and everyone had only the freedom to be "right."

> I am not arguing here for free anything—least of all free speech. I have always been very much amused by the advocates of free speech. In this harum-scarum world of ours, brought up as we are, the only person who ought to be allowed free speech is the parrot, because the parrot's words are not tied up with his bodily acts and do not stand as substitutes for his bodily acts. All true speech does stand substitutive for bodily acts, hence organized society has just as little right to allow free speech as it has to allow free action, which nobody advocates. When the agitator raises the roof because he hasn't free speech, he does it because he knows that he will be restrained if he attempts free action. He wants by his free speech to get some one else to do free acting—to do something he himself is afraid to do. The behaviorist, on the other hand, would like to develop his world of people from birth on, so that their speech and their bodily behavior could equally well be exhibited freely everywhere without running afoul of group standards.[92]

Aldous Huxley's *Brave New World* (1934) related some of the possibilities of this kind of behaviorist vision of the "good" society.

Watson might not have had "a dozen healthy infants" to bring up in his behaviorist faith, but he did have two healthy sons born to his wife, Rosalie. Together, they raised these youngsters according to what they believed was good behaviorist doctrine. *Psychological Care of Infant and Child*, which Rosalie helped Watson write, was as much a report of their experimentation on their own children as it was a report of the work they had done in the child laboratory at Johns Hopkins. They now had their own "little Alberts" on which to experiment. The book, written in layman's terms, turned out to be an instant success, selling over 100,000 copies in a few months.[93] Watson was rapidly becoming the Dr. Spock of his generation. Mothers were advised to start a child's toilet training at three to five weeks of age, and when it came time to touch their children, "Never hug and kiss them, never let them sit in your lap. If you must, kiss them once on the forehead when they say good night. Shake hands with them in the morning." Again he warned of the dangers of mother love: "In conclusion won't you then remember when you are tempted to pet your child that mother love is a dangerous instrument? An instrument which may inflict a never healing wound, a wound which may make infancy unhappy, adolescence a nightmare, an instrument which may wreck your adult son or daughter's vocational future and their chances for marital happiness."[94]

John and Rosalie Watson shaped their two sons as behaviorists would, always with an eye for making them rugged individuals who would not be dependent on parents or others for affection. The children were not coddled—mother and father maintained an emotional distance from their sons. John and Rosalie would shake hands with them rather than hug or kiss them. Watson's psychology, based on his reductionist conception of human nature, was adequately complemented by his sexist views of women, his macho view of life, and his view of himself as the "self made rugged, frontier type individualist."[95]

In the fall of 1930, the Watsons met their ideal type of man while traveling in Paris—one Ernest Hemingway. As Watson's biographer notes: "Hemingway was his kind of man, rough, rugged, boozing, cursing, a 'macho' man's 'macho' man."[96] Both men embraced the same kind of anachronistic, highly romanticized, frontier-type, rugged individualism; they both experienced periods of depression, stalked by the tempting shadow of suicide. Watson, however, would not succumb to an easy way out. By 1933, in spite of all the outer trappings of success, Watson slipped again into a state of depression. He overcame it by employing his usual technique: working on that which was bothering him. He made a study of the subject of suicide, and then wrote an article on the subject for *Cosmopolitan* magazine.

Watson did research for the article by asking his friends to write a fifty-word personal statement on "Why I don't commit suicide." The responses were disappointing, most reflecting a negative reason for continuing life; few reflected any positive reason for living at all, which confirmed Watson's beliefs about the condition of existing social institutions. He collated the resulting data, embellished them with his own analysis of the problematic world in which he lived, and ended his analysis by recommending his own tested behavioral techniques for overcoming depression. The editor of *Cosmopolitan* found the manuscript too depressing and refused to publish it. Shortly thereafter, that same editor committed suicide. The essay was Watson's last attempt at formal publication, and it remains unpublished.

In his essay on suicide, Watson noted the steady increase in the number of suicides, some of which were caused by the Great Depression, but most of which he felt were caused by a failure to restructure society. Behaviorism, he claimed, was on the side of youth.

> It has been the friend of youth—demanding that he be freed from the traditional bondage of the home—from undue attachments to parents—and that he be taught to face himself, his own weaknesses—freed from self adulation, self pity, and dependencies of social heritage. We have tried to teach him to find himself in battling with and in overcoming his environment. But I am afraid we have overlooked one thing. We haven't changed the world to receive these new individuals.[97]

We are, Watson believed, overburdened with the social heritage of millions of years. Our colleges continue to fail our young people, offering them less than a "practical and useful" curriculum, so that they become unemployed wanderers. Watson was discouraged by the younger generation, which had not been trained properly. In a highly critical manner, he said: "His [youth's] lack of responsibility, craftsmanship, his lack of ability to clean up his tools after the job is done and his lack of perseverance seem to me to become more apparent every day. He just will not work as hard as his father and grandfather worked."[98] These were all "thrilling" virtues Watson's father had taught him, but, he lamented, they no longer thrilled the younger generation. Two pages later he noted that although the family had declined in status, and the inner family ties such as mother love and father love had been weakened, all of which he believed were good trends, "nothing has come to replace them." The same was true in terms of the decline of church influence, an institution which in the past had maintained the community standards and values. The church in its prime was maintained by the methods now employed by behavioral psychologists. Said Watson, "Those values were based both upon hope of reward and fear of punishment, the most potent two factors for the control of behavior psychologists know."[99] The religious roots of Watson's behaviorism once again were made clear.

Watson went on to point to the declining marriage rate, rising divorce rate, and the unhappiness of parents and children as evidence that people were locked into anachronistic institutions. Under such circumstances the glamour and charm of life was lost, and it would be impossible, he surmised, to muster an army even in defense of the country. Modern youth not only had lost the thrill and glamour normally associated with doing things, but they now needed to have things "done for them." His old rugged individualist virtues were clearly in jeopardy. He argued that educational institutions should be changed, "to shape the youth for life—vocationally, artistically, practically." Business life, too, must be changed. The image of the old robber barons, who, though they made life unsafe for the weak, were in fact the real builders of society, must be reinstituted. Young people needed such heroic images; they needed to see these fellows at work: "It is the working with and alongside the big fellow in business that gives the kick to the youngster." Romance, glamour, and thrill must be put back into social institutions by creating the proper image with which youth might identify. The task was "herculean." It might require training up to at least two generations of young people. In the end, he argued, youth must be sold on "the romance that lies in every kind of honest work."[100]

In the meantime, what could be done with all the depressed people lingering on the brink of suicide? Watson was convinced that psychiatrists and psychologists could have prevented most of the 23,000 known suicides in 1932 if they had advocated his simple rule of thumb: "never make a serious decision—whether to change jobs, change husband or wife, or to commit suicide, when a depression state is on." Always wait until your courage returns, he advised, and until then, "run away for a week, a month or a year. There is no psychological medicine so potent in all the wide world as a *new environment*."[101] Watson knew this from experience.

Before Watson's brave new world would have a chance to take hold, it was necessary to develop survival techniques to maintain the necessary images for living. He was convinced that the children of the world—other people's children—had not been reared behavioristically and social institutions thus lagged behind as well.

We haven't changed the world to receive these new individuals. This was one of the important things I overlooked in trying to raise my own youngsters solely along behavioristic lines. I could raise them beautifully as long as I had them home— could shut out the outside world. But the world they had to enter at 3 or 4 years of age was not a behavioristic world. They had to mingle with a world which has a social heritage many millions of years old. To help counter-balance their behavioristic home training I sent them to the most conventional schools I could find.[102]

At Watson's insistence, both of his boys attended college, and Billy eventually became a Freudian psychiatrist. Jimmy recalled frequent father-son arguments over the proper psychiatry and, we might add, philosophy of life.[103] When Rosalie died in 1936, the boys, still in their adolescence, lost a lively friend who frequently shook hands with them before bedtime. Watson only managed to keep the boys on their career tracks by sending them to traditional schools. As adults, however, they found life difficult. Their problems may have stemmed from the failure of society to change and make way for the new, as Watson suggested earlier. Or perhaps they originated somewhere in the studied attempts of both parents to keep an emotional distance from their children; or the unusual toilet training both boys were subjected to; or the experimental games Rosalie and John liked to play on them; or a combination of these factors. Whatever the case, shortly after Watson died in the fall of 1958, Jimmy went into psychoanalysis and Billy committed suicide a few years later.[104]

In a happier moment during the fall of 1957, John Watson was asked if he would travel to New York City to receive the American Psychological Association Distinguished Service Award at their annual convention. The citation read: "To Dr. John B. Watson, whose work has been one of the vital determinants of the form and substance of modern psychology. He initiated a revolution in psychological thought, and his writings have been the point of departure for continuing lines of fruitful research."[105] Watson was excited by the thought of such an award. After thirty-seven years of relative estrangement from the profession, he felt that now he was going to be duly recognized. His secretary, Ruth Lieb, and sons accompanied him to New York, but when the time came to leave the hotel, Watson could not bring himself to go. He sent Billy instead to receive the award on his behalf.

Cohen suggests that this was Watson's last act of defiance, "a certain decent contempt" for the profession that had excluded him for so long. Those closer to him, like Ruth Lieb, recalled: "he said it was because he no longer had hand-made shoes or hand-made shirts"; Jimmy thought that his father was simply embarrassed by being overweight.[106] Although these latter reasons may seem superficial, they were important to Watson's self-image, and to the very end he was an image maker.

Appearances always counted more than substance in Watson's behavioristically oriented views. The psychology he had developed, the social philosophy he propounded, were based on the personality he had cultivated and the social reality he had conceived. Watson's personality helped him to see reality in terms of surface images, which in turn constituted for him the very fabric of reality. Whether it was his rats at Chicago, the children at Johns Hopkins, or the adult consumers on Madison Avenue, all were to be moved by images, shaped and molded by reward and punishment, toward his messianic vision of a new world. Early on, he recognized that the controlling image of the twentieth century was not the Baptist minister but the scientific psychologist who redefined human nature and pointed the way toward the "good" society.

Watson's sense of reality was one-dimensional, which made him appear empty and shallow and led his major professor to refer to him as "philosophically illiterate." That same kind of inner blindness earlier led Adolf Meyer to perceptively find in him a "dogma of exclusive salvation." Whether or not this was a consequence of Watson's Greenville experiences remains an open question. The evidence indicates that it was well developed throughout his adult life. In many ways, his one-dimensional Willie Loman sense of reality made possible the psychology and philosophy he propounded. While some attempted to separate behaviorism as a method from its social and ideological content, Watson could not. The method itself emerged out of his sense of reality and his conception of human nature.

John Dewey, it seems, was correct when he argued that means and ends are inevitably related. The behaviorist method itself requires the reduction of our conception of human nature to that of the animal world. The social experiment becomes a social experience in which the method shapes the end in view. When the method, derived from working on the lowest form of life, is dogmatically and exclusively applied to all human life, it reduces human life to nothing more than animal existence. Humans without "minds" are simply "mindless" creatures. This conception of human beings as empty animal organisms was no doubt part of the broader twentieth-century decline in respect for the dignity of human life and, as such, had powerful ramifications for the future.[107]

While we might be critical of Watson's reduction of human life to that of animal existence, and berate the kind of Willie Loman perspective he reflected, we could still make the case that his thought and values were close to the operational values of the average American of his day. Some might even view his overall life as a rags-to-riches American success story, the fulfillment of the American dream. Others might view it simply as an American tragedy. However the assessment is made, the fact remains that Watson had a powerful influence on the shaping of modern American life. The American Psychological Association was correct when they said that Watson's work was "one of the vital determinants of the form and substance of modern psychology." He had, indeed, "initiated a revolution in psychological thought," and his writings certainly proved to be "the point of departure for continuing lines of fruitful research." By the time Watson received this award, behaviorism had become the mainstream of American academic psychology. We can only speculate whether it was Watson's influence, his charisma, his message, or his image that most influenced the course of this mainstream development. Perhaps he was just riding the crest of a wave. I suspect that it was a bit of each. Nevertheless, in the end it was clear that Watson reflected many of the psychological and philosophical values of those who occupied the mainstream of American psychology.

By the time Watson began his second career, in advertising, it was clear that he had the personal values necessary for success and, once again, that he was riding the wave of modern American consumer consciousness. Whether reaching for a bar of candy or a pack of cigarettes, Watson's consumer was the experimental animal reaching for its reward. The revolution that Watson helped to initiate, both in psychology and in advertising, was based on the discovery that what constituted reward depended on one's associative image with respect to any given item. In controlling human behavior, those images were, in most cases, more important than the substantive content. As the peaks were recorded on Watson's sales charts, it was evident that image making was not only working, but that a growing population of Americans held values and a view of life similar to his own. This revolution in psychology and advertising carried over directly into American political life.

Media specialists had been involved in political campaigns in the past, but it was not until 1952 that an advertising agency was hired to play a major role in the election of a president. With the election of Dwight Eisenhower to the presidency, thanks in part to the firm of Batten, Barton, Durstine, and Osborn, the selling of the president took on its modern image-making character.[108] Even though Adlai Stevenson bitterly complained of being sold like soap, image making quickly became a part of American political life. By 1980, when image became more important than substance in politics, and training for the presidency shifted from the legal to the acting profession, it was clear that American politics had changed radically. As the average American stepped into the polling booth—or the "puzzle box"—and reached for a lever, they could not help but feel that someone was watching. Indeed, there was—a large cadre of behavioral psychologists monitoring the voters' moves and attempting to predict and control their behavior. While to some the issue of freedom appeared important, for many it was already dead.

By mid-century another behaviorist who also conceived of human nature in terms of it being an "empty organism"[109] and who also held a messianic social vision,[110] walking in the "scientific" tracks of Watson, concluded that a true science of human behavior did not need to assume that human beings were free. Thus did B. F. Skinner resolve the problem of freedom and determinism, by simply eliminating the concept of freedom. While Watson had some difficulty defining freedom, Skinner had no such problem. "The hypothesis that man is not free is essential to the application of scientific method to the study of human behavior. The free inner man who is held responsible for the behavior of the external biological organism is only a prescientific substitute for the kinds of causes which are discovered in the course of a scientific analysis."[111] Skinner went on to suggest that while the conception of the individual, "which emerges from a scientific analysis is distasteful to most of those who have been strongly affected by democratic philosophies,"[112] much of our difficulty arises because "we have not wholly abandoned the traditional philosophy of human nature; at the same time we are far from adapting a scientific point of view without reservation.

We have accepted the assumption of determinism in part; yet
we allow our sympathies, our first allegiances, and our personal
aspirations to rise to the defense of the traditional view."[113] Like
Watson before him, who once hypothesized a future scientific
moral ethic, Skinner, too, thought that the way out of the twentieth-century moral dilemma was science.

Skinner believed that science might eventually develop the
moral standard upon which humankind could agree: "If a science
of behavior can discover those conditions of life which make for
the ultimate strength of men, it may provide a set of 'moral
values' which, because they are independent of the history and
culture of any one group, may be generally accepted."[114] The
difficulty, however, was that the behavioral science to which
Watson and Skinner subscribed, the method employed, as well
as the conception of human nature upon which it was based,
were not "independent of the history and culture of any one
group." In both Watson's and Skinner's behaviorist methodology,
one lost the freedom and dignity of human life. In criticism of
their behaviorism, Joseph Wood Krutch said:

> There remains, nevertheless, the cheerful possibility that we
> actually know less about the Science of Man than we do of
> the less difficult sciences of matter and that we may, just
> in time, learn more. Perhaps Hamlet was nearer right than
> Pavlov. Perhaps the exclamation "How like a god!" is actually
> more appropriate than "How like a dog! How like a rat! How
> like a machine!" Perhaps we have been deluded by the fact
> that the methods employed for the study of man have been
> for the most part those originally devised for the study of
> machines or the study of rats, and are capable, therefore, of
> detecting and measuring only those characteristics which
> the three do have in common.[115]

Some years later, in response to Krutch, Skinner said: "Krutch
has argued that whereas the traditional view supports Hamlet's
exclamation, 'How like a God!,' Pavlov, the behavioral scientist,
emphasized 'How like a dog!' But that was a step forward. A god
is the archetypal pattern of an explanatory fiction, of a miracle-
working mind, of the metaphysical. Man is much more than a
dog, but like a dog he is within range of scientific analysis."[116]
Bringing man into the range of scientific analysis—Watson would
have exclaimed "How like a rat!"

Reflecting on the state of American psychology in 1961, Gordon
Allport reminded his colleagues that in an earlier day, when

psychology and philosophy were still a single discipline, William James, in his own work, seemed to have wisely warned "psychologists that by their own theories of human nature they have the power of elevating or degrading this same nature. Debasing assumptions debase the mind; generous assumptions exalt the mind."[117] Regrettably, so few have heeded this warning.

Notes

1. Letter from Meyer to Watson, May 29, 1916, p. 2, Adolph Meyer Papers, Alan Mason Chesney Medical Archives of the Johns Hopkins Medical Institutions. For all the letters from the Adolf Meyer papers used in this chapter, I am indebted to the research of Christine Shea.

2. Although Meyer did not go into this issue extensively, it was a problem throughout Watson's earlier work. It appeared in his Ph.D. thesis at Chicago, as well as in his book *Psychology from the Standpoint of a Behaviorist*. Meyer's warning was wisely put: psychobiology ought to use the "data as they present themselves" (Meyer to Watson, May 29, 1916, p. 4) in order to make its case, rather than to enter with a new and different jargon of biology and thereby allow the introduction of one's "own uncontrollable pet notions under the haze of a new terminology." It was precisely between the physiological description of the organism and the description of behavior that the personal ideology of Watson often emerged. Although they are more sophisticated, the same problems still essentially occur in the works of the present-day social biologists.

3. Letter from Meyer to Watson, May 29, 1916, p. 4.

4. Letter from Watson to Meyer, June 1, 1916, pp. 1, 2.

5. Ibid., p. 2.

6. Letter from Meyer to Watson, June 2, 1916, p. 1.

7. Letter from Meyer to Watson, June 3, 1916, p. 3.

8. Ibid., p. 4.

9. See letter from Watson to Meyer, Aug. 13, 1920. In this letter Watson detailed, from his perspective, the unhappy problems and events involving his marriage with Mary Ickes and sought Meyer's advice on how to handle the problem with the university.

10. Quoted in David Cohen, *J. B. Watson: The Founder of Behaviorism* (London: Routledge and Kegan Paul, 1979), p. 156.

11. This is surmised from the fact that Watson kept a fairly cordial professional correspondence with Meyer throughout the 1920s; and at times, Watson also arranged to have Meyer lecture to selected groups in New York City. See, for example, letters from Watson to Meyer dated Jan. 19, 1922, Oct. 2, 1926, Dec. 13, 1926.

12. See Cohen, *J. B. Watson*.

13. See ibid., p. 6.

14. Ibid.

15. Paul G. Creelan, "Watsonian Behaviorism and the Calvinist Conscience," *Journal of the History of the Behavioral Sciences* 10(Jan. 1974): 100.

16. John B. Watson, "The Place of Kinaesthetic, Visceral and Laryngeal Organization in Thinking," *Psychological Review* 31(Sept. 1924): 345.

17. The use of public confession is a powerful psychic tool which can effectively break down the independence of the individual self and expose that self to ready manipulation. Whether it was the medieval church, which required public confession on its steps, and later in the quasi privacy of the confessional before a priest; or the Young Pioneers, which requires it of all its members in the Russian schools; or the Chinese, who used it in group meetings and on American prisoners of war in Korea; or Jim Jones, who made ample use of the practice in the jungles of Guyana; or the Moonies, who use it effectively on American campuses; or the fundamentalist Baptists, like Bob Jones and others, who have incorporated it as part of their religious practice—all are using the same psychological technique as employed in most group psychotherapy sessions.

18. Carl Murchison, ed., *A History of Psychology in Autobiography*, 3 vols. (Worcester, Mass.: Clark University Press, 1936), 3:271. It is interesting to note that later in life, during his second marriage, John achieved a degree of rapport with his children through teaching them manual skills and the care and feeding of animals. As a professional psychologist he often recommended that fathers ought to teach such things to their children.

19. Cohen, *J. B. Watson*, pp. 9–10.

20. Murchison, *History of Psychology in Autobiography*, 3:271.

21. Cohen, *J. B. Watson*, p. 11.

22. Ibid., p. 15.

23. Murchison, *History of Psychology in Autobiography*, 3:272.

24. Ibid.

25. Ibid., pp. 272–73.

26. Cohen, *J. B. Watson*, p. 19.

27. Murchison, *History of Psychology in Autobiography*, 3:273.

28. Ibid., p. 274.

29. Ibid., p. 276.

30. See Cohen, *J. B. Watson*, pp. 33–34.

31. Murchison, *History of Psychology in Autobiography*, 3:274.

32. Ibid.

33. It is interesting to note that Freud overcame his "Rome" phobia by going to Rome, while Watson never did overcome his fear of the dark. To be fair to Watson, however, we might argue that Freud would readily admit he never completely got over his neurosis. He was still sublimating it when he wrote his last book, *Moses and Monotheism*.

34. John B. Watson, "Why I Don't Commit Suicide," p. 16 (unpublished ms., ca. 1933), National Archives, J. B. Watson Collection.

35. At times, Watson went to this extreme, especially when he argued that we think with our vocal cords. There were other times, however, when he wrote as if the overall state of the organism influenced the meaning of the stimulus. In this case, he appeared to be taking some of Dewey's criticism into account. Nevertheless, the overall thrust of his work went the other way, to the extreme.

36. Murchison, *History of Psychology in Autobiography*, 3:275. The last line here seems strange. We might normally have expected it to read, "If I failed him on logic, it was not his fault." Did he mean that Angell failed Watson in a course on logic, or that Angell failed to catch Watson's flaws in logic because he (Watson) was really cutting a new path, toward a new psychology? It is difficult to tell.

37. John B. Watson, *Animal Education* (Chicago: University of Chicago Press, 1903), p. 7.

38. Ibid.

39. Ibid., p. 122.

40. Ibid., p. 86.

41. For example: On p. 28 of his thesis, *Animal Education*, he refers to "these little fellows"; on p. 18, they seemed "much puzzled"; on pp. 28–29 he says, "But in the living cage this activity takes the form of play. Their conduct at this age reminds one very much of young children"; on p. 31, he sees his rats working "with all their might"; on p. 32, we find his rats working out problems which require an "advanced stage of intelligence"; on p. 39, one rat takes a long time to "make up his mind"; on p. 48, "it suited their fancy"; and on p. 57, the rat's "choice was then recorded." Watson's biographer, David Cohen, was clearly in error when he suggested that "Watson was careful not to ascribe to the rats anthropomorphic feelings" (Cohen, *J. B. Watson*, p. 32). Cohen also quotes Watson's incorrect title of his thesis "Animal Behavior" (ibid., p. 33).

42. Cohen, *J. B. Watson*, p. 34.

43. Although Ivan Pavlov was awarded the Nobel Prize in 1904, it is not known just when Watson became aware of his conditioning experiments. Whenever it occurred, however, it must have been a bracing experience for Watson and a significant reinforcement for later work on child conditioning experiments.

44. Letter from Watson to Meyer, Aug. 13, 1920, pp. 1, 2.

45. Quoted in part in Cohen, *J. B. Watson*, p. 55.

46. Ibid., p. 53.

47. Ibid.

48. See ibid., pp. 59–71.

49. John B. Watson, "Psychology as the Behaviorist Views It," *Psychological Review* 20(1913): 158.

50. Charles Darwin, *The Descent of Man and Selection in Relation to Sex*, 2 vols. (New York: D. Appleton and Co., 1872), 1:35.

51. Interestingly, Watson remained on cordial terms with Titchener throughout his life. See Cedric A. Larson and John J. Sullivan, "Watson's Relation to Titchener," *Journal of the History of the Behavioral Sciences* 1(Oct. 1965): 338–54.

52. Ibid., pp. 341, 348, 341–42.

53. Ibid., p. 342.

54. See John B. Watson, "The Place of the Conditioned-Reflex in Psychology," *Psychological Review* 23(Mar. 1916): 92.

55. For a psychoanalytic interpretation of this event, see Creelan, "Watsonian Behaviorism and the Calvinist Conscience," p. 95.

56. Quoted in Cohen, *J. B. Watson*, p. 142.

57. John B. Watson and Rosalie Rayner, "Conditioned Emotional Reactions," *Journal of Experimental Psychology* 3(1920): 14. For a detailed description of the Albert B. case, see ibid., pp. 1–14.

58. Mary Cover Jones, "Albert, Peter, and John B. Watson," *American Psychologist* 29(Aug. 1974): 581.

59. For a detailed description of Watson's and Jones's attempts at deconditioning fears, see Mary Cover Jones, "A Laboratory Study of Fear," *Pedagogical Seminary* 31(1924): 308–15. See also Mary Cover Jones, "The Elimination of Children's Fears," *Journal of Experimental Psychology* 7(1924): 383–90.

60. See, for example, John B. Watson and J. J. B. Morgan, "Emotional Reactions and Psychological Experimentation," *American Journal of Psychology* 28(Apr. 1917): 163–74.

61. It is striking how Watson managed to turn his professional studies toward his own personal problems of one kind or another—he was both a heavy drinker and a noted womanizer. By 1919, with Prohibition in full swing, he instituted studies on the effects of alcohol; during this same period he advocated the scientific study of human sexuality.

62. If it is the case that Mary began drinking and having affairs with other men, as Watson claimed in his letter to Meyer, then such behavior on her part may indicate an earlier reaction to his frequent affairs over the years. See letter from Watson to Meyer, Aug. 13, 1920.

63. For a detailed description of the ensuing events, see Cohen, *J. B. Watson*, pp. 145–67.

64. Ibid., p. 156.

65. Ibid., p. 185.

66. Murchison, *History of Psychology in Autobiography*, 3:280.

67. Quoted in Cohen, *J. B. Watson*, p. 187.

68. For Watson's research on V.D. films, see John B. Watson and Karl S. Lashley, "A Psychological Study of Motion Pictures in Relation to Venereal Disease Campaigns" (Washington, D.C.: U.S. Interdepartmental Social Hygiene Board, 1922).

69. See Frank Presbrey, *The History and Development of Advertising* (Garden City, N.Y.: Doubleday, Doran and Co., 1929).

70. Cohen, *J. B. Watson*, p. 176.

71. John B. Watson, "Advertising by Radio," p. 11, J. Walter Thompson Co. Archives, New York.

72. See Cohen, *J. B. Watson*, p. 179.

73. Ibid., p. 184.

74. Ibid., p. 179.

75. Ibid., p. 188.

76. Ibid., pp. 188–89.

77. Ibid., p. 270.

78. Ibid., p. 170.

79. For further discussion of the shaping of this image, see Stuart Ewen, *Captains of Consciousness: Advertising and the Social Roots of the Consumer Culture* (New York: McGraw-Hill Book Co., 1976).

80. John B. Watson, "The Weakness of Women," *Nation* 125(July 6, 1927): 10.

81. Ibid.

82. John B. Watson, "Men Won't Marry Fifty Years from Now," *Cosmopolitan* 86(June 1929): 71. It is perhaps worth noting that Watson was married twice and each wife bore him two children while still in her twenties.

83. Ibid., p. 104. Watson gave no source for the data that 80% of all married women were sexually unsatisfied.

84. Ibid., p. 106.

85. Ibid., p. 104. It is interesting that Watson was very much taken with William Graham Sumner's *Folkways*; his social-ethical relativisms appealed to Watson.

86. Ibid., pp. 104, 106.

87. "Urges Rotary Plan to train children. Dr. J. B. Watson, Psychologist, would change mothers every three weeks, to develop independence." *N.Y. Times*, Mar. 4, 1928.

88. John B. Watson, *Behaviorism* (Chicago: University of Chicago Press, 1924), pp. 103, 104.

89. "John B. Watson vs. Will Durant, 'Is Man a Machine?' " *Forum* 82(Nov. 1929): 265.

90. Watson, *Behaviorism*, p. 303.

91. Ibid., pp. 303–4.

92. Ibid., p. 303. We are reminded here of Rousseau's *Social Contract*, where individuals are forced to be free.

93. See Cohen, *J. B. Watson*, p. 217.

94. John B. Watson, *Psychological Care of Infant and Child* (New York: W. W. Norton and Co., 1928), pp. 128, 81–82, 87.

95. For a broader analysis of that image, see Irvin G. Wyllie, *The Self-Made Man in America: The Myth of Rags to Riches* (New Brunswick, N.J.: Rutgers University Press, 1954).

96. Cohen, *J. B. Watson*, p. 258.
97. Watson, "Why I Don't Commit Suicide," pp. 2–3.
98. Ibid., p. 4.
99. Ibid., p. 6. To Watson, the "religious tradition" of John Albert Broadus, his namesake, was thus linked by the method of reward and punishment to the "scientific" behavioral psychology he propounded.
100. Ibid., pp. 13, 14.
101. Ibid., pp. 15, 16.
102. Ibid., p. 3.
103. Cohen, *J. B. Watson*, p. 279.
104. See ibid., p. 281. As noted earlier, both John and Rosalie were peculiarly insensitive to the experimental consequences of their work on Albert B. It seems reasonable to assume that if they maintained that same insensitivity with the experimental work on their own children, problems would ensue. Ironically, John and Rosalie made light of Albert's condition and jokingly suggested what a Freudian psychologist might find in him under an analysis as an adult. We can only speculate what the Freudian analyst helped Jimmy find.
105. Watson, *Behaviorism*, p. iii.
106. Cohen, *J. B. Watson*, p. 280.
107. See Richard L. Rubenstein, *The Cunning of History: Mass Death and the American Future* (New York: Harper and Row, 1975).
108. See Dan Nimmo, *The Political Persuaders* (Englewood Cliffs, N.J.: Prentice-Hall, 1970), pp. 112–13. See also Joe McGinniss, *The Selling of the President 1968* (New York: Simon and Schuster, 1969), pp. 20–21.
109. Edwin G. Boring, *A History of Experimental Psychology* (New York: Appleton-Century-Crofts, 1950), pp. 650–51.
110. See B. F. Skinner, *Walden Two* (New York: Macmillan Co., 1962).
111. B. F. Skinner, *Science and Human Behavior* (New York: Macmillan Co., 1953), p. 447.
112. Ibid., p. 449.
113. Ibid., p. 9.
114. Ibid., p. 445.
115. Joseph Wood Krutch, *The Measure of Man* (Indianapolis: Bobbs-Merrill Co., 1954), pp. 32–33.
116. B. F. Skinner, *Beyond Freedom and Dignity* (New York: Random House, 1971), p. 192.
117. Gordon Allport, ed., *William James' Psychology: The Briefer Course* (New York: Harper and Brothers Co., 1961), p. xxiii.

5

G. STANLEY HALL [1844–1924]

Priestly Prophet of a New Dispensation

Shortly before his death in 1924, G. Stanley Hall, a leading figure in American psychology wrote:

> In the views I have attained of man, his place in nature, his origin and destiny, I believe I have become a riper product of the present stage of civilization than most of my contemporaries, have outgrown more superstitions, attained clearer insights, and have a deeper sense of peace with myself. I love but perhaps still more pity mankind, groping and stumbling, often slipping backward along the upward Path, which I believe I see just as clearly as Jesus or Buddha did, the two greatest souls that ever walked this earth and whom I supremely revere.[1]

Hall had been to the mountaintop, had seen the promised land, and had, as it were, "achieved another new birth superimposed on that of adolescence," the birth of a "superman."[2] He believed that, like Jesus and Buddha before him, he had been called to preach a new gospel, a new dispensation that would lift "Mansoul"

Portions of this chapter originally appeared in the *Journal of Libertarian Studies*, 7(1), Spring 1983, and are reprinted here by permission of the Journal of Libertarian Studies, Inc.

to its next higher stage of evolutionary development. For Hall, that dispensation was the "New Psychology" he would help to structure and create. In the end, Hall saw himself as a prophet of a new faith, indeed, a new religion. He had pierced the veil of appearances, had seen the path that "Mansoul" must take if it was going to avoid "slipping backward along the upward Path."

A year after Hall wrote those words, his body lay in state. The local minister rose to eulogize Hall, with every apparent intent of praising him, but he lost control of himself and ended by severely attacking Hall, thereby creating a small scandal. It probably was appropriate, if not customarily proper, for a Christian minister to attack Hall for the beliefs he had propagated. The man had passed beyond Christianity, beyond the faith of his fathers, toward a new heretical faith which he thoroughly believed represented the wave of the future. When Hall had published his two-volume work on *Jesus, the Christ, in the Light of Psychology* (1917), a close friend advised him "that it were better that he had died than write so blasphemous a book."[3] It isn't surprising, then, that the minister lost his composure and unleashed a controversy that, in itself, very well symbolized Hall's life.

Never a stranger to controversy, Hall once stood up in a professional meeting and pointed out to Josiah Royce that his "theory of idealism was similar to, and no better than, masturbation."[4] The same Hall, as a bright young student with unconventional ideas, so startled a congregation of faculty and students with his trial sermon at Union Theological Seminary, that the faculty member whose custom it was to criticize, despairing of mere criticism, knelt and prayed for Hall's soul.[5] Well he might have, for neither the mind nor the soul of G. Stanley Hall would ever long embrace orthodoxy or be free of controversy.

Aside from his unconventional religious ideas, Hall was unquestionably a trailblazer in American psychology. He was the first person in the United States to receive a Ph.D. in psychology (under William James), the founder and first president of Clark University, the founder of the psychological laboratory at Johns Hopkins, the founder of the American Psychological Association, and the originator of a number of journals, including the *American Journal of Psychology, Pedagogical Seminary*, the *Journal of Religious Psychology*, and the *Journal of Applied Psychology*. More importantly, from the standpoint of education, he can be considered one of the founders of educational psychology and, more specifically, of the child study movement, which by the twentieth century had evolved into the field of child psychology. A good case can be made as well that Hall was one of the key founders of genetic psychology in America. His studies of the child, the adolescent, and the adult were all conducted within the structural framework of biological and cultural evolution. For good or ill, his primary research method remained historical. However, he was just as much a purveyor of unconventional psychoreligious pedagogical thought as he was a founder of organizations.

Through his eleven books, hundreds of articles, and 2,500 lectures in over forty states, as well as in the effect his teaching had on thousands of students, Hall had a powerful and lasting impact on American educational thought.[6] As founder of the child-study movement, which led to the Department of Child Study of the National Education Association, in 1893, Hall directed the attention of educators toward child growth and development. When this movement began to decline in the early 1900s, many of his students became leaders in the new field of child psychology. Among the most important of these was Arnold Gesell, who not only fully adopted his mentor's view of the recapitulation theory, but also went on to coin the term "maturation," which reflected Hall's emphasis on the integration of physiological and social growth.

Perhaps Hall's most important work came in 1904, when he helped shape America's conception of adolescence with his massive two-volume work *Adolescence, Its Psychology and Its Relations to Physiology, Anthropology, Sociology, Sex, Crime, Religion and Education.* Over 25,000 copies of the 1,337-page text were sold.[7] The most influential books on psychology, however, were still those written by William James. Merle Curti has, it seems, correctly estimated that nine-tenths of American teachers who studied psychology in the period 1890–1910 read James. If his two-volume *The Principles of Psychology* and his *Psychology: The Briefer Course* are taken as benchmarks for the field of psychology in the 1890s, it is important to recognize that the term "adolescence" does not appear as a significant category in either work. In spite of James's extensive influence on that period, it was Hall, rather than James, who fostered adolescence as a distinct discipline of psychology and in turn substantially shaped its content.

The professionalization of the category of adolescence took place at approximately the same time that child labor laws were being enacted and compulsory education laws were being enforced. The high school was coming into existence as the most rapidly growing educational institution of the first half of the twentieth century. Delayed entrance into the job market meant delayed entrance into adulthood. Adolescence meant that awkward state of being sexually mature according to nature, while remaining socially immature according to the needs of society. The professional psychologist of the twentieth century not only helped mediate the problem by propounding the "scientific" existence of adolescence, but also propagated the illusion that it was in fact caused by nature itself. More than any other individual, Hall helped to conceptualize that development. To be sure, not all of his ideas were accepted by other educators, yet in a very real sense he pointed the way. William H. Kilpatrick was probably correct when he asserted, "America believes, as does no other country, that education must be based on a study of psychology. That this is so is due in no small degree to the influence of President Hall."[8]

Hall's profound influence on the fields of psychology and education was a result of his extensive organizational activities and writings as well as, and perhaps more importantly, his teaching and lecturing. He had a charismatic personality, one that left a significant imprint on his students. One of them, Lewis M. Terman, who influenced the testing movement and the study of the gifted child, spoke of Hall as a "source of inspiration." Another, Arnold Gesell, who left his mark on early childhood study, said of Hall, "There were giants in them thair days!"[9] There were still others who felt more attuned to the Hall student who said, "I only touched the hem of his garment, and yet it was a healing touch. I would not give the months I spent at Clark for any other period of my life."[10] As hundreds, and then thousands, of his students who "touched the hem of his garment" took up posts in normal schools, universities, and child development institutes around the country, they invited Hall to give literally thousands of sermonlike lectures to growing audiences of uninitiated early childhood teachers.[11] This priestly prophet of a new dispensation preached a gospel of a new psychology, a new faith, indeed, a new religion across an economic, social, and religiously troubled cultural landscape.

In this chapter I focus primarily on some key tenets of Hall's psychoreligious ideology, considering both the personal and cultural conditions that seemed to play a part in the development of his new dispensation. I also attempt to critically analyze the social significance of these ideas in the context of twentieth-century history.

G. Stanley Hall, like his mentor William James, lived and felt the tension existing between a God-centered worldview, which appeared to be on the wane, and a man-centered scientific world-view, which appeared to be on the rise. Although both men perceived the same problem, each responded to it differently. James's peculiar personality structure, as well as his unique personal family experience, led him in his search for resolution to the tension between these two worldviews. He adopted a pragmatic, therapeutic justification for religious beliefs, perhaps out of his own admitted need to have meaning inherent in his universe. His "God," his "more," was a "helping," a healing "more," which made it possible for James to travel that dark lonely road back to mental well-being. Pragmatically, he opened wide the door of religious belief, where virtually anything could be counted as true so long as it "worked." From James's perspective, Hall seemed to seek an "ultra-phenomenal identity." Hall, on the other hand, believed that James was a mystic who was "hungry for the supernatural," whose very "splendid individuality also passionately crave[d] immortality." Hall complained that James virtually expelled "every sexual element from religion,"[12] whereas he pictured himself as laying considerable stress on the subject. He thoroughly rejected James's pragmatic epistemology as well as his personal quest for immortality.

As a naturalist evolutionist, Hall believed "that the soul is freighted with traces of everything that life has experienced from its first dawn, that the experience of the individual now is the tiniest outcrop in consciousness of his entire psychic life. Hence he does not bank much upon the philosophy of experience, but regards the mind from the natural history point of view and says that nine-tenths of all our processes are submerged."[13] In this way Hall accounted for all the strange religious rites, practices, and beliefs of humankind as links in the great evolutionary chain of being. He saw Christianity as just one "consummate religion" based on love which could not adequately be studied or fully understood without taking into account the great ethnic religions and "the very lowest savage forms" as well. Hall believed that James saw religion as primarily the individual's "inner life and struggle from the efforts of the soul to become at one with itself."

While Hall conceded that such was also the case for him, he insisted that religion was "the largest thing in the world including all aspects for truth which the scientist feels and the desire for purity."[14]

Thus, Hall passed beyond Christianity, beyond a belief in the supernatural, beyond a belief in personal immortality. In *Jesus, the Christ, in the Light of Psychology* he sought to psychoanalytically explain away the divinity of Christ. The new faith that Hall came to preach was the faith that "man is the only divinity, or at least God is only a collective term for man."[15] What immortality might be gained was only a collective immortality to be found in the concept of "Mansoul." To Hall, all scientific evidence pointed to the fact that the only life that existed after death was to be found in the next generation, which carried with it the whole history of the racial experience. With a Vico-like timelessness, Hall, as scientific genetic psychologist, as high priest of "Mansoul," could read and ultimately understand the total anthropological record of life from the lowest forms to the development of a super-race. Through a superior scientific knowledge of the past, the present might be understood and the next higher stage of evolution might yet be collectively realized. This was a glimpse of that "ultra-phenomenal identity" James thought he saw in Hall.

Hall's disagreement with James was more than a personality difference. In philosophical and religious outlooks they were poles apart. As early as 1891, when reviewing James's *The Principles of Psychology*, Hall praised him for his breadth of view and numerous insights but criticized his work for being too introspective and not based substantially enough on hard experimental data. The new psychologist, he insisted, must be a scientific researcher imbued with the "spirit of reverence, and a sense of unity and law at the root of things," which is "religious to the core, in every sense which the best philosophy of religion makes basal." "Psychology," he asserted,

> is even to be the means of rescuing religious oracles from degradation and re-revealing them as sublime ethnic verbal editions of God's primative revelation in his works. It will also show what is in man, and may some day become veritable anthropology, the science of man in fact as well as in name, a gospel of love and work, where the heart is not subordinated to the head, and the emotions are not slighted, or the great ethical lesson of hereditary good and ill, psychogenesis and

adolescence doubted and disparaged. . . . the new psychology
of the present and future is based less upon introspection
than upon observation, experiment and experience, individual
and ancestral.[16]

He thus rejected James's psychology as largely misdirected.

By the beginning of the century, James had lent support to
both psychical research and Emmanuelism. In a draft article on
"Eddyism and Emmanuelism" (1909), Hall critically and pointedly
attacked James's pragmatic solution to the religious crisis of the
times. Pragmatism, Hall argued, is "roughly speaking the doctrine
that the criterion of truth is practicality, as we said, that is true
that works well and that is truest that works best. This is a new
touch-stone or test of truth very distinct from many others that
have been proposed: viz., the easiest and simplest way of thinking
the universe coherent, with a system of reason, clearness and
certainty, and all the rest."[17] What "works well" is ultimately
that which helps one "attain pleasure and escape pain; to live
and not to die." If a belief in God, the virgin birth, St. Christopher,
or any kind of fetish worship, has a healing effect, it works and
is therefore true.

Hall was convinced that James's pragmatic test of truth,
when applied to religious experience, would lead directly to the
justification of Eddyism and Emmanuelism, as well as any other
kind of faith-healing cult. "Just as Eddyism is absolute idealism
taken literally and put to work, so Emmanuelism is pragmatism
taken literally and put to work. Just as pragmatism is the inevitable
consequence of absolute idealism, so Emmanuelism is the inevitable consequence of Eddyism. Both are the shadows of things
academic thrown athwart the popular mind."[18] Continuing in
this vein, he argued that the church might open "a department
of comparative therapeutics" where definite information might
be obtained to determine the healing power of "fetishism, atomism,
invocation of ancestors, incantation, or Christian doctrines."
Pushing his point even further, Hall said, "In a word, if Hoodooism
works better, then if we converted the Hoodooist into an Emmanuelist and his patients into church patients, so that the healing
power would be lost, would not some truth also be lost if pragmatism be sound?" He concluded that in the field of therapeutics,
"Emmanuelism is the department of applied pragmatism, the
theoretical part of which is on the other side of the Charles."[19]

The pragmatist, Hall insisted, holds a basically selfish view
of knowledge in which the investigator "goes in for truth because

of what he can get out of it." While the test of truth for James was to be found in its "cash value," the pragmatic investigator, according to Hall, invariably asks, "What is there in it for me or mine? . . . Its only possible morals is Eudaemonism. Its religion is to get post-mortem pleasure and avoid post-mortem pain. It seeks God to enjoy Him, to use Him, and profit by Him in this world and the next, to enlist Him to work serviceably." In contrast to James's therapeutic faith in something "more," Hall argued the case of the realist: that truth "is not a matter of taste or of personal edification; but that which holds for all, everywhere, at all times, and under all conditions."[20] In the end, truth may not heal but may, in fact, be nauseous if not lethal. In the broadest sense of the term, the "pure science" researcher functions beyond pleasure and pain, good or evil. Reflecting his own views, Hall said,

> No one has known what real truth is who is not convinced of something that is independent of all, even the highest anthropomorphization, something that would be the same for all conceivable persons or orders of being, the same if man had never existed or that would survive if he were to become extinct, something utterly indifferent to all his wants, prayers, or pains. Even if no such truth is yet attained, the belief that it exists, because possible, makes pragmatism only a philosophy of pedagogy, of the stages of Wärden, evolution, or recapitulation. It deals with the phenomena of the way and not with those of the goal.[21]

From the perspective of "true" philosophic thought, however, "man must believe in something absolute, non-relative, subspeciaternitis, something above volition and desire. He at least tends to believe in that which at its highest parallels and participates in being." The new scientific psychologist thus would not rest easy with pragmatic truth but would cut through the veil of appearances and continue the quest for "evolving a larger composite photograph of the entire kingdom of man's soul." Hall believed that the scientific psychologist had passed beyond the old philosophies of idealism, realism, and pragmatism, the latter of which only "fits old men and over-ripe civilizations." Turning directly to James and Dewey, Hall asserted that pragmatism

> is an asylum for those who have long and earnestly striven with the riddles of the Sphinx and found them insoluble, who have much preferred the pursuit of truth over its pos-

session and had but little experience with the latter, who have seen the fondest hopes of their prime decay, who have, to be more definite (like James), been ignored by their tribe in Germany, and who so condemn the choicest products and methods of Teutonic philosophy, or like Dewey have found that too many of the problems he most loved to cultivate were aborting, or like Schiller that the systems in which they were reared were slowly losing vitality and interest.[22]

While Hall seemed to confuse philosophy with personality, he firmly believed that his conception of the new psychologist as a scientific researcher was a conception born to a new stage of evolution, the superman stage, which was in tune with youth itself and the coming new order.

Hall's reaction to Eddyism and Emmanuelism was not just a reaction to James's pragmatic philosophy of religion. More importantly, it reflected Hall's sensitivity to what really was at stake in the contest between a scientific naturalistic interpretation of human experience and the traditional religious interpretation. For Hall, this most fundamental issue was reflected in the birth of the new Christian Science faith of Mary Baker Eddy. As evolutionary doctrines swept the cultural belief system of the West, the rising scientific secular explanation for human affairs seemed more and more plausible. Even the traditional conception of sinful behavior often seemed better explained as sickness. Under these circumstances, many in the traditional Christian faith reached back to attempt to recover the faith of the early church fathers, and with it the healing function of the early church. The teaching and preaching of Mary Baker Eddy fell on welcoming ears. The very use of the two terms which many found a contradiction—Christian and science—was a masterpiece in symbolic construction. Christian Science seemed to fit the times; it seemed appropriate for the American cultural landscape. Hall argued that the rise of Christian Science on American soil was entirely understandable—that it incorporated both the absolute idealism implicit in New England transcendentalism as well as the Yankee practicality that ideologically took the form of American pragmatism. When James spun out the pragmatic roots of his faith in terms of healing and Bronson Alcott asserted that "a thing is in fact only a think,"[23] the twin roots of Christian Science were thus firmly set in fertile American soil.

Hall felt that "if mind, idea, or God is all in all, it follows that there can be no real error or sin and so no true defect or disease." While most Christians believe evil is the absence of good, some also believe that like evil, defect or disease can have no intrinsic reality. Mrs. Eddy was the "boldest of idealists" because, as Hall noted, "She takes the idealistic theory of knowledge, on the one hand, and the healing ministry of Jesus, on the other, literally and puts them to work in the service of man. Never was there such a masterpiece of pragmatism. Not only is it true because it works well; but because it heals, it seems personally true to those who could never otherwise have understood."[24] Hall argued that Eddyism was the "crassification" of idealistic metaphysics and the healing ministry of the early church. The turning back to the early church, and its traditional function of faith healing by casting out demons and calling for divine intervention, was only a way of cutting behind the more excellent way of science and the more sophisticated, culturally complex theological interpretation of the Scriptures. "But for the masses and for the half cultured, it is a fortress of refuge. They can now be both Christian and scientist in a cheap and easy way, and glimpse and feel in their vague, dumb, essentially vulgar wise, the verities of both."[25] This movement, Hall believed, was propelled by the strongest of all motives, "to be well." Here, too, was to be found the impulse of the Yogas and the Mahatmas, as well as other "faith healers." Emmanuelism as a healer's ministry was only a weaker version of Eddy's idealism and faith healing. The Emmanuelists stopped short of Eddy's logic and fell back on the traditional Christian church practices when it was convenient.

The issue between a "man-centered" view of the universe and a "God-centered" view was implicit in the argument over whether Christian Scientists and other irregulars should be prohibited from practicing medicine. Exactly where the roles of the medical doctor and the religious doctor began, and where they left off, was not at all clear. Hall was highly critical of a practice in Boston that required Emmanuelists to receive no patients unless they were diagnosed beforehand and referred to them by the family physician. This made the psychotherapeutic healing ministry of that church dependent on the secular medical physician. Hall fully appreciated that the modern scientific approach to healing was at odds with the traditional function of the church. Clearly a supernatural versus a naturalistic diagnosis was at stake: was the afflicted individual to be accounted sinful or was he or she sick?

Standing on the brink of that wide and deep chasm separating a naturalistic worldview from a supernaturalistic one, Hall took his stand implicitly on the naturalistic side and went on to argue explicitly that it was the only "real" side. First he chided both factions for their failure to train their experts properly. Neither the minister nor the physician had the expertise necessary for the task, or so he argued. In these matters, "only the trained and experienced psychologist is competent. And it is to him and not the clergy that the chief appeal should be made."

> The patient's consciousness must often be operated on and reconstructed in the way demanding the utmost expert skill. The average medical practitioner is usually quite as incompetent to make this diagnosis as the clergyman is to apply the cure; and error is dangerous in both processes. This, then, is the place for the psychological clinic. Unfortunately, neither in theological seminaries nor in medical schools is psychology generally taught; and the members of each profession are therefore incompetent to orient themselves properly in this vast and complex field. It would seem almost a commonplace that those whose profession it is to cure or save souls should have given a little attention to the study of what the soul is; and it would seem equally obvious that, as there are mental complications in every disease almost no attention is paid to this subject in medical education.[26]

At the very time Hall was stating his views, William James was writing to John D. Rockefeller and asking for a million dollars to support the care of the insane. In the decades ahead, the mental hygiene movement would take form, supported by various foundations, just as the psychological training of doctors would be sponsored and nourished by those foundations, bringing into existence the professional psychiatrist.[27]

It was Hall's contention that the upper, more culturally sophisticated classes ought to learn an object lesson from the emergence within their midst of such sects as Christian Science and Emmanuelism. He believed that the three great dangers they must learn to resist in the future were: "1. the dreamy metaphysics that exalts mind as something supreme and aloof from matter rather than its yoke-fellow in the world; 2. a habit of gross, literal verbal interpretation of scripture that sometimes falsely passes for orthodoxy; 3. a medical therapy that, however erudite, addresses the body only." His solution to the problem was that, "Each camp—doctors, philosophists, religionists—should admit its own share of responsibility for this curious excrescence of culture, and also at the same time should profit by the modicum of truth in and go on to develop a therapy that does justice to the psyche, a thought system that does justice to the soma, and a faith that not only comports with but supports science."[28] Human beings were, as both Friedrich Schleiermacher and Georg Hegel had shown, delicately balanced upon a sense of utter dependence on the ultimate powers that ruled the world. Power was conceived of as "God or laws of nature, on the one hand, and a sense of freedom and independence, on the other." Hall felt that, "Man is the only divinity, or at least God is only a collective term for man. Now the average man oscillates more or less between, but usually well within, these extremes. Perhaps he is rather humble toward what he feels above and arrogant to what is beneath him. Religion inclines him toward the dependent, and science toward the independent, term of these antitheses."[29]

The faith-curist, Hall contended, might rely too much on supernatural intervention and thus would dissuade the sufferer from taking the hygienic action necessary to work out a cure. Often that cure depended upon strengthening individual character, and thus a religion of the heart which overflows into free and easy helping could be most destructive. Jesus freely healed the sick "without price and effort on their part."

> The new ecclesiastical dispensaries should surely now require more of their patients than Jesus did of His. To faith must be added works, and the diligent use of all the now multifarious means of betterment: regular living, wholesome diet, plucky, hand-to-hand fights with temptation, turning on of every interest and instinct, the assiduous development of poise and self-control, perhaps change of inveterate habits by a strong, imperious, old-fashioned act or resolve of pure will.[30]

This was Hall's regime of strong, robust, virile living which he later elaborated in a more categorical form in his *Morale*. For him, the fundamental role of the church was not one of healing: "Again, freedom from all suffering, distress, and even health itself, precious as it is,—these are not the highest things in the world. The church does not exist chiefly to relieve pain or to cure ailments. Its higher function is to minister to the betterment of the soul and to improve morals, to make men more manly and women more womanly, and to make the world nobler, kinder, and purer." While the church may act to relieve misery, it also must act to "advance righteousness; it must improve the best to elevate the race in every humanistic virtue. It should do its noblest work for those who are themselves best endowed and in the best health and environment, and be a potent agency in advancing the kingdom of the superman who is slowly evolving a higher human type from the finest specimens of the *genus homo* now existing. If it saves the weakest and worst only, it does perhaps a sorry service to human evolution."[31]

Often, Hall argued that pain was the best tonic or "pedagogue." What humankind really needed, he insisted, was a more "virile Christianity": hellfire, pain, and suffering would move most people to greater action. The church's mission, therefore, must be protected from those who would feminize the true Christian with a loving, easy-going, "mollycoddling Saviour that merely speaks peace to his soul without arousing and arming him to fight." The truly virile Christian "does not wish to be a chronic beggar, even for healing grace or any other favors from heaven."[32]

According to Hall, the new "therapeutic dispensation" must be brought into the service of an evolving "Mansoul." "Although science is rapidly enlarging its domain at the expense of faith the vast majority of Christian people do not and will not think rigorously or judge sensibly about biblical or ecclesiastical matters. So long indeed have men been forbidden to use their reason here in fields that they have grown unaccustomed to do so."[33] Thus, religion had become the cultivator of the irrational, flying in the face of common sense as well as science itself. Under these circumstances, Hall was not surprised that church people

> easily accept absurdities like spiritism and Eddyism; and it is they especially who consult those who advertise short and easy methods of cure, to the utter abandonment of all their critical faculties. Slowly expelled from physical nature, miraculous agencies have been driven to their last shelter in the subconscious regions of the human soul, and here in Emmanuelism, their refuge and stronghold, they resist the advances of the youngest and highest of all sciences, psychology, which is destined sooner or later to reign supreme and alone in this field.[34]

By contrast, James took a far more sympathetic attitude toward the Emmanuelist movement, arguing that some "healing" and therefore some possible "good" may come from ministers practicing therapy.

For Hall, the great chasm between the natural and the supernatural would be closed when scientific psychology, as the new dispensation, would supercede the whole domain of religion. Then, he believed, we would have one world in which the God of "Mansoul" was worshiped for what He truly was: man as a being, potentially capable of becoming a superhuman being. Psychology

> lays upon itself the problem of explaining on rational grounds even the lofty and intricate activities of faith, to understand inspiration, to give the *rationale* of all that is supernatural, to formulate the mysteries of atonement for the soul and therapy for the body, and to annex the whole domain of religion as its own, until most truly pious man will be most ashamed to believe what is intrinsically preposterous, and the laws of mental hygiene itself will forbid this type of thought now so common among exigites and apologists of accommodating and making surds seem rational, of peddling and compromising as if there were two very distinct world orders instead of one only, and keeping ignorance and superstition in countenance in place of better knowledge. Any natural, psychic activities can suspend or alter the laws of the cosmos.[35]

Unlike James, who stood at the same precipice but for whatever personal reasons thought he saw something "more," Hall knew that what he saw was only the mirror image of "Mansoul" in himself. James wished to straddle both worlds; Hall had passed beyond the world of his childhood and into the world of twentieth-century evolutionary, naturalistic humanism. Hall clarified his position best in saying, "When psychology has expelled the last vestige of magic from religion and taken its place, then only shall we have a psychotherapy that is true to its name."[36] William James could not have made this statement. In retrospect, it is clear that the directors of the Gifford lectures had missed a significant opportunity when they failed to invite G. Stanley Hall to lecture on the religious contours of "Mansoul," following the James lectures on *The Varieties of Religious Experience.* In many ways, Hall had much more to say on the subject of religion than James did.

It is not at all surprising that Hall's ideas about religion and psychology should turn out to be so very different from his mentor's. Even though both men were born and bred in that same bracing New England atmosphere that produced Ralph Waldo Emerson, Henry David Thoreau, Nathaniel Hawthorne, and Herman Melville, and both men could equally romanticize the plight of the poor,[37] James's personal and social environment was vastly different from Hall's. William James was born into wealth and suffered at the hands of an overzealous, permissive, yet all-controlling, loving father whom he could not bring himself to hate (see chap. 1). In striking contrast, G. Stanley Hall was brought up in a rural atmosphere on a number of farms near Ashfield, Massachusetts. His father was a hard-working, fairly aggressive, outspoken man who instilled in his family the Puritan virtues of work and thrift. Hall's mother was a loving, kind, religiously guilt-ridden, and highly puritanical woman with a keen sense of duty and a personality that compelled her to shrink from conflict. As a child, Hall learned just how difficult it was to eke out a living on the rocky, hilly countryside near Ashfield. He also learned to romanticize the harsher dimensions of life as he grew deeply attached to his mother.

Hall confided in his mother and romanticized her into virtual madonnahood. His adult conception of the proper role of women no doubt was dictated by the way he came to see her. From her, Hall surmised, he inherited his reluctance for combat; while from his father, he believed that he inherited his drive to do and act with determination. It is clear that Hall loved and idealized his mother, but had only respectful tolerance for his father. His mother urged him to study for the ministry; his father wanted him to work the farm. As a youngster, he went with his father on his daily chores and often listened to the barnyard chatter when neighbors gathered. Hall eventually would admit that growing up in a rural environment had been the very best educational experience possible. However, in his youth he was embarrassed whenever he and his father had to drive their hogs to market through the center of the town, or when his father spoke up in public gatherings. Later, he was embarrassed to introduce his parents to his teacher, Mark Hopkins, while attending Williams College. Such embarrassments, then as now, are not uncommon among lower-class youth who become socially mobile. Hall did nurture a lifelong, inordinate drive to succeed as a result of these and other social experiences.

While at Williams College, Hall had a religious conversion experience which did not turn out to be very traumatic. He received his A.B. degree in 1867 and went on to Union Theological

Seminary where he eventually received a B.D. degree in 1869.[38] At Union he was introduced to the New York urban environment. He did missionary work in the slums of New York, preaching to "fallen" women and attempting to persuade them to mend their ways. The famed preacher Henry Ward Beecher made it possible for Hall to visit Germany, which opened up a completely new way of life for him, both intellectually and socially. Upon his return to Union the following year, he stayed with the Seligman family of New York City, serving as a tutor, and then went on to teach at Antioch College. In 1876 he went to Harvard University, where he took the first Ph.D. degree in psychology under William James. On borrowed money, Hall returned to Germany, where he became deeply engrossed in the intellectual culture as well as the sexual and social life there. In contrast to the staid New England environment, life in Germany was a freeing, opening experience. Hall returned from Germany with an American bride, deeply in debt and barely able to make ends meet by lecturing at both Harvard and Williams. Later, both Charles Eliot Norton and William James helped to persuade the president of Johns Hopkins that Hall was the right man for the new job there. And so, at the age of thirty-eight, he settled into his first really permanent position, and founded the country's first psychological laboratory. By 1888, he had moved on to Worcester, Massachusetts, where, with the donations of Jonas Clark, he founded and became the first president of Clark University.

At last approaching the height of his career, misfortune befell Hall. Within a brief period of two years both his parents died, followed shortly by the accidental asphyxiation of his wife and daughter in their home. No sooner had all this happened than Jonas Clark began to withhold financial support from the university, and Hall found himself embroiled in a battle to maintain the university in spite of severely limited resources. Personnel problems multiplied as William Rainey Harper raided Hall's faculty for the new University of Chicago. Under such trying circumstances, Hall continued to manage Clark University, to work on the child study movement, and to found the *Pedagogical Seminar Journal*. He remarried in 1899, but ten years later his wife, Florence, had to be committed to an insane asylum due to arteriosclerosis.

Throughout these years of personal crises Hall maintained a very productive career, although he clashed over and over again with his professional colleagues on a variety of issues. While Hall did not suffer an emotional breakdown that would incapacitate him from his work, his biographer, Dorothy Ross, makes the case (largely from his autobiography) that he suffered from a manic-depressive problem. Hall admitted that he had moods and cycles to his life which, if carried to the extreme, could be pathological. But the significant point is that no real evidence indicates that Hall ever suffered a breakdown because of those moods. To be sure, Ross correctly notes that Hall passed through a crisis period in his life in the early 1890s, but that crisis was induced by a set of unfortunate personal circumstances for the most part unrelated to his personality. It is remarkable that Hall managed to stay as sane and productive as he did, given his trying personal circumstances.[39]

Hall was a very complex person. The product of a puritanically repressed background, and propelled by a distinct distaste for conflict, he learned to lie at a relatively early age. For example, while explaining and justifying to his father, on highly moral grounds, his learning to dance, he "overlooked" the fact that he was at the same time drinking beer and carrying on a very active sexual life with a number of women. Even as he matured, Hall carried on a secret life. He was at home in virtually all the bawdy redlight districts of the major cities of western Europe and America. He loved prizefights and took lessons in all kinds of exotic dancing, just to get the feel of it. While his secret excursions into the redlight district often smacked of voyeurism, he insisted that he was merely carrying out a scientific study of humanity from the underside. The psychologist, he claimed, must know humanity in its fullest, most complete form. Hall was always open to new and different experiences.

Considering this penchant of his, it is little wonder that through Hall's efforts Sigmund Freud and Carl Jung were brought to America and introduced to American audiences. Shortly after Freud's visit, Hall's seminars took up the topic of psychoanalysis and the interpretations of dreams. They studied the works of Freud, Janet, Jung, Adler, and others. Hall became so fascinated by the psychoanalytic process that he began to analyze himself; after some difficulty he decided to enlist expert help. He wrote a chapter for his autobiography that detailed this analysis, but apparently had second thoughts and decided to destroy it.

Although never the rational thinker that Freud was, nor ever as convinced as Freud of the importance of sex in the total analysis of the unconscious, Hall did experiment with psychoanalysis and attempted to make use of it. In 1913, for example, he wrote to Dr. William Allen White, "We had last year a Dream Club of advanced students, which resulted in all studying their dreams, out of which I got some genetic and other conceptions. We have a Freud and Catharsis Club too which is thrashing out considerable material." However, in response to White's request for an article, he said, "I do not feel mature enough in the subject yet."[40] In previous correspondence with White, it seemed clear that Hall was working toward his own particular brand of psychoanalysis. White wrote: "In your letter to me sometime ago you said that you felt that the Freudians had not seen the full application of their work in all its breadth, that in dream analysis for example they had not seen the genetic implications."[41]

Although Hall lacked clinical therapeutic experience, which he regretted, he pushed on in his study of the unconscious and its implications for his overall psychological study of the religion of "Mansoul." His efforts were uniquely different from Freud's:

> As Freudians find sex, so our analysis finds religion at the root of all. Religion is a passion of the soul comparable in universality and intensity with sex, like it subject to and even made morbific by repressions. Like sex too, religion has left the soul full of its secondary qualities which it originated and inculcated, but has often left later to stand for themselves, so that their *de facto* religious origin is not apparent. As much all over the aesthetic field is due to the long circuiting of sex, so speculative philosophy is only the long circuiting of religion, and its sublimation into the intellectual field. As the root impulse of sex is to propagate another generation, so the root impulse of religion is to prolong the life of the individual by getting his soul born into another world.[42]

Hall's efforts along these lines bore fruit in his major two-volume work on *Jesus, the Christ, in the Light of Psychology* (1917), in which he attempted to psychoanalyze away the divinity of Christ.[43] He was still experimenting with the use of psychoanalytic procedures when he wrote *Recreations of a Psychologist* (1920). Following in the well-worn path of Arthur Schopenhauer, Hall played with the psychological meaning of the double turned onto himself. Thus, in the chapter "How Johnnie's Vision Came True," we meet Hall's *anima* and *animus* atop Mt. Hatch, with the role of his father and mother clearly in view. For Hall, the two eventually were reconciled into one personhood.

During the later decades of his life, he made extensive use of the works of Freud, Adler, Jung, and other analysts, though never to the satisfaction of any one of them. In one of his last letters to Freud, Hall commented: "But your own achievements are far and away beyond those of any psychologist of modern times; in fact history will show that you have done for us a service which you are not at all extravagant in comparing with that of Darwin for biology." He continued, reflecting on his personal indebtedness to Freud: "I think I have read about everything you have ever written, although in my limitations, there is much that I did not understand, and a little which, if I did understand it aright I have to question. Nevertheless, I owe to you almost a new birth of intellectual interest in psychology, as is perhaps best shown in my Jesus Book, which, without this, would not have been written."[44]

Hall fashioned his own unique vision of "Mansoul" from material he freely borrowed from those who impressed him. In a real sense, his two-volume work on *Adolescence* (1904), his two-volume work on *Jesus* (1917), and his work on *Morale* (1920)—the latter correctly subtitled "The Supreme Standard of Life and Conduct"—while drawn from a variety of sources, can also be read as a comprehensive overview of Hall's faith in "Mansoul," of which he believed himself to be a prophet:

> The true psychologist born and bred, yearns with all his heart for a deeper understanding of man and of all his psychic life, past and present, normal and morbid, good and bad, at all stages of his life. . . . He feels a peculiar urge to be intensely human and to glimpse, feel, or strive in his own brief little life for everything possible to man's estate. . . . Thus he is called to-day to be a sort of high priest of souls as in an earlier age the great religious founders, reformers, and creators of cults and laws used to be, for the day of great leadership in these fields seems to have passed.[45]

As a prophet and high priest of a new faith, Hall embraced the evolving sciences of anthropology, ethology, and psychology. Further, he believed that the greatest knowledge the individual could command was that of the evolutionary stages of the race, implicit in each person's soul. For some, such knowledge was possible; for others, it was not.

Hall felt that each of us could look into our own soul and see the soul of all humanity. He railed vitriolic all his life against

absolute Berkeleyian idealism and the cultist mysticism to which
he thought it would lead. His own idealism was tuned into his
biologic nature, with its own "delicious mysticism" from which
he would read the "true" story of humankind, not from viewing
humanity from afar, but from the sensual biological inside. With
Hall we can begin to see what it means to think with our blood.
From inside the self, both the past and the future of humanity
were to be read. Just as many of the great nineteenth-century
figures (e.g., Hegel, Marx, Freud, Schopenhauer, and Wagner) believed that the key to humanity and its progress was to be found
in humankind's history, so too did Hall believe that the genetic
history of the race, from the slime of the sea to the temple of
the superhuman, held its highest knowledge. Some could read
that history correctly, while others could not: "Genetic sense or
the vitalistic category of *werden* is, in men of true sympathy,
so strong that they *have* to believe not only in anthropomor-
phization but in animism, if not, indeed, in hylozoism. This gives
us a new orientation toward both origins and destinies and shows
us that the highest knowledge of anything is a description of its
evolutionary stages."[46]

It was Hall's belief that when people lose their connection
with the past and with the spirit of the true *Volk*, they cannot
lead; with it, however, they can move mountains.

> Those who lack this sense have lost rapport with childhood,
> even their own, and with arrested and undeveloped souls
> everywhere. To maintain this vital contact is essential for
> all teachers and leaders of men or for success in literature,
> art, poetry, politics. Here one must know how life and the
> world seem from under the smallest and thickest skulls. It
> is the secret of the charm of writers like Goethe, Tolstoi,
> Dickens, Hugo, and Strindberg. . . . it enables us, when the
> problems of life become too hard, to retreat or regress to a
> more juvenile point of view and flee for a time from reality
> without the danger of becoming permanently arrested like
> dementia praecox cases, but rather to be refreshed and rein-
> vigorated as by an Antaeus touch of mother earth and to
> gain strength for a fresh advance, which thus gathers to itself
> a new supply of momentum from the whole upward push
> of the *élan vital*, which is behind us all.

Looking inward is to look backward in communion with mother
nature, "when the overstrained city man goes back to the farm
of his boyhood and reverts to the simple life, getting into close

contact with mother earth, children, and animals, and giving way to all the inherited reactions of the human soul to the fresh and first-hand impressions of nature."[47]

Hall had drunk deeply from that strange neo-romantic well of primitive German *Volk* culture and had applied it freely to his own New England countryside. He stayed in touch with his childhood, with his primitive savage ancestry, and throughout his life would return periodically to the family farm where he played as a child, stripping off all his clothes and rolling down the hillside. Thus he would tune himself into his true nature by turning off the "inherited reactions of the human soul," which were really only the more recent civilized accompaniments of his "Mansoul": "I finally several times enjoyed the great luxury of being in complete undress, and of feeling pricked, caressed, bitten and stung all over, reverting to savagery as I had often done as a boy by putting off civilization with all clothes and their philosophy. It was a curious experience of lightness and closeness to nature."[48]

While such experiences may have had some therapeutic validity for the fifty-five-year-old president of Clark University, they represented, in fact, his way of connecting his soul to "Mansoul" as it lay dormant in his rural childhood environment. They served as the vehicle by which he believed he could freely move back to the primitive, savage stage of the race, and even beyond, when life first took shape. Periodically, Hall pierced what he thought was the veil separating time-bound consciousness from timeless unconsciousness: he tuned into the cosmic landscape of "Mansoul." He described those trips into his childhood past with a remarkable vigor and clarity, which at times strikes the reader as almost photographic.[49] He had a tremendous desire and longing for the presumed safety and security of his romanticized past, a past he freely fabricated.

It may seem a bit strange for a university president to roll down a hillside in the nude, recapturing his youthful vigor, yet it is not so strange in light of the many unconventional psychotherapeutic practices that flowered in more recent popular culture. What Hall described was not new to those who had studied *Volk* culture in Germany, nor was it new to certain groups within the larger youth movement in Europe, much of which had its origins in the same impulse: the desire to be rid of the dead accretions of bourgeois civilization while experiencing the more authentic sensations of a primitive past. In many ways,

Hall's essays are reminiscent of Marcel Proust's *Remembrance of Things Past*. Proust, like Hall, was searching through the labyrinth of the Vico-like timelessness of the unconscious self for the reconstruction of a more real, true, universal world of being. Both men reflected the acute alienation that affected many sensitive souls at the turn of the century. Rural life was passing, and urban industrial life was literally laying waste to that which they believed to be more real. Hall thought he saw a way out, and therefore used the concept of evolution as the key to structure his story of "Mansoul," which gave him respite from the artificiality of civilization while he recaptured the youthful spirit of earlier savage cultures.

Although a complete analysis of the ideas Hall plugged into his evolutionary landscape is not possible here, we must consider some of them in order to catch the critical social thrust of his new dispensation. Hall tended to be open to many different trends, embellishing the overall structure of his thinking with whatever was current. Much of the basic structure of his thought appeared early in his career, however. Upon his return from a second student tour of Germany in the early 1880s, he gave lectures and wrote articles which reflected this developing structure. In his articles was evidence of the recapitulation theory, the conflict between science and religion, and his attempt to resolve this issue by way of suggesting the role of a new psychology.[50] His articles also reflected his conception of the child in need of a stern shaping of will and character. In later works he would talk about "coercing and breaking" the will of the child,[51] but the concept of *Dressur*,[52] which he believed necessary for certain stages of child development, was already quite evident in his highly significant essay on "The Education of the Will." He noted that "the only duty of small children is habitual and prompt obedience," and in sweeping Fichtian terms introduced the reader to "muscle-culture" (the need to develop strong bodies) and "will-culture" (the need to develop strong character).[53] Hall argued that character must be shaped and molded so that those people who are destined to become obedient servants will, in fact, become obedient servants.

While many people become fixated at the lower evolutionary stage of savagery or even barbarism, and therefore need "obedience" training, there are those few who go beyond the civilized stage itself—the rare moral geniuses who are destined for leadership, who can be trusted to be trained to follow their true nature:

> Thrice happy he who is so wisely trained that he comes to believe he believes what his soul deeply does believe, to say what he feels and feel what he really does feel, and chiefly whose express volitions square with the profounder drift of his will as the resultant of all he has desired or wished, expected, attended to or striven for. When such a one comes to his moral majority by standing for the first time upon his own careful conviction, against the popular cry, or against his own material interests or predacious passions, and feels the constraint and joy of pure obligation which comes up from this deep source, a new original force is brought into the world of wills.

Hall insisted that this kind of character formation for the masses would be an "impractical if not dangerous ideal." It was fit only for the "rarest moral genius." As Hall argued, most people are not fit for freedom.

> For most of us the best education is that which makes us the best and most obedient servants. This is the way of peace and the way of nature, for even if we seriously try to keep up a private conscience at all, apart from feeling, faction, party or class spirit, or even habit, which are our habitual guides, the difficulties are so great that most hasten, more or less consciously and voluntarily, to put themselves under authority again, reserving only the smallest margin of independence in material interests, choice of masters, etc., and yielding to the pleasing and easy illusion that inflates the minimum to seem the maximum of freedom, and uses the noblest ideal of history, viz., that of pure autonomous ought-ness, as a pedestal for idols of selfishness, caprice and conceit.[54]

Hall's estimate "for most of us" is strangely similar to that of another charismatic leader, Adolf Hitler. A decade after Hall died, Hitler took the public stage in Germany and announced: "Providence has ordained that I should be the greatest liberator of humanity. I am freeing man from the demands of a freedom and personal independence that only a few can sustain."[55] Both men saw the bulk of humanity as eager and willing to escape from freedom; they sensed the underlying yearning for security that had overcome the Westerner. Both were highly sensitive to the alienating effects of industrial progress and the renting of

Western consciousness from an agrarian to an urban life. And they each seemed intuitively aware of the kinds of symbolic uses of the past that would heal such a wound. While Vilfredo Pareto analyzed this need for "security" by the "Western mind" in what was becoming a fractured culture, others would write about the human condition as alienated from nature, God, and even humanity itself. Throughout Hall's work, from "The Education of the Will" (1882) to *Life and Confessions of a Psychologist* (1923), his last work, is a constant reference and reaction to the loss of the agrarian virtues and the growth of artificial urban life. Indeed, *The Content of Children's Minds* (1893), which catapulted him to educational fame, was based on an examination of urban youngsters' knowledge of rural life.

It was Hall's firm belief that the scientific study of children would reveal the vital stream of "Mansoul," which could ultimately overcome the devastating effects of urban civilization. Here again, however, we find that the ideological screen Hall used to study the child, the adolescent, or the adult invariably colored his findings. Through his "scientific" studies of human development came his elitism, his racism, his chauvinism, his penchant for primitivism, and his authoritarianism—the integral elements of his personal value system. We find him recommending that "there are many who ought not to be educated, and who would be better in mind, body, and morals if they knew no school." He also argued that to educate girls to be self-supporting is "wrong and vicious," for to scientifically follow nature, "every girl should be educated primarily to become a wife and mother."[56] He insisted that *Dressur* was necessary for elementary students because the preadolescent was passing through an abbreviated form of the savage stage. Similarly, he believed that the adolescent was passing through that stage when civilization and reason began to dawn; therefore, courses in "heroälogy" were appropriate to teach the noble lesson of service to the collective soul of the people. Long after the recapitulation theory had been discredited, he continued to cling to this evolutionary structure.

Hall fought a delaying action when confronting movements that ran counter to his belief system. His resistance to the women's rights movement was typical. In a variety of public arenas he argued that women belonged in the home. However, when women began to gain some entrance to higher education, he insisted that at Clark University they were treated fairly. Nevertheless, in a private letter to Col. George A. Bullock, he said, "I am strongly opposed to giving women the slightest foothold in the college, even if we could do so under the founder's will. I feel that they would crowd out the best men a little later." He was inclined to leave the doctoral degree open to women because so few had gone through in the last ten years. Besides, he added, "it would save us a good deal of pounding by feminists; and by depriving it we would needlessly shut off possible bequests from women who have borne a pretty large part in the endowment of universities."[57] Hall was practicing explicit institutional chauvinism. What would appear to some on the outside as a relatively open system was, in fact, highly discriminating in intent and practice.

Women had a place in society, but for Hall it was not in the advanced centers of learning. He romanticized women as something very special, close to nature, bearers of the race and, indeed, the conduit through which "Mansoul" might someday become a "super-Mansoul." His personal values were clearly revealed in his reaction to his son Robert's announcement that he had found the girl he wished to marry: "I hope she is physically strong and with good heredity. What's her complexion? Send me her photo."[58]

Hall had raised physical and mental health to a near cult. In his book on *Morale* (1920), he addressed the physical and moral athlete, calling for a new collective ideal firmly rooted in the collective *Volk:* "Thus my book is a plea for nothing less than a new criterion of all human worths and values. I would have the home, the state, the church, literature, science, industry, and every human institution, not excluding religion, and perhaps it most, rejudged and revaluated by the standard of what they contribute to individual, industrial and social morale. This would give us a new scale on which to measure real progress or regression" (p. 20). Hall's scale for measuring progress toward a new order was clearly a totalitarian one.

While the social system could thus be improved, Hall knew that heredity was more important. He argued that a pound of heredity was "worth a hundredweight of education."[59] It was necessary to pay attention to better breeding: "The nation that breeds best, be it Mongol, Slav, Teuton or Saxon, will rule the world in the future." Eugenics, he insisted, was not merely medical certificates for fitness to marry or taxing bachelors for failing to breed their kind, or even steps to prevent the unfit from propagation, but rather the constant encouragement of the "Abrahams" of the race to breed a better race. Surely, he argued, "If farmers who can breed good cattle, sheep and horses, can also learn how to breed good men and women, the problem is solved. Germ plasm is the most immortal thing in the physical world. Backward it connects us by direct and unbroken lines of continuity with our remotest ancestor, be it Adam, the anthropopithicus, the amoeba or whatever else the human life began in, and the most optimistic law in the world is that the best survive and the worst perish." His complete vision ultimately would include breeding for a super race.

> If God [one should be reminded here that "God" for Hall is a collective term for "Mansoul"], the great stirpiculturist of man, were to create or choose an ideal environment for improving the human stock where the pure air and water and right, simple living and high thinking with correct adjustment of all the influences that work for the right balance between those supreme human forces, individuation and genesis, is struck, and thus establish a nursery for the slow evolution of the superman who will in body and soul realize all the highest human ideals and make what we have already dreamed must sometime come to the world, a new paradise, what better cradle or nest in which to incubate the overman of the future could be found than here?[60]

The new Paradise Hall had in mind was the superstate,[61] portrayed in the "Fall of Atlantis." In his ideal kingdom the individual practiced religion in all forms, from fetish and nature worship to "Mansoul" worship, according to each person's development on the evolutionary scale. Everyone dedicated his or her total self to the interest and service of the society under the enlightened guidance of those Hall called "heartformers" (psychologists). The entire society was organized into groups according to their productive functions, with each group dedicated to the ideal of being the very best of what they were destined to be (similar to the way Mussolini organized Italy when he came to power). Thus, service was emblazoned on everyone's consciousness. At the top of the social hierarchy could be found the superhumans, in the form of scientific researchers, who constantly sought more and more knowledge of "Mansoul." Hall's message was clear: through selective breeding, genetic psychology, and a well-planned educational system, the real nature of "Mansoul" could flower in the superstate. Something went wrong, however, and Hall's idyllic state eventually ended in chaotic destruction. Individual freedom at the expense of the collective ideal had eaten away at the very foundation of his totalitarian collective ideal. Hall's second message became clear: if America was to arrive at the promised land of "Mansoul," it would have to learn to tighten up and discipline itself to the collective ideal of *Morale*. This was Hall's ultimate vision and promise for America. Charles Burgess best captures the sense of what Hall was striving for: "With morale as the new religion of coercion for virtue's sake, with the colossus of a Christ-like superman standing on Liberty's vacated pedestal, with sublimation of self to the State therefore permeating every hierarchical layer from the slave to the *uebermensch*, Hall would at last be able to say that his battle had ended. The dawn of the new day would be upon the world."[62]

Before World War I, Nietzsche's view of the *Uebermensch* often served as a model for Hall; in many ways his superhuman was virtually the same as Nietzsche's. However, after the disillusioning experience of the war, Hall came to believe that there was a difference—Nietzsche's *Uebermensch* had succumbed to German militarism; it had been a superhuman of sheer power. In contrast, he believed that his superhuman was more moral and cultural, more a Christ-like colossus, a product of the evolutionary "Mansoul." For Hall, the Germany he had loved so dearly had destroyed itself in its turn toward militarism, which he believed could also infect other cultures and nations and would ultimately lead, if not checked, to the destruction of all culture. While his ideal state was not a militarized one, it was clearly totalitarian. Hall not only envisioned a total culture where all would be subservient to the ideal, but a total humanity where ultimately the best would come to see, as he, Christ, and Buddha had also seen, that view from the mountaintop.

G. Stanley Hall preached a new religion, a totalitarian, naturalistic faith for twentieth-century man, in which the psychologist replaced the priest and sickness replaced the age-old concept of sin. He was a prophet of the twentieth-century totalitarian individual, tuned into the deeper undercurrents of Western culture and able to feel the pangs of our alienation. He intuitively sensed the reactionary symbolic structure for which such vulnerable people came to yearn and thus seemed to touch the future. Hall was not long in his grave when Westerners began to hear those strange themes of back to nature, soil, fatherland, hearth and home, health, strength through joy, agrarian virtue, world order, new order, charismatic leadership, superhumans and super-race, ancestral calling, thinking with one's blood, and ultimately the *Triumph of the Will*,[63] echoing off those cold gray walls of the sports colossus at Nuremberg. He had touched the symbolic structure that the national socialists would use to weld Germany into an iron-clad soul of "obedient servants."

Perhaps Hall was correct when he argued that it was not German cultural ideology that led Germany astray in World War I but rather the growth of German militarism. Nevertheless, the unanswered question remains: what role did these complex ideological, cultural currents play in keeping the trains running on time to Auschwitz and the fires burning in the crematoriums? It might be as Hall earlier argued that these cultural currents of "Mansoul" were innocent "victims" rather than "perpetrators" of the catastrophe that ensued. The fault, he would say, lies with a growing cancerous military mind. Then again, it just might be the case, as another enlightened utopian visionary named Karl Marx once claimed, that "the abolition of religion as the *illusory* happiness of men, is a demand for their *real* happiness. The call to abandon their illusions about their condition is a call to abandon a condition which requires illusions."[64] Perhaps if we look more carefully at those conditions requiring illusions, we might find those cultural ideological conditions that helped to propel Germany into national socialism as well as militarism. It is possible that Hall was wrong in blaming the military. Perhaps some combination of cultural conditions and militarism concocted that witch's brew. If so, America's current longing for a reactionary past, charismatic leadership, health cults, back to the soil, nature, religious cults, a search for our mystical roots, and the simple virtues of "manhood," "womanhood," and "motherhood," may all stand as veiled warnings of things to come. It may well be that such an ideological pallor in conjunction with the growth of American militarism in the atomic age will be the spark that lights the path of "Mansoul" to an even greater, if not final, catastrophe.

However one interprets current trends in America, Lawrence Cremin seems to have been correct when he said of Hall: "He injected into the mainstream of American educational thought some of the most radical—and I happen to think virulent—doctrines of the twentieth century, and there is no understanding the present apart from his contribution."[65] While many of Hall's doctrines can be viewed as "virulent" in the context of the twentieth century, it is equally—and perhaps more importantly—clear that the conditions which gave rise to such ideas need further, more intensive examination. Nevertheless, just when it seemed that America was about to lose her traditional religious moorings, G. Stanley Hall, priestly prophet of the twentieth century, did more than any single individual to help construct that new faith, that new religion of psychology, in which so many have come to believe.

Notes

1. G. Stanley Hall, *Life and Confessions of a Psychologist* (New York: D. Appleton and Co., 1923), p. 596.

2. Ibid.

3. Lorine Pruette, *G. Stanley Hall* (New York: D. Appleton and Co., 1926), p. 199.

4. Quoted in Dorothy Ross, *G. Stanley Hall, the Psychologist as Prophet* (Chicago: University of Chicago Press, 1972), p. 254.

5. Hall, *Life and Confessions of a Psychologist*, p. 178.

6. See Merle Curti, *The Social Ideas of American Educators*, rev. ed. (Paterson, N.J.: Littlefield, Adams and Co., 1960), p. 426. See also E. L. Thorndike, *Biographical Memoir of Granville Stanley Hall (1844–1924)*, National Academy of Sciences, Biographical Memoirs, vol. 12, 1928.

7. See Ross, *G. Stanley Hall*, p. 336.

8. Quoted in Curti, *Social Ideas of American Educators*, p. 396.

9. A response to Edwin G. Boring's inquiry "Whose Student Are You?" Clark University Archives, G. Stanley Hall Papers, box 32.

10. Quoted by Pruette, *G. Stanley Hall*, p. 7.

11. This practice of developing a network of students who in turn invite their major professor to lecture at their institutions, while not unique to the field of early childhood was, however, particularly well developed in this area and continues so to the present day.

12. G. Stanley Hall, "Dr. Hall's statement of the difference between his views of religious psychology and that of Professor William James," 249a, May 9, 1907, p. 1, Clark University Archives, Hall Papers.

13. Ibid.

14. Ibid., p. 2.

15. Hall, "Eddyism and Emmanuelism," May 1909, p. 14, Clark University Archives, Hall Papers, box 28, folder no. 1, p. 14.

16. G. Stanley Hall, "Miscellaneous," *American Journal of Psychology* 2(1891): 590.

17. Hall, "Eddyism and Emmanuelism," p. 29. Eddyism, the philosophy of Mary Baker Eddy, founder of the Christian Science faith, in part includes a pure idealism which asserts that there is only one reality—Mind, God, Good—and that matter and evil are unreal. This idealism is combined with a healing ministry which relies heavily on the power of faith. The Emmanuel movement, an attempt to employ moral treatment

for nervous disorders, was inaugurated by Rev. Elwood Worcester and
Rev. Samuel McComb in Emmanuel Church, Boston, 1906. The overall
aim has been to revive the church's ministry of healing in cooperation
with scientific medical practice.

18. Ibid.

19. Ibid., pp. 31, 32.

20. Ibid., pp. 36, 34.

21. Ibid., p. 35.

22. Ibid., pp. 35, 38, 44.

23. Ibid., p. 7.

24. Ibid., pp. 7, 8–9.

25. Ibid., p. 12.

26. Ibid., p. 6.

27. See Christine Mary Shea, "The Ideology of Mental Health and
the Emergence of the Therapeutic Liberal State: The American Mental
Hygiene Movement, 1900–1930," Ph.D., dissertation, University of Illinois
at Urbana-Champaign, 1980.

28. Hall, "Eddyism and Emmanuelism," p. 13.

29. Ibid., p. 14.

30. Ibid., p. 16.

31. Ibid., pp. 16, 17.

32. Ibid., p. 18.

33. Ibid., p. 19.

34. Ibid., p. 20.

35. Ibid., pp. 20–21.

36. Ibid., p. 21.

37. See Curti, *Social Ideas of American Educators*, pp. 434–35.
Consider the suggestion by Hall that lower-class children are not really
unfortunate because they are neglected. Lower-class children, he asserted,
"thrive well under a certain degree of neglect" (G. Stanley Hall, "What
Is to Become of Your Baby?" *Cosmopolitan* 48[Apr. 1910]: 664).

38. See Pruette, *G. Stanley Hall*, p. 265.

39. The evidence for Ross's case seems strained. The fact that Hall
wrote with a good deal of hyperbole does not indicate that Hall had a
hyper-personality condition. If so, we would have to indict an entire
generation of writers who also wrote in this grand style. Hall wrote in
a much-exaggerated fashion most of his life, just as he lectured—char-
ismatically, making ample use of emotionally charged symbols. While
it may be the case that Hall was emotionally repressed, as Ross further
claims, it also is the case that he had very clear outlets of expressing
his emotions in his teaching, lecturing, and writing. Given all the problems
he faced, it is amazing that he remained constantly open to new experiences. See Ross, *G. Stanley Hall*, pp. 435–36.

40. Letter from Hall to White, Feb. 18, 1913, Clark University Archives,
Hall Papers, box 26, folder no. 9 (1906–19).

41. Letter from White to Hall, Feb. 11, 1913.

42. G. Stanley Hall, "Why Kant Is Passing," *American Journal of Psychology* 23(July 1913): 421.

43. It is not the case, as Ross claims, that "Hall's picture of Jesus owed little to Freud" (*G. Stanley Hall*, p. 418); rather, Hall was significantly dependent on many Freudian insights.

44. Letter from Hall to Freud, Sept. 24, 1923, pp. 2–3, Hall Papers, box 24, folder no. 9. See also "Sigmund Freud and G. Stanley Hall: Exchange of Letters," John Chynoweth Burnham, ed., *Psychoanalytic Quarterly* 29(1960): 314–15. Ross follows Burnham's estimate that the Jesus book could have been written without Freud's influence. A careful reading of both volumes leads me to question this point, on which I believe Hall was essentially correct.

45. Hall, *Life and Confessions*, p. 436.

46. Hall, *Life and Confessions*, p. 461.

47. Ibid., pp. 462, 463.

48. G. Stanley Hall, "Note on Early Memories," *Pedagogical Seminary* 1(Dec. 1899): 504.

49. See, for example, G. Stanley Hall, "Bay Life in a Massachusetts Country Town Thirty Years Ago," *Proceedings of the American Antiquarian Society* 7(1892). See also Hall, "Note on Early Memories," p. 504.

50. See G. Stanley Hall, "The Moral and Religious Training of Children," *Princeton Review* (Jan.-June 1882): 32; and "The New Psychology," *Andover Review* 3(Feb. 1885): 247.

51. See G. Stanley Hall, "The Ideal School Based on Child Study," *Forum* 32(1902): 35.

52. The concept of unflinching obedience training is discussed in Hall, *Life and Confessions*, p. 514.

53. G. Stanley Hall, "The Education of the Will," *Princeton Review* (July-Dec. 1882): 310.

54. Ibid., pp. 321, 322.

55. Quoted in Herbert J. Muller, *Issues of Freedom* (New York: Harper and Co., 1960), p. 36.

56. Hall, "The Ideal School Based on Child Study," pp. 25, 35.

57. Letter from Hall to Bullock, Nov. 20, 1909, pp. 1, 2, Hall Papers, box 20. I am indebted to Chris Shea for first calling my attention to this letter.

58. Letter from G. Stanley Hall to Robert G. Hall, May 16, 1915, Hall Papers, box 2, folder no. 9.

59. Hall, "What Is to Become of Your Baby?" p. 661.

60. G. Stanley Hall, untitled and undated manuscript, in Articles and Addresses, 1902–17, pp. 24, 22–23, 25–26, 26–27. Hall Papers, box 29, folder no. 1.

61. Hall uses this term to describe his ideal state in the "Fall of Atlantis," *Recreations of a Psychologist* (New York: D. Appleton and Co., 1920), p. v.

62. Charles Burgess, "The Educational State in America," Ph.D. dissertation, University of Wisconsin, 1962, p. 222.

63. Leni Riefenstahl's vivid film portrayal "Triumph of the Will," was the official Nazi film of the Nuremberg Party Convention in 1934.

64. T. B. Bottomore, ed. and trans., *Karl Marx* (New York: McGraw Hill and Co., 1964), p. 45.

65. Charles E. Strickland and Charles Burgess, *Health, Growth, and Heredity: G. Stanley Hall on Natural Education* (New York: Teachers College Press, 1965), p. viii.

6

Sigmund Freud [1856–1939]

Religion as an Obsessional Neurosis

After considerable thought, Sigmund Freud selected the epigraph for what he believed was his most important work, *The Interpretation of Dreams*, from Virgil's *Aeneid*: "If I cannot move Heaven, I will stir up the underworld." His book did just that, and in the process launched the psychoanalytic movement, which eventually had a profound effect on the way Western culture would perceive itself in the twentieth century. *The Interpretation of Dreams* was written as the culmination of Freud's own psychoanalysis under the guidance of Wilhelm Fliess, from 1897 to 1900. This was a period of crisis in Freud's life, when his "creative neurosis"[1] came to full fruition. He would look back to that "once-in-a-lifetime" period as one of real creative discovery.

In Freud's view, his unique experience was a gradual descent into the underworld, into his unconscious, which turned out to be very much like a journey into hell where evil and sin are transformed into sickness and death.[2] In the depths of this hell he would find the origin for "all morality," indeed, the very basis for religion itself. He took this precarious journey, not out of sheer curiosity, but rather as a consequence of events and circumstances that had propelled him into a state of crisis. Freud was approaching his fortieth birthday, a time in life when most of us become a bit more self-reflective about our existence.

Early in life, Freud, like so many other Jews of his generation, began his migration from the rabbinical world of Talmudic studies to the gentile world of the gymnasium and the university. He was first in his class at the Sperl Gymnasium, where he studied Herbart,[3] a variety of languages, and the classics. He considered a possible career in law,[4] but was inspired by Johann Goethe's *On Nature* to move away from law and into a career in medical science. As a young man he was successful in physiological science. He helped to discover the medical usefulness of cocaine and did landmark work in the physiology of the nervous system. At this point in his career he became interested in Martha Bernays, of Hamburg, who was from a distinguished traditional Jewish family (her grandfather had been the chief rabbi of Hamburg). Eager to marry but financially hard-pressed, Freud began a shift in his career from that of empirical laboratory scientist to therapeutic physician, dealing with nervous disorders. He became interested in hysteria through the work of his former teacher and friend Josef Breuer. He won a scholarship to study with Jean-Martin Charcot at Paris, where his interest in hysteria was further stimulated. Upon his return to Vienna, he became associated with Breuer and those who were treating hysteria as well as other forms of mental illness. With the assistance of Breuer he opened his own private therapeutic practice and, with his career underway, married Martha Bernays and began a family.

All was not well with this brilliant young scholar, teacher, and physician, however. Freud's promotion to Professor was held up at the university, apparently for anti-Semitic reasons. He began to suffer severe migraine headaches and developed a troublesome heart condition.[5] He also was plagued by a travel phobia, a clear symptom of a larger obsessional neurosis. When required to travel, Freud found himself compelled to go to the train station well ahead of time and never alone. Increasingly, he longed to take a trip to Rome but found that he was always prevented from doing so "because of health reasons." Rome and death became the two major focal points of his obsessional neurosis. Whenever he thought that someone might be wishing him dead, he fainted.[6] He suffered as well from the guilt of wishing others dead, the effects of which were especially acute when his fantasy world actually broke through his unconscious barriers and became indistinguishable from reality (Freud reported to Fliess that there were times when he hesitated to even think certain thoughts for fear that they would became real). Freud's death problem took a number of other different forms as well. He was fascinated with dates when he supposedly might die; for example, he greeted the dawning twentieth century as the one that held his death date. He suffered from guilt associated with the death of a younger brother. Self-analysis revealed that his death problem critically shaped his own character and, in turn, conditioned the way he ultimately came to treat his professional colleagues. His Rome phobia appeared to be related to both his hatred of the Catholic church and a death wish directed toward his father, the latter being intimately tied to his view of religion as an obsessional neurosis.

All of these problems surfaced and began to intensify as Freud found himself suffering from anxiety attacks that increasingly interfered with his work. He was clearly shaken by his father's death on October 23, 1896, noting, "By one of the obscure routes behind the official consciousness the old man's death affected me deeply. I valued him highly and understood him very well indeed, and with his peculiar mixture of deep wisdom and imaginative lightheartedness he meant a great deal in my life. By the time he died his life had long been over, but at a death the whole past stirs within one. I feel now as if I had been torn up by the roots."[7] Cut off from the conventional world, Freud became more and more self-reflective, and his life entered a period of what he called "splendid isolation," increasingly dominated by a search for the causes of neurosis in his patients and, more importantly, in himself—he would become his "own patient." Fliess now became much more than just a close friend. As Freud assumed the role of patient, Fliess assumed the role of analyst. Over the coming years, their meetings—or "congresses"—gradually took on the appearance of therapeutic sessions. In letters to Fliess, Freud frequently expressed his "longing," "pining," and "need" for another "congress." Clearly, Freud considered Fliess his lifeline to the conscious world as he journeyed through the unconscious, making the most significant discoveries about himself and about that which he assumed could be universalized to all humanity.

In this chapter I focus on Freud's self-analysis, how he described that analysis, what he thought he discovered about himself and all humanity in the process, and how he, in part, overcame his own phobic problem through sublimation. I then consider Freud's life work, the psychoanalytic movement, as a form of his personal sublimation. Lastly, I turn to the new faith which Freud had created, how he saw himself as the new Moses of that faith, and how he saw that faith fitting into the Western religious tradition.[8]

Freud learned from his patients as well as from direct experience with self-analysis, the latter proving most important. He discovered the process of transference, the therapeutic usefulness of that process,[9] and his "own feminine side."[10] He also came to appreciate the nature of repression and the psychic pain that accompanies it. In interpreting his dreams and those of others, he made the critical distinction between what he called "manifest" content and the "latent" content of the dream. Thus he learned that only the patient could really discover the deeper meaning of the dream, and only in a free-association process— by following the dream and its intuited associative meanings. Deeply involved in this process, Freud discovered the function of screen memories, those fragmentary memories from the period of early childhood amnesia, and their utility for probing the unconscious.[11]

It was during self-analysis that Freud came to discard the seduction theory, the belief that all hysteria was caused by the sexually perverse acts of a parent or nurse committed against the child in his or her earliest formative years. He had questioned the theory's validity on several grounds. First, in using seduction theory, he had had difficulty bringing analyses with even his most "favorably inclined patients" to any real conclusions; second, he had had difficulty believing that the sexually perverted acts against children could be so widespread; and third, "there was the definite realization that there is no 'indication of reality' in the unconscious, so that it is impossible to distinguish between truth and emotionally-charged fiction."[12] Most importantly, the childhood seduction theory implicated his own father in the hysterical symptoms he detected in his and his sister's neuroses. Such considerations combined to incline Freud to drop the seduction theory for what might be termed the "fantasy" theory.[13] For the most part, then, he believed that he was dealing with the fantasies of his hysterical patients rather than the effects of actual seduction.

Once he accepted the fantasy theory, Freud's own analysis seemed to pick up both speed and some sense of direction. Using his screen memories, he worked back through adolescence to his early childhood experiences. For Freud the most critical years were the first three of his life. He was born in 1856,[14] in Freiberg, Moravia, to Kelemen Jacob Freud, age forty-one, who grew to manhood in the Galician *shtetl* of Tysmenintz, and to Amalia Nathanson, age twenty-one, from eastern Galicia. His father and great-grandfather were "registered as Galician wandering Jews (Wanderjuden). They travelled perpetually between Galicia and Freiberg, trading wool, woolen fabrics, suet, honey, anise, hides, salt, and similar raw products."[15] Freud's father had been married at least once before,[16] so his son's birth marked the beginning of a second family for him. However, as the first-born son of Amalia Nathanson Freud, and in accord with Jewish custom, Sigmund received very special treatment within the family circle. He held a favored place with his mother, who called him her "golden Sigi," her golden victory. Shortly after his birth, an old peasant woman prophesied to Amalia that her first-born "Sigi" would be a great man someday.

Amalia Freud was an East Galician Jew who, according to her grandson Martin, was born and reared of unique stock. Sigmund Freud's son wrote of his grandmother:

> [She] came from East Galicia, then still part of the Austrian Empire. She came of Jewish stock; and it might not be known by many people that Galician Jews were a peculiar race, not only different from any other races inhabiting Europe, but absolutely different from Jews who had lived in the West for some generations. They, these Galician Jews, had little grace and no manners; and their women were certainly not what we should call "ladies." They were highly emotional and easily carried away by their feelings. But, although in many respects they would seem to be untamed barbarians to more civilized people, they, alone of all minorities, stood up against the Nazis. It was men of Amalia's race who fought the German army on the ruins of Warsaw; and it might, indeed, be true to say that whenever you hear of Jews showing violence or belligerence, instead of that meekness and what seems poor-spirited acceptance of a hard fate sometimes associated with Jewish peoples, you may safely suspect the presence of men and women of Amalia's race.[17]

Freud's often-noted verbal coarseness might have been acquired from his mother's eastern European background as described by

Martin Freud, a background characterized as sensually direct, unencumbered by the niceties and civilities of the more modern secularized West. Freud's proclivity for exposing the harsh realities that lay behind the curtain of Western civilized culture may also have been acquired from his eastern Galician inheritance.[18]

Sigmund Freud was the first in his family to ever attend the gymnasium and the university. His father, reared in a "Hassidic milieu" and a Talmudic scholar in his own right, tutored the young boy and prepared him for his work in the gymnasium. Both intellectually and emotionally, then, Freud straddled two very different worlds: his childhood, as an eastern European Jew, and his adult life, as a Western modern Jew. The traditional behavior patterns of the eastern European Jewish family, especially those between a first-born son and his mother, are important in understanding Freud's deep, lifelong relationship with Amalia. In such families we can expect to find a great deal of public endearment, a relationship in which "demonstrativeness is allowed between mother and son, which mothers encourage." While the "marital obligations are fulfilled with the husband, the romance exists with the son." Indeed, "a young son often sleeps with her, unlike her husband who is prohibited by sacred law from remaining in her bed." "There is no avoidance between mother and son, except that intercourse is forbidden. Mother is the embodiment of warmth, intimacy, food, unconditional love, security, practical reality." The son's relationship with his father is best characterized as respectful, intellectual, somewhat distant and unemotional, with traces of fear. In such families it is not unusual to find that "rivalry between father and son is a familiar theme, expressed in large and small ways, privately and publicly."[19] Traditionally, the mother runs the household and reinforces these family roles. It is reasonable to presume that some of these relationships characterized the Freud family; and it is equally reasonable to suggest that Freud's discovery of the Oedipus complex and castration fears were not unrelated to his own early childhood experiences.

As Freud saw it, his childhood was complicated by the fact that he was the first-born son of his father's second family. By the time of his birth, Emanuel, the oldest of Jacob Freud's sons by his first marriage, had a son of his own, one-year-old John, and a newborn daughter, Pauline. Both families lived close together and shared a Catholic nurse named Monica Zajic.[20] Thus, while "Sigi's" special place in the family was assured by a young mother showering affection on her first-born, his place with respect to the extended family was not so secure.[21] He competed with both John and Pauline. His emotional security was jeopardized further by a brother, Julius, who was born around Freud's first birthday and who died some eight months later. Additional complications occurred at the age of two-and-a-half, when his sister Anna was born, concurrent with the loss of his nurse, who was imprisoned for stealing. In 1859, at the age of three, his family moved to Leipzig because of financial difficulties encountered by his father; his half-brother, Emanuel, moved with his children to Manchester, England. These moves were the result of economic changes wrought by the introduction of machinery into the textile industry and the consequent dislocation of the artisan life in which Jacob Freud had participated as a peddler.

The year at Leipzig and the next two or three years at Vienna were economically harsh for the Freuds, and their poverty must have had a traumatic effect on young Freud, to the point where later he could not remember anything from those years. Erich Fromm has suggested that Freud's life-long fear of poverty could be traced to those years (1859–63). He recounts one of the most dramatic moments of Freud's life when, in a smoke-filled hotel room in Nuremberg, in 1910, trying to get his Jewish colleagues to accept the leadership of the gentile Carl Jung to assure victory for his psychoanalytic movement, he regressed to the emotive reactions of those childhood days, tearfully exhorting: "My enemies would be willing to see me starve; they would tear my very coat off my back."[22] As Fromm aptly notes, at that point in his career Freud was not about to starve, but the effects of the insecurity of poverty from those early years of his life apparently were still with him.

Freud believed that his Freiberg childhood years (1856–59) were his most important ones; he could, at least, remember bits and pieces of that time. Overtly, they were happy years; and perhaps, considering the subsequent decline in the family fortune, that was the case. In a letter read at the unveiling of a tablet marking the house of his birth, Freud referred to himself "as the happy child of Freiberg, the first-born son of a youthful mother. . . ."[23] In reality, one suspects that the family was not as financially well off as Freud assumed; nor was "golden Sigi" all that socially secure. The family lived those Freiberg years in a single room, in which occurred three births, one death, and all the personal problems inherent in living in such close physical confinement. This was the context in which the young "Sigi" became conscious of the world about him.

As an adult, and with the aid of Wilhelm Fliess, Freud struggled to recall his earliest childhood years: "My own analysis is going on, and it remains my chief interest. Everything is still dark, including even the nature of the problems, but at the same time I have a reassuring feeling that one only has to put one's hand in one's own store-cupboard to be able to extract—in its own good time—what one needs."[24] That cupboard, both symbolically and literally, figured as a significant place in Freud's dream analysis and in his screen memories. Once, in one such dream, "full of animosity," he dreamed about a one-eyed doctor he had difficulty identifying, until his mother pointed out that he might be the doctor who sewed up a cut on young Sigmund's face as a result of a fall while climbing on a cupboard trying to obtain something pleasant. The feeling of "serves him right" for trying to overreach himself would recur whenever Freud recalled this moment.[25]

Another screen memory involving a cupboard would intermittently reappear in his consciousness for over twenty-nine years: "I was crying my heart out, because my mother was nowhere to be found. My brother Philipp (who is twenty years older than I) opened a cupboard for me, and when I found that mother was not there either I cried still more, until she came through the door, looking slim and beautiful. What can that mean?"[26] Freud associated this memory with the loss of his nurse, who had just been imprisoned for stealing (he also associated Philipp with the loss of his nurse). In a later analysis of the same screen memory, Freud made the association of the cupboard with his mother's womb and pointed to his unhappiness over the birth of his sister, Anna.[27] In describing this particular cupboard screen memory, Freud reported to Fleiss that "I have found love of the mother and jealousy of the father in my own case too, and now believe it to be a general phenomenon of early childhood."[28] He had, he thought, discovered the "gripping power" of Sophocles's Oedipus Rex, as well as William Shakespeare's Hamlet.

Painfully, Freud worked through his screen memories, as well as both the manifest and latent content of his dreams. As his father once taught him to read the Talmud, he now read his unconsous. He learned to appreciate the difficulties involved in breaking through repression: "I have been through some kind

of a neurotic experience, with odd states of mind not intelligible
to consciousness—cloudy thoughts and veiled doubts, with barely
here and there a ray of light."[29] Slowly he sought the rules he
believed must govern the memory distortions as well as the
creative fantasies. At times, he feared to think, for fear that the
very thought would become reality; at other times, he despaired
of ever knowing reality.

In his unconscious world Freud discovered his own sensual
longing for his mother and his bitter hatred for his father, or,
indeed, for anyone else who would dare stand in the way of
satisfying his cravings. The two greatest crimes a young man
might commit within the Judeo-Christian tradition are incest
and murder, and Freud found both in the depths of his soul. As
he approached this awareness, he said: "Another presentiment
tells me, as if I knew already—though I do not know anything
at all—that I am about to discover the source of morality."[30] He
was at the very center of that bridge spanning the river of human
relationships, a river separating the traditional religious culture
from the modern therapeutic society. On one side could be heard
a good deal about sin and evil; on the other, about sickness and
mental illness. Freud discovered for himself that in the very depth
of the unconscious, sin was transformed into sickness and religious
culture gave birth to the therapeutic society: "My recognition
that difficulties of treatment derive from the fact that in the last
resort one is laying bare the patient's *evil inclinations,* his *will
to remain ill,* is growing stronger and clearer."[31] Here, in mi-
crocosm, Freud found the juncture between the religiously oriented
culture in which he was reared and the secular medical-therapeutic
world in which he lived as an adult; he learned that morality
begins in the individual, with the guilt of sin. Here, too, he
thought, must be the source of his own obsessional neurosis and
its connection with his murderous death wishes, rooted in his
childhood, and his sensual desires.

Exploring his childhood experiences, Freud came to understand
the following relationships:

> I can only say that in my case my father played no active
> role, though I certainly projected on to him an analogy from
> myself; that my "primary originator" [of neurosis] was an
> ugly, elderly but clever woman who told me a great deal
> about God and hell, and gave me a high opinion of my own
> capacities; that later (between the ages of two and two-and-
> a-half) libido towards *matrem* was aroused; the occasion

must have been the journey with her from Leipzig to Vienna, during which we spent a night together and I must have had the opportunity of seeing her *nudam* (you have long since drawn the conclusions from this for your own son, as a remark of yours revealed); and that I welcomed my one-year-younger brother (who died within a few months) with ill wishes and real infantile jealousy, and that his death left the germ of guilt in me. I have long known that my companion in crime between the ages of one and two was a nephew of mine who is a year older than I am and now lives in Manchester; he visited us in Vienna when I was fourteen. We seem occasionally to have treated my niece, who was a year younger, shockingly. My nephew and younger brother determined, not only the neurotic side of all my friendships, but also their depth.[32]

He suggested that his travel anxiety was somehow connected to these childhood relationships as well as to his own hysteria, of which he still had not gotten to the "bottom."

Freud's perceptions of his childhood friendships and hatreds had a lasting, instrumental effect in shaping his own character, and in the end had a significant impact on the nature of his adult relationships. Repeatedly, the death wish involving his brother, Julius, who died, and that involving his nephew, John, who moved to Manchester, would reappear in Freud's dreams.[33] He came to believe that his death wish for Julius and his struggle for dominance over John interplayed in the way he ultimately came to use people.

In a certain sense all my friends are incarnations of this first figure, "which early appeared to my blurred sight"; they are all *revenants.* My nephew himself returned in the years of adolescence, and then we acted Caesar and Brutus. An intimate friend and a hated enemy have always been indispensable requirements for my emotional life; I have always been able to create them anew, and not infrequently my childish ideal has been so closely approached that friend and enemy coincided in the same person, not simultaneously, of course, nor in repeated alterations, as had been the case in my first childhood years.[34]

At the time Freud wrote these words, Josef Breuer was well on the way to becoming a *revenant* and Fliess was not far behind. With incredible insight into his own character, Freud prophetically revealed what would eventually come to characterize his relationships with his friends and colleagues for the next three generations. He found "no one is irreplaceable"; friends and enemies alike became usable, replaceable parts, true *revenants*. By the end of *The Interpretation of Dreams* and Freud's own analysis, Fliess had become one of Freud's *revenants*.[35] In his dream relationships, Freud found himself always willing to sacrifice "dear persons to my ambition."[36] It is striking how often his dream relationships became reality later in life.

Throughout his life Freud suffered from guilt, the consequences of which he struggled to avoid. In his *non vixit—non vivet* dream, in which he rejoiced over the death of a friend whose position he sought and had acquired after his death, Freud made the error of superimposing *non vixit* ("he did not live") for *non vivit* ("he is not alive"), thus relieving himself of the responsibility and guilt of having wished the man dead. Similarly, by saying his brother Julius did not live, Freud could not be responsible for his death. The problem of a death wish played itself out in virtually all of his relationships with his most intimate friends and followers. They became *revenants* for him so that he did not have to suffer the "guilt of the survivor," a dominant theme in his own analysis. If, then, Freud held a death wish for his own friends and followers who broke with his interpretation of the unconscious, it is little wonder that Freud would so readily faint at the first hint of a friend's death wish held toward him. He understood himself all too well. He loved and hated intensely.[37]

The problem of death was central to Freud's neurosis and in one sublimated form or another found its way into virtually all aspects of his life.[38] He desperately hoped to outlive his mother, so as to spare her the announcement of his death, while he feared that the angel of death might take him before he could fulfill his destiny. In spite of Fliess's constant warning about his cigar smoking being injurious to his health, Freud continued to smoke "a steady twenty a day."[39] He associated smoking with his own creativity. One might go further and suggest its association with his creative neurosis. Whatever the case, he continued to smoke even after his leukoplakia had turned to cancer. Later in life he would sublimate his death wish into his psychology as a natural "death instinct." It is not surprising that Freud made arrangements with his personal physician to terminate his life when he himself chose to do so.[40]

Freud was determined that his own death was not going to be like that of his father, who died a vegetable. Given all these circumstances, it is little wonder that his father's death triggered Freud's neurosis. Freud wrote:

> During the night before the funeral of my father I dreamed of a printed placard, a card or poster—perhaps something like signs in railway waiting-rooms which announce the prohibition of smoking—which reads either:
>
> It is requested to shut the eyes
>
> or
>
> It is requested to shut an eye
>
> which I am in the habit of representing in the following form:
>
> It is requested to shut $\genfrac{}{}{0pt}{}{\text{the}}{\text{an}}$ eye(s).
>
> Each of the two variations has its own particular meaning, and leads us along particular paths in the interpretation of the dream.[41]

It seems clear that Fliess's "no smoking" advice had become associated with Freud's travel phobia and his father's death, and in due time would become the vehicle through which he would satisfy his own death wish. Freud proceeded to give what might be described as a very simple or prosaic interpretation to this very important dream, however. He suggested that it was a response to relatives who were disappointed at the simplicity of his father's funeral arrangments; the "shutting of the eye or eyes" meant that one should show more consideration for the dead. The latent content of this very suggestive dream is not adequately revealed, and may be one of those parts of *The Interpretation of Dreams* that Freud and Fliess both agreed to leave out for personal reasons. In Freud's letter to Fliess about this dream, however, we get a bit closer to a possible interpretation: "I must tell you about a very pretty dream I had on the night after the funeral. I found myself in a shop where there was a notice up saying: 'You are requested / to close the eyes.' "[42] Note that this dream supposedly occurred not *before* the funeral, as mentioned in *The Interpretation of Dreams*, but *after* it, and the "eye" versus "eyes" problem no longer existed.

> I recognized the place as the barber's to which I go every day. On the day of the funeral I was kept waiting, and therefore arrived at the house of mourning rather late. The family

were displeased with me, because I had arranged for the funeral to be quiet and simple, which they later agreed was the best thing. They also took my lateness in rather bad part. The phrase on the notice-board has a double meaning. It means one should do one's duty toward the dead in two senses—an apology, as though I had not done my duty and my conduct needed overlooking, and the actual duty itself. The dream was thus an outlet for the feeling of self-reproach which a death generally leaves among the survivors.[43]

Freud at this point made no attempt at a deeper analysis. Had he done so, it might have led him back to his childhood when a one-eyed doctor sewed up his face after the fall from his mother's cupboard; when after wishing his brother dead, he in fact died; and when his sexual desires for his mother led him face-to-face with his own wish for his father's death. One might note further that his father, like Freud's one-eyed childhood doctor, was also one-eyed—late in life he suffered from glaucoma in one eye. Freud obviously had some difficulty determining whose eye or eyes he was shutting and what episode of his life he was really closing.

Amid all the censorship and doubt (see note 8), it seems certain that Freud's neurosis was vitally connected with his father, whom he deeply loved and deeply hated. After all, Jacob Freud, a Talmudic scholar in his own right, taught his brilliant young son how to think and privately prepared him for his work in Sperl Gymnasium, from which he was graduated summa cum laude. Freud looked back from time to time and saw his mother's influence as the driving force behind his success: ". . . if a man has been his mother's undisputed darling he retains throughout life the triumphant feeling, the confidence in success, which not seldom brings actual success along with it."[44] However, his father taught him the extended meaning of the Word and, in rabbinical fashion, how to follow the intuitive flashes of the Holy Spirit to interpret the meaning of the Word expressed in dreams and the conscious use of the Word in everyday life. Freud learned from his father the value of free-associative thought through his interpretation of Talmudic law, and he applied this process to the interpretation of dreams: "We have attached no less importance in interpreting dreams to every shade of the form of words in which they were laid before us. And even when it happened that the text of the dream as we had it was meaningless or inadequate—

as though the effort to give a correct account of it had been unsuccessful—we have taken this defect into account as well. In short, *we have treated as Holy Writ what previous writers have regarded as an arbitrary improvisation."*[45]

Jacob Freud more than likely introduced his son to the vast Jewish mystical tradition as well. His home of "Tysmenica was the seat of one of the several dynasties of Hasidic rabbis,"[46] and his wish was to teach young Sigmund to be a great man, a great rabbi—indeed, a great teacher of humanity. Max Schur correctly suggests that nothing better reflected Jacob Freud's attitude than this inscription in Hebrew in the Bible he gave Sigmund for his thirty-fifth birthday:

My dear Son,

> It was in the seventh year of your age that the spirit of God began to move you to learning. I would say the spirit of God speaketh to you: "Read in My book; there will be opened to thee sources of knowledge and of the intellect." It is the Book of Books; it is the well that wise men have digged and from which lawgivers have drawn the waters of their knowledge.

> Thou hast seen in this Book the vision of the Almighty, thou hast heard willingly, thou hast done and hast tried to fly high upon the wings of the Holy Spirit. Since then I have preserved the same Bible. Now, on your thirty-fifth birthday I have brought it out from its retirement and I send it to you as a token of love from your old father.[47]

Five years later he was dead, and his son was "torn up by his roots," forced to look into himself and read his own unconscious, as a Talmudic scholar might read the Bible, to discover what evil had wrought the illness that afflicted him.

Freud's immediate, most disabling phobia concerned travel to Rome. While he wanted very much to go there, he found it impossible to do so for many years. Associated with Rome were his feelings for his father, his lifework as it was then emerging, and his awareness of being Jewish in a gentile world. Like so many other eastern European Jews who attempted to enter the gentile world, he felt like a pariah among the *goyim*—in a state of virtual anti-Semitic siege. While some, like Heinrich Heine, attempted to gain acceptance and success in the *goyim* culture through baptism, others, like Freud, remained steadfastly Jewish. While studying under Charcot in Paris, Freud was asked his nationality; he immediately responded "Jewish." Later, his own son would become an active Zionist; Freud remained a lifelong member of B'nai B'rith Lodge, and became one of the trustees of the Hebrew University. Although he denied any belief in God, he never denied his Jewish cultural background. He thought of himself as preserving the best of Judaism and carrying those elements over into the new scientific humanism he espoused. In December 1930, in the Hebrew translation of his preface to *Totem and Taboo*, Freud wrote: "If the question were put to him: 'Since you have abandoned all these common characteristics of your countrymen, what is there left to you that is Jewish?' he [Freud] would reply: 'A very great deal, and probably its very essence.' He could not now express that essence clearly in words; but some day, no doubt, it will become accessible to the scientific mind."[48]

Thus, Freud never abandoned what he believed to be the essence of Judaism. He hated the *goyim* world of anti-Semitism. He detested the citadel of Christian irrationalism, the Catholic church, which toward the end of his life was both his acknowledged enemy and his practical protector. Yet he desperately wanted to conquer that world on his own terms. Rome thus became his phobic symptom and symbol, and he began to see himself as a conquistador. In a letter to Fliess, just after finishing *The Interpretation of Dreams*, Freud wrote: "I am actually not at all a man of science, not an observer, not an experimenter, not a thinker. I am by temperament nothing but a *conquistador*, an adventurer, if you want to translate this term—with all the inquisitiveness, daring, and tenacity characteristic of such a man. Such people are customarily valued only if they have been successful, have really discovered something; otherwise they are thrown by the wayside."[49] Believing he had "really discovered something," and having conquered himself and his own phobia, Freud believed he could now go to Rome. He further believed that eventually he would conquer that city and dispel the irrationalism of Christianity, replacing it with his own rational scientific humanism. A lifetime of work remained to fulfill that destiny.

It is important, however, to first consider how Freud explained his conquest of his inner world. In the midst of self-analysis he had written Fliess: "Incidentally, my longing for Rome is deeply neurotic. It is connected with my schoolboy hero-worship of the Semitic Hannibal, and in fact this year I have no more reached

Rome than he did from Lake Trasimene."[50] Repeatedly, he wrestled with his "demon" within; it was Rome he sought.[51] In his "hunger for greatness,"[52] he identified with Hannibal because he was impressed, in his adolescent youth, with the way the Semitic Hannibal wreaked revenge on Rome. Describing the reason for this identification, Freud related a story his father told him when he was twelve years old:

> While I was a young man, I was walking one Saturday on a street in the village where you were born; I was handsomely dressed and wore a new fur cap. Along comes a Christian, who knocks my cap into the mud with one blow and shouts: "Jew, get off the sidewalk." "And what did you do?" "I went into the street and picked up the cap," was the calm answer.

> That did not seem heroic on the part of the big strong man, who was leading me, a little fellow, by the hand. I contrasted this situation, which did not please me, with another more in harmony with my feelings—the scene in which Hannibal's father, Hamilcar [sic] Barka made his boy swear at the domestic altar to take vengeance on the Romans. Since that time Hannibal has had a place in my phantasies.[53]

Freud interpreted his father's actions as cowardice in the face of the enemy. As he grew to manhood, he became aware of what it meant to be a member of an "alien race," and this connected with his emotional life and his career goals. Ultimately, like Hannibal, he would be called upon to conquer Rome himself.

> Then, when I came finally to understand the consequences of belonging to an alien race, and was forced by the anti-semitic sentiment among my class-mates to assume a definite attitude, the figure of the semitic commander assumed still greater proportions in my eyes. Hannibal and Rome symbolised for me as a youth the antithesis between the tenaciousness of the Jews and the organisation of the Catholic Church. The significance for our emotional life which the anti-semitic movement has since assumed helped to fix the thoughts and impressions of that earlier time. Thus the wish to get to Rome has become the cover and symbol in my dream-life for several warmly cherished wishes, for the realisation of which one might work with the perseverance and single-mindedness of the Punic general, and whose fulfilment sometimes seems as little favoured by fortune as the wish of Hannibal's life to enter Rome.[54]

Freud also identified with Johann Joachim Winckelmann, a German

Jewish archaeologist and art historian who joined the Roman Church and became a librarian to Cardinal Archinto of Rome, and with Andre Massena, who Freud had presumed to be a Jewish general under Napoleon.[55] In the end, both Massena and Hannibal were defeated and Winckelmann was murdered. Thus, for Freud, Rome became a forbidden city.

On a more neurotic level, Rome also symbolized Freud's Catholic nurse, who, by his own admission, taught him about God and hell. She was a substitute mother, one who first awakened in him his libidinal drives.[56] While his mother listened to an old peasant woman's prophecy of his potential greatness, and nurtured in him a longing for that greatness, his father chastized him for urinating in his parent's bedroom, remarking, "That boy will never amount to anything." That remark, Freud recalled, "terribly mortified my ambition, for allusions to this scene return again and again in my dreams."[57] In the end, Amalia's "golden Sigi" would conquer his Rome phobia by setting out on a lifetime mission to dominate the entire gentile world.

By the time Freud finished *The Interpretation of Dreams*, and had overcome his phobia, he had learned how to use the process of tranference. At the same time, he came to accept Fliess's theory of bisexuality, as well as his own more "feminine-side of me." As his self-analysis drew to a close, Freud recognized "gaps in the treatment" and knew that he could have gone further, but he nevertheless was satisfied with his "dung-heap."[58] He ended his treatment by breaking his transference relationship with Fliess, turning his friend into an enemy, into a *revenant* he could hate.

Freud knew that Fliess was the originator of the theory of bisexuality and that he was particularly possessive in that regard. As early as 1898, Freud had created the ambiguity that would set the stage for the eventual break. He wrote Fliess, "I seized eagerly on *your* notion of bisexuality, which I regard as the most significant for *my* subject since that of defence."[59] Just a few years later, at the breaking point with Fliess, Freud announced that his next book would be on the "Bisexuality in Man." He knew exactly what it would take to anger Fliess and used it when he felt the final break was necessary.[60] Having finally passed through his crisis and conquered his problem, Freud no longer needed Fliess: "No one can help me in what oppresses me, it is my cross, which I must bear."[61] They would not meet that Easter because he no longer needed help. A month later Freud proclaimed,

" 'Next Easter in Rome,' I should feel like a pious Jew."[62] His internal conquest was over; his lifework, the psychoanalytic movement, was about to begin.

Convinced that he had journeyed where no mortal had ever before set foot, Freud feared that the angel of death would take him before he was recognized as the authentic lawgiver who had seen "the promised land": ". . . it will be a fitting punishment for me that none of the unexplored regions of the mind in which I have been the first mortal to set foot will ever bear my name or submit to my laws. When breath threatened to fail me in the struggle I prayed the angel to desist, and that is what he has done since then."[63] Although he had walked through hell and back again, much still remained. Some two months later he remarked: "The big problems are still unsettled. It is an intellectual hell, layer upon layer of it, with everything fitfully gleaming and pulsating; and the outline of Lucifer-Amor coming into sight at the darkest centre."[64]

Fliess's differences with Freud increased until the final breaking point. When Fliess suggested that, in the end, "the thought-reader merely reads his own thoughts into other people,"[65] Freud immediately took this remark to deprive all of his work of any value. The end of his relationship with Fliess was at hand. Nevertheless, Freud's journey into the unconscious had already been accomplished. *The Interpretation of Dreams* would stand as Freud's most important achievement. He was now free to go to Rome. He wrote to Fliess about Rome on September 19, 1901.

> I ought to write to you about Rome, but it is difficult. It was an overwhelming experience for me, and, as you know, the fulfillment of a long-cherished wish. It was slightly dis-appointing, as all such fulfillments are when one has waited for them too long, but it was a high-spot in my life all the same. But, while I contemplated ancient Rome undisturbed (I could have worshipped the humble and mutilated remnant of the Temple of Minerva near the forum of Nerva), I found I could not freely enjoy the second Rome; [mediaeval as distinct from ancient and modern Rome] I was disturbed by its meaning, and, being incapable of putting out of my mind my own misery and all the other misery which I know to exist, I found almost intolerable the lie of the salvation of mankind which rears its head so proudly to heaven.
> I found the third, Italian, Rome hopeful and likeable.[66]

The Catholic church and all that it stood for disturbed Freud deeply. While he had overcome his Rome phobia, he had yet to conquer Rome.

With his phobic reaction out of the way, Freud turned to face another *goyim* problem. He believed that his promotion to "Professor Extraordinarius" had been refused for anti-Semitic reasons. In his last letter to Fliess he reported that he had made a decision: "So I made up my mind to break with my strict scruples and take appropriate steps, as others do after all. One must look somewhere for one's salvation, and the salvation I chose was the title of professor."[67] Through a former teacher and two socially influential former patients, Freud exerted counter-influence against those who had held up his promotion for some five years. In 1902 he became "Professor Extraordinarius" and finally decided to drop his "strict scruples." He had played the *goyim* game and won: "I have learned that the old world is governed by authority just as the new is governed by the dollar. I have made my first bow to authority, and am entitled to hope to reap my reward." Toward the end of his relationship with Fliess—and, indeed, the end of this part of his creative analysis—he concluded: "If I had taken those few steps three years ago I should have been appointed three years earlier, and should have spared myself much. Others are just as clever, without having to go to Rome first."[68]

When Freud advised his patients that "a great deal will be gained if we succeed in 'transforming your hysterical misery into everyday unhappiness,' which is the usual lot of mankind,"[69] he was only reminding them not to expect a complete cure from the neuroses underlying their phobias. He knew from personal experience that sublimating a neurosis was not the same as curing it; the root problem would reappear in a variety of forms throughout life. While *The Interpretation of Dreams* (1900) and *The Psychopathology of Everyday Life* (1901) clearly marked the end of Freud's Rome phobia, neither marked the end of his neurosis or eliminated the need to return again and again to self-analysis. Years later, he would stand on the Acropolis with his younger brother and feel the cold chill of the "guilt of survivors."[70] He also would be reminded of the depth of his neurosis when he fainted into the arms of his prodigy, Carl Jung, upon suspecting that Jung harbored a death wish against him.

Even though his neurosis did not dissipate, Freud's life underwent a significant shift from "splendid isolation" to leadership of a psychological movement. The field of psychoanalysis was developed out of what Freud discovered in his patients and in his own soul, and what he came to believe was universally true for humankind. Just as he had found a death wish for his father buried in the depths of his unconscious, so did he find in all people "a savage beast to whom consideration towards his own kind is something alien."[71] Psychoanalysis was thus to be ideologically structured out of his own neurosis, sublimation, and "truths," which he believed lay at the heart of his problem. His sexual etiology must be treated as "dogma," even as Adler, Jung, and others would begin to doubt it. The Oedipus complex was not a scientific hypothesis to be tested with potentially shattering critical questioning, but rather an incontrovertible religious "dogma," to be held on faith in the lawgiver, who had been to the mountaintop. Fifteen years after writing *The Interpretation of Dreams*, Freud told one of his very close disciples, Sandor Ferenczi, "We possess the truth; I am as sure of it as fifteen years ago."[72]

Freud believed he had trod a unique path, and his disciples also came to believe that. Ernest Jones insisted that Freud was the true leader, the one who had seen things that no one had seen before. Max Schur, Freud's private physician and a devoted follower, went even further, insisting that Freud's exploits "can never be duplicated."[73] To the young men attracted to this genius, Freud was a lawgiver, prophet of a new faith. In 1902, Wilhelm Stekel—who said, "I was the apostle of Freud who was my Christ!"[74]—first suggested weekly meetings for Freud and a select group of his followers. Thus, the Wednesday Society, which a few years later became the Vienna Psychoanalytic Society, was started.[75] Stekel described those early meetings: "On the first night, we spoke about the psychological implications of smoking. There was complete harmony among the five, no dissonances; we were like pioneers in a newly discovered land, and Freud was the leader. A spark seemed to jump from one mind to the other, and every evening was like a revelation. We were so enthralled by these meetings that we decided new members could be added to our circle only by unanimous consent."[76] Soon to be added were such young men as Otto Rank, Alfred Adler, Sandor Ferenczi, and Ernest Jones. Max Graf, another early participant, said of the meetings that there was

an atmosphere of the foundation of a religion in that room.

Freud himself was its new prophet who made the theretofore prevailing methods of psychological investigation appear superficial. Freud's pupils—all inspired and convinced—were his apostles. . . . However, after the first dreamy period and the unquestioning faith of the first group of apostles, the time came when the church was founded. Freud began to organize his church with great energy. He was serious and strict in the demands he made of his pupils; he permitted no deviations from his orthodox teaching. Subjectively, Freud was of course right, for that which he worked out with so much energy and sequence, and which was as yet to be defended against the opposition of the world, could not be rendered inept by hesitations, weakening, and tasteless ornamentations. Good-hearted and considerate though he was in private life, Freud was hard and relentless in the presentation of his ideas.[77]

As a prophet, Freud had discoverd new truths about humanity, and he needed followers who would preach and propagate his ideas, not test them for their scientific validity. Within a few decades, Freud had built a loyal following around an inner circle especially chosen to guide the movement. He gave those in his inner circle special rings to signify their roles within the movement. As it emerged, the movement was not without its human loss, the list of suicides being remarkable, if not revealing. Federn, Stekel, Tausk, and Silberer were among the more well-known followers who took their own lives; the large number of relatively unknown analysts who also committed suicide included Karin Stephen, Eugenia Sokolnicka, Tatiana Rosenthal, Karl Schrötter, Monroe Meyer, Martin Peck, Max Kahane, and Johann Honnegger. Writing to Jung about the situation, Freud said, "I think we wear out quite a few men."[78]

The inner circle was enlarged to sixteen members, and many other analysts became lifelong devoted followers. However, an increasing number of individuals defected and adopted what to Freud were heretical positions. Eric Fromm has suggested (commenting on the table of contents of Ernest Jones's biography of Freud) that the movement seemed more political or religious than scientific.[79] In the many battles and skirmishes that ensued, Alfred Adler discovered and developed his notion of an inferiority complex; Carl Jung structured his own gnostic beliefs; and Otto Rank held fast to his Schopenhauer-based belief that in the end all is illusion. Others abandoned the sexual etiology Freud insisted

211

upon, and even went so far as to eliminate the genetic basis of psychoanalysis—a move to make the current social environment the most important one.

For Freud, perhaps the most bitter defection was Jung's. Freud had argued intensely against his Jewish followers in Vienna who had resisted making Carl Jung, a Swiss Gentile, the "Crown Prince" of the psychoanalytic movement. Freud had insisted that Jung's leadership was absolutely essential if the movement was ever to conquer the gentile world and be freed of the stigma of being "Jewish." Yet, both Freud and his close Jewish followers from Vienna knew that in method as well as in substantial content, the movement was essentially Jewish in origin.[80] Freud prevailed, but no sooner had he installed the new "Crown Prince" than it became apparent that Jung had his own mystical faith with which he was intent on replacing Christianity. His loss to Freud's movement was serious but ultimately not disabling.

While the psychoanalytic movement survived both its friends and its enemies, it was all too clear that in Freud's mind the defections meant far more than mere intellectual differences. Freud reacted emotionally, calling Stekel a "pig," Adler a "pygmy" and a "Jew-boy," and Jung simply "crazy." The supposedly passionless analytic "science" of psychoanalysis was fraught with passion, and the same intense reaction that had characterized earlier breaks with Breuer and Fliess was repeated again and again. Freud had analyzed himself as a user of people, and he continued to require "intimate friends and hated enemies" to fill his emotional life. He never stopped turning his friends into hated enemies, and then into *revenants*, who in the end were replaceable.

The psychoanalytic movement as a religious movement passed through what Graf clearly recognized as a heretical period: "Within the space of a few years I lived through the whole development of church history; from the first sermons to a small group of apostles, to the strife between Arius and Athanasius." Hanns Sachs cast it in personal terms, saying that his faith in the movement "... burned with a steady and all-consuming flame. Like every other faith, it imposed on the life of the believer severe restrictions and regulations. Everything from the small details of everyday routine to the most momentous decisions was shaped by its dictation."[81] Freud had established a new faith, destined to change humanity's perception of itself, and as far as he was concerned it required total discipline in thought and action on the part of his followers.

Early on, followers like Eugen Bleuler had mistakenly assumed that the psychoanalytic movement was a scientific movement wherein open, critical analysis of the various propositions implicit in the movement might occur. Freud, however, made it very clear in his essay "*On the History of the Psycho-Analytic Movement*" (1914), that it was *his* movement, and it needed protection from imposters and deviants.[82] Bleuler put his finger on a very real problem when he told Freud:

> Scientifically, . . . I still do not understand why for you it is so important that the whole edifice [of psychoanalysis] should be accepted. But I remember I told you once that no matter how great your scientific accomplishments are, psychologically you impress me as an artist. From this point of view it is understandable that you do not want your art product to be destroyed. In art we have a unit which cannot be torn apart. In science you made a great discovery which has to stay. How much of what is loosely connected with it will survive is not important.[83]

It is interesting to note that the only international award Freud received during his lifetime was the Goethe Prize, in 1930, for his "creative work . . . worthy of an honour dedicated to Goethe's memory."[84] He readily accepted the award, not only out of respect for Goethe, who was a lifelong favorite, but because he knew all along that artists like Sophocles, Shakespeare, Dostoyevski, and Goethe were nearer to the heart from whence he spoke than any of the traditional men of science. Creative writers, Freud said, are "valuable allies and their evidence is to be prized highly, for they are apt to know a whole host of things between heaven and earth of which our philosophy has not yet let us dream. In their knowledge of the mind they are far in advance of us everyday people, for they draw upon sources which we have not yet opened up for science."[85] He believed that science might one day catch up.

Freud was doing some things that scientists were reluctant to do. Even though he was trained as a laboratory scientist, and spent over half of his career in that area, when he took up self-analysis and entered his fantasy world, he adopted by necessity the method of the poet and the Talmudic scholar—in fact, the method of free association.[86] In interpreting dreams or unconscious thought through the process of free association, it is ultimately the dreamer alone who can discover and verify the "real" meaning of the dream. This subjective insight, this "ah-ha" experience, while perhaps valid for the individual dreamer, is nonetheless not publicly verifiable or falsifiable.[87] The method of free association, then, which worked so well in leading Freud and the poets into the underworld, was not readily amenable to empirical scientific verification. It required the mind to abandon logical reflection, and thus allow thoughts to spontaneously emerge—in short, to follow the dream. This intersubjective method is hermeneutically a powerful one, very useful in understanding literary and poetic truth. But taken alone, unchecked by publicly verifiable empirical tests, it more often than not makes bad history.

While Freud considered himself a scientist akin to Darwin, he also saw himself as the creator of a new science, one that would effect the crossover from the world of the poetic artist to that of the empirical scientist, from the unconscious to the conscious. "Nature" would in this sense finally be "one." Ultimately, Freud's method of following the dream was, as Bleuler had suspected, that of the artist, creating a metaphysical dream to fulfill a wish. The realm of the unconscious was not the realm of publicly verifiable, rationalistic science, where understanding led to belief, but rather the Augustinian world of faith, where it was necessary to believe in order to understand.[88]

Freud often spoke of psychoanalysis as a form of reeducating the individual at a deeper level, lifting the conscious mind to yet another, higher level. This reeducation required the adoption of a certain set of beliefs and values about human nature, as well as about civilization itself, some of which Freud described in *Totem and Taboo* (1913). He argued that all civilization began with the primal crime, the murder of the father by the sons, who wished to have sexual relations with their mother. Thus, at the origin of culture, he found the same problem that existed in his own soul, the one that lay at the very heart of his neurosis: all the artifacts of civilization, its sciences, arts, philosophies, and religions, were a consequence of sexual repression.

For Freud, religion itself was a compulsive neurosis. Reflecting on *Totem and Taboo* in *Moses and Monotheism* (1939), Freud said: "From then on [1912] I have never doubted that religious phenomena are to be understood only on the model of the neurotic symptoms of the individual, which are so familiar to us, as a return of long-forgotten important happenings in the primeval history of the human family, that they owe their obsessive character to that very origin and therefore derive their effect on mankind from the historical truth they contain."[89] Throughout *Totem and Taboo*, in sublimated form, runs a thinly veiled chronicle of Freud's own neurosis, his own death wishes, his own view of "guilt of the survivors," as well as his own view of morality and its origins. In creating this work, Freud had relied on such sources as Sir James Frazer's *The Golden Bough* and William Robertson Smith's *Lectures on the Religion of the Semites;* but the most important source was clearly his own book *The Interpretation of Dreams.*

While many anthropologists took issue with *Totem and Taboo*, and set out to prove scientifically that there was no solid empirical evidence to indicate that civilization or religion originated in the way he described, for the most part they missed the point. Freud was not saying that empirically this is the way it happened; rather, he was saying that artistically or metaphorically—or indeed, psychoanalytically—this is the way it *must* have happened. Empirical verification is not possible in much of the prehistory of civilization, just as it is not possible in much of the prehistory of the individual's unconscious. Nevertheless, for Freud, psychoanalysis filled in the blanks in both cases.

When Freud gave up the seduction theory and adopted the fantasy theory to understand neurosis, he also forfeited the notion of the empirical validation of the history of the individual, as well as the origin of civilization itself. Emprical validation was not necessary to artistically capture the meaning of a dream. Similarly, psychoanalytic history may be heuristically interesting, but without the empirical canon of "what actually happened," it can only turn out to be bad history. In following the dream, fiction may replace fact; the beautiful, the aesthetically pleasing, takes precedence over the more ragged empirical test.[90] Many cultural anthropologists, in reviewing *Totem and Taboo*, felt that they had effectively proven Freud wrong; late in life, however, while writing *Moses and Monotheism*, Freud found his theories to be as "true as ever." Into his overarching model he swept both Judaism and Christianity. He argued that Christians, who in their Mass drink Christ's blood and eat his flesh, are simply assuaging what was originally the primal crime for both Jew and Christian alike. Freud ended his metaphysical journey of reinterpretation of the Old Testament by suggesting that, "In the beginning was the deed."[91]

Shortly after completing *Totem and Taboo*, Freud again went to Rome, to sit for three weeks at the feet of Michelangelo's Moses. After careful study, he concluded that Michelangelo had created a new image of Moses, contrary to the old biblical notion of a Moses who had lost his temper and broken the tablets. Michelangelo's Moses, in Freud's view, had sublimated his anger in the service of a cause. "Michelangelo has placed a different Moses on the tomb of the Pope, one superior to the historical or traditional Moses," a lawgiver who met uncomprehending opposition by sublimating his anger: "In this way he has added something new and more than human to the figure of Moses; so that the giant frame with its tremendous physical power becomes only a concrete expression of the highest mental achievement that is possible in a man, that of struggling successfully against an inward passion for the sake of a cause to which he has devoted himself."[92]

Freud, too, had devoted himself to such a cause—the psychoanalytic movement. The figure with whom he now identified was not Hannibal but the new Moses. Freud, with his new faith, would lead the children of Israel, and of all the civilized world, out of bondage.[93] His new faith incorporated the ancient Hebraic doctrine of original sin, which Christianity had adopted; it was, in fact, the bedrock, the "dogma," as Freud put it, upon which he built his faith. During self-analysis he had discovered the source of "all morality" in the structure of guilt; to him, God was merely "an infantile wish," and religion itself but a variant of an obsessional neurosis.[94] Freud knew from experience that neither the individual nor civilization was easily cured, that humankind had a long way to go before it could be freed—if, indeed, it ever would be—from this bondage of neurosis. Against the irrationality of religion he posed his own God of Reason.

> Our God, Λόγος [Logos], will fulfil whichever of these wishes nature outside us allows, but he will do it very gradually, only in the unforeseeable future, and for a new generation of men. He promises no compensation for us, who suffer grievously from life. On the way to this distant goal your religious doctrines will have to be discarded, no matter whether the first attempts fail, or whether the first substitutes prove to be untenable. You know why: in the long run nothing

can withstand reason and experience, and the contradiction which religion offers to both is all too palpable.[95]

Freud insisted that the God of his science would ultimately conquer the obsessional neurosis on which religion depended. He confidently wrote: "our science is no illusion. But an illusion it would be to suppose that what science cannot give us we can get elsewhere."[96]

In his last work, *Moses and Monotheism*, Freud again turned to religion as an obsessional neurosis, reaffirming much of his faith expressed earlier in *Totem and Taboo* and *The Future of an Illusion*.[97] In *Moses and Monotheism*, Freud rewrote biblical history to fit the overall psychoanalytic beliefs he had propounded over the years, interpreting Moses as an Egyptian who brought monotheism to the Jewish people, led them out of bondage, and was shortly thereafter murdered by them. The expiation of guilt for the killing of the primal father was still not assuaged. Nevertheless, the extreme "instinctual renunciation" of the Jewish people led them to "ethical heights that had remained inaccessible to the other people of antiquity." That renunciation, according to Freud, was the source of their ability to accept monotheism: "The origin, however, of this ethics in feelings of guilt, due to the repressed hostility to God, cannot be gainsaid. It bears the characteristic of being never concluded and never able to be concluded with which we are familiar in the reaction-formations of obsessional neurosis."[98] Christianity thus emerged, at least in Freud's view, as a reaction formation to ease the heavy guilt acquired by the higher ethical development of Jewish monotheism. While Christianity also tended, in theory, to be monotheistic, its God the Father, God the Son, and God the Holy Ghost made it polytheistic and therefore less ethically demanding. To Freud, Christianity was not only a retrograde religion, but a "Son" religion in which God the Son had been murdered to pay for the original murder of God the Father. Christians, according to Freud, disliked Jews, not only because Jews believed themselves to be the chosen people of God, with a higher sense of ethics, but also because Christians saw Jews as Christ-killers, who would "not admit that they killed God, whereas we do and are cleansed from the guilt of it."[99]

Christian polytheism, with its promise of salvation, was a step backward for Freud in the great chain of religious progress.

A great step forward he believed, would come from the mono-theistic world of Judaism, when the world would leave behind the polytheistic belief system of Christianity and step into the God-free world of psychoanalytic "science." Such was Freud's mission. Ultimately, living or dead, he would conquer Christianity and, in the end, save the Jewish people.[100] Freud, the Moses of the new law, would lead both Jew and Gentile out of the land of their irrational neuroses and into the promised land of science and reason. Judaism and Christianity thus would fall into their proper places, each becoming the dialectical stepping-stone for the next great religious synthesis of the world.

As empirically oriented biblical scholars turned the pages of *Moses and Monotheism*, they found embarrassingly few verifiable "truths." Like the anthropologists before them who came away from *Totem and Taboo* empty-handed, they also had missed the point. When intuitive insight is used to light the path of the unconscious or the prehistoric past, that past takes on a logic all its own, one that is confirmed not by an external world of raw data but rather by internal flashes of aesthetic truth. While some biblical scholars attempted to prove Freud wrong in claiming that Moses was an "Egyptian," other scholars, such as George Steiner, suggested that Freud knew that claim to be false and was frantically trying to shift the heavy burden of monotheism from his people, thereby saving them from the fiery holocaust he sensed was coming.[101]

It is equally plausible that, given the context of Freud's overall life, he made Moses an Egyptian because he was following his own dream—for him, Moses simply had to be an Egyptian, not a Jew, who led the children of Israel out of bondage. That being the case, it would then be Sigmund Freud, the Jew, who would lead both Christians and Jews out of the irrationalism of their obsessional neuroses and into the promised land of scientific humanism. He had become the rabbi of the West, fulfilling both his father's and his mother's dreams—as well as the old peasant woman's vision of his greatness.

Notes

1. Henri F. Ellenberger uses this term in *The Discovery of the Unconscious* (New York: Basic Books, 1970).

2. Marie Bonaparte, Anna Freud, and Ernst Kris, eds., *The Origins*

of *Psychoanalysis: Sigmund Freud. Letters, Drafts and Notes to Wilhelm Fliess, 1887–1902* (New York: Doubleday Books, 1957), p. 324.

3. Ibid., p. 47.

4. Carl E. Schorske suggests in his *Fin-De-Siecle Vienna: Politics and Culture* (New York: Alfred A. Knopf, 1980), pp. 181–203, that Freud moved away from politics because of anti-Semitism; and further, that much of the political life of Vienna figured significantly in Freud's own neurosis.

5. See Max Schur, *Freud: Living and Dying* (New York: International Universities Press, 1972), p. 41.

6. For a discussion of the instance of these spells, see Ernest Jones, *The Life and Work of Sigmund Freud*, 3 vols. (New York: Basic Books, 1953, 1955, 1957); see also Paul Roazen, *Freud and His Followers* (New York: Alfred A. Knopf, 1975).

7. Bonaparte et al., *Origins of Psychoanalysis*, p. 173.

8. On a number of occasions Freud destroyed his personal papers to throw his future biographers off the track: ". . . let them worry, we have no desire to make it too easy for them. . . . I am already looking forward to seeing them go astray" (quoted in Edward Rothstein, "The Scar of Sigmund Freud," *New York Review* [Oct. 9, 1980]: 17). Under the circumstances, my analysis is tentative, based solely on documents now available. Fliess's letters to Freud, written during Freud's analysis, have never been found and are assumed destroyed. Freud's letters to Fliess were found by Marie Bonaparte and, over Freud's objection, were preserved. Many of these letters, carefully censored, are published in *The Origins of Psychoanalysis*. There are, however, over one hundred letters remaining to be published, and it has been publicly announced that this will occur in the near future. My analysis, then, is precariously based on such censored primary source material as Bonaparte et al.'s *The Origins of Psychoanalysis*, Freud's *The Interpretation of Dreams*, and other of his translated works, as well as important secondary sources such as Erich Fromm's *Sigmund Freud's Mission* (New York: Harper and Brothers Co., 1959); Alexander Grinstein's *On Sigmund Freud's Dreams* (Detroit: Wayne State University Press, 1968); David Bakan's *Sigmund Freud and the Jewish Mystical Tradition* (New York: Schocken Books, 1969); Henri F. Ellenberger's *The Discovery of the Unconscious*; Ronald W. Clark's *Freud the Man and the Cause* (New York: Random House, 1980); Frank J. Sulloway's *Freud, Biologist of the Mind* (New York: Basic Books, 1979); Ernest Jones's *The Life and Work of Sigmund Freud*; Paul Roazen's *Freud and His Followers*; and Max Schur's *Freud: Living and Dying*. The latter was particularly important, not only because it is a substantial work, but also because Schur had the opportunity to read all the Fliess correspondence. He treats Freud's relationship with Fliess very much as one of patient and analyst. It is likely, however, that no clear critique of Freud's analysis may ever be achieved, since

Freud saved many of his thoughts for the verbal "congresses" and Fliess and Freud both heavily censored *The Interpretation of Dreams* for personal reasons.

9. See Schur, *Freud: Living and Dying*, pp. 77–79.

10. Bonaparte et al., *Origins of Psychoanalysis*, p. 320.

11. See Philip Rieff, ed., *Sigmund Freud: Early Psychoanalytic Writings* (New York: Collier Books, 1963).

12. Bonaparte et al., *Origins of Psychoanalysis*, pp. 218–19.

13. The claim has been made in Jeffrey Masson, *The Assault on Truth* (New York: Farrar, Straus and Giroux, 1984), that Freud abandoned the seduction theory because of a lack of courage in the face of political and social pressure. Masson points to Freud's highly questionable behavior involving the Emma Eckstein case. Freud's exhibition of cowardice and crude attempts to protect Fliess in that case do not, however, in any way prove that this was the reason for Freud's abandonment of the seduction theory. Max Schur, in *Freud: Living and Dying*, has shown the relationship of this case to Freud's famous dream about "Irma's injection," and his discussion is most persuasive. Some of the letters which Masson published, which begin "Dearest Wilhelm," reflect the passionate transference relationship that existed between the two men. Freud was clearly undergoing a state of analysis at the time. Masson proved, as so many others have, that Freud was authoritarian and held his ideas in a most dogmatic, unscientific manner. In general, Schur's treatment of this crucial period in the development of psychoanalysis is by far the best. Given what little actual, new, hard evidence has emerged amid the recent controversy surrounding the seduction theory, Freud's explanation for his abandonment of the theory and Schur's interpretation of the events surrounding those explanations still remain most convincing.

14. There is some doubt as to the exact day. Some evidence seems to suggest that Freud's mother may have changed the date so that her first-born son could celebrate his birthday in more pleasant weather. However, his birth certificate indicates that he was born in May 1856, while other reports seem to indicate March 1856.

15. Renée Gicklhorn, "The Freiberg Period of the Freud Family," *Journal of the History of Medicine and Allied Sciences* 24(Jan. 1969): 38.

16. There are some indications from an 1852 document that Freud's father may have been involved with Rebecca, age thirty-two, after the death of his first wife and before his marriage to Freud's mother. The records are scanty, and many commentators suspect a family secret. See Renée Gicklhorn, "The Freiberg Period of the Freud Family," p. 41.

17. Martin Freud, *Sigmund Freud: Man and Father* (New York: Vanguard Press, 1958), p. 11.

18. John Murray Cuddihy, in *The Ordeal of Civility* (New York:

Basic Books, 1974), makes this point but goes on to explain virtually all of Freud's ideas, as well as other Jewish contributions to Western thought, in terms of this eastern European phenomena. While much of what Cuddihy suggests is heuristically interesting and in some cases very plausible, he ultimately overdraws the case almost to grotesque proportions. There can be little doubt, however, that the infusion of eastern European Jewry into the emerging liberal secularized West at the end of the nineteenth century resulted in a tremendous release of Jewish talent and intelligence for cultural production. Without it the Western world today would be very different and much the poorer. The varieties of directions that talent took tended to be functionally creative and reformist in spirit. Edmund Wilson put it well when, after describing how "nobody but a Jew such as Marx could have fought so uncompromisingly for the victory of the dispossessed classes," went on to say:

> The great Jewish minds of these first generations that had been liberated from the closed Judaic world, still remembered the mediaeval captivity, and they were likely to present themselves as champions of other social groups or doctrines which had not been freed or vindicated yet. ... so Einstein became preoccupied with the few unemphasized anomalies in the well-operating system of Newton and made them the cornerstone that the builder had rejected on which to build a new system that should shake the authority of the old. So Lassalle took up the cause of feminism at a time when German women were largely at the mercy of their fathers and their husbands; and so Proust transferred from a persecuted race to the artist and the homosexual, both that race's tragic fate in society and its inner conviction of moral superiority. [And so did Freud see] the vital importance of those sexual impulses that civilization had outlawed or that puritanism had tried to suppress, and forced psychiatric science to take account of them.

Wilson is quoted in Ronald W. Clark, *Freud: The Man and the Cause* (New York: Random House, 1980), pp. 242–43.

19. Ruth Landes and Mark Zborowski, "Hypotheses Concerning the Eastern European Jewish Family," *Psychiatry* 13(Aug. 1950): 453, 454. For further discussion see Mark Zborowski and Elizabeth Herzog, *Life Is with People* (New York: International Universities Press, 1952); see also Mark Zborowski, "The Children of the Covenant," *Social Forces* 29(May 1951): 351–64. For more material on *shtetl* life see Moshe Decter, "The Study of Man," *Commentary* 13(Jan.–June 1952): 600–604; see also Theodore Bienenstok, "Antiauthoritarian Attitudes in the Eastern Shtetl Community," *American Journal of Sociology* 59(July–May 1951–52): 150–58, and "Social Life in the East European Jewish Shtetl Community," *Southwestern Journal of Anthropology* 6(1950): 238–54.

20. Gicklhorn, "The Freiberg Period of the Freud Family," p. 42.

21. While Freud eventually did attain his "rightful," traditional place in the family circle, it was not without some resentment on the

part of the children who followed. See, for example, Anna Freud Bernays, "My Brother, Sigmund Freud," *American Mercury* 2(201, Sept. 1940).

22. Quoted in Fromm, *Sigmund Freud's Mission*, p. 17.

23. Siegfried Bernfeld and Suzanne Cassirer Bernfeld, "Freud's Early Childhood," *Bulletin of the Menninger Clinic* 7(1943): 110.

24. Bonaparte et al., *Origins of Psychoanalysis*, p. 230.

25. This cut left a life-long scar, both physically and psychologically. See Edward Rothstein, "The Scar of Sigmund Freud," *New York Review* (Oct. 9, 1980): 16.

26. Bonaparte et al., *Origins of Psychoanalysis*, pp. 225–26.

27. See James Strachey, ed., "The Psychopathology of Everyday Life," *The Standard Edition of the Complete Psychological Works of Sigmund Freud*, 24 vols. (London: Hogarth Press, 1960), 6:51.

28. Bonaparte et al., *Origins of Psychoanalysis*, p. 226.

29. Ibid., p. 214.

30. Ibid., p. 209.

31. Ibid., p. 223 (emphasis added).

32. Ibid., p. 222.

33. See, for example, Freud, *Interpretation of Dreams*, pp. 213, 331, 385, 387, 388, 407.

34. Ibid., p. 385. What should not go unnoticed here is that not only did Brutus kill Julius Caesar, but Caesar's first name was the same as that of Freud's dead brother, whom he had wished dead and who did die.

35. This idea begins to appear in *The Interpretation of Dreams* when Freud associates Pauline, the niece he treated so shockingly as a childhood playmate, with Fleiss's daughter Pauline. See ibid., p. 388.

36. Freud, *Interpretation of Dreams*, p. 331.

37. Freud's conception of love was always neurotic, for which Erich Fromm criticizes him in *The Art of Loving* (New York: Bantam Books, 1963).

38. See Schur, *Freud: Living and Dying*.

39. Clark, *Freud: The Man and the Cause*, p. 284. While Schur and others point to Freud's cigar smoking as an addiction, the figure of twenty a day does seem very high. The smoking problem appears related to his own death wish.

40. See Schur, *Freud: Living and Dying*, p. 529.

41. Freud, *Interpretation of Dreams*, p. 295.

42. Bonaparte et al., *Origins of Psychoanalysis*, p. 174.

43. Ibid.

44. Quoted in Clark, *Freud: The Man and the Cause*, p. 3.

45. Quoted in Bakan, *Sigmund Freud and the Jewish Mystical Tradition*, p. 251 (emphasis added). For an insightful discussion of the Jewish origins of free association as a technique and of psychoanalysis itself, see ibid., pp. 246–69; see also Ernst Simon, "Sigmund Freud, the Jew,"

in Robert Weltsch, ed., *Year Book II* (London: East and West Library, published for the Leo Baeck Institute of Jews from Germany, 1957).

46. Schur, *Freud: Living and Dying*, p. 26.

47. Quoted in ibid., p. 24.

48. James Strachey, ed. *The Complete Psychological Works of Sigmund Freud*, 13:xv.

49. Quoted in Schur, *Freud: Living and Dying*, p. 201.

50. Bonaparte et al., *Origins of Psychoanalysis*, pp. 239–40.

51. See ibid., pp. 239, 272, 282, 283, 319.

52. Freud, *Interpretation of Dreams*, p. 161.

53. Ibid., p. 165. Freud made a slip of the pen in the first edition of *The Interpretation of Dreams* by substituting the name Hasdrubal, Hannibal's brother, for Hamilcar, Hannibal's father. He described this slip in rather superficial, if not misleading, terms in *The Psychopathology of Everyday Life*, pp. 219–20. What Freud failed to report was that Hasdrubal was beheaded in one of Hannibal's battles for Rome, and his head was served on a platter to Hannibal. When writing *The Interpretation of Dreams*, Freud still unconsciously wished his father dead for his slackness in facing up to the *goyim*. See Grinstein, *On Sigmund Freud's Dreams*, p. 82.

54. Ibid., pp. 164–65. Note that while Freud was writing this, his promotion was being held up for anti-Semitic reasons.

55. Massena's Jewish origins are in doubt. See Grinstein, *On Sigmund Freud's Dreams*, p. 88.

56. Ibid., p. 91.

57. Freud, *Interpretation of Dreams*, p. 182.

58. Bonaparte et al., *Origins of Psychoanalysis*, pp. 320, 284.

59. Ibid., p. 245 (emphasis added).

60. For the author who first developed this idea, see Edith Buxbaum, "Freud's Dream Interpretation in the Light of His Letters to Fleiss," *Bulletin of the Menninger Clinic* 15(Nov. 1951): 197–212. For the relevant letters see Bonaparte et al., *Origins of Psychoanalysis*, pp. 334–37.

61. Bonaparte et al., *Origins of Psychoanalysis*, p. 316.

62. Ibid., p. 319. The editors noted that "at the end of the Passover service Jews wish each other: 'Next year in Jerusalem!' " See ibid., note 388. In Freud's case Rome had replaced Jerusalem.

63. Ibid., p. 320.

64. Ibid., p. 324.

65. Ibid., p. 335.

66. Ibid., p. 336.

67. Ibid., p. 343.

68. Ibid., p. 345.

69. Quoted in Clarence Karier, *Man, Society, and Education* (Glenview, Ill.: Scott, Foresman and Co., 1967), p. 161.

70. See Sigmund Freud, "A Disturbance of Memory on the Acropolis,"

in James Strachey, *Sigmund Freud: Collected Papers* (London: Hogarth Press, 1950), 5:302–12.

71. Sigmund Freud, *Civilization and Its Discontents*, James Strachey, trans. and ed. (New York: W. W. Norton and Co., 1962), p. 59.

72. Jones, *Life and Works of Sigmund Freud*, 2:148.

73. Schur, *Freud: Living and Dying*, p. 221.

74. Quoted in Clark, *Freud: The Man and the Cause*, p. 213.

75. Rothstein, "The Scar of Sigmund Freud," p. 14.

76. Clark, *Freud: The Man and the Cause*, p. 213.

77. Quoted in ibid., pp. 217–18.

78. Rothstein, "The Scar of Sigmund Freud," p. 14.

79. See Fromm, *Sigmund Freud's Mission*, p. 83.

80. See, for example, Clark's discussion in *Freud: The Man and the Cause*, pp. 123, 243.

81. Both passages quoted in ibid., p. 312.

82. Ibid., p. 292.

83. Ibid., p. 294.

84. See Strachey, *Standard Edition of the Complete Psychological Works*, 21:206–14. Freud maintained a powerful style of writing throughout his career. In attempting to persuade his readers he would invariably introduce them to controversial and questionable topics by first discussing how outlandish the particular idea might appear to the reader; a few pages later, he would present his very best arguments as to why the reader should accept the questionable idea. It was a most effective approach.

85. Clark, *Freud: The Man and the Cause*, p. 116.

86. While not all of the work of the Talmudic scholar is best characterized as free association—indeed, much of it is very tight authoritative reasoning—there remains a significant portion of the process that is based on free associative conceptualizing.

87. There has been an extensive debate in and around this issue. See, for example, Karl R. Popper, *Conjectures and Refutations* (New York: Harper and Row, 1962). See also Hans J. Eysenck, *The Effects of Psychotherapy* (New York: International Science Press, 1966); and Adolf Grünbaum, "Is Psychoanalytic Theory Pseudo-scientific by Karl Popper's Criterion of Demarcation?" *American Philosophical Quarterly* 16(Apr. 1979): 131–41. See also Jane Flax, "Psychoanalysis and the Philosophy of Science: Critique or Resistance?" *Journal of Philosophy* 78(Oct. 1981): 561–69; and Edward Erwin, "The Truth About Psychoanalysis," ibid., pp. 549–60. For an attempt at evaluating psychotherapeutic practice, see Leslie Prioleau, Martha Murdock, and Nathan Brody, "An Analysis of Psychotherapy Versus Placebo Studies," *Behavioral and Brain Sciences* 6(1983): 275–310. For an attempt to publicly verify what takes place in a therapeutic session, see Robert E. Pittenger, *The First Five Minutes* (New York: Paul Martineau, 1960). While some attempts to verify/falsify psychoanalysis have reconstructed and distorted Freud's psychology into

a form of social behaviorism, others, such as Grünbaum and Popper, clearly misrepresent vital aspects of Freud's theory, as Flax points out. She correctly notes that psychoanalytic method and the knowledge derived therefrom do challenge, if not undercut, many of our traditional notions of science. Nevertheless, while the poetic truths derived from the subjective states of a patient engaged in a tranference relationship with an analyst may be true, they still remain, as a whole, very much outside the traditional canons by which certain kinds of knowledge are "scientifically" verified or falsified.

88. We are reminded of the oft-repeated claim by those who have been analyzed and have adopted the canon of that particular faith, namely, that others cannot readily understand psychoanalysis until they have been analyzed, or in other words, have adopted that faith.

89. Sigmund Freud, *Moses and Monotheism* (New York: Vintage Books, 1967), p. 71.

90. See, for example, David E. Stannard, *Shrinking History: On Freud and the Failure of Psychohistory* (New York: Oxford University Press, 1980).

91. Sigmund Freud, *Totem and Taboo* (New York: Vintage Books, 1946), p. 207.

92. Sigmund Freud, "The Moses of Michelangelo," in Ernest Jones, ed., *Sigmund Freud: Collected Papers* (London: Hogarth Press, 1956), 4:283.

93. Symbolically, then it is understandable how and why Freud decorated the desk in his study with statuary of the ancient gods.

94. See Sigmund Freud, *The Future of an Illusion* (New York: Anchor Books, 1964); see also *Totem and Taboo.*

95. Freud, *Future of an Illusion*, pp. 88–89.

96. Ibid., p. 92.

97. As Freud put it in *Moses and Monotheism*, "That conviction I acquired a quarter of a century ago, when I wrote my book on *Totem and Taboo* (in 1912), and it has only become stronger since" (p. 71). Schur, in *Freud: Living and Dying*, had difficulty toward the end trying to explain why, as late as 1939, Freud still held on to the recapitulation theory. He misses the point here. For Freud, the idea of recapitulation was part of his overall metaphysical model, built by following the dream. It did not need the verification of the empirical world; indeed, it fit the overall model beautifully, and intuitively one knew it was true. For an example of this exchange of fantasy for reality, see Freud, *Moses and Monotheism*, p. 111.

98. Freud, *Moses and Monotheism*, p. 173.

99. Ibid., p. 176.

100. For a similar interpretation, see Simon, "Sigmund Freud, the Jew," pp. 270–305.

101. See George Steiner, *In Bluebeard's Castle* (New Haven: Yale University Press, 1971), pp. 38–39.

7

ALFRED ADLER [1870–1937]

Social Interest as Religion

In the early morning hours of a day in late May 1937, Alfred Adler lay prostrate on a cobblestone street in Aberdeen, Scotland, stricken by a fatal heart attack. When, very much moved by the news, Arnold Zweig reported Adler's death to Sigmund Freud, the latter is said to have replied: "I don't understand your sympathy for Adler. For a Jew boy out of a Viennese suburb a death in Aberdeen is an unheard-of career in itself and a proof of how far he had got on. The world really rewarded him richly for his service in having contradicted psychoanalysis."[1] For twenty-six years, Freud had nurtured a bitter hatred for Alfred Adler, cringing with each report of his former pupil's success. Why this was so is a complicated issue, owing to the existential circumstances and the characters and personalities of the people involved.

Adler was noteworthy on Freud's long list of friends who became his enemies. He was the first to break ranks from the Wednesday Society (later the Vienna Psychoanalytic Society) and the first to create a counter-movement. From 1902, when the Wednesday Society was formed, until 1911, when the final break with Freud came, Adler was an active, regular participant in Freud's inner circle. In the context of those weekly discussions, however, he gradually tested and shaped his own views about psychology.[2] Particularly distressing for Freud was his belief that Adler not only was creating a complete system of character formation, something Freud thought impossible at the time, but that he seemed to be "creating" his system from many of Freud's constructs, loosely altering the terminology and simply watering down some of his teacher's most important ideas. The latter deceit moved Freud to write the "History of the Psychoanalytic Movement," and in it to proclaim to the world that "psychoanalysis is my creation."[3] Freud never rested easy with what his students did with his "creation." Likening them to dogs, he complained, "They take a bone from the table, and chew it independently in a corner. But it is my bone!"[4]

Adler's deviations were bitterly resented by Freud, who repeatedly referred to his once highly respected student as a "malicious paranoiac."[5] As time went on, Freud described Adler as a shallow thinker who constantly reduced psychoanalysis to the "commonsense" simplicity of the man in the street. Although Adler would not have been insulted by such a remark, Freud meant it disparagingly. Reflecting on nine years of association with Adler, Freud regretfully concluded, "I have made a pygmy great."[6] The intensity of his reaction is reminiscent of earlier conflicts with Josef Breuer and Wilhelm Fliess. In fact, Freud himself made the association. Shortly before Adler's final break, he wrote to Carl Jung: "It is getting really bad with Adler. You see a resemblance to Bleuler; in me he awakens the memory of Fliess, but an octave lower. The same paranoia." And a few days later: "I am very glad that you see Adler as I do. The only reason the affair upsets me so much is that it has opened up the wounds of the Fliess affair. It was the same feeling that disturbed the peace I otherwise enjoyed during my work on paranoia; this time I am not sure to what extent I have been able to exclude my own complexes, and shall be glad to accept criticism."[7]

At this point one cannot help but be reminded of the nature of Freud's "own complexes" and of his analysis as to how his own childhood problems ultimately affected his adult relationships.[8] Freud had clearly described how his death wish for his brother Julius, as well as his struggle for dominance with his nephew, John, would be reenacted over and over again with respect to any future close friends, turning them into enemies. They would all become ghostly figures, or *revenants*, out of his past. As Freud put it, "In a certain sense all my friends are incarnations of this first figure, 'which early appeared to my blurred sight'; they are all *revenants*."[9] Breuer had become a *revenant*, while Fliess was just about to become one. The time when Adler and then Jung would join Freud's menagerie of ghostly figures remained in the not-too-distant future. While Freud's analysis of his attitude toward friends and foes is helpful in explaining the intensity of the break with Adler, it is so only in a partial sense. The other aspects of this dynamic situation are to be found in Adler's own personal history, in his character, and in the vast differences in fundamental ideas, values, and beliefs that existed between the two men. Alfred Adler's personality, life history, life-style, and fundamental values were all the near opposite of Freud's.

The very style of cognition to which Freud and Adler each adhered was quite different. Adler rejected the significance of dreams and the unconscious, calling dreams "the adversary of common sense."[10] Common sense, on the other hand, was the key to cooperation and, in turn, the key to solving most of the world's problems. People who dream a lot, Adler insisted, are simply people who like to practice a form of self-hypnosis, deluding themselves into thinking they have found answers to their problems when they really have not. Adler disliked metaphors and symbols, complaining that they were too often used to hide the real meaning of our thinking because we lacked the courage to be forthright. He was a literalist, distrustful and unhappy with the playful world of the poet. As such, he attempted to destroy the significance that Freud attached to both the dream and the unconscious.[11] Little wonder that Freud was angry. Adler argued that the poetic world of Freudian analysis was nothing more than the imaginary world of those spoiled and pampered children who lack the courage to speak in commonsensical terms: "If we speak plainly, without metaphors or symbols, we cannot escape common sense."[12] In cognitive style as well as personality, character, life history, and fundamental social values, both men were near opposites.[13] It is understandable why Adler's individual psychology turned out to be so very different from Freud's psychoanalysis.

In certain respects, however, Freud and Adler were similar. Both men looked deeply into their own troubled souls and found problems that also afflicted their patients and all of humanity. Both men created quasi-religious movements in an attempt to conquer the world: Freud, the Jew, wanted to lead the children of Israel and Rome out of their irrational bondage (by overcoming through sublimation his own obsessional neurosis, which he universalized to the world); Adler, the Jew turned Christian, wanted to overcome his own inferiority complex, which he also universalized to the world, by practicing the virtue of courage and preaching the gospel of social interest.

Alfred Adler was born of prosperous Jewish middle-class parents in 1870, in Penzing, a suburb of Vienna. His parents hailed from Burgenland, the home of composers Haydn and Liszt and a somewhat unique area of the Austro-Hungarian Empire, in that Jews there enjoyed a most liberal social status, relatively untouched by anti-Semitism. Perhaps, as Henri Ellenberger suggests, that is why Adler never complained about anti-Semitism.[14] Whatever the case, it is clear that his father's occupation as a prosperous corn dealer led Alfred into personal contact with both the rural, predominantly gentile, peasant population and the urban, modern, religiously diverse Viennese. Adler grew up in a suburb of Vienna in which there were few Jews, and most of his playmates were of the lower class. His family was musically inclined, affluent, and non-Orthodox, leaning in the direction of assimilation into a gentile world. Unlike Freud, Adler grew up in an environment that was conducive to crossing cultural as well as religious and social-economic class lines.

In contrast to Freud, who wrote of the "happy child of Frieberg," Adler often spoke of his childhood as having been most unhappy. Part of his suffering he attributed to the misfortunes of being a second-born son.[15] He saw himself in the undesirable position of forever, either literally or symbolically, having to compete with his older, always successful brother. Toward the end of his life, Adler reported to Phyllis Bottome, "My eldest brother . . . is a good industrious fellow—he was always ahead of me—and for the matter of that, he is *still* ahead of me."[16] From early childhood on, Alfred was no match for sibling competition. Suffering from a severe case of rickets, he could only watch his healthy older brother run and jump freely, with no pain and little effort. Adler also suffered from spasms of the glottis, which brought him near suffocation when he cried.

During Alfred's early years, a younger brother, Rudolph, drew the family's attention, especially his mother's, away from him. Then, when Alfred was almost four years old, his one-and-a-half-year-old brother died in the bed next to him. At that same age "he decided" to cure himself of spasms by refusing to cry or scream anymore.[17] The traumatic experience of his brother's death seemed to have affected him deeply. Recall that Freud's brother's death in early childhood also deeply affected him. However, it affected Adler in a significantly different way than it had affected Freud. Whereas Freud took on the heavy burden of guilt associated with having wished his brother's death, Adler focused his feelings of resentment onto his mother, whom he believed had failed to give him the kind of pampered attention he had become accustomed to receiving before his younger brother's birth,[18] and who now smiled too readily after his brother's death. Bottome notes: "Alfred had always been much less attached to his mother than to his father. She was colder in her nature, and it is probable that she preferred her first-born to Alfred. Alfred did not understand, and never quite forgave her for smiling soon—he thought far too soon—after the sudden death of a little brother."[19] Such a mother was not to be trusted, especially by a youngster who faced the daily competition of a more-favored brother, and who just as often faced the danger of suffocation whenever he cried.

No sooner had Adler decided to cure himself of his glottal spasms—by refusing to cry or scream ever again[20]—than he, himself, faced imminent death. Suffering from a severe case of pneumonia, the five-year-old accidentally overheard the doctor advise his father that there was "no point in going to the trouble of looking after [him] as there was no hope of [his] living." Adler recalled: "At once a frightful terror came over me and a few days later when I was well I decided definitely to become a doctor so that I should have a better defence against the danger of death and weapons to combat it superior to my doctor's."[21] Thus, at an early age, Adler chose an occupation that would help him in adult life to overcompensate for the insecurities of his childhood. In Adlerian terms he chose a life-style that would overcome his "organ inferiority." This kind of childhood experience later led him to write his first major book, *Studies of Organ Inferiority* (1907). Few would disagree with his professional claim, "I *am* the legitimate father of the Inferiority Complex."[22]

As an adult, Adler admitted that his feelings toward his mother were mistaken, although this was the error upon which he had creatively built his own inferiority complex. Throughout his life, he identified most closely with his father, whom he thought was plentifully supplied with ego strength. In contrast to Freud's father, who meekly picked his new hat out of the gutter when an anti-Semite flicked it into the street with his cane, it is reported that Adler's father, "when he saw people with their legs crossed on a tram, . . . would push one foot down with his walking stick, saying politely, with a charming smile: 'I do not like to clean my trousers on your shoes as I pass!' "[23] In later years, Adler would write a good deal about the necessity of "courage" in overcoming one's feelings of inferiority. Throughout his childhood, his father symbolized for him a courageous man who did everything he could to overcome his own physical and psychical defects. He made a lasting impression on his young son, especially when he took him on early morning strolls, during which time he taught him a variety of life's lessons.[24] One such lesson, often repeated, was, "Never believe what anyone tells you!" Skepticism thus became a necessary trait for the young rebel.

Alfred Adler was a complex person whose childhood history was in many ways transparently related to the course of his adult life. Feeling a lack of support and warmth in his home, the youthful Adler took to the streets and found the needed support in the camaraderie of the street gang. It became for him an important window to the world, one that allowed him to study the diversity of human character and satisfy his psychic need for security. When Adler later developed individual psychology as a movement, he did so in the cafes of Vienna, not in the relative cloister of the academic community. He insisted throughout, even at the cost of some followers, that individual psychology must be kept free of the unnecessary abstract trappings of intellectuals and be clearly understandable to the people on the streets.

Some years after Freud graduated at the top of his class at the Sperl Gymnasium, Adler flunked mathematics there and had to repeat his form. "His teacher advised his father to take him out of school and apprentice him to a shoemaker because he was not fit enough to do anything else."[25] His father left him in school, however, and the next year young Alfred conquered his problem and became, by his own description, one of the best mathematics students in his class. He went on to pass all his examinations and entered the University of Vienna to study medicine, where his academic record was average. In 1895 he passed the university examinations without distinction and went to work in the Vienna hospital. At this point in his career he seemed to drift from being an eye specialist to becoming a general practitioner, although in the latter role he was uncomfortable, suffering a sinking feeling of helplessness every time a young patient died.[26] In a sense, each terminal case was a special failing of a calling that had its roots in his childhood. Gradually, he shifted his attention to psychology and philosophy, and later he became a practicing psychiatric therapist. Aside from attending a few Kraft-Ebing lectures, Adler did not have any formal training in psychiatry. He was successful as a therapist, however; his personal characteristics allowed people to relate easily to him.

From the time Adler received his medical degree in 1895 until 1902, when he joined the Freudian circle, he served a short term in the Hungarian army, shifted careers into psychotherapy, became interested in the social causes of disease, and wrote a monograph entitled *A Health Book for the Tailoring Trade*, in which he outlined the social conditions leading to the particular diseases afflicting tailors. During this same period, Adler wrote a series of short articles dealing with a variety of human ailments and their possible social causes and cures. One such article, "The Physician as Educator" (1904), written shortly after joining the Freudian circle, clearly reveals the direction he would take later, after breaking with Freud in 1911. Adler's concern for courage in overcoming feelings of inferiority, and the need he felt to educate children so as to build their self-confidence, are themes he explicitly developed.[27]

During his student days at the University of Vienna, Adler became interested in socialism and attended socialist meetings. At one such meeting he met Raissa Timofeyevna Epstein, whom he married in 1897. Raissa came from a wealthy Jewish merchant family of Moscow; she had studied in Switzerland and now was a student in Vienna (females were not permitted to formally register, although they were permitted to attend lectures). Raissa was a strong-willed, beautiful young girl, notable for her fanatic honesty as much as for her neglected interest in formal dress. She knew that the world needed changing, and she was interested in changing it. An active, liberated woman, Raissa's social beliefs lay considerably to the left of her young doctor-husband. When the Leon Trotzkys lived in Vienna from 1907 to 1914, they frequently visited the Adlers, and Trotzky's wife became a close friend of Raissa's. During this period Adler accepted Yoffe, a Russian revolutionary, as one of his patients.[28]

Early on, the Adler marriage seemed most happy and stable, blessed by the births of Valentine in 1898 and Alexandra in 1901. However, as the years passed, and with the births of Kurt in 1905 and Nelly in 1909, the marriage seemed to falter. Small conflicts surfaced, and Alfred and Raissa became increasingly estranged.

Although their specific problems remain obscure, we can postulate a number of possible reasons for their difficulties. Obviously, considerable cultural differences existed between the middle-class Austrian concerned with liberal social reform and the upper-class Russian interested in radical revolution. Also, while Adler espoused equality for women, there were many practical differences between his theory and his life with a liberated woman. There is reason to believe that Adler had some difficulty making the transition between theory and practice.

Throughout his career, Adler insisted that women were not only equal but in many respects were superior to men. He perceptively analyzed the repressed role of women and the psychic consequences for both sexes. Nevertheless, his values with respect to the ideal family remained structurally typical, idealized, and middle-class. Nowhere in his work did Adler ever propose a radical restructuring of the family unit or the functional roles of husbands and wives. It is interesting to note that when he finally broke with Freud, Adler was giving a paper before the Vienna Psychoanalytic Society that dealt with what he called the "Masculine Protest." In it he suggested that sex-role competition, behind which could be found deep feelings of inferiority and superiority, was more important in explaining one's character development than Freud's Oedipus complex. Adler's life with Raissa, a very strong-willed person, no doubt made him aware of the importance of this concept.

The Adlers seemed destined to be on opposite sides. When, for example, Alfred was baptized in 1904 into the Protestant faith, along with his two daughters, Valentine and Alexandra, Raissa refused to join them. When World War I broke out, Raissa supported the cause of the Allies against the Austro-Hungarian Empire; once the war was over, Raissa supported the Russian revolution. Alfred, however, came out against the violence of the communists and predicted the ultimate failure of the revolution. Serious grounds thus existed for the estrangement between Alfred and Raissa that would last throughout most of the remaining years of their marriage. Not until late in life, when Adler took ill in America, did he and Raissa seem to reconcile their differences.

As Adler formulated his views about individual psychology within the Freudian circle, he found the Jewish faith too limiting and wished to "share a common deity with the universal faith of man."[29] He gradually developed his own psychology and his own faith, both of which not only separated him from Raissa but clearly enabled him to become the most serious competitor of Freud's psychoanalytic movement.

The years (1902–11) that Adler spent within the Freudian circle were important developmental ones for him. During this time he published the *Studies of Organ Inferiority* (1907), which Freud believed supported his own ideas, and he also put together his unique ideas about neurosis. Thus, only a year after resigning from the Vienna Psychoanalytic Society, Adler was able to publish his most important work, *The Nervous Character* (1912), which laid the groundwork for the individual psychology movement.

While many Freudian psychoanalysts have insisted that Adler was one of Freud's students, Adlerian psychologists have insisted that he was not. The issue ultimately depends on one's conception of the teacher-student relationship. If that relationship is such that the student learns and incorporates the teacher's ideas, then Adler was, indeed, not a student of Freud—or he was a very poor one. If, however, the proper teacher role is to act as a catalytic agent, spurring the student to develop his or her own ideas, then the Freud-Adler relationship was that of teacher-student, albeit, from Freud's standpoint, unintentional. Freud and his inner circle did serve as a counterfoil against which Adler could test his ideas. Clearly, many of his ideas had already germinated, having been expressed in a variety of forms before he actually joined the group in 1902. However, in the smoke-filled crucible of those heated Wednesday night discussions, Adler tested and sharpened his ideas against some of the very best critics.

Out of this experience Adler proposed a psychology that was the opposite of Freud's on virtually every issue. Freud believed that dreams were "wish fulfillments" which could be decoded in understanding the unconscious; Adler believed that dreams were little more than unnecessary distortions of the more important conscious world. Freud emphasized the role of the unconscious in determining behavior; Adler emphasized the role of consciousness. Freud looked for the causes of neurosis in the libido; Adler looked to the ego. Freud universalized his idea about the Oedipus complex to all humankind; Adler universalized his own inferiority complex to all humanity—"to be a human being means to feel oneself inferior."[30] Freud's movement was to be theoretical and abstract, given to a heavy use of metaphor and poetic, symbolic interpretations; Adler's movement was common-sensical, concrete, and given to simple, practical interpretations.

Freud saw the neurotic individual as divided against himself; Adler saw that same individual as a unity. Freud's psychoanalytic movement sought a causal explanation for neurosis; Adler's individual psychology sought a teleological explanation. And so on.

Although shortly after their break, Freud complained that "Adler's system is founded entirely upon the impulse of aggression. It leaves no room at all for love,"[31] later in life Freud himself wrote more about aggression, suggesting that there was, in fact, a "beast" in men and women to whom sparing their own kind was something alien.[32] Adler, by contrast, eventually emphasized cooperation, insisting that human nature, if not innately good, carried the urge for perfection which was valued as good. To Freud, women occupied an inferior position in society for biological reasons; whereas Adler assumed that women were by nature superior, but because of faulty social reason, men dominated. Both men and women suffer, Adler insisted, from the masculine protest. While the woman errs in wanting to be a man, the man errs in his fear of not being manly enough. Striving for superiority, as a reflection of their drive for perfection, men become mixed up in the competition of the sexes and this symbolically affects all of their sexual behavior, even to the extent of their insistence on being on top during intercourse. The masculine versus feminine problem was not sexual, Adler insisted, but social, an issue of inferiority versus superiority within society's framework.

Adler's relationship with his wife no doubt helped him clarify his theory of masculine protest, just as his relationship with his mother initially helped him understand his own inferiority complex. His will to power grew from his sense of inferiority, which resulted not only from his own organ inferiority, but also from his mother's withdrawal of her pampering support for him at the birth of his younger brother. He grew up distrusting his mother, and later came to believe that this was the error upon which he created the notion of an inferiority complex, which in turn set into motion his own life-style. It is notable that his adult relationship with his mother was characterized by overprotectiveness. Friends were very surprised at the extent to which Adler would interrupt his routine work to accompany his mother whenever she left the house. When asked why,

He answered gravely, "But I cannot let my mother go out alone; she is not used to that." He was especially careful in helping his mother to cross the street. He noticed later that though he crossed the street quietly when he was alone, he was always very careful about the person he was accompanying, and directed them right and left. Finally he found out that he wanted to over-compensate an old insecurity in this way. He had been run over twice when he was a child; that is to say, had had bad experiences, and wanted to demonstrate that he was the only one who could lead others across the street correctly. This insight enabled him to rid himself of this disagreeable habit.[33]

While this incident reflects Adler's insecurity stemming from his childhood accidents, it also very much reflects the insecurity he felt toward his mother. Although she had deserted him in those crucial childhood years, he was not going to desert her! Significantly, when it came time to select a mate, he chose someone he perceived in most respects to be the opposite of his mother, someone he felt he could trust. In Raissa he found an honest, forthright person. Still, she did not readily give him the mothering he had missed as a child.

A significant portion of individual psychology clearly grew out of Adler's personal problems. He saw in himself and in his patients a deep-seated feeling of inferiority, and he observed that both he and his patients attempted to overcompensate, playing tricks on themselves and the community through a variety of devices. He found his way out through a process of extending his "social interest." Like Freud, Adler expressed in his final work a religiouslike faith. Freud's bore the mark of a stoic, fundamentally Hebraic kind of moral system, while Adler's led to a kind of humanized Christian dictum of "love thy neighbor as thyself." Freud, in *Civilization and Its Discontents*, had ridiculed this dictum as an impossible ideal, just as Friedrich Nietzsche once portrayed the same notion as the groveling weakness of spineless Christians. Clearly, Freud and Adler drew on vastly different ethical codes.

As opposed to Freud, who saw neurosis as the almost inevitable price we pay for civilization, Adler thought neurosis was a correctable error. Adler would sit facing his patients, and his brand of therapy led to a much quicker assessment of the patient's lifestyle, the errors made in its development, and the practical steps necessary for remediation. Errors in life-style were to be determined by the therapist's personal experiences, knowledge of individual psychology, and "a guess." This added method of guessing was viewed by Adler's followers as a distinctive contribution to the "science" of individual psychological therapy. One such follower, Rudolf Dreikurs, noted: "Adler frankly admitted that he used guessing in this procedure, thereby introducing into science a technique which up to then was considered the most 'unscientific' approach to a problem. But Adler demonstrated that we can learn to 'guess in the right direction.' "[34] While a "guess in the right direction" may or may not enhance the "scientific" validity of a diagnosis, it is clear from the standpoint of most observers that it did increase the speed with which any diagnosis could be made.

In comparison to Freudian therapy, Adlerian therapy was a "quick fix." In this regard Freud could say of Adler's therapy what he once had said of Otto Rank's therapy: it was designed to suit an American clientele. Americans, Freud believed, were not prepared to accept lengthy, drawn-out, expensive therapeutic practices. The issue here, however, is not so much one of European versus American as one of social and economic class differences. The upper classes Freud serviced could afford the cost of protracted analysis, while the middle and lower classes Adler—and later Otto Rank (see chap. 10)—serviced could ill afford such a lengthy process. Isidor Wassermann, of the Psychiatric Clinic of the Medical Academy, in Wroclaw, Poland, did a comparative study of the socioeconomic class differences of Freud's and Adler's patients and concluded that not only was the ability to pay significantly different in the two therapies, but also the very content appeared to be class-determined.[35] In general, Adlerian concerns involving inferiority and the desire for power are typically lower- and middle-class problems; those involving sexual sublimation for cultural purposes are of more central concern to the upper classes, who have already overcome an inferior social position.[36] The great bulk of Adler's patients were situated within or very near to the middle class. The middle-class values that permeated Adler's psychology clearly fit the class he was serving, while the upper-class elite values that permeated Freud's psychology were similarly appropriate for the class he served.

Although Freud evidently created a movement designed to serve the elite groups in society, and built this movement with a select priesthood of analysts possessing esoteric knowledge, he repeatedly argued for a "lay" movement. However, Freud did not want a movement that was simple and easily understood by all concerned, which might include the lower classes; rather, he wished to keep psychoanalysis out of the controlling hands of medical doctors. Freud lectured to medical students at the university, but that served his personal status needs more than anything else. He wanted to create a new lay cadre of analysts unencumbered by established medical practice. Had the rise of fascism not occurred and the holocaust not wiped out Freud's "lay" movement in Europe, that thrust of psychoanalysis might well still exist. Very much to the dislike of Freud, psychoanalysis in America developed as the special domain of medical doctors. Thus, as a consequence of World War II, America became the stronghold of psychoanalysis and the field became dominated by the medical profession.

While Freud failed to develop a lay movement free of medical practitioners in America, he did develop a select group of lay elite expert analysts in Europe. Adler, on the other hand, created a lay movement on both sides of the Atlantic that was clearly geared away from the notion of a select priesthood possessing expert, esoteric knowledge. While he would have liked to lecture to medical students, as Freud did, he purposely designed and championed a movement that would be easily and clearly understood by all concerned. Indeed, when his individual psychology movement was well underway, there were several among his followers who pushed hard to create a more esoteric knowledge and thus a functional role for a new priesthood. At the price of some defectors, Adler insisted on keeping his analysis simple, unabstract, practical, and guided by common sense. He intended to create a truly lay movement, to spread his gospel among the people as far as possible. While Freud lectured to medical students at the university, Adler lectured in cafes and eventually to larger groups at the Pedagogical Institute of Vienna, as well as the city's schools and guidance clinics. His audiences were composed primarily of teachers, teacher trainees, parents, child guidance counselors, and rank-and-file mental health workers from the growing therapeutic community.

Given the remarkable, vast differences between Alfred Adler and Sigmund Freud, we might seriously wonder what was in Adler's mind during the nine years he was a member of Freud's Psychoanalytic Society. Ernest Jones's impression of him during those days was that he was argumentative, "a morose and cantankerous person, whose behavior oscillated between contentiousness and sulkiness. He was evidently very ambitious and constantly quarreling with the others over points of priority in his ideas."[37] Inasmuch as Adler used the group to clarify his own contrasting ideas, then this view seems reasonable. Many years after their initial encounters, Jones noticed a change in Adler: "I observed that success had brought him a certain benignity of which there had been little sign in his earlier years."[38] Success no doubt helped Adler overcome his inferiority complex and thus bring under control the inordinate drive for superiority that was so much a part of his personal character. Competitive from childhood, hating to stand in the shadow of his older brother, Sigmund, Adler reportedly told Freud at the end, "Do you believe that it is such a great pleasure for me to stand in your shadow my whole life?"[39] We can only speculate as to which Sigmund's shadow Adler felt most heavily.

The break with Freud was not a clean one. As it dragged on people took sides, and when Adler finally resigned from the Psychoanalytic Society, he and those who left with him created a competing organization with the unfortunate name "Society for Free Psychoanalysis" (rather quickly changed to "Society for Individual Psychology"). There were some who wished to remain active in both organizations, which Adler permitted; Freud, however, moved his organization to exclude any member who attended Adler's group, with the exception of a very special friend, Lou Andreas-Saloné. She kept Freud informed as to what the renegade group was doing, while at the same time pursuing her own course of psychological inquiry.

Shortly after Adler published *The Nervous Character* in 1912, he wrote to Hertha Orgler, "With this book, ... I have founded the school of Individual Psychology."[40] In it he described what he believed to be the origin of neurosis, the development of feelings of inferiority, the development of psychic compensations to overcome that inferiority, as well as the fictions individual neurotics choose to create, around which they build a life-style. Throughout this and other works, Adler attempted to create distance between himself and Freud, suggesting that while Freud sought causal factors for neurosis, he (Adler) was more concerned with the life-style the individual created as a consequence of some early childhood problematic experience.

Adler argued that early experiences were so laced with fictions that precise causal factors could not be determined. Furthermore, even if we could know the exact causal factor or factors, we could not change the original experience, only evaluate our present life-style, constructed over time, and its supporting operational fictions. In this stance, Adler aligned himself with typical twentieth-century ahistorical thinking. He treated the patient's lifestyle as the cause of his or her current ailment, and usually traced the creation of that life-style back to the age of three to five years, where, in the context of too much or too little pampering by father, mother, sister, or brother, a certain life-style was chosen. For the neurotic personality the choice was an error, but one that could ultimately be corrected by therapy.

While Adler claimed he did not deal with exact causal factors, whenever he spoke about the "correct" or the "best" child-rearing practices, he implicitly assumed that certain causal factors were productive of the neurotic personality. Even so, he repeatedly turned away from what he considered to be the fictitious history of the patient, stressing instead the current fictions and possible pragmatic consequences for the future of the patient. Thus Adler insisted that the teleological purposes or "fictitious goals" of the individual could tell us more about the individual's problems than any lengthy inquiry into the unconscious, itself laced with imaginative creations.

Throughout this work and in his later exposition of individual psychology, Adler relied on H. Varhinger's *The Philosophy of "As If"* for the key to interpreting neurotic behavior. Adler saw the individual almost as a monad, always situated in a social environment in which he or she acted and reacted. In this life process the individual creates ideas and self-conceptions that collectively reflect his or her overall life-style. Within this lifestyle, purposes emerge that serve as teleological goals, which become so when the individual acts upon them as if they were, in fact, real. Thus individual "fictions" are created about self and world, and by acting "as if" these fictions were true, individuals create their own meaningful, unified world. Whether neurotic or normal, the world of the individual is always unified.

The individual was thus never completely determined by the environment but was actively shaping that environment. Paraphrasing Johann Pestalozzi to that effect, Adler said, "The environment molds man, but man molds the environment."[41] Heinz and Rowena Ansbacher point out that Adler's position here is similar to the one taken by Marx and Engels: "The circumstances make men just as men make the circumstances."[42] Like Marx, Adler saw individuals as creative actors who shaped not only their physical but also their psychical and spiritual worlds. Neurosis occurs when individuals err in their psychic creations and generate a sense of self that leads them away from legitimate social interest. The issue is not so much whether a particular idea about one's self is true or false, but more importantly, where that particular idea may lead. The neurotic's ideas about self usually lead toward an increasingly alienated state, until insanity and death ultimately ensue. Neurosis can be cured, Adler believed, if the individual can be taught to see and understand the error of these "fictions," be encouraged to create new, more socially desirable fictions, and to act on *those* ideas "as if" they were true—in effect, to be reeducated to an entirely new life-style.

Adler's psychology was a holistic one which combined both material and spiritual concerns. It was a total way of life. His psychology touched upon all aspects of human character formation: avarice, sloth, and envy, as well as spiritual virtue and the meaning of God. *The Nervous Character* began Adler's movement, which he preached throughout Europe and America from 1912 to 1937. He was bent on replacing psychoanalysis with a total psychology, created from a theory about character formation that was based on a view of aggression as involving the struggle for superiority, especially in terms of the sexes. Freud's key concept of a universal Oedipal complex, around which all psychosexual repression occurs, was, from Adler's standpoint, nothing more than his own notion of the masculine protest dressed up in mother's clothing: "A proper insight for instance into the 'Oedipus complex' shows us that it is nothing more nor less than a figurative, sexually clothed conception of what constitutes masculine self-consciousness, superiority over woman. . . ."[43] Adler described these neurotics, like Freud, who suffered from an Oedipus complex, as nothing more than "pampered children," spoiled by a doting mother who ill prepared them for the world of cooperation and social interest. Thus Adler not only attempted to replace Freud's psychology, but he thereby attempted to explain away Freud's own neurosis as well.

Once the individual psychology movement was underway, Adler applied for the title of *Privat Dozent* at the University of Vienna, so that he also might lecture to medical students. He submitted *The Nervous Character* as evidence of his scholarship, but in 1915 a faculty of twenty-five voted unanimously against his apppointment. Although they found his ideas imaginative, facile, and ingenious, they also found them totally lacking in any kind of rigorous, scientific, disciplined methodology: ". . . it is dangerous for research when it is only ingenious. The products of imagination must undergo the refining process of criticism, which Adler's writings show themselves not even to have begun."[44] The door to the medical students of Vienna was closed to Adler from the beginning of his movement.

The bitterness of this rejection faded from Adler's immediate consciousness as he faced more pressing problems. As war clouds gathered, Raissa took their four children for a visit to Russia. When the Archduke was shot, Adler telegraphed Raissa to return home at once. At first she refused; then she became entrapped,[45] and it took five months to arrange return passage for her and the children. Raissa returned from Russia a pro-ally; Alfred left for the Russian front to do his duty for Austria-Hungary. Their strained marriage was not helped when Russia sued for a separate peace and slid into the communist revolution which Raissa supported. When Adler returned to his beloved Vienna after the war, he became actively involved in the Social Democratic party and the reform committees which swept political radicals into office. Raissa took up the cause of the Trotzky revolutionaries; Alfred argued against their violent methods. Pitting himself against his wife, as well as many of his radical friends, Adler argued in the cafes and in print that violence would breed violence, and in the end, the communist revolution would fail, unable to achieve its dreamed-of goals. Adler slowly but clearly steered his individual psychology movement away from the choppy waters of radical revolution and toward the calmer waters of liberal reform, where it eventually took anchor.

As the old group congregated at the Cafe Central, after the war, to hear and discuss with Adler his ideas about psychology and philosophy, it became apparent that they all had passed through the portals of the twentieth century. Each person was different; the world they faced was different. Adler himself sounded different, insisting that what the world needed and wanted was *Gemeinschaftsgefühl,* "community feeling." Over the next twenty years he would develop the meaning of that term, teaching and preaching his gospel of social interest, the new religious faith of Alfred Adler. While some thought it to be a bland oversimplification, and walked away in disgust, others stayed and listened. His new faith was interpreted by one of his critical followers in this way:

there was a law binding man to the universe, moving always in the same direction, and towards a goal that could never be reached, but which never varied; and as man obeyed this law and co-operated with it, he would develop in a direction that furthered universal welfare—but his co-operation with others was the price he must pay for this development. The egocentric goal must be broken up. Social Interest *was* the only goal for mankind; and every human being must be trained towards it in childhood, until it became as natural to him "as breathing or the upright gait."[46]

Although both Marx and Adler dreamed the impossible dream of a perfect social order, Marx saw the road to his vision paved with class conflict, while Adler insisted that it must be paved with cooperation. Unlike Marx, who turned to revolutionary praxis to change his world, Adler turned to educational praxis. He and his followers now became actively engaged in educational reform in Vienna. Through the influence of a close friend and follower, Carl Furtmüller, Adler was introduced to the new minister of education, Otto Glöckel. Glöckel was impressed with Adler and his small band of followers and thus gave them entrance to the school system, where they fostered on-going educational reforms. They helped make the Vienna school system the educational showplace of Europe in the 1920s. Adler's group was directly involved in creating experimental schools, which attracted international attention, and in developing institutes and workshops for teacher training, on a regular basis. They formed and supervised over thirty child guidance clinics, attached to the Vienna schools. Through his forthright lectures to both parents and teachers, Adler helped to develop a strong attitude toward the use and acceptance of therapeutic practices in educating children in both the school and the home. Adler assumed the post of lecturer at the Institute of Pedagogical Studies in Vienna, clearly reaching the high-water mark of his career. All Vienna seemed to react positively to his ideas. His fame spread from Vienna to Germany, England, France, and America, and in 1930 his beloved city awarded him the title "Citizen of Vienna."

From 1926 to 1934, Adler divided his time between American and Viennese audiences. New Adlerian groups were forming in America, and he was rapidly finding a second home there. He talked to overflowing, appreciative audiences in some of the major academic centers, lecturing in extension courses at Columbia University from 1929 to 1931. His friends there prematurely put him up for a chair, for which he was rejected. By 1932 he was teaching as a regular member of the faculty at Long Island Medical College. Although his individual psychology, especially its "born-again-of-the-spirit" message, did not set well with the established Freudians in the United States, Adler made an impact on social workers, penal institution officers, guidance counselors, mental health workers, family therapists, and parents and teachers. While his American lectures received limited coverage in the more-established psychotherapeutic journals, they received extensive coverage in the *Police Journal, Good Housekeeping*, and *Parents Magazine*.

By 1934, Adler's divided home life between America and Vienna came to a close. The national socialists had taken power in Vienna, and all his reform work was halted. In that same year he became seriously ill with an untreated carbuncle and was hospitalized. Raissa, hearing of his illness, immediately joined him, and the results were therapeutic for both his physical health and their marriage. "His illness and Raissa's instant response to his need of her changed both their lives. For the first time, Adler realized how deep his wife's devotion to him really was; and his whole nature responded to it, and to her care for him."[47] Recall that illness had played an important role in Adler's own early childhood character formation. His inferiority feelings, as he had analyzed them, lay in his response to his mother's inability to satisfy his need for attention when ill. He had married someone he thought was different, but through the years her emancipated outlook tended to undercut his overwhelming need for security. Yet when Raissa quickly responded to his need for attention during his first and only illness as an adult, their marriage was at last reconciled, and they remained together until Adler's death three years later.

The three great problems of life, or so Adler argued, were community feeling, work and occupation, love and marriage. *Gemeinschaftsgefühl*, "community feeling," must permeate all activities of life. We must turn away from our selfish ways, not through self-sacrifice so much as through self-development— indeed, through the continuing expansion of social interest. The key word in all this was "cooperation": men and women must learn to cooperate, for their own individual good and for the good of humanity. Problems with friends, work, or family always could be solved by increasing cooperation, or social interest. Individual problems of crime, delinquency, drug addiction, alcoholism, and sexual perversion were all similar, in the sense that each showed a lack of social responsibility and each erred against any true social interest. In response to a critic who had accused him of making a religion out of his notion of social interest, Adler said, "I have propounded religion as a constructive step towards the advancement of co-operation so much that I was frequently suspected of being a Philistine. . . . I refuse to teach religion being not qualified for it, and leave it to others. I only represent the viewpoint of science which, in its application in fact often corresponds with the commandments of religion. We do not demand anything, however, we merely explain."[48]

Adler was doing something much more than explaining, however; he was, in fact, preaching a particular way of life, a kind of middle-class, liberal, religious humanism. In *Understanding Human Nature* (1927), *What Life Should Mean to You* (1931), *Religion and Individual Psychologie* (with Ernest Jahn, 1933), and *Social Interest: A Challenge to Mankind* (1936), Adler detailed the values that "ought" to be taught in the home, the school, the workplace, and the general community. All of this led Freud, late in his life, to refer to the Adlerians as "buffoons . . . publishing books about the meaning of life(!)"[49] Buffoons or not, Adler and his followers were preaching a religious faith laced with conventional middle-class values: the ideal family was based on a monogamous marriage in which the role of motherhood was exhorted; masculine and feminine social roles remained separate and distinct, by nature. "The bisexuality of the human race conditions another division of labor. Woman, by virtue of her physical construction, is excluded from certain activities, while on the other hand, there are certain labors which are not given to man, because man could better be employed at other tasks."[50]

Although the term "individual" in Adler's individual psychology placed emphasis on the individual as a choosing being, Adler did not see individuals as an end in themselves; rather, their very value or worth was to be determined by a communal measure: "Any man's value . . . is determined by his attitude toward his fellow men, and by the degree in which he partakes of the division of labor which communal life demands."[51] A productive system requiring ever-greater divisions of labor reflected, to Adler, a system that was evolutionary, advancing, and progressing; it reflected increasing degrees of cooperation and therefore was viewed in a positive way. The problem facing the individual was simply to find a place within this vast system of work in which to satisfy his or her need to contribute to the social interest. All occupations, Adler argued, were equally useful, and therefore the wishes of the child must be honored in the selection of an occupation. "We must let him value as he chooses; since we ourselves have no means of saying which occupation is higher and which is lower. If he really does his work and occupies himself in a contribution to others, he is on the same level of usefulness as any one else. His only task is to train himself, try to support himself, and set his interest in the framework of the division of labor."[52]

Repeatedly, Adler treated the productive system as a positive "given" that was socially desirable and fundamentally sound. In 1931, Adler viewed the unemployment situation with "alarm." Dangerous, antisocial interests lurked in the large army of unemployed persons who did not fit into the existing division of labor. One of the worst effects of unemployment was that it impeded those who were "trying to improve cooperation."[53] When Adler himself considered what should be done, he did not advocate changing the means of production or the economic system of distributing wealth; rather, he called for training the unemployed to improve their skills and their social interest, so that they might better fit into the prevailing division of labor. In his analysis of work, he escaped reality through a process of idealization. For example, Adler felt that if we all do our jobs, then somehow we are all equal, because we are all contributing to the commonweal. This may be true in an ideal society but not in the real world of sharply differentiated pay scales. To suggest, as Adler did, that we have "no means of saying which occupation is higher or lower" is pure idealization. A similar kind of false consciousness emerged when Adler blamed unemployment on the unemployed, rather than on the economic system and its failure to provide work opportunities. This displacement of blame occurred when he sought solutions to the unemployment problem in education rather than the economic system. This same false consciousness has served repeatedly to protect our current economic system from critical scrutiny.

Significantly, this therapy, which presumes to be so heavily oriented toward practical, ongoing life, repeatedly returns at critical junctures to a benign idealization of that social existence. The net consequence was an obfuscation of social reality. In the midst of severe economic dislocation in the monopoly-capitalist system of the West, Adler called for group cooperation in place of class struggle. "What we must disagree with is the view of life in which people are looking only for what is given them, looking only for a personal advantage. This is the greatest conceivable obstacle to individual and common progress. It is only through our interest in our fellows that any of our human capacities develop."[54] The solution, then, to all problems was to expand one's social interest. Neurosis itself would thus be overcome. Adler said, "As soon as he can connect himself with his fellow men on an equal and cooperative footing, he is cured."[55] He urged teachers, psychological counselors, and mental health workers to teach the values of cooperation: "All that we demand of a human being, and the highest praise that we can give him, is that he should be a good fellow worker, a friend to all other men, and a true partner in love and marriage. If we are to put it in a word, we may say that he should prove himself a fellow man."[56]

As Adler's audiences increased in size and he received more support, it was almost possible to sense in him a growing confusion between the world as he thought it ought to be and the way it actually was. With the dark clouds of fascism gathering on the near horizon, Freud wrote about human nature "as a savage beast to whom consideration towards his own kind is something alien,"[57] while Adler insisted that human nature was basically good:

> Thus the long-standing dispute as to whether man is good or evil by nature is settled. The growing, irresistible evolutionary advance of social feeling warrants us in assuming that the existence of humanity is inseparably bound up with "goodness". Anything that seems to contradict this is to be considered as a failure in evolution; it can be traced back to mistakes that have been made—just as in the vast experiments of nature there has always been material in the bodies of animals that could not be used.[58]

Adler often quoted Christ's command, "Thou shalt love thy neighbor as thyself," which Freud had concluded was a false expectation that ran counter to human nature itself. Given man's beastly aggressiveness, Freud suggested, Heinrich Heine's dictum, "One must, it is true, forgive one's enemies—but not before they have been hanged,"[59] was perhaps more appropriate. Adler, of course, charged that Freud's psychology was derived from a "pampered child," and that it was fundamentally unethical and immoral.

At times, however, Adler seemed to waver regarding his conception of human nature. For example, he said, "Man is not born good or evil, but he can be trained in either direction. Whose fault is greater? That of the erring community or that of the erring child?"[60] In general, however, he returned to his normative ideal of social interest, which he found implanted in the evolutionary progress of humankind. Just as individuals carried with them a goal for perfection, so did the collective community carry within its evolution a guiding normative goal of perfection. For Adler, this idealized goal lay beyond immediate experience; it rested in a new, yet-unborn, ultimate synthesizing of ideas. He said, "I must admit that those who find a piece of metaphysics in Individual Psychology are right." His faith was total, resting on a metaphysics of his own creation; the very purpose of life was perfection. Adler continued: "We conceive the idea of social interest, social feeling, as the ultimate form of mankind, a condition in which we imagine all questions of life, all relationship to the external world as solved. It is a normative ideal, a direction-giving goal. This goal of perfection must contain the goal of an ideal community, because everything we find valuable in life, what exists and what will remain, is forever a product of this social feeling."[61]

Thus, for Adler, humankind's quest for superiority was in reality an evolutionary quest for perfection, directed at "mastering the environment." However, it errs—indeed, fails—when it is directed at people.

> Individual Psychology has uncovered the fact that the deviations and failures of the human character—neurosis, psychosis, crime, drug addiction etc.—are nothing but forms of expression and symptoms of the striving for superiority directed against fellowmanship, which presents itself in one case as striving for power, in another case as an evasion of accomplishments by which another might benefit. Such erroneous striving leads to the psychological decline and fall of the individual, as any biological erroneous striving has led to the physical decline and fall of entire species and races.[62]

Errors on the part of the individual in creating his or her guiding fictions lead to psychological decline just as errors in biological development lead to the disappearance of the species. Under Adler's leadership, individual psychology had discovered a special formula for overcoming the errors that would lead to the decline of human civilization: "Individual Psychology has found a special formula for the correct striving for perfection of man: The goal which the individual must pursue must lie in the direction which leads to the perfection of *all of mankind sub specie aeternitatis.*" Virtue was defined as the advancement toward the common goal of the cooperating community, not as in the existing community, but in the yet-unborn ideal community where all people would be striving for perfection. "This is how the Individual Psychology concept of social interest (*Gemeinschaftsgefühl*) is to be understood."[63]

God could be found in this individual and collective quest for perfection, in this final and ultimate goal which sheds grace on humankind in its continual upward striving on the path of life. "Whether one calls the highest effective goal deity, or socialism, or, as we do, the pure idea of social interest, or as others call it in obvious connection with social interest, ego ideal, it always reflects the same ruling, perfection-promising, grace-giving goal of overcoming."[64] Adler's individual psychology would light the path to the "sanctification of human relations." While the true *Gemeinschaftsgefühl* had not yet arrived, it was on its way. The psychology advanced by Adler would replace traditional religion when its most profound insights were acted upon and lived, as if true. He wrote: ". . . profound recognition of interconnectedness, which closes all doors to error and proves that virtue is teachable, has not as yet become realized by many. Religious faith is alive and will continue to live until it is replaced by *this* most profound insight and the religious feeling which stems from it. It will not be enough only to taste from this insight; mankind will have to devour and digest it completely."[65]

Adler perceived the promised land as a place where "error" was no more and "virtue" abounded. For him and his followers, individual psychology was the holistic faith that would lead men and women out of the bondage of antisocial errors. In Adler's world, sin had disappeared and was replaced by error. His social message was well within that eighteenth-century Enlightenment tradition which saw human nature as "good, but susceptible to error." Ignorance would eventually be banished and all evil thus would be overcome. In Adler's quasi-religious-therapeutic world, we would no longer suffer from the Christian sense of guilt but from the anxiety of having erred. Adler believed people were trying to escape the responsibility of those errors in the lifestyles they had created for themselves, just as Cain had attempted to escape the error of his sin by asking, "Am I my brother's keeper?" Adler's answer would have been "Yes!"

In the unified but insulated world that neurotics tend to create, Adler saw their escape from responsibility as an escape from community, one that would lead them away from humanity and toward individual isolation, insanity, and ultimately death, for both themselves and the community. In the real, alienating world of industrial capitalism, where "competition," not "co-operation," reigns supreme and we are each pitted against the other for our very physical existence, the path we tread is clearly not one of Adlerian neighborly love, but that of a sickly, alienating society where the term *Gemeinschaftsgefühl* is difficult, if not impossible, to comprehend. This loss of community is clearly reflected in much of the literature of the Western world—in Marx's radical utopian vision, in Dewey's liberal view of community,[66] or in Adler's *Gemeinschaftsgefühl*.

In Adler's beloved Vienna, the "City of Dreams," where Martin Buber studied philosophy and art and discovered the communal values of Hasidism, and where Theodor Herzel cultivated his liberal philosophy and discovered Zionism as a way toward a Jewish community, Adolf Hitler, during his Viennese years, cultivated his early hatred of the Jewish people. As Hitler's anti-Semitism gradually bore its bitter fruit, Adler's voice could still be heard urging his fellow citizens to "love thy neighbor as thyself." It was much like listening to Norman Vincent Peale's varied claims for the power of positive thinking during the time of the holocaust. As Adler lectured in cafes about "loving thy neighbor," the violent sounds of the fascists taking over the streets of Vienna were clear enough for all to hear. His benign, nonrevolutionary, nonviolent social gospel of cooperation might have been harmlessly incongruous, except that Adler's faith created for him a social cocoon, one that in the end insulated him from the noise of the streets. Early on, Raissa had sensed the problem— by ignoring the political and economic roots of the pending disaster and ministering to the psychological needs of the victims, and by ignoring the social roots of the disease and preaching an idealized metaphysical future, Adler was creating a consciousness which, in the end, can and often does easily lead one to blame the victims. It also creates the necessary social blindness that allows one to preach brotherly love during the very birth of Austrian fascism.

While we are struck by the distance between Adler's benign cooperative world and the actual competitive world of the streets he thought he understood, we are also struck by the fact that the psychologist who prided himself on his "commonsense" philosophy and his psychology of "practical solutions" in the end propounded a faith for humanity that was far afield from where men and women actually lived and died. In the modern world of alienated existence, a one-eyed psychology of praxis, blind in the other eye to the social-economic vested interests of power, is a psychology that can be expected to create a world of false security by creating a world of false consciousness. The philosophy of "as if," as applied in Adlerian psychology, thus easily slips into a kind of consciousness which, through its idealization of the cooperative way, actually protects the nihilistic competitiveness it abhors.

The legacy left by Alfred Adler is a strange one. While, on the one hand, there are today relatively few Adlerians—or at least people who admit to being Adlerians—on the other hand, his ideas heavily permeate the modern therapeutic community as well as the general public.[67] Adler was clearly an important forerunner in the field of psychosomatic medicine, thanks to his original work on the psychic effects of organ inferiority, but in general, his most lasting impact can be found in the Adlerian concepts and terms that have become commonplace. In psychiatric hospitals or on the streets, we hear about "inferiority complex," "overcompensation," "life-style," "masculine versus feminine psychosexual roles," "ego psychology," "the child's place in the family," the psychology of "as if," and "organ inferiority." It is ironic that the term Adler believed to be most important—*Gemeinschaftsgefühl*—*the* key to his therapy, did not take hold.

In many ways the religion that Adler ended up preaching in the cafes of Vienna and the lecture halls of America was, in the end, just another failed religion—a "quick fix," an opiate to help people produce an "as if" fiction, an optimistic euphoria that momentarily overcame the "soulless conditions" of a "heartless world." Nevertheless, those who continue to struggle to overcome the crippling effects of alienation in American society, with its growing signs of fascism, by preaching a gospel of practical "social relatedness," "interpersonal relations," and "communication," devoid of any serious social critique, do not appear to be far afield.

Notes

1. Ernest Jones, *The Life and Work of Sigmund Freud*, 3 vols. (New York: Basic Books, 1957), 3:208.

2. For the gradual development of Adler's deviations, see Herman Nunberg and Ernst Federn, eds., *Minutes of the Vienna Psychoanalytic Society*, 3 vols. (New York: International Universities Press, 1962, 1967, 1974).

3. A. A. Brill, ed., *The Basic Writings of Sigmund Freud* (New York: Modern Library, 1938), p. 933.

4. Quoted in Paul Roazen, *Freud and His Followers* (New York: Alfred A. Knopf, 1975), p. 191.

5. See Nathan G. Hale, Jr., ed., *James Jackson Putnam and Psychoanalysis* (Cambridge, Mass.: Harvard University Press, 1971), p. 146; see also William McGuire, ed., *The Freud/Jung Letters* (Princeton, N.J.: Princeton University Press, 1974), pp. 231, 373, 376, 422.

6. Fritz Wittels, *Sigmund Freud: His Personality, His Teaching, and His School* (London: Allen and Unwin, 1924), p. 225.

7. McGuire, *Freud/Jung Letters*, pp. 376, 382.

8. See chap. 6.

9. Sigmund Freud, *The Interpretation of Dreams* (New York: Macmillan Co., 1913), p. 385.

10. Alfred Adler, *What Life Should Mean to You*. ed. Alan Porter (New York: Capricorn Books, 1931), p. 101.

11. See ibid., pp. 101–19.

12. Ibid., p. 102.

13. Paul Roazen seriously errs when he suggests in *Freud and His Followers* that the argument between these two men appears as a "narcissism of small differences—a dispute between men who are so close to each other that they feel obliged to compare themselves, but who regard their differences as an implied reproach or criticism" (p. 206).

14. See Henri F. Ellenberger, *The Discovery of the Unconscious* (New York: Basic Books, 1970), p. 573.

15. There is some disagreement here as to whether Adler was a second child or a third child. Carl Furtmüller refers to him as "the third child in a family of five boys and two girls, the oldest child a boy, the second a girl" (quoted in Heinz L. Ansbacher and Rowena R. Ansbacher, eds., *Alfred Adler: Superiority and Social Interest* [Evanston, Ill.: Northwestern University Press, 1964], p. 330). Hertha Orgler, in *Alfred Adler: The Man and His Work* (London: Sidgwick and Jackson, 1963), p. 1, reports that "Alfred was the second of six children." Phyllis Bottome, in *Alfred Adler: A Portrait from Life* (New York: Vanguard Press, 1957), p. 28, suggests that Orgler is correct: "Adler's immediate family consisted of four brothers (including himself) and two sisters." Whatever the case, it should be clear that Adler was still the second-born *son*. It is ironic

to see this kind of discrepancy creep into the biography of a man whose psychology put so much importance in the place one had in the family birth order.

16. Bottome, *Alfred Adler: A Portrait from Life*, p. 27.

17. See Orgler, *Alfred Adler: The Man and His Work*, p. 1.

18. Ibid., p. 2.

19. Bottome, *Alfred Adler: A Portrait from Life*, p. 30.

20. Orgler, *Alfred Adler: The Man and His Work*, p. 1.

21. Bottome, *Alfred Adler: A Portrait from Life*, pp. 32, 33.

22. Quoted in ibid., p. 19.

23. Ibid., p. 29.

24. Interestingly, it was on an early morning stroll that Alfred Adler died on the streets of Aberdeen. As a young theological student rushed to give him first aid, the last word he was said to have murmured was "Kurt," his only son's name.

25. Orgler, *Alfred Adler: The Man and His Work*, p. 3.

26. Ibid., p. 5.

27. See Ellenberger, *Discovery of the Unconscious*, pp. 602–3.

28. See ibid., p. 585.

29. Quoted from Bottome, in ibid., p. 584.

30. Alfred Adler, *Social Interest: A Challenge to Mankind* (New York: Capricorn Books, 1964), p. 96.

31. Brill, *Basic Writings of Sigmund Freud*, p. 970.

32. Sigmund Freud, *Civilization and Its Discontents* (New York: W. W. Norton and Co., 1961), p. 59.

33. Orgler, *Alfred Adler: The Man and His Work*, p. 6.

34. Rudolf Dreikurs, "Case Interpretation," *Individual Psychology Bulletin* 2(Oct. 1941): 1.

35. See Isidor Wassermann, "Letter to the Editor," *American Journal of Psychotherapy* 12(1958): 623–27. Wassermann's study indicates that 74 percent of Freud's patients were upper class, 23 percent middle class, and only 3 percent came from the lower working class. In contrast, 25 percent of Adler's patients came from the upper class, 40 percent came from the middle class, and 35 percent from the working class.

36. For an extended discussion of this point, with an additional analysis emphasizing the personality differences between Freud and Adler, see Heinz L. Ansbacher, "The Significance of the Socio-Economic Status of the Patients of Freud and of Adler," *American Journal of Psychotherapy* 13(Apr. 1959).

37. Jones, *Life and Work of Sigmund Freud*, 2:130.

38. Ibid.

39. Brill, *Basic Writings of Sigmund Freud*, p. 965.

40. Orgler, *Alfred Adler: The Man and His Work*, p. 13. It should be noted that Orgler cites *The Neurotic Constitution*, which is the same as *The Nervous Character* and is often cited as such.

41. Ansbacher and Ansbacher, *Alfred Adler: Superiority and Social Interest*, p. 28.

42. Ibid., p. 322.

43. Alfred Adler, *The Neurotic Constitution* (New York: Maffat, Yard and Co., 1917), p. 64.

44. Wagner V. Jauregg, *Unsere He Imat* (Vienna) 36(10/12; 1965, Beckh-Widmanstatter, H. A. Zur, Geschichte Der Individual Psychologie . . .): 188; I thank Steve Tozer for the translation. For a more extended sympathetic treatment, see Ellenberger, *Discovery of the Unconscious*, pp. 585–86.

45. See Bottome, *Alfred Adler: A Portrait from Life*, pp. 117–19.

46. Quoted in ibid., p. 121.

47. Ibid., p. 224.

48. Orgler, *Alfred Adler: The Man and His Work*, pp. 85–86.

49. Quoted in Roazen, *Freud and His Followers*, p. 204.

50. Alfred Adler, *Understanding Human Nature* (Greenwich, Conn.: Fawcett Publications, 1927), p. 103.

51. Ibid., p. 102.

52. Adler, *What Life Should Mean to You*, p. 244.

53. Ibid., p. 251.

54. Ibid., p. 254.

55. Ibid., p. 260.

56. Ibid., p. 262.

57. Freud, *Civilization and Its Discontents*, p. 59.

58. Adler, *Social Interest: A Challenge to Mankind*, p. 48.

59. Quoted in Freud, *Civilization and Its Discontents*, p. 57.

60. Ansbacher and Ansbacher, *Alfred Adler: Superiority and Social Interest*, p. 307.

61. Ibid., p. 35.

62. Ibid., p. 39.

63. Ibid., p. 40.

64. Ibid., pp. 277, 278.

65. Ibid., p. 279 (emphasis added).

66. See John Dewey, *The Public and Its Problems* (New York: Henry Holt and Co., 1927).

67. See Ellenberger, *Discovery of the Unconscious*, pp. 636–48.

8

CARL G. JUNG [1875–1961]

The Ethics
of a Therapeutic Man

The sound of machine guns across the frozen moun-
tain ridges of Korea had not yet faded into the stillness of history
when Hermann Hesse, writing to his friends from the peace and
tranquillity of the Engadine, reflected on the feeling of guilt that
attacks people of his generation whenever they think of the
peaceful times before 1914.

> Whoever has been awakened and shaken by world history
> since the first collapse of the peaceful world will never be
> entirely free from the feeling of complicity, although it is
> more appropriate to the young, for age and experience should
> have taught us that this question is the same as that of our
> share in original sin and should not disquiet us; we can leave
> it to the theologians and philosophers. But since within my
> lifetime the world in which I live has changed from a pretty,
> sportive, somewhat self-indulgent world of peace to a place
> of horror, I will no doubt suffer occasional relapses into this
> state of bad conscience.[1]

Portions of this chapter orginally appeared in *Psychoanalytic Review*, 63(1),
1976, and are reprinted here by permission of Human Sciences Press, 72 Fifth
Avenue, New York, N.Y. 10011.

Throughout his life, Hesse and other intellectuals like him suffered occasional relapses into that "state of bad conscience," during which they would feel themselves responsible for the ills of the world. They were, after all, men and women *of* the world, not just *in* the world, helping to structure and shape the evolving future of Western culture, and their remorse perhaps was justified.

As alienated observers, however, merely describing the chaos and perhaps insightfully but prophetically predicting the holocaust of World War I or the rise of national socialism, these men and women could and often did claim innocence. For the truly sensitive artist, the thin line between describing a social movement and becoming a functional part of that movement is necessarily subtle and frequently obscure. The artist's work can become the conceptual lens through which people perceive the events around them, which in turn can significantly influence the future course of events. In many ways, the truly sensitive artist who claims to be unpolitical is doomed to be an unwilling prophet of a new politics for a new age. Ironically, the unpolitical artists who touch on those issues about which a people feel deeply may turn out to be far more politically significant than those who consciously set out to change the world.

Whether guilty or innocent of influencing world events, one of the responsibilities of those who played *The Glass Bead Game* in the Castilian world of Hermann Hesse was, in the end, to forsake the world of art for art's sake and return to the world of action in order to at least warn of the impending danger. Surely, the artist who senses the fire within and gives warning of the coming social conflagration cannot be held responsible for that fire. The problem remains, however, as to what extent the very analysis of both the ideal and the real form the combustible material out of which the fire developed in the first place. What are the functions of knowledge, and to what extent are the producers of that knowledge accountable for the ways such knowledge is used to shape our social destiny? What are the moral responsibilities of the artist as creative thinker to the human community? To what extent should the artist feel responsible for a world that went from one "of peace to a place of horror"?

Unanswered, and perhaps unanswerable, these questions are not easily dismissed. Their substantive nature strikes at the very heart of the moral function of imaginative art, whether in the form of painting, sculpture, literature, philosophy, or psychology. In this chapter I will examine critically the philosophical assumptions about human nature and the social order held by Carl G. Jung within a historical context and consider the possible implications these ideas had in terms of Hermann Hesse's therapeutic analysis. I will further consider the role these ideas may have played in helping to shape the world, and again raise the thorny question of responsibility.

Alienated from the bourgeois values that increasingly structured a mechanized industrial bureaucratic society, artists such as Hermann Hesse, seeking a more authentic existence, saw in the outbreak of World War I the hoped-for death of the old order and the birth of the new. They promptly volunteered their services to the cause,[2] but for Hesse and others disillusionment came quickly. The war did not bring an end to the unauthentic, fraudulent, bourgeois world; instead, it seemed to infuse new life into a decaying civilization. By 1918 the naive but desperate hope that somehow the new order might emerge from the ravages of war lay buried with the blood of ten million dead in the muddy trenches in Europe.

During these nightmarish years, Thomas Mann espoused a form of *Kultur* jingoism while pronouncing in *Betrachtengen eines Unpolitischen* that he was an unpolitical man and proud of it.[3] Profoundly shaken by the course of world events, and disillusioned with the liberal Enlightenment world of political action, Mann moved away from the world of politics at a critical moment in history: "I hate politics and the belief in politics, because it makes men arrogant, doctrinaire, obstinate, and inhuman."[4] Although he later changed his position and urged artists to return to politics, the course he set was essentially that of Hesse and others like him. In a world gone insanely barbaric, the meaning of life was no longer to be found in reforming sociopolitical institutions, but rather in the depths of the individual soul.

The revolt against middle-class values expressed in art, drama, literature, and youth culture at the fin de siècle in Europe eventually fused with the moral nihilism of World War I. As is always the case, the legitimacy of authority could not withstand the corrosive effects of the lies and deceptions so necessary to mobilize and sustain a people for the actions of war. While most expressionists were repelled by the horror of the trenches,[5] and the Dadaists mocked the *Kultur* that led men to their deaths in the trenches,[6] others such as Ernst Juenger, in *Thunder of Steel* (1919), found in the blind fury of the bloody violence the instinctual basis for a "new man" and a "new order" that would transcend the unauthentic bourgeois sense of good and evil. Many more artists turned away from the war in profound disgust. Paul Valéry perhaps was speaking for those disillusioned men and women when he said: "We do not know what will be born, and we fear the future, not without reason, we hope vaguely, we dread precisely; our fears are more precise than our hopes; we confess that the charm of life is behind us, but doubt and disorder are in us and with us."[7] It was little wonder that so many sensitive artists turned away from the outer world and sought the meaning of life in their inner souls.

Somehow humankind sensed that this was one of the rare moments of history when a transformation of values was about to occur. What remained of the Enlightenment faith in reason, whether expressed in a Comtean positivism or a Spencerian science, was declared bankrupt by Ferdinand Brunetière; what was left of Condorcet's faith in progress was declared dead by Georges Sorel, in his *Reflections on Violence*. The traditional Enlightenment faith in progress, science, technology, and reason—which for more than a century had cut deeper and deeper into the Judeo-Christian mythology that sustained Westerners with meaningful assumptions about their personal and collective existence—would no longer suffice.[8]

In a mass-technological society, which tends to obscure meaning, destroy identity, and degrade human value, the quest for meaning, identity, and value becomes all the more significant. The individual's guide in this quest was not the theologian or the philosopher, but the psychologist. Theologians such as St. Augustine and Jonathan Edwards, in the past and under the old faith, defined human nature, good and evil, and psychologically ministered to the existential loneliness of the individual. Now the psychotherapist defined human nature, sickness and health, and spiritually ministered to that same existential condition within a vastly changed social environment. As in the past, when diverse and competing theological positions on the nature of men and women and their place in the universe had emerged, in the modern era a wide range of psychological positions also emerged, defining human nature and our place in the universe. Competing assumptions about the nature of human nature and that reality lay at the base of most of the doctrinal disputes dividing the therapeutic community. Such assumptions shaped both diagnosis and therapy.[9] The life of the therapeutic individual, whether therapist or client, was dominated by an impulse for healing, for dispensing curative remedies to gain a sense of well-being; the life of the theological individual had been dominated most often by an impulse for salvation. Philip Rieff noted: "Religious man was born to be saved; psychological man is born to be pleased. The difference was established long ago, when 'I believe,' the cry of the ascetic, lost precedence to 'one feels,' the caveat of the therapeutic. And if the therapeutic is to win out, then surely the psychotherapist will be his secular spiritual guide."[10]

In 1909, when Sigmund Freud, Carl Jung, William James, G. Stanley Hall, and others met at Clark University, the age of the "therapeutic" was about to dawn, and with it the role of the psychotherapist as spiritual guide in the secular society. Earlier Goethe had sensed this trend: "Speaking for myself, I too believe that humanity will win in the long run; I am only afraid that at the same time the world will have turned into one huge hospital where everyone is everybody else's humane nurse."[11]

By the twentieth century, Christian theology and the mythology upon which it was based seemed to crumble under the weight of scientific investigation.[12] While some people turned to a scientific humanism as a substitute faith,[13] others vested their faith in a Comtean positivism, and still others turned to psychoanalysis. Although Freud, in an apparently anti-positivistic stance, argued that since humans think in terms of perceptions and everything must be translated in terms of those perceptions, of which we cannot free ourselves, "reality will forever be unknowable."[14] Ultimately he did place his faith in science and rationality, believing that it was an illusion to suppose that anything, including religion, could give us what science could not.[15]

Carl Jung based his psychology on the reality of what Freud called illusions. He argued that many of our modern neuroses stem from our inability to believe in the sacred myths of religion. Speaking before the Alsatian Pastoral Conference at Strasbourg, Germany, in 1932, Jung noted: "Courageous and upright persons [had the] feeling that our religious truths have somehow become hollow. Either they cannot reconcile the scientific and the religious outlook, or the Christian tenets have lost their authority and their psychological justification. People no longer feel redeemed by the death of Christ; they cannot believe—for although it is a lucky man who *can* believe, it is not possible to compel belief."[16]

Jung had experienced this problem in his immediate family—his father "suffered from religious doubts,"[17] which Jung believed contributed to, if not caused, his mental illness. He attributed his father's debilitating psychological condition, as well as his failure as a theologian, to his growing loss of faith in the fundamental Christian tenets. Several times the elder Jung advised his son, "Be anything you like except a theologian." Much of his youth, Jung recalled, was spent trying to come to grips with the religious beliefs of his father, whom he grew not only to disrespect but to "pity."[18]

In his youth Carl Jung experienced what he believed was "the grace of God." He had a secret vision which set the course of his "modern consciousness" and Gnostic beliefs, indeed of his entire youth. His vision left little to the imagination: "I saw before me the cathedral, the blue sky. God sits on His golden throne, high above the world—and from under the throne an enormous turd falls upon the sparkling new roof, shatters it, and breaks the walls of the cathedral asunder."[19] He experienced "illumination"; the "miracle of grace" had clarified his life. Jung now understood why and how his father's faith was so "empty and hollow," why his father "did not know the immediate living God who stands, omnipotent and free, above His Bible and His Church, who calls upon man to partake of His freedom, and can force him to renounce his own views and convictions in order to fulfill without reserve the command of God. In his trial of human courage God refuses to abide by traditions, no matter how sacred."[20]

Without this kind of direct experience, Jung felt that his father would never know that God ultimately was the author of evil as well as good. Spiritually enlightened by this Gnostic illumination, Jung's fate came sharply into focus.[21] Keenly sensitive to the inadequacies of his father's theology, and accepting his father's admonition to stay away from theology, Jung became not a doctor of theology but rather a "doctor of the soul." Traveling in his father's footsteps, he attended his father's university, joined his father's fraternity, and upon his father's death occupied his room and took over his position in the family, all of which gave him a feeling of "manliness and freedom."[22] His divinely guided fate would lead him to succeed where his father had failed. He believed that he had been spiritually called to minister to the needs of the therapeutic individual by cultivating a new, yet very ancient Gnostic theology. Jung's mother seemed to sense this when, shortly after her husband's death, she told Carl, "He died in time for you," which Carl interpreted to mean, "You did not understand each other and he might have become a hindrance to you."[23] His father's death freed him to develop a kind of faith that rejected the traditional dogmas of the church and adopted a system of beliefs based on the psychological experiences of religious mysticism once considered heresy.

Unlike Freud, who found an explanation for mysticism in repressed sexuality, Jung found the explanation rooted in the real demands of the collective unconscious and the darker spirits of the cosmic universe.[24] Traditional Christianity at its best could successfully deal with only half a world; the other half, the side of evil, occult, and darkness, could not be interpreted correctly. Evil was not, as most traditional Christians defined it, a mere absence of good; according to Jung, it was to be accorded its place in the universe with good. The God of the universe was not the God of good and light alone, but of evil and darkness as well. Jung's therapeutic faith included a process by which men and women could come to accept the evil that was in their shadow as well as in their God. They would overcome their alienation by being reunited to their true selves, properly rooted in the mystical archetypes of the cosmic universe. The universe Jung envisioned was Gnostic and Neoplatonic.

As the Western mind seemed to lose confidence in itself, and as the issue of decadence again became viable, historians such as Arnold Toynbee and Oswald Spengler reached back to the past to redevelop the classic cyclical theories of history. Jung also reached back to the pre-Christian era to recreate his Gnostic Neoplatonism for the modern world. Martin Buber recognized that Jung's psychoreligious therapy was more than a simple process of psychological healing—it was a fundamental challenge to the Judeo-Christian tradition.

> Gnosis is not to be understood as only a historical category, but as a universal one. It—and not atheism, which annihilates God because it must reject the hitherto existing images of God—is the real antagonist of the reality of faith. Its modern manifestation concerns me specifically not only because of its resumption of the Carpocratian motif. This motif, which it teaches as psychotherapy, is that of mystically deifying the instincts instead of hallowing them in faith. That we

must see C. G. Jung in connection with this modern man-
ifestation of Gnosis I have proved from his statements and
can do so in addition far more abundantly.[25]

Jung's Gnosticism not only challenged traditional beliefs, but in
the context of the modern world posed this basic moral issue:
Can we be held responsible for acting out the evil will of God?
Jung realized that his "new consciousness" reopened the biblical
problem of Job for himself and others who adopted his faith.[26]
This problem would recur repeatedly in his work, as well as in
that of Hesse and others who had taken this therapeutic path to
salvation.

As the therapeutic individual replaced the theological individual as spiritual guide to modern consciousness, the therapist
defined the psychological boundaries of health and sickness in
much the same way as the theologian had defined good and evil.[27]
Both delineated the boundaries of the mind or soul, and both
had to come to grips with the way that mind or soul interacted
with the world—a world often viewed as humanly destructive.
While therapists such as Alfred Adler advocated a kind of cooperative "social interest," which they thought might alleviate
the psychic as well as the physical suffering of humanity, others
took the more stoic path of Freud. To them, happiness was not
attainable, for ultimately the fault did not lie with society or
the individual but was inherent in the very unchanging nature
of men and women themselves. All culture, Freud believed, was
created out of libidinal restraint and sublimation. Universalizing
the reality principle based on human nature, Freud offered little
solace for the suffering soul: "A great deal will be gained if we
succeed in 'transforming your hysterical misery into everyday
unhappiness,' which is the usual lot of mankind."[28]

Wilhelm Reich, R. D. Laing, and others challenged the repressive social environment and advocated changing the reality
principle itself. Yet most therapists, in one way or another, made
peace with the world by helping their clients adjust, if only in
a suffering way, to the existing world. A part of that adjustment
included a definition of the neurotic person as that individual
who persists in suffering guilt and anxiety feelings derived from
a world which cannot be controlled. In this sense the well-balanced
individual is the one who loses little sleep over such things; the
person who does lose sleep is neurotic and can be treated. Hermann
Hesse spoke as a therapeutic man when he said:

Presumably this feeling of shared responsibility for the state of the world, which those who have it sometimes like to interpret as a sign of an especially sensitive conscience and a higher humanity, is only a sickness or, to be specific, a lack of innocence and faith. The completely well-balanced person will not hit upon the arrogant idea that he must share responsibility for the crimes and sickness of the world, for its inertia in peace and its barbarity in war, unless he is important and influential enough to be able to increase or lessen its suffering and guilt.[29]

What happens, however, to the unpolitical artist who is alienated from society, repelled by politics, and who turns inward in a search for meaning? Does he or she become increasingly powerless to control events and less responsible for the "crimes and sickness of the world"? Under such circumstances, the more alienated such persons become, the less likely they are to influence the course of political action and, in turn, the less guilt they should feel. The therapeutic individual thus can survive the bad feelings that erupt from time to time when remembering what took place at Buchenwald, Dachau, Belsen, Dresden, Hiroshima, or My Lai. Such was the moral dilemma—indeed, the moral tragedy—not only for Hermann Hesse, but for all imaginative artists who turned inward to find their authentic soul and in the end therapeutically lost their social conscience.

Psychotherapy requires a fundamental reeducation of the person and usually includes the adoption of the basic assumptions undergirding the therapist's philosophy of person, society, and nature. Thus, the kind of therapy a person undergoes is critical in shaping both what that person finds in his or her inner soul and the particular perspective from which he or she perceives the world of action. From May 1916 to November 1917, Hermann Hesse underwent seventy-two therapeutic sessions with Dr. Joseph Lang, a student of Carl Jung. The immediate literary consequence was the writing of his prize-winning novel *Demian*, which he is said to have written in 1917 in just a few weeks.[30] Published in 1919, *Demian* exerted an electrifying influence on German youth in the early years of the Weimar Republic. Thomas Mann wrote in a preface to a later edition: "With uncanny accuracy this poetic work struck the nerve of the times and called forth grateful rapture from a whole youthful generation who believed that an interpreter of their innermost life had risen from their own midst—whereas it was a man already forty-two years old who gave them what they sought."[31] While we might wonder just what it was that German youth in the 1920s found so attractive about *Demian*, it is clear that Jung's philosophy of life had profoundly shaped both Hesse's perspective of his own life and his writing.

Demian is the story of Emil Sinclair's youth and his struggle to "live in accord with the promptings which came from his true self." The story exemplifies the Jungian process of individuation. The young Sinclair struggles to free himself from the "persona," or social roles, that he is expected to play within a middle-class culture. In time, and with the assistance of Pistorius,[32] Sinclair confronts his "shadow" and finds the evil in his soul to be ultimately sparked by Abraxas, the Gnostic God of good and evil. Pistorius advises Sinclair, "Gaze into the fire, into the clouds, and as soon as the inner voices begin to speak, surrender to them, don't ask whether it's permitted or would please your teachers or father, or some god. You will ruin yourself if you do that. . . . Sinclair, our god's name is Abraxas and he is God and Satan and he contains both the luminous and dark world."[33] Young Sinclair then is led to discover that he is one of the children of Cain, who murdered his brother, to be sure, but only because he had the courage to follow his inner destiny, which God had willed. So it was with the two thieves crucified with Christ. Certainly the so-called good thief was not to be respected—he was nothing but a "sniveling convert." No, the real man of character was the thief who remained a thief, following his destiny to the appointed end.[34] The children of Cain, and all who bore the inner mark of Cain, could accept the evil within themselves and follow their destiny. As Sinclair's personal growth continued, he came to grips with Anima, Frau Eva, the archetypal feminine, maternal figure within his own soul. Accepting this femininity, Sinclair's process of individuation continued, until he eventually came to sense, feel, and then know his personal destiny. That destiny involved the destruction of the old order and the painful birth of the new. As one of the marked children of Cain, Sinclair was prepared to face and participate in the attendant evil and destruction.

Just as Jung found the traditional beliefs of Christianity wanting, so would Sinclair's Demian argue that Europe was dominated by the "herd instinct": "A whole society composed of men afraid of the unknown within them! They all sense that the rules they live by are no longer valid, that they live according to archaic laws—neither their religion nor their morality is in any way suited to the needs of the present. For a hundred years or more Europe has done nothing but study and build factories! They know exactly how many ounces of powder it takes to kill a man but they don't know how to pray to God." To be sure, Demian insisted that the coming revolution would be bloody and could not improve the world; but it would not be in vain. The bloodletting would "reveal the bankruptcy of present-day ideals, there will be a sweeping away of Stone Age gods. The world, as it is now, wants to die, wants to perish—and it will."[35]

There is remarkable similarity here between the way Jung and Hesse viewed their world. For example, in 1918, Jung prophetically predicted: "As the Christian view of the world loses its authority, the more menacingly will the 'blond beast' be heard prowling about in its underground prison, ready at any moment to burst out with devastating consequences. When this happens in the individual it brings about a psychological revolution, but it can also take a social form."[36] Hesse also sensed the imminent collapse of the present world: "What will come is beyond imagining. The soul of Europe is a beast that has lain fettered for an infinitely long time. And when it's free its first movements won't be the gentlest. But the means are unimportant if only the real needs of the soul—which has for so long been repeatedly stunted and anesthetized—come to light." Demian continues:

> Then our day will come, then we will be needed. Not as leaders and lawgivers—we won't be there to see the new laws—but rather as those who are willing, as men who are ready to go forth and stand prepared wherever fate may need them. Look, all men are prepared to accomplish the incredible if their ideals are threatened. But no one is ready when a new ideal, a new and perhaps dangerous and ominous impulse, makes itself felt. The few who will be ready at that time and who will go forth—will be us. That is why we are marked—as Cain was—to arouse fear and hatred and drive men out of a confining idyl into more dangerous reaches.[37]

The future clearly belonged to the children of Cain who were ready and willing to bloody themselves and others for the new ideal—indeed, the new order—that was coming.[38] Hesse had found his Demian, his inner voice, his destiny, his "master."[39] This was the expression of a philosophy of life appropriate for youth ready to ignore bloody violence in the process of giving birth to the new order. In the name of sincerity he insisted that we must reject the facade of bourgeois values. While the war had shaken the political institutions of the herd, Hesse found therapeutic salvation in a nihilistic world by listening to his inner voice echoing from the dark unconscious world that determined his fate. God really hadn't died after all—He had been rediscovered in the unconscious. He was, however, different from the traditional God. For Hesse He was, as Jung also had found Him, a Gnostic God of both good and evil.

Hesse, like others who adopted Jung's perspective of life, ran into the same problem: How could the individual be held responsible for acting out the evil will of God? Fate, destiny, and predetermination were central in this therapeutic philosophy, which not only allowed those in a humanly destructive world to engage in that world without suffering the pangs of what Hesse called a bad conscience, but also to further that destruction. How, then, is it possible to judge the ethics of such therapeutic individuals? Are they merely following their inner voice, prophetically acting as midwife to the evolving predetermined future? Or are their ideas, including that inner voice, the very stuff of which world events are shaped? The therapeutic, quasi-religious philosophy of Hesse and Jung cannot be judged in a social vacuum. It must be considered in not only the social matrix out of which it grew but also the social forces to which it contributed.

Jung's faith was created partly out of his personal need to overcome his father's inadequate faith as he saw those inadequacies projected across the religious conscience of the Western mind. It was further constructed out of a longing to overcome the alienation of technological urban existence by returning to a more authentic rural existence where the spiritual—indeed, the occult and demonic—myths were still creditable. Late in life Jung commented: "Plainly the urban world knew nothing about the country world, the real world of mountains, woods, and rivers, of animals and 'God's thoughts.' "[40] He imbibed deeply of the neo-romantic German nectar that allowed him to appreciate the primitive and the occult in a *Volk* culture, which he found rooted in the chthonic qualities of the soil.[41] The divine spirits literally lived in the earth, where they spiritually, psychically, and even physically influence our lives.[42] Relying on Franz Boas as an anthropological source, Jung pointed out that the American immigrant family underwent anatomical changes as a result of trespassing on Indian soil: "Thus the American presents a strange picture: A European with Negro behavior and an Indian soul. He shares the fate of all usurpers of foreign soil." To be personally authentic, he continued, we must be rooted to the earth. "He who is rooted in the soil endures. Alienation from the unconscious and from its historical conditions spells rootlessness. That is the danger that lies in wait for the conqueror of foreign lands, and for every individual who, through one-sided allegiance to any kind of -ism, loses touch with the dark, maternal, earthy ground of his being."[43]

Freud and the Jews were examples of those rootless individuals who adopted the -ism of materialism and lost touch with the earthy ground of their being. The problem with the Jews, Jung argued, was twofold. First, they represented an ancient civilization with a rationalized psyche which was abstract, spent, and so thoroughly developed that they had little if any youthful vigor or potential for future development. Second, they were wanderers, rootless, and therefore incapable of independent culture. Without the maternal earth to gain vital spiritual sustenance, Jews inevitably existed in a parasitical fashion. Speaking in Nazi Germany in 1934, Jung characterized a Jew as one "who is something of a nomad, has never yet created a cultural form of his own and as far as we can see never will, since all his instincts and talents require a more or less civilized nation to act as host for their development."[44] Given such overdeveloped consciousness and "soulless rationalism," reinforced by a narrow "materialistic outlook," the Jew's dominant role as therapist for the German people, Jung insisted, could only lead to the corruption of the true German psyche.[45] Jung argued that Freudian Jewish psychology ought to be abandoned for the more Aryan, racially conscious psychotherapy he espoused. As early as 1918, clearly identifying himself with the Germanic soul, Jung said:

> [Freud and Adler] are thoroughly unsatisfying to the Germanic mentality: *we* still have a genuine barbarian in *us* who is not to be trifled with, and whose manifestation is no comfort for *us* and not a pleasant way of passing the time. Would that people could learn the lesson of this war! The fact is *our* unconscious is not to be got at with over-ingenious and grotesque interpretations. The psychotherapist with a Jewish background awakens in the German psyche not those wistful and whimsical residues from the time of David but the barbarian of yesterday, a being for whom matters suddenly become serious in the most unpleasant way.[46]

Although after World War I Jung identified his soul with that of the Germans, which contained a barbarian character yet to be developed culturally, after World War II his identification shifted. In "After the Catastrophe" (1945), he accepted the guilt that went with being European, but he no longer wrote of "our" German soul; rather, he spoke of "his" Swiss background. As he put it: "Living as we do in the middle of Europe, *we* Swiss feel comfortably far removed from the foul vapours that arise from the morass of German guilt."[47]

Jewish stereotyping, which marked Jung's earlier work, tended to disappear from his writings after World War II, as did his references to a *Volk* Germanic soul. Instead, he tended to universalize his mysticism and write in terms of archetypes appropriate for all humans. Whether this shift was conscious or not is unknown. Nowhere did he seem to seriously entertain the possibility, however, that the *Volk* religious philosophy he espoused was part of the broader ideological Zeitgeist marking national socialism itself. On the contrary, he often pointed to his early discovery of the "blond beast" in the German soul as confirmation of his belief system. The beast now had broken out of its underground prison, and Jung saw himself as the one who had correctly warned Westerners what might happen.

The events in Germany from 1932 to 1945 confirmed in Jung's mind the belief about the chthonic, albeit demonic, qualities embedded in the unconscious soul of the German people. He saw Adolf Hitler as the "mirror of every German's unconscious": "He is the first man to tell every German what he has been thinking and feeling all along in his unconscious about German fate."[48] Jung asserted that Hitler's power was not political but "magical"—he was a mystic and prophet of the Third Reich, with all its trappings from Wotan to storm troopers. Hitler was a "true" leader, a charismatic leader, who spoke with the divine authority of the Gnostic God which lived in the unconscious soul of the German people. As Jung said:

> Now, the secret of Hitler's power is not that Hitler has an unconscious more plentifully stored than yours or mine. Hitler's secret is twofold: first, that his unconcious has exceptional access to his consciousness, and second, that he allows himself to be moved by it. He is like a man who listens intently to a stream of suggestions in a whispered voice from a mysterious source and then acts upon them. In our case, even if occasionally our unconscious does reach us as through dreams, we have too much rationality, too much cerebrum to obey it. This is doubtless the case with

Chamberlain, but Hitler listens and obeys. The true leader is always led.[49]

Just as Hesse's Demian advised the young Sinclair to "listen within yourself" to find the voice of fate, good, and evil—his "master"—so did Hitler act on his inner voice when he made the decision to march into the Rhineland, Austria, and Czechoslovakia. In those situations, Jung argued, "Hitler's unconscious knew—it didn't guess or feel, it *knew*—that Britain would not risk war."[50] Hitler listened and obeyed his own Demian. National socialism itself was an inevitable expression of the demonic divine.

With Hitler's rise to power in Germany, Freud and those Jews who dominated the field of psychotherapy came under direct attack. On April 6, 1933, Ernst Kretschmer, editor of the *Zentralblatt fürr Psychotherapie* and president of the International Medical Society for Psychotherapy, and all other Jewish members of his staff were forced to resign. Jung, the Society's vice-president, took over as president and as editor of the Aryanized journal.[51] He later argued that he did so to save psychotherapy from being completely wiped out because it was perceived as a Jewish discipline. Sharply criticized at the time by G. Bally, Jung responded that just as the totalitarian church had had its day and presently was in a state of decline, now the totalitarian state would have its day. He argued, "The 'metamorphosis of the gods' rolls rumbling on and the State becomes Lord of this world."[52] Under such inevitable circumstances, scientists must learn to "adapt themselves." Indeed, he insisted, "To protest is ridiculous—how protest an avalanche? It is better to look out. Science has no interest in calling down avalanches; it must preserve its intellectual heritage even under the changed conditions."[53] He was all for "render[ing] unto Caesar the things that are Caesar's and unto God the things that are God's. . . . There is no sense in us as doctors facing the National Socialist regime as if we were a party. As doctors we are first and foremost men who serve our fellows, if necessary under all aggravations of a given political situation. We are neither obliged nor called upon to make protests from a sudden access of untimely political zeal and thus gravely endanger our medical activity."[54]

A basic part of Jung's philosophy was not to protest, not to confront, but to allow the unconscious to find expression and then to moderate, if possible, the extremes.[55] He often had counseled not to face the national socialist movement directly. This was not so much a matter of tactics as of philosophy. National socialism, he believed, was an expression of the demonic religious spirit that welled up from the deeper reaches of the unconscious. Maintaining his Gnostic perspective, he commented to a friend: "Religions are not necessarily lovely or good. They are powerful manifestations of the spirit and we have no power to check the spirit."[56]

Jung's role in the Aryanization of the *Zentralblatt* was no doubt stimulated by his psychoreligious philosophy, which helped him see the rise of national socialism as inevitable, and also by his own personal distaste for Freud, as well as his long-standing stereotyped view of Jews. More significant, perhaps, was the role he believed Freud and his Jewish colleagues had played in profoundly misinterpreting, and thereby corrupting, the true German spirit. Writing in *Zentralblatt* (1934), an Aryanized journal to be read in a country where Jews were being beaten, tortured, and murdered on the streets, Jung described what he saw as the Jewish problem in psychotherapy:

> Freud and Adler have beheld very clearly the shadow that accompanies us all. The Jews have this peculiarity in common with women: being physically weaker, they have to aim at the chinks in the armour of their adversary, and thanks to this technique which has been forced on them through the centuries, the Jews themselves are best protected where others are most vulnerable. Because, again, of their civilization, more than twice as ancient as ours, they are vastly more conscious than we of human weaknesses, of the shadow-side of things, and hence in this respect much less vulnerable than we are. Thanks to their experience of an old culture, they are able, while fully conscious of their frailties, to live on friendly and even tolerant terms with them, whereas we are still too young not to have "illusions" about ourselves. Moreover, we have been entrusted by fate with the task of creating a civilization—and indeed we have need of it—and for this "illusions" in the form of one-sided ideals, convictions, plans, etc., are indispensable. As a member of a race with a three-thousand-year-old civilization, the Jew, like the cultured Chinese, has a wider area of psychological consciousness than we. Consequently it is *in general* less dangerous for the Jew to put a negative value on his unconscious. The "Aryan" unconscious, on the other hand, contains explosive forces and seeds of a future yet to be born, and these may

not be devalued as nursery romanticism without psychic danger. The still youthful Germanic peoples are fully capable of creating new cultural forms that still lie dormant in the darkness of the unconscious of every individual—seeds bursting with energy and capable of mighty expansion. The Jew, who is something of a nomad, has never yet created a cultural form of his own and as far as we can see never will, since all his instincts and talents require a more or less civilized nation to act as host for their development.

The Jewish race as a whole—at least this is my experience—possesses an unconscious which can be compared with the "Aryan" only with reserve. Creative individuals apart, the average Jew is far too conscious and differentiated to go about pregnant with the tensions of unborn futures. The "Aryan" unconscious has a higher potential than the Jewish; that is both the advantage and the disadvantage of a youthfulness not yet fully weaned from barbarism. In my opinion it has been a grave error in medical psychology up till now to apply Jewish categories—which are not even binding on all Jews—indiscriminately to Germanic and Slavic Christendom. Because of this the most precious secret of the Germanic peoples—their creative and intuitive depth of soul—has been explained as a morass of banal infantilism, while my own warning voice has for decades been suspected of anti-Semitism. This suspicion emanated from Freud. He did not understand the Germanic psyche any more than did his Germanic followers. Has the formidable phenomenon of National Socialism, on which the whole world gazes with astonished eyes, taught them better? Where was that unparalleled tension and energy while as yet no National Socialism existed? Deep in the Germanic psyche, in a pit that is anything but a garbage-bin of unrealizable infantile wishes and unresolved family resentments. A movement that grips a whole nation must have matured in every individual as well. That is why I say that the Germanic unconscious contains tensions and potentialities which medical psychology must consider in its evaluation of the unconscious.[57]

Jung denied repeatedly the charge of anti-Semitism that Freud, Bally, Reik, and many others made against him.[58] He frequently pointed out that some of his best students were Jewish and that he had written introductions for their books.[59] Adamantly he insisted that he was not against the Jews but against Freud and the application of his psychology, which was Jewish, to non-Jews: "I am absolutely not an opponent of the Jews even though

I am an opponent of Freud's. I criticize him because of his materialistic and intellectualistic and—last but not least—irreligious attitude and not because he is a Jew. In so far as his theory is based in certain respects on Jewish premises, it is not valid for non-Jews."[60] Throughout his life, however, Jung had stereotyped the Jew as rootless, burned out, overly conscious, materialistic, rationalistic, intellectualistic, abstract, and parasitic, someone unable to communicate with the chthonic qualities of the true Aryan soul. By contrast, he had stereotyped the Aryan as barbarian, youthful, creative, powerful, and dangerous, with a fantastic potential for building new cultural forms. Did such stereotyping make him anti-Jewish and pro-Aryan? Not at all, he argued. He merely was describing "scientifically" the psychological characteristics of two different races and pointing out the implications those differences had for therapeutic practice.[61]

Jung's racial psychology argument here is very close to the one that men like Arthur Jensen and Richard Herrnstein have used in America in recent years with respect to the cognitive abilities of blacks. They, too, claim they are not anti-black but merely are describing scientifically the cognitive differences between the races. They deny any responsibility for claiming one race to be superior to another, insisting that the society at large makes that judgment by determining those values they most cherish. In other words, in a racially oriented America, not only the stereotype—in this case "cognitive ability"—is determined by the white majority, but the value of the stereotype itself is determined by that majority. Such was the case in a racially oriented Germany. The racial psychologist absolves his or her conscience of the responsibility for both the stereotype and its social value, and under the guise of "science" proceeds to make recommendations for social action. By this reasoning, Arthur Jensen recommended that Americans should stop trying to teach cognitive skills to black preschool children, just as Jung called for action against Jewish psychotherapy as the corrupter of the German psyche.

While we must question the empirical validity of the stereotype being used and ask for solid evidence to demonstrate whether Jews are, in fact, materialistic, rootless, and so on—or blacks are, in fact, cognitively inferior—it is perhaps at least as important to question what a particular stereotype actually means within a historical context. Social stereotypes invariably carry

loaded meanings within a given culture. For a nation like pre–
World War II Germany, which had maintained a youth movement
for more than three decades,[62] the stereotype of the Aryan as
youthful, vigorous, alive, and creative, in juxtaposition to the
Jew as rationalized, materialistic, culturally spent, and old, carried
a profound if not deadly meaning. It is difficult to maintain the
position that Jung, Jensen, and Herrnstein have—that stereotypes
of Jews, and of blacks, are merely descriptive and therefore not
anti-Jew or anti-black. Whether or not a particular category in
which a people are placed is seen as positive, negative, or neutral
is a function of the normative beliefs of the society using those
terms.

Ultimately, then, the only way to judge whether or not Jung's
statements about Jews were anti-Semitic is to view them within
an established social context. While we might give him the benefit
of the doubt and recognize that he did not stereotype Jews so
that they could be burned in ovens, it is clear nevertheless that
he believed his stereotype of the Jew to be correct, and he stereotyped them specifically to show the damaging effects their
psychology had when applied to the German nation. At issue is
not the empirical truth or falsity of his statements about Jews,
or whether his intent was to counteract the damaging effect
Jewish psychology had on the German nation. In the historic
context of national socialism, Jung's statements must be assessed
as anti-Semitic in consequence. At the very least, he was guilty,
along with many others, of cultivating the intellectual climate
through which the "final solution" to the Jewish problem ultimately was made possible.

Why did Jung act as he did? Was he carried away with the
Zeitgeist and emotional trappings of the national socialist movement, making personal choices contrary to his stated philosophy
and a lifetime of work? On the contrary:

> The assertion that I acknowledge racial psychology only at
> this present juncture [1934] is incorrect. In 1927 I wrote:
> "Thus it is a quite unpardonable mistake to accept the con-
> clusions of a Jewish psychology as generally valid. Nobody
> would dream of taking Chinese or Indian psychology as binding
> upon ourselves . . ." and in 1928 I wrote . . ., "He [the Jew]
> is domesticated to a higher degree than we are, but he is
> badly at a loss for that quality in man which roots him to

the earth and draws new strength from below. This chthonic quality is found in dangerous concentration in the German People. . . . The Jew has too little of this quality."[63]

Built into Jung's philosophy from the very early days of his career was a racial stereotype cultivated in his youth. Recall that he associated his father's mental weakness with his inability to defend himself and his faith "against the ridiculous materialism of the psychiatrists." Jung's father had taken to reading Freud's translation of Bernheim's book on suggestion, the effect of which was negative: "But his psychiatric reading made him no happier. His depressive moods increased in frequency and intensity, and so did his hypochondria."[64] During those years, Jung's relations with his father were strained; he saw him as a man whose view of himself and the world had become rationalized and soured by attempts to live a life based on indefensible dogma. Jung's stereotype of the Jews and the condition of his father's theological beliefs are strikingly similar. He objected to his father's acceptance of dogmatic theology without the direct experience of "grace," yet after his father's death he studied dogmatic theology from his father's mentor, before a series of divine interventions led him to become a "doctor of the soul."

Jung also studied the dogma of the world with his father figure, Freud: "I can still recall vividly how Freud said to me: 'My dear Jung, promise me never to abandon the sexual theory. That is the most essential thing of all. You see, we must make a dogma of it, an unshakable bulwark.' He said that to me with great emotion, in the tone of a father saying, 'And promise me this one thing, my dear son: that you will go to church every Sunday!' "[65] Later, he would publicly reject Freud for requiring dogmatic belief in sexual theory, just as he secretly rejected his father's theological beliefs as dogmatic without benefit of grace. Shortly before his final break with Freud, Jung had a dream about an elderly man in the uniform of an Imperial Austrian customs officer; he recounted: "His expression was peevish, rather melancholic and vexed. There were other persons present, and someone informed me that the old man was not really there, but was the ghost of a customs official who had died three years ago. 'He is one of those who still couldn't die properly.' That was the first part of the dream."[66] Interpreting the border passing as part of Freud's censorship and control over the field of psychoanalysis, Jung continued: "As for the old customs official, his work had

obviously brought him so little that was pleasurable and satisfactory that he took a sour view of the world. I could not refuse
to see the analogy with Freud."

Much of Jung's analysis of this dream could have applied to
his own father as well as to Freud. The very words "sour view
of the world" were ones he used to describe his father's condition
shortly before he died. Jung later sensed this connection when
he wrote: "At that time Freud had lost much of his authority
for me. But he still meant to me a superior personality, upon
whom I projected the father, and at the time of the dream this
projection was still far from eliminated."[67] He proceeded to question whether or not his own revolt against Freud's strong personal
control over his public statements included that "death-wish
which Freud had insinuated I felt toward him."[68] On two occasions—once in Bremen in 1909 and again in Munich in 1912—
Freud suffered a fainting spell while Jung was speaking;[69] in both
cases, the subject of patricide was part of his speech. Freud explained his fainting behavior (albeit neurotic) as reading in Jung's
unconscious a death wish for him. Although Jung said that he
could not find any part of himself that reflected such a wish, he
was "distinctly shocked" by his dream about the Austrian customs
official.

We might hypothesize that Freud was correct—that Jung
did project a death wish for Freud, his "adopted" father. After
all, Jung had had some difficulty accepting his real father in both
life and death. It is also conceivable that Jung unconsciously
projected a death wish for Freud to all of Jewish psychology.
More than two decades after his break with Freud, Jung's father
problem still appeared in his public statements. Responding to
Bally's criticism of his role in helping to Aryanize the *Zentralblatt*,
Jung said: "I am grateful to my theological forebears for having
passed on to me the Christian premise, and I also admit my so-
called 'father complex': I do not want to knuckle under to any
'fathers' and never shall."[70]

Jung refused to knuckle under to Freud and "Jewish psychology" and continued his battle with his "fathers" into the
national socialist era. He saw nothing wrong with raising the
question of the effect of Jewish psychology on the German psyche
during one of the most virulent anti-Semitic periods of Western
history—"I must confess my total inability to understand why
it should be a crime to speak of 'Jewish' psychology."[71] The

psychologist who gave us such stereotypical categories as introvert and extrovert seemed unable—or unwilling—to understand the social consequences of stereotyping people. While the evidence does not warrant the assertion that Jung sought the destruction of Jews per se, he did actively seek the demise of Freudian and Jewish influence in psychology in Germany, and the consequences of such activities in some measure did contribute to the ensuing holocaust. Clearly, the Gnostic faith Jung developed allowed him to interpret Adolf Hitler as an expression of the demonic-divine, and therefore permitted him to caution others against direct opposition. No doubt, his relations, real and projected, with his "fathers" helped him frame his attitude toward Jewish psychology, which partly explains the choices he made throughout the tragic era of national socialism.

Whether we analyze Jung's philosophic-religious position or consider his personal psychological relation with his father, each analysis reveals part of the complicated process by which he made choices and asserted his own freedom. Such analyses may help us to better understand how and why a specific course of action was taken, but they should not be used to justify that action. Jung was responsible for the choices he made; in the end, he need not have remained true to his ideological commitments or his psychological hang-ups, except by choice. Even neurotics know that they need not act on fear, although they most often do. For some individuals more than others, the ideological sets and unconscious pressures generated in a repressive culture form the anesthesia that protects them from what Søren Kierkegaard knew to be the "fear and trembling" of moral choice.[72] The twentieth-century therapeutic individual chooses a form of therapy in much the same way his or her predecessors chose religious help—and in so doing assumes responsibility for the social consequences of that choice. "Man is nothing else but that which he makes of himself," Jean-Paul Sartre wrote:

> When we say that man chooses himself, we do mean that every one of us must choose himself; but by that we also mean that in choosing for himself he chooses for all men. For in effect, of all the actions a man may take in order to create himself as he wills to be, there is not one which is not creative, at the same time, of an image of man such as he believes he ought to be. . . . I am thus responsible for myself and for all men, and I am creating a certain image

of man as I would have him to be. In fashioning myself I fashion man.[73]

While Freud and his followers found the nature of modern illness rooted in a reality principle that in turn was embedded in human nature, and called for a form of stoic resignation, others like Jung rediscovered the ancient Gnostic God at work in the deep recesses of the unconscious of the modern individual's soul, and called for resignation to one's fate. Still others, such as Wilhelm Reich, sought to change the Freudian reality principle by calling for a sexual revolutuion. For many, however, neither the illness nor the cure was to be found in the individual per se. Speaking as a therapeutic man, Sartre argued that the roots of illness lay not in our nature, our soul, or our unconscious, but in the capitalist organization of society itself. He was in fundamental agreement with Friedrich Engels, who argued in *The Condition of the Working Classes in England* (1845) that capitalist industrialization inevitably developed a social system "in which a race of people could feel at home only if it were dehumanized, degraded, intellectually and morally depressed to the level of animals, and physically morbid."[74] Sartre agreed that capitalist society was a sick society, and illness was the only possible form of life under such a system. Thus, psychiatrists who try to help their clients adjust to the social ills of the world are themselves ill.

> In reality the psychiatrist who is a wage earner is sick like every one of us. The ruling class merely gives him the power of "cure" and of commital to institutions. It is self-evident that "cure" in our system cannot mean the *abolition* of illness: it serves exclusively the maintenance of work capacity, whereby one continues to remain ill. In our society there thus exists the healthy and the cured (two categories of the unconsciously sick who adapt to norms of production) and on the other hand the avowedly sick, those whom aimless rebellion incapacitates for work and who are delivered over to the psychiatrist.[75]

Psychotherapists who lead their clients to adjust to such a system serve as policemen for that system, whereas psychotherapists who seek a real cure—meaning the "abolition of the illness" itself—must become social revolutionaries.

The psychological therapy, philosophy, and religion—indeed, the life-style—we choose has important consequences for what we become individually and what influence we have collectively. Neither the Gnostic faith, *Volk* mysticism, occult beliefs, and Jewish stereotypes of Jung, nor the Gnostic Demian of Hesse's children of Cain were neutral concepts. Within the historical context of the twentieth century, these concepts were functionally useful parts of the ideological Zeitgeist that culminated in national socialism. To the extent that these concepts were freely chosen, and to the extent that they actually influenced people to act in a certain way, is the extent to which Jung's therapeutic individual was responsible for helping move the world from one of peace to a "place of horror." While it is difficult, if not presumptuous, to ascribe guilt for those crimes that have plagued humanity, it is clear that in the twentieth century neither art nor the artist has been unpolitical, as the artist so often claims.

Notes

1. Hermann Hesse, *Autobiographical Writings* (New York: Farrar, Straus and Giroux, 1972), p. 286.

2. Although Hesse had been living in Switzerland for over two years, he went to the German Consulate in Berne to volunteer for military service. See Bernhard Zeller, *Portrait of Hesse* (New York: Herder and Herder, 1971), p. 80.

3. See Peter Gay, *Weimar Culture: The Outsider as Insider* (New York: Harper Torchbooks, 1968), p. 73. See also George L. Mosse, *The Crisis of German Ideology* (New York: Grosset and Dunlap, 1964), p. 4, and *Germans and Jews* (New York: Fertig, 1970), p. 218.

4. Gay, *Weimar Culture*, p. 74.

5. The expressionist film *The Cabinet of Dr. Caligari*, as it was originally created by Hans Janowitz and Carl Mayer, focused explicitly on the issue of the legitimacy of all authority. As the play came under the direction of Robert Weine, however, the focus of the film was changed to only one kind of authority. See Gay, *Weimar Culture*, pp. 102–3.

6. The Dadaists of World War I might be favorably compared to the American Crazies during the Vietnam War. Both mocked the existing dominant culture.

7. Hans Kohn, *The Making of the Modern Mind* (New York: Van Nostrand, 1955), p. 79.

8. "Myth" is used in this chapter in a sociological way, as any idea or cluster of ideas that people believe in enough to use as a rationale for action. The critical question, then, is not whether the myth is true or false, but whether or not it works in shaping behavior.

9. Consider, for example, the competing philosophic assumptions explicit in such twentieth-century therapeutic approaches as those practiced by Sigmund Freud, George H. Mead, and B. F. Skinner.

10. Throughout this chapter I am using the term "therapeutic" as a broad category in much the same way as Philip Rieff uses the term to include such very diverse thinkers who sought remedies for the diseased Western mind as Freud, Jung, Reich, and Lawrence. See Philip Rieff, *The Triumph of the Therapeutic* (New York: Harper and Row, 1966), pp. 24–25. In this chapter our focus will be restricted to only one therapeutic man, C. G. Jung, and the way his ideas are reflected in the work of others such as Herman Hesse.

11. Quoted in Rieff, *Triumph of the Therapeutic*, p. 24.

12. See Carl G. Jung, *Psychology and Religion: West and East* (London: Routledge and Kegan Paul, 1958).

13. See John Dewey, *Common Faith* (New Haven, Conn.: Yale University Press, 1934).

14. Quoted in George L. Mosse, *The Culture of Western Europe* (Chicago: Rand McNally, 1961), p. 268.

15. Sigmund Freud, *The Future of an Illusion* (New York: Doubleday Anchor, 1964), p. 92.

16. Jung, *Psychology and Religion*, p. 337.

17. Carl G. Jung, *Memories, Dreams, Reflections*, A. Jaffe, ed. (New York: Vintage, 1963), p. 92.

18. Ibid., pp. 75, 55.

19. Ibid., p. 39.

20. Ibid., p. 40.

21. After this vision, other divine signs also steered Jung toward his chosen profession. One sign was the cracking of a solid walnut table; another was the breaking of a bread knife by mystical occult forces into several pieces. The latter, which occurred in 1898, helped him to decide not to be a surgeon. See Jung, *Memories, Dreams, Reflections*, pp. 104–9. For a picture of the knife, which he saved all his life, see his *Letters*, vol. 1, Gerhard Adler and Aniela Jaffe, eds. (Princeton, N.J.: Princeton University Press, 1973), p. 181.

22. Jung, *Memories, Dreams, Reflections*, pp. 94–96.

23. Ibid., p. 96.

24. While Jung interpreted his vision of God on a throne as a message from the divine, Freud probably would have interpreted it in terms of Jung's conflict with his father. The difference between the two positions is profound.

25. Martin Buber, *Eclipse of God* (New York: Harper Torchbook, 1952), pp. 136–37.

26. Jung, *Psychology and Religion*, pp. 357–470.

27. R. D. Laing, *The Politics of Experience* (New York: Random House, 1967).

279

28. Quoted in Herbert Marcuse, *Eros and Civilization* (Boston: Beacon, 1955), pp. 246–47.

29. Hesse, *Autobiographical Writings*, p. 286.

30. See Joseph Milek, *Hermann Hesse and His Critics* (Chapel Hill: University of North Carolina Press, 1958), p. 298. See also Clarence Boersma, "The Educational Ideal in the Major Works of Herman Hesse," Ph.D. dissertation, University of Michigan, 1948, p. 28; Hesse, *Autobiographical Writings*, p. xxiii.

31. Thomas Mann, "Preface," in Hermann Hesse, *Demian* (New York: Bantam, 1970), p. ix.

32. Most literary authorities agree that Sinclair was Hesse and Pistorius was Lang.

33. Hesse, *Demian*, p. 93.

34. Ibid., p. 52.

35. Ibid., pp. 115, 116.

36. Carl G. Jung, *Civilization in Transition* (London: Routledge and Kegan Paul, 1964), p. 13.

37. Hesse, *Demian*, p. 124.

38. Hermann Hesse was not a pacifist, as some seem to think. He had volunteered to serve in World War I but was rejected. Later he became disillusioned with the consequences of the war and publicly advocated detachment for the artist in order to preserve culture, for which he was severely criticized. However in 1914, in *If the War Goes On*, he said: "Since shooting is the order of the day, let there be shooting— not, however, for its own sake and not out of hatred for the execrable enemy but with a view of resuming as soon as possible a higher and better type of activity."

39. Hesse, *Demian*, p. 141.

40. Jung, *Memories, Dreams, Reflections*, p. 100.

41. I am using *Volk* as George Mosse defines the term in *The Crisis of German Ideology*, p. 4: "'Volk' is one of those perplexing German terms which connotes far more than its specific meaning. 'Volk' is a much more comprehensive term than 'people,' for to German thinkers ever since the birth of German romanticism in the late eighteenth century 'Volk' signified the union of a group of people with a transcendental 'essence.' This 'essence' might be called 'nature' or 'cosmos' or 'mythos,' but in each instance it was fused to man's innermost nature, and represented the source of his creativity, his depth of feeling, his individuality, and his unity with other members of the Volk."

42. Jung's doctoral thesis was entitled "On the Psychology and Pathology of So-Called Occult Phenomena" (1902).

43. Jung, *Civilization in Transition*, p. 49.

44. Ibid., p. 166.

45. The abstract materialism with which Jung stereotyped the Jew and Jewish psychology also appeared in his association with his father's

problem of faith: "He could not even defend himself against the ridiculous materialism of the psychiatrists. This, too, was something one had to believe, just like theology, only in the opposite sense." Jung, *Memories, Dreams, Reflections,* p. 74.

46. Jung, *Civilization in Transition,* p. 14 (italics added).

47. Ibid., p. 196 (italics added).

48. Hubert R. Knickerbocker, "Diagnosing the Dictators," *Hearst's International Cosmopolitan* (Jan. 1939): 116.

49. Ibid.

50. Ibid.

51. For a sympathetic treatment of Jung's role in this event, see E. Harms, "Carl Gustav Jung: Defender of Freud and the Jews," *Psychiatric Quarterly* (Apr. 1946): 199–230. For a more critical review, see Edward Glover, *Freud or Jung* (New York: Meridian, 1956), pp. 141–53. For personal letters relevant to the issue, see Jung, *Letters,* 1:131–65.

52. Jung, *Civilization in Transition,* p. 537.

53. Ibid., p. 538. Hermann Hesse did not protest either, and under the circumstances, the Third Reich neither banned nor burned his books. From 1933 to 1945, Hesse had twenty books in print in Germany, which sold some 481,000 copies. See Zeller, *Portrait of Hesse,* pp. 131–32.

54. Jung, *Civilization in Transition,* p. 539.

55. While the *Zentralblatt* was reorganized during his presidency of the International Medical Society for Psychotherapy, Jung was also instrumental in getting the international association to adopt an enabling clause to allow German Jewish doctors to become members of other national groups. See Jung, *Letters,* 1:149.

56. Ibid., p. 159.

57. Jung, *Civilization in Transition,* pp. 165–66.

58. See Sigmund Freud, "On the History of the Psychoanalytic Movement" (1914), *Collected Papers,* vol. 1 (London: Hogarth, 1953); G. Bally, "Deutschstammige Psychotherapie," *Neue Zurcher Zeitung* 154(1934); Glover, *Freud or Jung;* see also E. Freeman, "Theodor Reik," *Psychology Today* (Apr. 1972): 50.

59. Erich Neumann was one such example. See Jung, *Letters,* 1:167.

60. Ibid., p. 154.

61. Throughout this discussion, I use the term "stereotype" in a sociological sense, as a fixed ideological matrix into which groups of people are categorized and objectified, not in a pejorative sense.

62. See David C. Poteet, "The Nazi Youth Movement (1920–1927)," Ph.D. dissertation, University of Georgia, 1972; Walter Z. Laqueur, *Young Germany* (New York: Basic Books, 1962). See also Mosse, *Germans and Jews.*

63. Jung, *Civilization in Transition,* p. 544.

64. Jung, *Memories, Dreams, Reflections,* p. 94.

65. Ibid., p. 150.

66. Ibid., p. 163.

67. Ibid.

68. Ibid., p. 164.

69. Ibid., pp. 156–57.

70. Jung, *Civilization in Transition*, p. 540.

71. William McGuire, *The Freud-Jung Letters* (Princeton, N.J.: Princeton University Press, 1974), p. 541. Since this chapter was originally given as a paper at the University of Pennsylvania, the correspondence between Freud and Jung has been published. Jung's father problem and his association of that problem with both the religion of his father and Freud as a father figure are clearly reflected in the correspondence between the two men, as well as between Freud and Jung's wife, Emma. For example, see ibid., pp. 94–95, 157–60, 186–87, 215–17, 218–19, 232–33, 300–301, 328–30, 455–57, 534–35.

72. Jean-Paul Sartre, in his essay on "Self-Deception," warns about using the unconscious to escape the burden of choice. George Mosse also correctly points out that the danger in psychohistory lies not only in the tendency to move to a single cause, but also in the tendency to fall into a predetermination analysis. See Mosse, "Commentary," *History of Childhood Quarterly* 1(1973): 230–33.

73. Quoted in William Kaufman, *Existentialism from Dostoyevsky to Sartre* (New York: Meridian, 1963), pp. 291–92.

74. Jean-Paul Sartre, *Socialist Patients Collective*, p. 3, mimeographed pamphlet, 1972.

75. Ibid.

9

MARGARET NAUMBERG [1890–1983]

WALDO FRANK [1889–1967]

Art in a Therapeutic Age

If, as the Frankfurt school of thought suggests, the modern age suffers from a widespread disease diagnosed as "alienation," then it seems reasonable also to characterize that age in terms that incorporate the human attempt to overcome estrangement, as Philip Rieff did in *The Triumph of the Therapeutic* (1966). In this context, artistic creation itself, whether performing, literary, or visual, is perceived as taking on a therapeutic function. Sigmund Freud suggested as much when he said: "If the individual who is displeased with reality is in possession of that artistic talent which is still a psychological riddle, he can transform his phantasies into artistic creations. So he escapes the fate of a neurosis and wins back his connection by this roundabout way."[1] In past ages, when the artist was considered more a purveyor of beautiful and useful things and when the many-sided relatedness of that artist's creative work to a living community was clear, Freud's words would have fallen on deaf ears. In the present age, however, when alienation has become widespread and much individual and collective human activity resembles neurotic forms of escape, viewing the artistic act of creation as a healing process is commonly accepted.

The role of the artist in any given culture depends upon

various historic circumstances. In one and the same age, some artists may openly work as courtiers of the dominant elite, while others serve the cause of social upheaval; some may romantically claim to divorce themselves from all social utility and practice art for art's sake, while others may claim to possess the eternal verities of the past. Whatever position is espoused and whatever art is pursued, these artists all are participants in the historic age in which they live; and in one form or another, all are engaged in the process of creating a consciousness of reality which ultimately characterizes their age by setting the peculiar aesthetic boundaries in which the collective community exists. In this sense, the creative artist is both an inheritor of a historically determined consciousness and a creator of a new consciousness.

Karl Marx suggested that the artist creates the consciousness of an age out of the economic-social matrix: "The mode of production of material life determines the general character of the social political and spiritual processes of life. It is not the consciousness of men that determines their being, but, on the contrary, their social being determines their consciousness."[2] However, we might move beyond Marx and suggest that the consciousness derived from a given mode of production may itself become a creator of a new reality, one that transactionally relates to a new means of production in the forthcoming age. Sensitive artists,[3] whether performing, literary, or visual, estranged or connected, thus play a crucial role in our lives. Waldo Frank noted that even in a dying civilization, "creation is revolution."[4] The kind of art nurtured in any given age helps us understand not only that civilization but, in a real sense, possible futures as well.

The modern age was born when the national state and capitalism emerged as the undisputed successors to the medieval worldview. With that historic development came a fundamental transformation in values: poverty became less a virtue and more a vice; work itself progressively lessened as an act of creation and became more an act designed for profit. As the notion of usury faded into the dusty pages of medieval history and the profit motive came to dominate the workplace, the factory system and the machine industry gradually replaced artistic minds and skilled artisan hands. In the social context of the nineteenth-century industrial revolution, the new middle class, which had led the eighteenth-century liberal revolutions and established its own ideological political position in terms of parliamentary government, increased in power, size, and significance. In urban areas nourished by the factory system, the new wealthy classes lived and cultivated the arts. Great political and economic centers of the West thus became cultural centers where the arts were patronized. In Europe, growing metropolitan areas such as London, Paris, and Vienna were the cultural focus of the European bourgeoisie.

By the third quarter of the nineteenth century a new style of visual art was coming to the fore: impressionism began to attract the attention of younger artists.[5] For various political reasons, however, impressionism as a literary art made itself felt somewhat later. In either form, impressionism was first an urban art form and second an art form that began to erode the traditional structure of reality which had dominated the Western mind since the Middle Ages. Visually, impressionists would accomplish with colors what those in literature achieved with words and conceptual meanings. In a very real sense, impressionism expressed for the children of the urban, affluent middle class an emerging sense of reality, which ultimately evolved in terms of an identity crisis for those individuals. Impressionism, at a deeper level, also represented a new ordering of reality which would set the world into motion, and lead to chaos for many. The world of the machine was one of whirling speed and an atomized competitive existence in which process became more important than product, becoming more important than being.[6] As social structures eroded before this driving force, and as one social sanctuary after another collapsed into a Heraclitean stream of evolutionary consciousness, it became clear that humankind was about to undergo the most significant aesthetic revolution since the Renaissance. Out of this revolution emerged the radically different conceptions of time and space that would ultimately shape modern existence.

Those who entered this Heraclitean stream of consciousness— William James, Henri Bergson, Friedrich Nietzsche, Fydor Dostoyevski, and Franz Kafka among them—did not step into it in precisely the same place, nor did they interpret reality in precisely the same manner. All, however, eventually sought to leave that stream for more solid ground.[7] In rejecting the facade of bourgeois appearance in the name of a new sincerity, they each sought a new form of spiritual security amid a nihilistic social reality. The aesthetic revolution in bourgeois culture, which began with impressionism and continued into postimpressionism, symbolism, cubism, dadaism, and surrealism, clearly reflected a profound wrenching of Western culture.

It matters little whether we agree with Max Weber, who analyzed the social functions of mechanized and reified institutions in the form of bureaucracies, or with Freud, who explored the symbolic meaning at work in the unconscious, for both thinkers constructed their analyses out of a reality structure that took for granted the dissolving certainties of bourgeois culture. As the nineteenth century came to a close, some seemed to confuse that fin de siècle with the end of civilization itself; others viewed the art, literature, and poetry of the young *bohème* of Munich, Vienna, and Paris as clear evidence of the decadence that had overtaken Western civilization. Sexual freedom, psychoanalysis, unconscious expressionism, drug consciousness, atonal music, group psychic manipulation, and occult spiritualism were all part of the new bohemianism that existed in virtually every major cultural center of western Europe at the end of the nineteenth century, each a form of revolt, mocking the older established order.

In the decade prior to World War I, America developed its own bohemian culture in Greenwich Village. Here, too, it was nurtured in an urban setting by the sons and daughters of the affluent bourgeoisie. Impressionism, postimpressionism, and cubism were introduced through the efforts of Alfred Stieglitz and those associated with a variety of salons in and around the Village. The first major showing of modern art for American audiences was the Armory Show of 1913.[8] Oddly enough, impressionism and postimpressionism appeared in America three to four decades later than it had in Europe. Although we might readily account for the lag as a consequence of the late development of an American *bohème* capable of supporting such art, a more exact explanation might be found in the metaphor of "progress" that tended to dominate American literary and artistic history. This metaphor, implicitly assumed in the Puritan concept of the "city on a hill," had become the belief that America was a redeemer nation. It surfaced politically in the nineteenth century as "manifest destiny" and in the twentieth century as "making the world safe for democracy." In a practical sense, this metaphor undergirded the frontier thesis and the westward movement.

In American literature, the overriding optimism of progress seems to have delayed the discovery of the more pessimistic genius of Herman Melville, for example, until well into the twentieth century. The arcadian myth and the pastoral image corollary to the belief in frontier progress dominated much artistic expression until then.[9] America was viewed as a new garden where a second Adam would be born—indeed, the last great hope of humanity. The arcadian discussion of the American metaphor of progress stimulated the development of playgrounds and national and city parks when the western frontier closed and emphasis was shifted to urban industrial frontiers.[10] This very metaphor had been shaken by the thundering sounds of the locomotive in Thoreau's *Walden Pond* and had become an empty, illusory promise for Nick Carraway in Fitzgerald's *The Great Gatsby*. Throughout much of the nineteenth century and part of the twentieth, the future still held the real promise of American life, as demonstrated in Walt Whitman's *Democratic Vistas*. American literary artists were not very publicly introspective. Nevertheless, at the beginning of the twentieth century, certain young writers, such as Waldo Frank, who struggled to find a spiritual promise in what he later came to characterize as *The American Jungle*, felt the time was ripe for self-reflection.

Sensitive young artists like Frank flocked to the Village, in rebellion against their bourgeois parents and their life-styles, as well as the materialistic values undergirding American industrialism and the alienation they had experienced while growing up in a business-oriented urban world. These new American bohemians readily mixed radical and reactionary protest and experimented with whatever seemed to challenge the existing mores of what they perceived to be mainstream America. Prior to World War I, as Malcolm Cowley points out in *Exile's Return*, both the politically radical and bohemian currents flowed side by side through Greenwich Village.[11] The artist and the revolutionary, though often distinct, were carrying on an open dialogue. Whether at Alfred Stieglitz's small gallery at 291 Fifth Avenue or at any of the numerous bohemian meeting places in the Village, you were as apt to run into Big Bill Haywood, Alexander Berkman, or Emma Goldman, as you were to meet Sherwood Anderson, John R. Dos Passos, Margaret Naumberg, or Waldo Frank. The Village was alive with dissenters, political as well as artistic, challenging the social values of the traditional community.[12]

For the most part, those who emerged as leaders in this setting were no ordinary revolutionaries. Many came from affluent, professional, upper-middle-class families who had sent their offspring to Harvard, Yale, Princeton, Radcliffe, or Barnard, as well as on frequent and extended trips abroad, where they came in direct contact with their European counterparts. For some, what transpired in those years was only a youthful interlude on the way to becoming part of the established mainstream; for others, the revolt that began in the Village would continue throughout their lives. Walter Lippman, for example, participated in his youth in the radical *bohème* and flirted with their ideas, but in the end he made a pragmatic compromise with the requirements for success in the mainstream of American liberalism. Others, such as Waldo Frank and Margaret Naumberg, traveled a somewhat different course. They both imbibed heavily of the spirits of postimpressionistic art and reality; both refused to accept the world as they knew it; and both were governed by an impassioned idealism to make that world over, which in turn led them into revolt and resistance against family, friends, class, and country. Each adopted psychoanalysis as an instrumental philosophy of life by which to therapeutically make sense of their existence. In the end, they found spiritual certainty in the deeper recesses of the unconscious and, in turn, anchored their psychic beings in a cosmic sense of reality.

This chapter explores and analyzes the beginnings of the use of psychoanalysis as exemplified by Waldo Frank in his literature, and then considers Margaret Naumberg's application of psycho-analysis, first in therapeutic education and later in her work in the field of art therapy. The reality principle generated by both individuals also will be critically analyzed.

Although impressionism in art originated within the middle class as a sensual revolt against clumsy materialism, it employed a process that broke with the traditional use of colors and, when developed further in both literature and art, exploded our spatial sense of reality as well as our linear concept of time. As modern men and women stepped into the Heraclitean stream of con-sciousness, the future, the present, and the past all seemed to dissolve into the consciousness of the unconscious, where only the past held any real meaning. Impressionism in literature was reflected in such classic psychological novels as Marcel Proust's *Remembrance of Things Past*. As the very structure and form of reality dissolved into the unconscious stream, and as the search for positive knowledge became a quest for self-knowledge, expressionism in art and literature took the form of a self-centered search for reality through a critical analysis of the meanings behind the symbolism at work in the unconscious mind. Although Freud had declared that "reality will forever be unknowable,"[13] he nonetheless sought to discover the laws that govern the process of reality construction in the human mind. Psychoanalysis is itself a form of analytic symbolism with a variety of turns. Although Freud knew that "wherever id goes there too goes ego," he remained convinced that only the delicate and fragile voice of reason would light the pathways of the subterranean world of the human soul. Jung, by contrast, took a more spiritualistic path through the soul to find a cosmic reality in a Gnostic God. Waldo Frank came to know the ideas of both men through the influence of his wife, Margaret Naumberg.

Frank, the son of a successful New York lawyer, attended a private preparatory school in Lausanne, Switzerland, and in 1911 was graduated Phi Beta Kappa from Yale. From 1911 to 1913 he worked as a reporter for the *New York Evening Post* and the *New York Times*. In 1913 he lived in Paris among the avant garde. Unlike the ordinary expatriate who found a home away from home in Paris, however, Frank could not remain there. "I was happy here (in Paris) but I was not *needed*. I was being nourished by what other men, through centuries and ages had created. I was a parasite."[14] He returned to America, not only to discover his native roots, but in a larger measure to help fulfill a promise. He felt strongly impelled to answer the clarion call of Walt Whitman for an American literary artistry, one that could meet the challenge of *Democratic Vistas*. Frank wrote: "This then is our task. Whitman foresaw it and sang of it and warned us. We must go through a period of static suffering, of inner cultivation. We must break our impotent habit of constant issuances into petty deed. We must begin to generate within ourselves the energy which is love of life. For that energy, to whatever form the mind consigns it, is religious. Its act is creation and in a dying world, creation is revolution."[15] By 1914, Frank had settled down with Margaret Naumberg in Greenwich Village to begin a professional writing career.

It was clear to Frank that the old Puritan values, which had sustained and made possible the affluent condition of his own class, had become life-destroying values from which he must free himself and his country. If a new America was to be born, a new consciousness would be required, one that would overcome the materialism, the mechanization, and the very alienation of humankind from itself, from its fellows, and from its spiritual roots. The creative artist, struggling to transcend this condition of alienation, must become a critic.

> In ages of cultural stability, of cultural integrity, the creative
> writer may more or less keep his critical activities to himself:
> the standard by which he lives and works may be implicitly
> accepted. In an age like ours in which the accepted forms
> of all values have broken down and the critical field is noisily
> preempted by shallow and false men, every true literary artist
> feels the need of re-establishing his cultural roots, of developing
> and articulating his cultural values in terms of his own time.
> Irresistibly, he becomes a critic.[16]

For Waldo Frank, the battle for authenticity, sincerity, and life
itself was fought to understand himself, while at the same time
establishing his cultural roots, free of the fear of life emblazoned
on his soul so early in life: "I hope that this present state of not
being afraid of life will not pass away. The direst of all the
horrible heritages of the class of society in which I was born is
this fear of life—this rotting conservatism. I trust to God my
bones and my heart are free of it. But one can never be sure.
One never gets over one's early legacies. All one can do is to
sublimate or to counter-act them."[17]

Frank's struggle to free himself from his upbringing was
enhanced by his wife's knowledge of psychoanalysis, which she
had gained through recent analysis with Beatrice Hinkle, one of
the leading female psychoanalytic therapists in New York City.[18]
Hinkle knew well the difference between Freud and Jung, having
studied with both; respectful of Freud, she preferred Jung's treatment of the unconscious. The Jungian influence was critically
significant to the lives of such young people as Margaret Naumberg
and Waldo Frank (albeit secondhand). His brand of psychoanalysis
would provide the conceptual vehicle through which the alienated
soul could be reconnected with life and the universe.

Jungian analysis meant, in part at least, the rediscovery of
the Neoplatonic "great chain of being" that exists in the soul
and both mystically connects us with the timeless cosmic forces
of the universe and integrates the disparate sides of our conscious
self. Through this process, its adherents believed, we might overcome modern life's damaging effects on our sense of belonging.
Jung's psychology was built on a philosophy that carried all the
earmarks of a modern revival of ancient gnosticism (see chap.
8). We may assume that many persons who, in the course of
Jungian therapy, adopted the philosophical assumptions underlying
his psychological (if not his religious) perspective, did so for a
variety of personally satisfying reasons. But it also should be

clear that a Jungian view of life offered peculiar attractions for those seeking a certain kind of perspective—to those troubled by modernity, by the erosion of custom and tradition, and by the feeling of rootlessness attendant on urban and industrial developments. Such people found solace, if not roots, in the primitive archaic unconscious, where time was eliminated and where in the eternal present, the cosmic present, they might truly commune with the noble dead. For Waldo Frank and others, this Jungian philosophy at least temporarily provided the psychospiritual haven from which they could sail forth and do battle with the world. Frank's mystical discovery provided the anchorage that would free him to espouse a variety of socially radical causes.

Jungian philosophy also offered welcome relief for those in revolt against the repressive character of the patriarchal society that undergirded Freud's worldview. Jung's discussion of anima and animus, the feminine and masculine, allowed for a break with the masculine dominance of Freudian psychology without blurring or collapsing the traditional distinctions between masculine and feminine psychosexual roles.[19] Jung also postulated the mother as the really dominant figure in a child's life, an idea that attracted young women to his therapeutic approach to psychoanalysis. Hinkle noted: "Jung's development of this point of view shows very clearly that, just as the problem of the father is the great fact of Freud's psychology, the problem of the mother is the essence of Jung's, with the struggle carried on between the two great forces of love and power."[20]

Combining a Freudian view of rationalization and sublimation with a Jungian view of the role of mother in one's psychic life, Margaret Naumberg guided Waldo Frank's self-analysis and search for the spiritual meaning of existence.[21] Between 1917 and 1920, while undergoing such an analysis, Frank composed a deeply moving novel, entitled *The Dark Mother*, which he dedicated to Naumberg. In that novel he described and analyzed in expressionist form the psychological rebirth of David Markand, who suffered from an Oedipus complex. Themes reflecting the generation gap, rebirth, anti-modernity, alienation, anti-materialism, and the dread of anomie, all cast in a basic structure of Jungian archetypal characters, abound in Frank's book. The young Markand worked out his feelings toward himself and developed a truly integrated personality—the ultimate goal of therapy and of the novel. Recall that a Jungian analytical approach to therapy calls for working through the evil, or the "shadow," which exists in the deeper levels of one's unconscious by allowing it to surface to a conscious level where it can be treated. In this process one must also deal with the feminine and masculine characteristics of one's own nature. Opposites, whether good or evil, masculine or feminine, must not be repressed but rather must be allowed to express themselves in a conscious form. It should also be noted that Jungian therapy thus easily lends itself to expressionist forms in literature. Frank's novel is just such a form.[22]

In *The Dark Mother*, Jungian archetypal characters are brought to the foreground of consciousness and played out as a part of David Markand's personality. The two major characters besides David are Tom and Cornelia Rennard, who serve as the anima and animus, mirrorlike images of different parts of David's personality. These masculine and feminine characteristics are reflected in David's life as he attempts to free himself from the womb, to be born anew. At times, Tom represents both the dark shadow with which David must come to grips and the homosexual desires with which he must learn to deal. Cornelia, in turn, represents David's need to deal with the feminine side of his personality and his incestuous desires, all within a psychosymbolic womb: "The world was a Dark Mother. The Night of the miracle of worlds was fleshed and was a Mother. She moved in infinite directions as infinite path. She was moveless. And he within her, moving with the world toward the movelessness of birth."[23] Apparently, Frank was profoundly disturbed while writing this novel, yet he worked his way through a kind of self-analysis to gradually and symbolically overcome what both Tom and Cornelia represent. In the novel, Tom fades out of existence, and Cornelia, in therapist-like fashion, encourages David to take up with a young woman named Helen Daindrie. Then Cornelia, who had painted the inner reflections of her soul in water colors, burns her paintings and commits suicide.[24]

The Dark Mother is a heavy psychological work, combining elements of social protest with the central Jungian structure of analytic psychology, all cast in an expressionist novel. This was not the first time, nor would it be the last, that a novel was used as a therapeutic outlet. Herman Hesse's *Demian*, which so captured the imagination of German youth in the 1920s, was written shortly after Hesse had completed a period of Jungian analysis (see chap. 8). It, too, contained many Jungian archetypal symbols, but with a difference. After reading *Demian*, it is rather clear that Hesse was well on his way to resolving his personal difficulties.

Frank's *The Dark Mother*, however, reveals so many deeply disturbing psychological problems that we can never really be confident that he adequately worked his way through his problems. It is not unreasonable to assume that at least part of the subtle but distinctive Jungian structure of *The Dark Mother* was influenced by Margaret Naumberg who introduced her husband to psychoanalysis.[25]

Although in his later years Frank was associated with the Communist Party, that association tended to be peripheral. He pursued a distinguished writing career that reflected his own quest for social justice: from commentaries on his experiences when he posed as a black man in the South, to the Harlan County coal strike in Kentucky, and fascism in Argentina, to a portrait of Fidel Castro's Cuba. Naumberg, on the other hand, was more thoroughly disenchanted with collective reform after their divorce in 1926. Within a few years after leaving the school she had established, which was committed to applying psychoanalysis to childhood education,[26] she pursued a distinguished career in the field of art therapy. More therapist than social activist, she came to view social reform and the possibility of collective political action as fruitless ventures. Public schools, she concluded late in her life, continue to be in a hopeless bureaucratic shambles, more often serving the cause of anti-education than education.[27]

Like so many other sensitive young people, Naumberg became disillusioned with political action. Unlike many of her peers, however, she was not a critic without a program. She wanted to reform individuals rather than institutions. Psychoanalysis would light the path through the inner life, making it possible, quite literally, to commune with the living thoughts of the noble dead.[28] Those who followed this path could overcome the superficiality and rootlessness of modern life and build an integrated psychic existence in spite of the failings so apparent in the larger social order. Naumberg had not always believed that direct institutional reform was hopeless, however. In her college days she had been head of the Socialist Club and had repeatedly called for major political and institutional reforms. While at Barnard, she roomed with Evelyn Dewey, took courses with John Dewey (she found them boring), counted Walter Lippmann as one of her "closest men friends,"[29] and tried to move the Socialist Club to take more aggressive stands against social injustice. Dissatisfied with the middle-class urban life in which she had been reared, Naumberg became actively involved in attempts to change that world. She was by temperament an experimenter, committed to trying the new in the interest of what she believed was a better world. Frank described her in those days as "a beautiful woman, dark, with great luminous eyes and a dynamic compassion that was not ready to settle for less than a totally new world."[30]

In revolt against both her parents and society, she found herself in difficult psychological waters upon graduation from college. Given her inclination to try the experimental and the novel, she turned to psychoanalysis, first with Jungian analyst Beatrice Hinkle and some time later with A. A. Brill, a Freudian analyst.[31] Shortly after her period of analysis with Hinkle, Naumberg left for England to study at the London School of Economics under the direction of Sidney and Beatrice Webb. She took courses in economics with Graham Wallas and wrote a paper on the beginnings of the motion picture industry in London. During her stay she met Maria Montessori, who was lecturing on her own new methods of education. Naumberg traveled to Rome to study these methods further, and upon her return to New York City, she opened a Montessori school in the Henry Street Settlement House. Dissatisfied with the overt structuring inherent in Montessori's method, however, she abandoned the approach and moved to create her own school. By 1914, when that school opened, she was living openly with Waldo Frank in Greenwich Village.[32] Revolting against the social mores of the time, as well as the traditional approaches to education, Naumberg set out to create a school that would utilize psychoanalysis as a guiding philosophy.

Margaret Naumberg's Walden School, having begun in 1914 as a nursery school for two-year-olds, added new students at that level each year and graduated its first high school class in 1928. By 1940, 126 students had graduated from the school, 114 of whom went on to college.[33] With Central Park at its door, the school drew students from the wealthy professional upper-middle class; nevertheless, it was always short of funds. From 1914 until 1922, when she withdrew from the directorship, Naumberg invested not only her time and energy but also her personal wealth. The school was, by most reports, a success. Using an extremely diversified curriculum, it provided learning situations from technical shopwork to lectures on anthropology by professors from the New School for Social Research.

Central to the curriculum of Walden School was the art program, directed by Naumberg's sister, Florence Cane. The philosophical assumptions about human nature, reality, and society through which the art experiences of the child were interpreted and guided were clearly Jungian—Florence Cane also had been analyzed by Beatrice Hinkle. For those who adopted Jung's philosophy, art was a critical vehicle for coming to know the individual unconscious as well as the collective unconscious, and involved the discovery of Platonic universals existing in archetypal forms within the deeper recesses of the soul.[34] The problem of anomie, resulting in part from the onrush of industrialism, might be overcome through a rediscovery of our primitive cosmic roots.[35] Whether treated as therapeutic art or therapeutic education, this was no romantic laissez-faire approach; rather, it was a psychoanalytic approach, which directed by interpretation and suggestion on an individual basis. Cane clearly reflected her Jungian interpretative assumptions about the world of reality and of children's art in this remark: "As the child matures the art becomes more than a balance wheel it becomes a means for searching through the self for things beyond the self, a search for archetypal forms, for universal concepts, for truth emerging through beauty so as the child travels and widens his horizon, the art grows with him."[36]

The function of interpretation and suggestion as a channeling process is critical in the use of psychoanalytic techniques as applied to education. Human growth and development consists of not only integrating our internal life but also searching through the self for archetypal forms that allow us to connect with the more universal cosmic reality. This is no free and easy wandering through the unconscious; on the contrary, it is a directed, guided tour. The influence of symbols and their interpretation, whether we look for them, as Freud did, in dreams or, as Naumberg and Cane did, in art as an expression of the unconscious, must be critically examined. At this point the philosophy and values of the teacher-therapist come directly into play. The process, then, is not just a matter of discovering what is there. What is asserted to be there is in part a function of the instruments of that discovery. Thus the instrument inevitably affects the outcome, or what is discovered. The basic instruments the psychoanalyst uses are his or her conceptions of human nature, of the nature of reality, and of the social order. Thus, the philosophy of Naumberg and Cane is critically important here in helping to understand what is discovered.

Centrally concerned with the deeper psychic character of

personality, and using a quasi-religious medical model, Naumberg saw the teacher-therapist as ministering to the spiritual health of childhood. "If modern medicine has come to realize that one of its most profound duties is the healing of sick souls, how much more should modern education realize its responsibility of maintaining the spiritual health of childhood! For this, the new teachers need a deeper knowledge of their own unconscious emotional life, as well as that of their pupils." The teacher and parent as therapists, ministering to the "spiritual health of childhood," needed special training. Naumberg repeatedly argued that "the problem of a modern school is not the development of its children, but the right training and adjustment of its teachers and parents."[37] Both teachers and the parents should undergo analysis so that they would have the correct psychophilosophical structure through which to interpret the development of the inner life of their children. This notion of "spiritual health" was important, not only as an idealized norm toward which to strive, but as a touchstone in the reconciliation of opposites as one explores the deeper recesses of his or her psyche. Naumberg and Cane knew what "spiritual health" looked like. The ideal for these Jungian teacher-therapists was the integrated person who had worked through the problem of opposites in harmony with a universe where time ultimately disappeared and all psychic existence was unified. The teacher as a therapist was to be a guide, interpreting the unconscious through a Jungian prism that showed character as dualistically divided but searching for an integrated soul. As the psychologist in Naumberg's "Sixth Dialogue" asked: "Why, the importance of the analytic technique as a means of uncovering the hidden motives, the real wishes, that are governing the lives of all of us; and the obvious conclusions that opposite types respond in their unconscious as well as their conscious life to the self same stimuli in radically different ways."[38] To Naumberg, the "chief problem of education" was the identification of personality types and the construction of an educational environment to aid the child in fulfilling the potentiality of that type. "Until we truly comprehend the fundamental differences in psychic mechanisms between the jolly, outgoing, sociable child and the acutely reticent, overmoody one, we can't help them educationally to fulfill their own potentialities or to overcome their psychic difficulties."[39]

Naumberg argued, as did many Western educators from Plato to Rousseau, that the child must be true to his or her self—a self that is in many ways preordained by nature. If children were, in Jungian terms, really to discover their true selves, the opposites of their personalities must be allowed to surface in consciousness and be expressed in overt behavior so as to be interpreted and integrated into the child's personality. It is at this point that many scholars have seriously misinterpreted both Naumberg and Jung as having advocated a kind of romantic freedom for the child that borders on license. Such was not the case. The freedom Naumberg advocated was not license but the freedom essential for Jungian sublimation to function and to allow for the emergence of an integrated personality.[40] The leopard was not free to change its spots, nor was the child free to change his or her personality type. Naumberg's educational philosophy advocated a highly sophisticated, well-thought-through socialization process that called into play a far more effective control mechanism than had previously been employed.

As did Plato in the *Republic*, Naumberg argued that the school group must replace the family as a necessary step in socialization. Highly critical of the ineffective traditional methods of socializing the child, Naumberg said: "My own experience with the new psychologic method has convinced me that a great part of the so-called socialization in our modern schools is an external form superimposed by the teacher, and that underneath the appearance of a social group, the fundamental interests of the children may still remain attached to primary ego-centric sources; may, in other words, not have been socialized at all." She was not calling for less socialization of the individual to the group, but a more effective socialization process at the personality level. "Whatever work he may do, if it is to be satisfactory to him and to his fellows, he must express himself and become a means toward living in a creative way. All work must serve as a channel whereby the individual's particular life-energy may flow undiminished into the life of the group." In Platonic fashion, Naumberg concluded, "It is a mistake, moreover, to consider the individual and the group concepts as really antagonistic."[41] She assumed there could be no real conflict between the authentically true individual and the true society.

If the true individual is known, then what appear to be adult controls in channeling the development of personality are quickly translated into helping children fulfill their own "real" needs. This is not a rhetorical attempt to dodge responsibility for directing the child but an expression of a kind of Neoplatonic philosophy that assumes, first, the true nature of the child is discoverable and, second, the chief role of the adult is to construct an environment suitable to the fulfillment of that child's nature. The will of the teacher and the wishes and impulses of the children are merged. Naumberg best expressed this view in summarizing her Walden School experiment:

> this experiment is based on the consideration of the child as a threefold organism to be led to integration by "positive channeling." Thus, the rounding out of personality becomes a means of true socialization from within the group. We have come to know that the real group life of children cannot be directed by adults from above. For the moving center of socialization in a school lies not within the will of the teacher, but within the wishes and impulses of the children. These we have sought to direct according to our aim.[42]

The aim of the teacher and the wishes and impulses of the children had, indeed, become one. Personalities were to be shaped, positively channeled, and integrated along the presumed needs of the child as interpreted through the philosophical value-screen of a Jungian analyst.

It seems that John Dewey missed this point when, in his criticism of many progressive schools, he stated the question in terms of "How much Freedom in the New Schools?" rather than in terms of the psychological basis of freedom. Although he did not directly address himself to Naumberg's school, he did level his criticism at those in the child-centered schools who "are still obsessed by the personal factor; they conceive of no alternative to adult dictation save child dictation. . . . Some of these schools indulge pupils in unrestrained freedom of action, of manners and lack of manners. Schools farthest to the left (and there are many parents who share the fallacy) carry the thing they call freedom nearly to the point of anarchy."[43] Many scholars unfairly interpreted Naumberg's school in these terms. Neither Freudian nor Jungian psychology lends itself, either in theory or in practice, to educational anarchy. It is important to recognize, however, that the casual observer of Naumberg's school easily might have concluded that it was very permissive, with the child having free rein to express whatever surfaced from his or her unconscious. A more studied examination would have revealed that in the process of analytic interpretation of what the child had in fact expressed, the adults—whether teachers, therapists, or parents—played a very important controlling role. This is why Naumberg repeatedly emphasized the need for the adults who interacted with the child to undergo analysis.

Dewey's own social behaviorism seems to have been a conceptual block to his coming to grips with either Freudian or Jungian psychology as applied to education. It was Dewey as a social behaviorist who said: "When the child proposes or suggests what to do, some consequences to be attained, whence is the suggestion supposed to spring from? There is no spontaneous germination in the mental life. If he does not get the suggestion from the teacher, he gets it from somebody or something in the home or the street or from what some more vigorous fellow pupil is doing."[44] A true Jungian would urge the student to listen to the voice within. While Dewey and Naumberg were conceptual worlds apart, he did sense perhaps the major weakness of many of the progressive schools, including Naumberg's, when he argued that progressive education "cannot be secured by the study of children alone. It requires a searching study of society and its moving forces."[45]

Although Dewey did not focus his attack directly on Naumberg, she aimed her criticism at him by accusing him of cultivating a philosophy and psychology that would lead to a herd existence.[46] Naumberg asserted that Dewey had made his peace with modern industrialism and that his attempt at curriculum reconstruction meant little more than a pragmatic acquiesence to some of its worst consequences. More importantly, she argued, when it came to his treatment of individual development, he viewed subjective states as something from which we must move away. For Naumberg, this aspect of Dewey's psychology marked his perspective as not only inadequate but basically reactionary.[47] He had failed to develop a psychology that fully integrated the human personality: "Here Dr. Dewey is being the American of Americans. A dull and gloomy picture, this technological utopia, to those of us who still hope for a richer and socially balanced individualism— the flowering of a more equitable society. In his new world, if a man is no longer pitted against man in the purely economic struggle for existence, man will vie with man to create and construct for others as well as himself."[48] Like so many other utopian revolutionaries of the twentieth century, Naumberg's vision was not to be realized through party action, social organization, or confrontation with the power structure. Naumberg believed that the problems created by modernity, rootlessness, and alienation could be overcome only by educating the individual in such a way as to integrate and adjust the inner and outer life with the cosmic collective unconscious that sprang from the depths of the soul.

What had happened to the young woman who Waldo Frank said was "not ready to settle for less than a totally new world"? The hope of social action, albeit the only action by which any revolution is ever effectively sustained, had died with World War I. Social reform, obtainable through any of the current organizations, was largely rejected by Naumberg: "Any possibility of an immediate social or economic escape from the impasse of our civilization has become quite remote and rather absurd to me now. I've lived to see that whether people fought to save democracy or imperialism does not make the profound difference I had once hoped. I've wakened to a complete realization that all social and economic groups have identical methods of acting and reasoning, according to whether they are in or out of power."[49] While the one hope she nurtured was to educate the individual, the possibility for collective political action had disappeared. She found in the traditions of the past and in the soil from which the chthonic qualities emerged a degree of compensation for the failure of her utopian dream. As she turned inward, she saw the power and beauty of a "real" tradition. Recalling her first trip to Oxford, with its Gothic buildings, Naumberg wrote:

> I remember how at the sight of those cloistered Gothic buildings set within carpets of greensward and English gardens, I said, "Now at last I can feel and understand what it might mean to be born where one's roots would naturally draw sustenance from the soil of the past." From that moment, the brittle efficiency and surface speed of our American psyche became evident to me. With all that can be said in favor of our vitality and power, I still feel as I did then, many years ago, that we lack that spiritual equilibrium of those who grow from their native soil. This very want is, I think, what makes us Americans subject to tides of slavish imitation. Our system of education is no more indigenous than our fashions or our arts.[50]

Naumberg added her voice to those of Gertrude Stein's "lost generation."[51] Disillusioned with political and social reform, rootless, alienated, and fundamentally at odds with the ongoing rush of urban modernity, which daily reminded her of the severed ties to soil, Naumberg joined many others of her generation in turning to psychoanalysis to find her roots.

Having withdrawn in 1922 from the directorship of the school she founded, Margaret Naumberg increasingly turned her attention to the new field of art therapy. What began as an interest in her Walden School turned into a full commitment to art therapy as a career. Lecturing and teaching in hundreds of medical schools, art schools, and psychiatric research centers, and authoring numerous articles and books, Naumberg ended her career at the New School for Social Research as perhaps one of the most distinguished leaders in the field of art therapy. A number of questions that had been problematic in Walden School activities persisted in her later work. Just who created the meaning of the symbols that were being interpreted in art therapy? Was it the therapist or the patient, or was it merely a function of the particular social interaction that occurred? Assuming there was a defensible answer, then we might ask, Just what was the nature of the reality issuing from this therapeutic engagement? Was that reality invented or discovered?

Naumberg believed that what she was doing with art symbols was very much akin to what Freud had been doing with language symbols. She explained, "It is sometimes difficult to convey to psychoanalysts accustomed only to communication through words that a primary nonverbal technique such as art therapy can effectively release many repressed feelings of a patient more directly and more swiftly than words."

> Regardless of the fact that Freud rejected and Jung accepted the use of symbolic art expression in psychotherapy, dynamically oriented art therapy cannot be tied to any one specific interpretation of the significance of spontaneous art or dream productions. Dynamically oriented art therapy leaves a patient free to direct his associations to the images he creates in any direction that he chooses. It therefore frees the patient from overdependence on the art therapist and also speeds up the therapeutic procedure.[52]

Naumberg's therapeutic education, as well as her art therapy, employed the same principle. The student discovered the meaning of his or her education, just as the patient discovered the meaning of his or her artistic creations. As late as 1966, Naumberg insisted that "unlike the psychoanalyst, the art therapist does not interpret a patient's imaged projections but encourages the patient to assume the active role of explaining his creations."[53] When the patient did not know the meaning of his or her paintings, a series of questions might be asked by the analyst, focusing on the conditions or mood under which the drawings were created. Thus the hidden meaning of the artwork could be spontaneously released. Dynamically oriented art therapy proceeded with the end in view of self-analysis and of an ultimate understanding of one's self.

Although Naumberg thought of her work in terms of Freudian analytic free association, she felt that the art therapist necessarily had to be more active: "An art therapist, however, cannot remain as passive as a Freudian analyst, for the role of an art therapist is comparable to that of such psychoanalysts as Sullivan, Horney, Fromm and others who place emphasis on the active interpersonal relation between analyst and analysand." Ultimately, it was a process of freeing the client through the use of certain techniques: "The art therapist introduces patients to certain techniques that will help free them—rather than, as Dr. Spitz implies, 'manipulate the patient'—in the spontaneous expression of their thoughts, feelings and memories. These techniques include ways of relaxing muscles, freeing spontaneous body movements and demonstrations of the 'scribble' technique."[54] In this way therapist and patient together could discover the reality of the problem at hand—a joint discovery of a reality that existed prior to either's search. Freedom came when that hidden reality became conscious.

Fundamentally, then, what was the nature of that reality which was to be discovered? It was the reality of what S. Giedion called the "eternal present,"[55] which saw, in the early strivings of the child, *all* its history and *all* its future. It was that same notion of reality in which, deep in the unconscious, the collective cosmic unconscious meets the personal unconscious; in which wholeness, unity, and true reality were to be found. The child recapitulates in symbolic form the yearnings of the primitive, just as the creative modern artist who is guided by voices from the deeper recesses of the human soul may recapitulate primitive art.[56] Within such a frame of reality, time itself becomes obsolete. Surrealism and expressionism were in part attempts to reach down to the mystical depths of the human soul and experience what William James called something "more" and what Jung called a collective unified spirit. Naumberg made these same connections:

We know now that distortion, for instance, may be due to purposeful emphasis, not to ignorance or pathology. We can also recognize that simultaneity of focus in a head by Picasso or primitive man, although differing from external appearance, may nevertheless intensify an inner meaning. Acceptance of such direct and simultaneous expression of multiple aspects of human or other forms is conclusive confirmation of the significance of recurrent symbolic imagery in man's art, for in such projections—whether made by the primitive, the child or the modern artist—there are, in the choice and arrangement of these nonliteral, universally valid formulations, certain deep psychological laws at work.[57]

For Naumberg, then, there was a cosmic reality, one that was indeed timeless. In 1974 she related to me that while in a deep trance she had communed with some artists in the Hittite culture.[58] Like so many others in the twentieth-century reified world of positive science, she had discovered a new cosmic reality. Naumberg had undertaken special research in parapsychology with Dr. William McDougall in London and at Duke University, and with Dr. William Brown, who directed the experimental Laboratory of Psychology in Oxford.[59] The psychoanalytic path she followed led her to discover that mystical basis for reality which others, such as William James, G. Stanley Hall, and Gertrude Stein, had sensed and with which N. O. Brown and Carl Jung seem to have communed.

In the years following the publication of *Dark Mother*, and after his divorce from Margaret Naumberg in 1926, Waldo Frank also had a number of mystical experiences that led him to see the organic wholeness of the universe and, indeed, to find God. He said the mystic "is a man who *knows*, by immediate experience, the organic continuity between his self and the cosmos."[60] Frank himself was such a man. Like Naumberg, he had discovered the mystical center of reality about which he would later say, "We can have no adequate politics, no adequate aesthetics, no adequate ethics in our time without an adequate metaphysics and religion."[61] While both Naumberg and Frank appeared to have settled on a similar notion of reality, and while both explicitly accepted and highly respected the wisdom of Freud and Jung, they both favored Jung in describing the depth of the unconscious.

Frank and Naumberg differed fundamentally, however, on the role of the therapist in modern society. Even though Frank used psychoanalysis to develop and construct his personal philosophy of life and, in turn, used the novel as therapeutic art in understanding himself,[62] he held a strong antipathy toward the role he saw emerging for the therapist within his social system. In his novel *The Bridegroom Cometh* (1939), he portrayed the work of a therapist, Dr. Cariss, thusly:

> But pretty women, idle women, sex-unhappy women phys-iologically right, were a good part of his practice and the dramatic realization of the suppressed needs of all of them . . . to go to bed with the analyst . . . often crystalized their problem and hastened the cure. When they say that what they had done was to go to bed with their dream (the imago of the father for the most part), they were ready to Face Reality (his favorite phrase). Meantime the analyst was nour-ished . . . and paid for his nourishment at from twenty-five to fifty dollars the session. Facing reality that was![63]

In a similar vein he sketched the character of Dr. A. A. Brill in the context of his own Greenwich Village days:

> Psychoanalysis! Who that lived them can forget those days in which the souls of our American youth flowed without benefit of liquor? Not then, as now in our prohibition era, did men and girls gather about the hip flask. All they needed was water, to wet their lips parched with too long talking. They met in club, in salon, in bed—and "psyched" each other. They discussed. Above all, they confessed. Women roamed about, dreams gushing from their unrouged lips. Young girls wore passionate avowals like posies in their hair, like lurid gems on their breasts. Strong men, inspired by Dream-interpretation, abandoned wife and career, seeking the Mate of a Complex. Plays, poems, novels, critiques lifted into glamorous light all the dark ways of our souls. And schools sprang up—and philosophies—and religions. For the slow-evolving Europeans, there had been the Age of Darwin: for ourselves this Psychoanalytic Age, a saturnalia of sex talk.[64]

Accepting the insights and wisdom of Freud and Jung, Frank rejected the role of the therapist in a therapeutic society.[65] In so doing, he made a clear distinction between what he believed was the wisdom of Freud and Jung and their work as therapists, which he argued was the least important aspect of their thought. His quarrel with the idea of therapy rested not with the fact that therapists helped individuals discover the nature of their problems, but rather that they helped people live with those problems rather than solve them.

Most of the ills of personal maladjustment which the Freudian analysis may cure are symptoms of the disorder, economic, social, cultural, of the contemporary world. The right way to overcome them is to attack the disease, not its individual symbols. In this task, the light thrown by Freud on the human psyche is of great importance; the actual relief given to a few persons is immaterial. The time required by an analysis, and the expense, make the method (under our present system) available chiefly to the type of idle woman and parasite man who are not worth saving at the price of the lengthy effort which the analyst must devote to readjusting them in a morbid world.[66]

Reminiscent of Karl Marx's suggestion that "the philosophers have only interpreted the world in different ways; the point is to *change* it,"[67] Frank believed that what the world needed was not therapy but revolution; indeed, a revolution in fundamental values. He also clearly recognized that the therapist who claims neutrality in therapy is merely tacitly accepting the world as it is. For Frank, the world needed changing, not resignation. If men and women were sick from alienation, the point was not to help them live with their sickness but to change the causes of their alienation. Reminiscent of Jean-Paul Sartre's discussion of this issue (see chap. 8), Frank argued:

The man who disclaims any individual norm of values and yet deals with the subtlest problems of human adjustment, implicitly accepts the values that are current and actively rejects what lies outside his measure. The patient is sick because he does not fit into the world as he finds it; the analyst who cures him helps him into this world, which means that he has set up, as the desired norm, the values of the world. If the analyst is not aware of this, his acceptance is merely the more blind and his work upon the soul of the patient the more irresponsible. This is a serious criticism to be made against psychoanalysis from the viewpoint of a world sorely in need of revolution in the domain of values. And it may well be that the maladjusted neurotic of today is closer to the norm of healthy social transformation than the neurotic whom Freudian analysis has made "fit and content" within a society of false individualism and cultural decay.[68]

Recognizing the problem of therapy in an age of cultural decay, Frank appreciated the work of Freud as the classic work of genius, reaching to the timeless universal depths of the human soul. Yet he believed that Freud's rationalism went too far, that it excised "the cosmic connection" and, in the end, proved the irrationality of the rationalist dogma. Of Jung, Frank said: "although he lacks Freud's intellectual genius and although his work is not, like Freud's, a great esthetic body, [he] is more logical, calling the id the 'collective unconscious' and finding there the cosmic seed that can explain the human fruit."[69]

Frank came to know, through psychoanalysis, what Jung had understood all along: that in the beginning was to be found the end. For Frank, while Freud had begun the discovery of a new world, it was Jung who completed the mystical journey. Unlike other children of the sun who tended to acquiesce to the demands of the world as they contemplated the truths of the "eternal present," Frank remained a social revolutionary. While both he and Margaret Naumberg used psychoanalysis to discover that timeless reality they knew existed in the human soul, they both also used their creative, artistic talents to therapeutically overcome the sickness of their age, the alienation they felt so deeply. The spiritual discovery both believed they had made had echoed and re-echoed down through the Neoplatonic corridors of time. Was that reality really discovered, or was it invented? To those of us in the modern world who struggle with similar problems and, through that very Jamesian impressionistic stream of consciousness, are rediscovering, as Jung did, the spiritual nature of reality, the answer is clear. To others of us who still have doubts, we may well wish to reflect on Freud's suggestion that in this culture the artist escapes neuroses by transforming "his phantasies into artistic creations."

Notes

1. From Freud's "Clark Lectures," quoted in Beatrice Hinkle, *The Recreating of the Individual* (New York: Harcourt, 1923), p. 348.

2. From Marx's "Preface to Contribution to the Critique of Political Economy," quoted in T. B. Bottomore, ed., *Karl Marx: Selected Writings in Sociology and Social Philosophy* (New York: McGraw-Hill, 1956), p. 51.

3. By "sensitive" I mean someone very much in tune with the key generating forces of his or her historic period.

4. Waldo Frank, *Our America* (New York: Boni and Liveright, 1919), p. 232.

5. The first showing of impressionistic art took place in 1874. See

Arnold Hauser, *The Social History of Art*, 4 vols. (New York: Vintage Books, undated), 4:174. See also John Rewald, *The History of Impressionism* (New York: Museum of Modern Art, 1946), pp. 6–7.

6. See Hauser, *Social History of Art*, 4:169.

7. A leading American psychologist who suffered from the anxiety issuing from a Hericlitean universe without meaning was William James. He overcame his existential loneliness by discovering a spiritual something "more" in the human soul, which served, interestingly enough, a therapeutic function. For an analysis of his position, see Clarence J. Karier, "The Ethics of a Therapeutic Man: C. G. Jung," *Psychoanalytic Review* 63(1976): 120. See also chap. 1 of this book.

8. See Milton Brown, *The Story of the Armory Show* (New York: Hirshorn Foundation, 1963).

9. See Leo Marx, *The Machine in the Garden* (New York: Oxford University Press, 1964).

10. On national parks, see Peter J. Schmitt, *Back to Nature* (New York: Oxford University Press, 1969); for playgrounds, see Paul Violas, *The Training of the Urban Working Class: A History of 20th Century American Education* (Chicago: Rand McNally, 1978), chap. 4.

11. Malcolm Cowley, *Exile's Return* (New York: Viking, 1951), pp. 66–67. See also Henry F. May, *The End of American Innocence* (New York: Knopf, 1959).

12. See Paul Rosenfeld, *Port of New York* (Urbana: University of Illinois Press, 1961). See also Caroline F. Ware, *Greenwich Village of 1920–1930* (Boston: Houghton Mifflin, 1935).

13. Quoted in George L. Mosse, *The Culture of Western Europe* (Chicago: Rand McNally, 1961), p. 268.

14. Waldo Frank, *In the American Jungle* (New York: Farrar and Rinehart, 1937), p. 10.

15. Frank, *Our America*, pp. 231–32.

16. Quoted in Jerome W. Klousek, "Waldo Frank: The Ground of His Mind and Art," Ph.D. dissertation, Northwestern University, Evanston, Ill., 1958, p. 389.

17. Letter from Frank to Sherwood Anderson, Nov. 7, 1917, in ibid., p. 259.

18. Beatrice Hinkle received her M.D. degree from Stanford's Cooper Medical College in 1899. Shortly thereafter she became the "city physician" in San Francisco, the first woman in the country to hold such an office. After the death of her first husband, who had been the city's district attorney, Hinkle moved to New York City and in 1908 opened a psychotherapeutic clinic at Cornell Medical College, the first of its kind in the United States. The following year, she went to Europe to study under Freud and Jung. See Anne O'Hagan, "Beatrice Hinkle, Mind Explorer," *Woman Citizen* 12(July 1927): 47.

19. A significant segment of the women's liberation movement was

sustained at more than a suffragette level by female Jungian therapists who responded positively to his characterization of masculine and feminine. For example, consider the works of Beatrice Hinkle, *The Re-creating of the Individual* (1923); Frances Wicks, *The Inner World of Childhood* (1927); Eleanor Bertine, *Woman's Press*, "Must Women Weep?" *Human Relationships, Jung's Contribution to Our Time* (1967); M. Esther Harding, *Woman's Mysteries Ancient and Modern* (1935), *The Way of All Women* (1933), *The "I" and the Not-"I": A Study in the Development of Consciousness* (1965), *The Parental Image: A Study in Analytical Psychology* (1965), *Psychic Energy* (1947); Constance E. Long, *Collected Papers on the Psychology of Phantasy* (1920).

20. Hinkle, *Re-Creating of the Individual*, pp. 10–11.

21. Naumberg reported that she analyzed Frank, in a letter from Margaret Naumberg to Clarence J. Karier, Sept. 3, 1974.

22. *The Dark Mother* has been reviewed by a number of people as a confused kind of expressionist novel. See, for example, Paul Rosenfeld, "The Novels of Waldo Frank," *Dial* 7(Jan.-June 1921): 95–105.

23. Waldo Frank, *The Dark Mother* (New York: Boni and Liveright, 1920), p. 249.

24. This act might be interpreted as overcoming the feminine in Frank's personality, just as the knifing of Hermine in Hermann Hesse's *Steppenwolf* might be seen as the symbolic overcoming the feminine in Hesse's personality. Note that both Hesse and Frank wrote under Jungian therapeutic influence. We might further speculate that Cornelia in part represents Margaret Naumberg, and her death symbolizes Frank's lessening need for therapeutic direction. At that time, Naumberg was interested in art therapy and later became a leader in that field.

25. In a letter to the author, dated Sept. 3, 1974, Margaret Naumberg reflected on her therapeutic role: "He [Frank] was very emotionally disturbed in his tie-up with his mother and later in an unconscious deep tie-up with a man. Both of these complications I helped to unravel over the years through my own psychiatric training. . . . I had to use my own personal experience through psychoanalysis to untangle many of the emotional conflicts of his life, both with his personal family and his endless love affairs."

26. The school, which Naumberg ran from 1914 to 1928, was called "The Children's School," but was renamed "Walden School." It was the first of its kind in America.

27. From a taped interview of Margaret Naumberg by Martha and Joseph Hamilton, Feb. 6, 1971, New York.

28. See, for example, Carl G. Jung, *Memories, Dreams, Reflections* (New York: Random House, 1961).

29. Letter from Naumberg to the author, Sept. 3, 1974.

30. Alan Trachtenberg, ed., *Memoirs of Waldo Frank* (Boston: University of Massachusetts Press, 1973), p. 199.

31. Brill's child attended Naumberg's school. While Naumberg defines her position as Freudian, certain characteristics of Jungian psychology are clearly reflected in her thought. See Margaret Naumberg, *An Introduction to Art Therapy* (New York: Teachers College Press, 1973). Her interpretation of the primitive in art therapy, her belief in the mystical, her use of time and recapitulation, all seem to be closer at times to Jung than to Freud.

32. In an interview with the author, on June 10, 1974, Naumberg reported that she had actually married Frank twice—once secretly, because her sister was so upset by their relationship, and later publicly, in 1916, to satisfy the demands of her parents. They were formally divorced in 1926. Both Frank and Naumberg later described their ten-year marriage in terms that, today, would indicate an "open" marriage.

33. *Walden School, Parent Brochure*, 1939–40, New York, N.Y.

34. See Hinkle, *Re-Creating of the Individual*, esp. chap. 7 on "The Psychology of the Artist and the Significance of Artistic Creation."

35. See Naumberg, *Introduction to Art Therapy*; see also Florence Cane, *The Artist in Each of Us* (New York: Pantheon, 1951).

36. Florence Cane, "Teaching Years: Walden School Experiences," p. 3, unpublished ms.; quoted in Robert H. Beck, "American Progressive Education," Ph.D. dissertation, Yale University, New Haven, Conn., 1942, p. 171.

37. Margaret Naumberg, *The Child and the World* (New York: Harcourt, Brace, 1928), pp. 35–36.

38. Ibid., p. 145.

39. Ibid., p. 118.

40. See ibid., pp. 46–54.

41. Margaret Naumberg, "A Direct Method of Education," *Bureau of Educational Experiments* (N. 4) *Bulletin* 12(1917–22): 9, 11.

42. Margaret Naumberg, "The Walden School," *NSSE Yearbook 1926*, chap. 23, p. 339.

43. John Dewey, "How Much Freedom in New Schools?" *New Republic* 63(July 9, 1930): 204, 205.

44. John Dewey, *Art and Education* (New York: Barnes Foundation Press, 1939), pp. 180–81.

45. Dewey, "How Much Freedom?" p. 206.

46. See Naumberg, *Child and the World*, p. 115.

47. Some years later, in a taped interview with Joseph and Martha Hamilton in New York City, Feb. 1971, Naumberg bitterly complained that John Dewey had avoided responding to her criticism. She characterized him as a "polite reactionary."

48. Margaret Naumberg, "The Crux of Progressive Education," *New Republic* 63(June 25, 1930): 146.

49. Naumberg, *Child and the World*, p. 40.

50. Ibid., p. 26.

51. In protest against bourgeois values, Gertrude Stein, herself an expatriate and a student of William James, also stepped into that post-impressionist stream of consciousness and came up with "automatic writing," which assumedly was a pure, uncontaminated voice of expression from the unconscious. See Mable Dodge, "Speculations, on Post Impressionism in Prose," *Arts and Decoration* (Mar. 1913): 172–74.

52. Margaret Naumberg, *Dynamically Oriented Art Therapy: Its Principles and Practice* (New York: Grune and Stratton, 1966), pp. 18, 22.

53. Ibid., p. 8.

54. Ibid., pp. 16, 17.

55. See S. Giedion, *The Eternal Present: The Beginnings of Art*, Bollingen Series (New York: Pantheon, 1962).

56. See ibid.; see also Naumberg, *Dynamically Oriented Art Therapy*.

57. Naumberg, *Dynamically Oriented Art Therapy*, p. 46.

58. The interview was conducted in Naumberg's apartment in Boston, on June 10, 1974.

59. Margaret Naumberg, "Professional Record in Relation to Art Therapy, Psychotherapy, Research and Teaching," professional vita, p. 3.

60. Waldo Frank, ed., *The Collected Poems of Hart Crane* (New York: Liveright, 1933), p. xiii.

61. Waldo Frank, *Chart for Rough Waters* (New York: Doubleday, 1940), p. 100.

62. See, for example, Waldo Frank, *The Dark Mother* (1920), *Rahab* (New York: Boni and Liveright, 1922), *City Block* (Darien, Conn.: by the author, 1922), and *The Death and Birth of David Markand* (New York: C. Scribners and Sons, 1934).

63. Waldo Frank, *The Bridegroom Cometh* (New York: Doubleday, 1938–39), pp. 548–49.

64. Waldo Frank, *Time Exposures* (New York: Boni and Liveright, 1926), pp. 97–98.

65. For a more extensive treatment of this point, see Frederick F. Hoffman, *Freudianism and the Literary Mind* (Baton Rouge: Louisiana State University Press, 1945), pp. 256–76.

66. Waldo Frank, *In the American Jungle*, pp. 88–89.

67. Theses on Feuerbach, 1845; quoted in Bottomore, *Karl Marx: Selected Writings in Sociology and Social Philosophy*, p. 69.

68. Frank, *In the American Jungle*, p. 91.

69. Ibid., p. 92.

10

OTTO RANK [1884–1939]

Therapeutic Uses of Illusions

Shortly before Otto Rank died in 1939, Erich Fromm published an article in which he argued that "the basic trend of Rank's philosophy is akin to Fascist philosophy." Fromm believed this to be true, even though Rank himself was not politically a fascist; nor did he appear to have any "intention of copying the Nazi formula." Fromm puzzled over possible reasons why so many American social workers had found Rank's ideas so attractive, and then closed his analysis with two intriguing hypotheses: first, "that this acceptance of Rank seems to indicate the inroads that Fascist philosophy can make, if only it avoids mention of those political symbols which made it unacceptable to liberals and Jews"; and second, that Rank's thought might appear attractive to psychiatric social workers who, amid the day-to-day frustration of attempting to help their clients overcome emotional problems, were often confronted with insolvable economic difficulties.[1] Given these social circumstances, Rank's "will therapy," which suggested that the patient must learn to live with his or her illusions, might appear to be a welcome panacea.

Portions of this chapter originally appeared in James V. Smith and David Hamilton, eds., *The Meritocratic Intellect: Studies in the History of Educational Research* (New York: Pergamon Press, 1980), pp. 97–114, and are reprinted here by permission of the publisher.

In the forty-six years since Fromm published his critique, America has engaged in a hot war against fascism and a cold war against communism, out of which has emerged a highly militarized, multinational, corporate superstructure. Within this economic structure, a complementary therapeutic social welfare–oriented society has developed with its thousands of "helping" psychosocial services. In this context, it would be profitable to consider again some of the issues raised by Fromm's analysis and critically examine both the philosophical underpinnings of Rank's psychology and its possible social implications. In this chapter I will analyze what Fromm believed to be the "fascist philosophy" he saw in Rank's thought; consider these ideas in a broader nineteenth- and twentieth-century cultural context; discuss the problem of definition; analyze Rank's psychosocial ideas as they were developed historically; and suggest possible ways that Rankian thought and therapy might be interpreted as reflecting deeper historic currents of the modern therapeutically oriented welfare society.

In analyzing Rank, Fromm made no attempt at a compre-hensive description of fascist philosophy; instead, he confined his argument to what he considered to be some of the "essential features" and demonstrated that these ideas appeared in Rank's philosophy.[2] The fascist, Fromm argued, lives in a nihilistic world where the search for truth is not only vain but harmful for most people. Reality itself is thought to be illusory. In such a basically nonrational world, leadership emerges that creatively welds the illusions of the masses for action, and thus the power and strength of arms replaces the power of truth, while the realities of injustice and suffering are taken as givens, not susceptible to rational reform. Fascists pride themselves on being "realists," funda-mentally accepting the world of power relationships as given and readily adapting to its demands. Idealism rests with creative leaders who bring the herd along. Within this view emerges a thoroughly authoritarian outlook, one that sees the social world in terms of powerful and powerless, superior and inferior, strong and weak. Leadership thus rests not on truth, education, or rational social values, but rather on proven ability to creatively use the illusions of the masses to exercise power.

Was Rank a closet fascist, or was he possibly a fascist without knowing it? He personally did not approve of the label, telling Jessie Taft, in no uncertain terms, "I don't like it."[3] Whether we agree or disagree with Fromm depends on how we define a fascist. Fromm was not claiming that Rank was politically a fascist, nor was he claiming that Rank himself would agree with his analysis. Fromm was insisting, however, that there was such a thing as a fascist philosophy and that Rank held many of its basic tenets. In the context of the times, when many people thought they knew what fascism was, this argument might have seemed straightforward enough. However, in the present day, such a charge might appear highly questionable, due at least in part to our usage of the term over the last four decades—a usage that has served to obfuscate its meaning so as to make many people altogether wary of using it at all.

In the intervening years, the term "fascism" has become for many of us a synonym for all that is evil, eliciting painful memories of such infamous centers of human degradation as Auschwitz, Buchenwald, Dachau, and Belsen. In this sense the term describes a specific period in history, and its use beyond that specific time frame may significantly detract from the memorialization of its victims. Others among us prefer to bury the term with the historic dead, assuming that history will not repeat itself, that fascism came to an end with the defeat of the Axis powers in 1945. Still others render the term useless by making it applicable to virtually any and all of our enemies.[4] And there are some people who define fascism in terms that are dialectically related to their own ideological positions. Ernst Nolte, for example, in *The Three Faces of Fascism* (1966), points out how our ideology influences our definition of fascism.

> Christian theorists see fascism as part of the secularization of society as man turns from God, but this implies that the antidote to fascism is theocracy. Conservatives regard fascism as the revolt of the masses against current values, yearning with pessimistic nostalgia for the "good old days". Liberals regard fascism as a form of totalitarianism, and are, as a result, incapable of distinguishing between fascism and Stalinism. Nationalists look upon fascism as either a high or a low point in national history, and are therefore prey to conservative or ultra-right nostalgia for an earlier epoch. Marxists view fascism as the product of the contradictions in advanced capitalism, and hence see the abolition of bourgeois society as the necessary precondition for the elimination of fascist tendencies.[5]

In lieu of all these ideological interpretations, Nolte offers his own "non-partisan theory," which "sees fascism as a specific and supra-national phenomenon of a particular epoch." He does this, he asserts, so as to make possible "discarding the burden of the past." His "nonpartisan theory" does essentially that, effectively burying the term in a particular epoch and thus freeing the present from the "burden of the past."[6]

The issue of definition is complicated not only by the ideology of the interpreter but also by the particular discipline of the interpreter. Thus it seems clear that Nicos Poulantzas's exceptional political-economic treatment in *Fascism and Dictatorism* fails to treat the intellectual and cultural dimensions of fascism just as George Mosse's excellent treatment of the intellectual and cultural roots of this subject in *The Crisis of German Ideology* fails to relate the intellectual roots to the emerging corporate structure which played such an important practical role in the rise and success of national socialism.[7] Monopoly capitalism, in the form of multinational corporations and cartel arrangements, provided the economic superstructure within which fascism was nourished and the spread of communism checked. It was and still is a vital part of the economic framework within which the fascist state has emerged in the twentieth century. Any comprehensive treatment of fascism in this century must take into account the developing economic structure of the West, with all its tensions, and relate those tensions to the current political, intellectual, and cultural trends.[8] Leon Trotsky was correct in arguing in *The Struggle Against Fascism in Germany* that even though the economic structure and fascism were intimately related, it was just as much a mistake to view fascism as inevitably flowing from monopoly capitalism in some predetermined sense as it was to see fascism in virtually all political and social movements. It also seems to be as much an error to divorce monopoly capitalism from fascism as it is to refrain from using the term altogether. The relationships might better be recognized as complex, subtle, and at times transactional, limited by considerable historical contingencies.

As historians and social scientists develop a more adequate picture of fascism, the term appears to be best treated as a composite picture of a many-sided condition of humans in the stream of twentieth-century history. Within that stream there exists a meta-culture, dynamically born anew with the passing of each generation, helping to define and structure the conscious realities of the emerging world. Given this overarching structure, we can isolate people, movements, and institutions for analytic purposes and thus recognize those people who perhaps were more sensitive to some of the ideological currents that logically could, and in many ways historically did, seem ultimately to support the political and economic development of fascism, without themselves being fascist. By the same token, we may analyze the ideology of a particular person without making any causal claims about either that ideology or its existing social structure and merely assume an unexplored transactional relationship to exist between culture, economic structure, and political action. In this respect, many of the ideas of such notable people as G. Stanley Hall, D. H. Lawrence, and, indeed, Otto Rank, as Erich Fromm saw him, can be viewed as expressing some of the main cultural currents that tended to shape our developing fascist world.

While in a very real sense fascism was a response to the conditions of life in the twentieth century, it was also a culmination of a larger nineteenth-century revolution against Enlightenment values. That European liberal bourgeoisie which so confidently manned the barricades of social change at the beginning of the nineteenth century, stood frozen in narcissistic contemplation of its own destruction at the end of that century. What began as a romantic reaction to the rationalism of the Enlightenment eventually culminated in a storm of intellectual nihilism. Disillusioned, wearily searching for certainty in an uncertain world, Western society experienced an irrationalism more profound and despairing than anything it had experienced since the decline of the ancient world. Literate intelligence henceforth would focus not on the meaning of life and the future millennium but on the crisis of death and the absurd existence of the individual alienated from "culture," "nature," or "God." By the time Nietzsche had passed beyond tragedy, beyond good and evil, Søren Kirkegaard had discovered the value of *Fear and Trembling*, Herman Melville had emphasized the indestructible nature of evil, Fydor Dostoyevski had written, "There are three powers, three powers alone, able to conquer and to hold captive forever the conscience of these impotent rebels for their happiness—those forces are miracle, mystery, and authority."[9] A transformation of values had occurred, culminating in a focus on the absurdity of life and the irrational well-spring of human motivations and actions. The alienated, unfulfilled world of the bourgeoisie held little promise for coming generations.

315

Individual existence was to be secured, not by fulfilling our duties to the mass or herd, which lived by illusions, nor by placing our faith in the humanitarian future or in the rationalistic past, but rather by asserting the self in a nihilistic world. In the name of sincerity and authenticity, all ideology had to be rejected. Youth without banner, youth without cause became the rallying cry of the new generation. Representative democracy came to mean nothing more than a bourgeois facade behind which petty, selfish, vested interests developed. Democracy appeared to be a sham when we passed beyond appearances to the reality of nihilism. Even science, the goddess of the Enlightenment, which once offered so much rational hope for suffering humanity, came to be viewed as a Frankenstein, ushering in an age of mass organization and mass culture that threatened to destroy individual identity.

Within this Zeitgeist, Otto Rank, as a youth of nineteen, mused, "if anything could drive me to suicide, it would be the stupidity and commonness of mankind."[10] Born into a lower-middle-class, culturally barren, unhappy home, with a father who drank too much and a family that fought too much,[11] Otto Rank developed an image of himself that provided the personality structure upon which he hung the ideological values that sustained him throughout his life. In many ways his was to be a life of escape. So distasteful was his family experience that he could not bear to carry his father's name, changing it as quickly as he could from Rosenfeld to Rank. As a youth, he escaped his unfortunate family situation by delving into poetry, music, and philosophy, and by nurturing an inflated conception of himself as a creative, artistic genius who would one day stand against the commonness of humankind, who felt "for most people no sympathy, only for animals."[12] He believed he had been called to commune with the truly great: "Just as whole races of average men prepare unconsciously for the possibility of the coming of the one superior being, so must I slowly and unconscious of the goal go through a lot of average works in order to reach the worthwhile ones."[13]

Rank eventually found those "worthwhile ones" when he encountered the works of Arthur Schopenhauer, Richard Wagner, and Friedrich Nietzsche. In Schopenhauer he discovered the negative side of the "will," buried deep in the recesses of the unconscious mind; in Nietzsche he found the Dionysian "will," which could carry him beyond the good and evil of the herd;

and in Wagner he communed with the creative artist who could so admirably unite "tone and word" with "dramatic action." All confirmed in their own way his youthful contempt for humanity, as well as his search for a super soul, or what late in life he called a "God-man." Throughout Rank's life these three men provided much of the basic foundation upon which he constructed his philosophy, which was congruent with his personal psychological temperament—one that consistently propelled him into extreme states of elation or depression. Nietzsche served him well when he was at the mountaintop enjoying his grandiose view; Schopenhauer guided his path in the darker valleys of depression.

Much of what Rank wrote about the creative genius can be easily translated as autobiographical. From his youthful conception of the artist, to his *Der Kunstler*, with which he introduced himself to Freud, and on to his more mature work, *Art and Artist*, the basic structure of his conception of the artistic act of creation remained the same. On April 29, 1905, he wrote in his diary:

> One can't bring up an artist. . . . The artist in the act of their creation fluctuates for the most part between life and death; he "chooses" between suicide and creating, between art and hysteria; if there is a grain too much of resistance, if the delivery does not occur at the right time, then the artist falls. But even if all that were possible, who would unburden on his son so many severe hardships, suffering that goes psychically as well as physically to the uttermost limits of life, which are, however, necessary to many a great artist.

Rank considered himself a great artist, and it is clear that at that point in time a complete organization of his views was occurring. On May 10, 1905, Rank wrote, "It comes only to this, that one has the courage to universalize his experience; whoever has this courage, his generalizations are correct." *Der Kunstler* was born on May 13, 1905: "Now I see everything clearly: the world process is no longer a riddle; I can explain the whole culture, yes, I can explain everything. What shall I be able to do with the remainder of my life?"[14] It became Rank's statement of his ideological beliefs, one to which he would return again and again during his professional career.

When Alfred Adler, Rank's family physician, introduced him to Freud, Rank gave Freud an early draft of *Der Kunstler*. Freud recalled: "One day a young man who had passed through the technical training school introduced himself with a manuscript which showed very unusual comprehension. We induced him to go through the Gymnasium and the University and to devote himself to the nonmedical side of psychoanalytic investigation. The little society acquired in him a zealous and dependable secretary and I gained in Otto Rank a faithful helper and co-worker."[15] For the next twenty years Rank served Freud as his "research worker, his proof reader, and his adopted son."[16] Freud saw to Rank's education, sending him to the University of Vienna, where he completed his Ph.D. thesis on Richard Wagner, entitled *Die Lohengrin Sage.* He moved quickly into Freud's secret inner circle which, after Jung's and Adler's disaffections, had become so important in directing the psychoanalytic movement.[17] Concerned with the practical application of psychoanalysis, Hanns Sachs and Rank founded the *Imago,* and shortly thereafter Rank became editor of *Zeitschrift.* A bright, intuitively inclined young man, Rank grew very close to Freud, at times acting as his corresponding secretary and personal aide. Freud regarded him so highly that he put Rank in charge of four revised editions of *The Interpretations of Dreams.* Educated in the field of psychoanalysis by Freud himself, perceived as creative, hardworking, and trustworthy in every respect, it seemed clear to many people around Freud that Rank was being groomed to succeed him as the leader of the psychoanalytic movement.

Throughout these very productive years (1905–25) both men profited from each other's thoughts. Freud came especially to appreciate Rank's intuitive insights. As Rank did imaginative work on "The Double" in literature and published *The Myth of the Birth of the Hero,* in which Freud contributed an essay, it was apparent that Freud saw Rank's work as an extension of much of his own. Rank was exactly what Freud hoped for: someone to imaginatively develop the powerful and fruitful concepts embedded in the psychoanalytic paradigm. Perhaps this wish led him to seriously misjudge the direction his young student had taken from the very start. Rank was not content with simply exploring the nonmedical side of the psychoanalytic paradigm but, rather, was developing his own paradigm, one based not on the rationalized poetic world of Freud but on the irrational world of Schopenhauer, Wagner, and Nietzsche. The difference was fundamental.

The inevitable break began when Rank presented a completed manuscript to Freud in 1923, called *The Trauma of Birth,* in honor of his birthday; the break was completed three years later when Rank sent the seventy-year-old Freud a decoratively bound copy of Nietzsche's work. The meaning of the latter gift was made clear in Rank's *Truth and Reality* (1929): "Nietzsche, who experienced thoroughly the whole tragedy of the creative man and admitted in his 'amor fati' the willingness to pay for it, is in my opinion the first and has been up to now the only psychologist."[18]

In *The Trauma of Birth*, Rank was following Freud's earlier suggestion that the source of anxiety might possibly originate in the act of birth. However, he went considerably further when he put critical emphasis on the mother and the infant's relationship to the mother. Karl Abraham, Ernest Jones, and others within the inner circle were quick to sense a serious heresy in the making. Freud, however, was reluctant to make a clear-cut judgment; while he hesitated, he entertained Rank's thesis, argued, discussed, and attempted to persuade. Almost to the very end, Freud held out hope that Rank could be returned to his way of thinking.[19] Once again Freud was wrong. Rank set out on his own, establishing his practice in Paris and then taking an extended trip to America, where he lectured, gave seminars, and presented what in effect were his own ideas about psychoanalysis and therapy. There followed an agonizing period in which Rank swung from the position of a rebellious son back to one of total submissiveness, and from publicly recanting his deviation, to again rejecting Freud's position outright. In the midst of severe depression, Rank returned to Vienna, where in many hours of consultation with Freud, both men became convinced that Rank's rebellion was brought about because of his "manic state," which had been triggered by the announcement of Freud's dangerous illness.[20] Rank sent a letter of apology to the inner circle; Freud wrote optimistically that he believed much of the problem had been resolved, which, of course, it was not. Freud suggested that Rank continue to undergo analysis, but Rank refused, and the letters between the two became biting and bitter.

As he increasingly engaged Rank in heated debate, Freud vacillated in his interpretation of what was actually taking place. Initially, he refused to recognize what was clearly a highly significant deviation, attempting to explain the situation in terms of Rank's neurotic reaction to the announcement of his (Freud's) cancer.[21] Later he accounted for much of the problem in terms of Rank's need for money, which had led him to establish an independent practice in Paris and New York City. In *Moses and Monotheism*, Freud described Rank as "a young man whose fate it was to grow up beside a worthless father [who] began by developing, in defiance of him, into a capable, trustworthy and honorable person. In the prime of life his character was reversed, and thenceforward he behaved as though he had taken this same father as a model. In . . . the beginning of such a course of events there is always an identification with the father in early childhood. This is afterwards repudiated, and even overcompensated, but in the end establishes itself once more."[22] At one time, Freud also suggested that their conflict was precipitated by the excessive spending habits of Rank's wife, Tola[23]; or that it was another patterned, stoically tragic case of fathers (real or adopted) and sons (see *Moses and Monotheism*). Jessie Taft, Rank's biographer, saw it as a case of a creative young scholar growing beyond his teacher and the teacher not being able to adjust graciously to the situation. Perhaps Taft was even more correct when she suggested that the adoption of a particular psychology was more like an adoption of a religion than a science, and the conflict between Freud and Rank was unavoidable.[24]

While many of these reasons are not mutually exclusive and may be viewed as interactive factors in the events that transpired, it is clear that the announcement of Freud's cancer and Rank's deviation made for an unfortunate coincidence that allowed some interpreters to put negative connotations on Rank's motivations. The news of Freud's illness in April 1923 could not have influenced Rank's writing of *The Trauma of Birth*, which was finished in that same month. The ideas he put forth in that book had been developed over a long period of time, even though they had not been fully discussed within the inner circle. Highly charged individual reactions to the conflict and the strong personal ties of those involved at times clouded the issues. Objectively, we must recognize that, from the very outset, Rank was following a basically different ideological position, and as a consequence he clearly developed a profoundly different psychology. His psychology ultimately had to be rejected by Freud, regardless of personal attachments. It was not just a matter of growth and development, either; much of what was implicit in Rank's earlier thought was later simply made explicit.

Psychoanalysis provided Rank with a vehicle to imaginatively play with religious symbols, literature, philosophy, and anthropological data, but it was not the core structure out of which his view of the universe was built. While psychoanalysis could be used to embellish that universe, the basic organization was derived from Schopenhauer, Wagner, and Nietzsche, not from Freud. Where Freud emphasized the importance of a poetic reason, Rank emphasized the importance of will; where Freud saw the search for truth and its ultimate acceptance as constructively therapeutic, Rank saw it as ultimately destructive—for him, the creation and acceptance of illusions were therapeutic. These were not minor misunderstandings. Rank came to emphasize the role of the mother over that of the father in the life of the child long before it was made more fashionable to do so by others such as Erik Erickson. And he gradually came to argue, as did Sandor Ferenczi and others, that therapy was more important than theory, that understanding the immediate present of the patient was far more important for therapeutic purposes than understanding the patient's past. On virtually every significant construct, Rank reversed positions with Freud. He was not simply a youthful rebel bent on upstaging his former mentor at any price. Rather, the cleavage between the two men represented a fundamental rift in modern Western thinking which has persisted to the present day.

The idea that reason could light the path to truth within the human soul as well as the social order, and that such was the desired path to virtue, was the ideological keystone in the Enlightenment's arch of progress, under which so many Western thinkers have passed. By the end of the nineteenth century, however, that keystone gave way under the pressure of contradictions inherent in alienated bourgeois life. Rank's thought was an expression of a "modern" twentieth-century consciousness. It also reflected a fundamental break with the Enlightenment belief in rational progress. That belief was firmly based on the ancient Socratic dictum that the unexamined life was not worth living, that truth was possible and its pursuit was a valued "good" because, in the end, both the individual and the community would benefit. Both Freud and Marx clearly worked within this tradition; Otto Rank did not.

For Socrates and for many Western thinkers, the examination of life meant an analysis of the individual and, equally as important, an analysis of the community in which the individual developed. No Greek could have conceived of the current notion of self as separate from community. Since Rousseau, that ancient conceptual unity of self and society has gradually weakened. Early in the nineteenth century, Marx reacted to the growing estrangement; whereas later in the century, Freud was conceptually working within it. Both men lived and thought within the broader Zeitgeist of a nineteenth-century economic world that in revolutionizing production and consumption was simultaneously profoundly shaking the roots of the Western mind. The crisis of the nineteenth-century bourgeoisie, translated into European romanticism and/or American transcendentalism, reflected both the conceptual estrangement of self from society and the varied attempts to overcome that estrangement through abstract constructions of reality.

By the end of the century, the individual was increasingly conceived as being separate and apart from the social order and the social order as being separate and apart from the individual. In this context, Marx's analysis of the social order in the earlier part of the century and Freud's analysis of the individual at the end of the century were both influenced by this problem. In this sense, Marx, to a limited extent, and Freud, to a much greater extent, were doing something no Greek could have done. Both worked within a developing worldview which, beginning with Rousseau, could mentally separate the individual from society. To be sure, neither Freud nor Marx could conceive of the individual as humanly possible without society. Nevertheless, the entire corpus of their works stands as a benchmark of the extent to which the Zeitgeist of the romantic's splintered view of life had managed to penetrate Western rationalistic consciousness. Marx saw the problem as alienation and constantly insisted on conceptually restoring humanity to history. He searched to understand the dynamics of social relations, which he believed was the cause of the alienation that now existed. While Marx, in the early part of the century, sought to discover the social conditions that gave rise to the phenomenon of alienation as reflected in the earlier romantic literature as well as in Hegelian philosophy, Freud created psychoanalysis in the context of the latter neo-romantic Zeitgeist, at the end of the century. By Freud's time, the separation of the individual from society had become even more obvious to Western consciousness.[25]

Psychoanalysis can be, and often is, viewed as akin to the romantic frame of mind because its approach to mental phenomena relies on the unconscious as the most genuine source of truth. The emphasis on free association can also be viewed as a variant of the romantic's inner voice. The Freudian idea of individual happiness as necessarily antagonistic to the social order formed the basis from which mental energy was sublimated and was, itself, not readily conceivable, without the romantic's original sense of alienated reality.[26] Under these circumstances, even the creative activity of the artist can be viewed as rooted in estrangement and therefore a variant of neurotic behavior. All these characteristics of psychoanalysis clearly suggest romantic underpinnings. Nevertheless, Freud and his psychoanalytic views of the human condition were also firmly rooted in a biological science which entailed an Enlightenment faith in science and the promise of the intelligibility of truth. However, Freud had extended the meaning of science to include the poetic epistemological understanding of the unconscious. Still, both Freud and Marx believed that the quest for public knowledge was desirable. This, then, was the common ground upon which these two great thinkers of the nineteenth century worked. While Marx sought to understand the social dynamic governing the creation of our social system, and Freud sought to understand the patterns and structures governing the individual psyche, both assumed that a truth existed behind the facade of appearances which was intelligible and worth knowing.[27] As sons of the Enlightenment they believed that illusions were the chains that kept humanity in bondage. Where Marx saw the damaging effects of "false consciousness," Freud saw the crippling consequences of "rationalizations." Both believed in the therapeutic value of truth. When Marx wrote of religion as the "opium of the people," he argued that "the abolition of religion, as the illusory happiness of men, is a demand for their real happiness. The call to abandon their illusions about their condition is a call to abandon a condition which requires illusions."[28] So too, after a lengthy discussion of religion as a form of illusion, Freud ended his work by insisting, "No, our science is no illusion. But an illusion it would be to suppose that what science cannot give us we can get elsewere."[29]

Standing in the midst of the crumbling ideological ruins of the Christian society at the dawn of a secular order, both Freud and Marx knew the power of illusions and the varied ways false consciousness could be manipulated for the happiness of what Dostoyevski's Grand Inquisitor called those "impotent rebels." While Marx was more optimistic than Freud with respect to the amelioration of these conditions, each rested his case on the therapeutic value of truth. Although this conception of the value of truth remains alive in isolated segments of modern secular society, it clearly does not represent the mainstream of thought. This society tends more and more to survive on varied forms of manufactured opiates, ideological as well as psychological. From this perspective, Western Enlightenment tradition was fractured, first through a process of alienation, which helped people to conceive of the individual as separate from society, and second, through a conception of truth, either in the individual soul or in society, which was at bottom found to be only another illusion. The former is a condition for the latter; yet the latter represents the more profound breakdown of Western rationalistic culture.

This breakdown was reflected clearly in the work of Arthur Schopenhauer (1788–1860), among others, who found the quest for truth to be only another of life's illusions. His anti-rationalism undercut Enlightenment faith in reason; for him, philosophy ended in silence.[30] Ultimately, he believed that the illusory phenomenal world is escaped only by a mystical "turning of the will" against itself, as the ascetics and mystics have done throughout history. This death of personality led Schopenhauer to end his quest in Buddhist mysticism. His philosophy of will thus moved into stark pessimism because, for him, the search for truth was a search through a labyrinth of illusion, an impossible dream that was ultimately destructive. Thus Otto Rank, heavily influenced by Schopenhauer, concluded that the real lesson to be learned from "Oedipus Rex" was that the search for truth was ultimately destructive.

Rank borrowed significantly from Schopenhauer for his own understanding of the negative will, the working of the unconscious, and the theory of double knowledge, as well as for his pessimistic, anti-rationalistic view of the world. It was Schopenhauer's worldview that Rank discovered in Richard Wagner's *Tristan und Isolde*, just as selected characteristics of the Nietzschean overman can be found in Rank's use of the creative will and his analysis of the creative artist. Rank had drunk deeply of Schopenhauer's pessimistic romantic nectar, brewed in the underworld of strange gods and mythlike creatures, which had intoxicated so many of the bourgeoisie at the end of the nineteenth century. Thoroughly alienated from any real sense of effective social action, this class looked within its own soul to find the secrets of the universe. In search of inner authenticity behind a veil of appearances, the brutish world of action thus could be escaped. In the name of sincerity, Enlightenment values were rejected as illusions.

When Rank broke with Freud and made his own psychology explicit, he was rejecting Freudian psychoanalysis as too ideological and rationalistic. His psychology was to be based on therapy, not theory. Denying the importance of the patient's history in the therapeutic situation, Rank focused on the immediate present. It was not necessary for patient and analyst to attempt to discover what really happened because, as Rank argued, the truth was purely subjective and relative to what "I want to believe."[31] The world of human behavior was one of necessary illusions, which protected and shielded us from seeing the world too well. Rank believed that the neurotic suffered not from living with illusions, but from attempting to live without them. His therapeutic ideas about "will therapy" were not only anti-Freudian but were a fundamental denial of the broader Socratic Western rationalistic tradition. The good life was to be found not in knowing thyself, but in learning to believe in illusions. As Rank said, not truth but illusion was the goal of therapy:

> It is to the effect that our seeking the truth in human motives for acting and thinking is destructive. With the truth, one cannot live. To be able to live one needs illusions, not only outer illusions such as art, religion, philosophy, science and love afford, but inner illusions which first condition the outer. The more a man can take reality as truth, appearance as essence, the sounder, the better adjusted, the happier will he be. At the moment when we begin to search after truth we destroy reality and our relation to it.[32]

For Rank, self-deception was a necessary condition of life. It was the function of the therapist, as a creative artist, to enter the world of the patient by transference and help that individual turn off his or her overactive, negative will, which was allowing truth to destroy illusions, and to help the patient make use of his or her creative will to generate effective illusions. The reality behind the displacement was not important—the displacement itself was. To live effectively and to be therapeutically healed was to learn to live with lies.[33] Rank noted: "This displacement, if it succeeds, we regard and rightly so as healing, for this constantly effective process of self-deceiving, pretending and blundering, is no psychopathological mechanism, but the essence of reality, the—as it were—continuous blunder."[34]

In Rank's "will therapy," the search for truth and the construction of theory to explain behavior were rejected for a quicker and simpler creation of a patchwork set of illusions with which the patient might live. Under such circumstances it is clear how it was possible for Rank to introduce his therapy as uniquely shortened, with a prescribed termination date for the overall process. Although Freud described this shortened therapy as "designed to accelerate the tempo of analytic therapy to suit the rush to American life,"[35] and others saw it as an accommodation to modern urban existence, Rank insisted that it was genuinely an integral part of his overall dynamic psychology, which was more attuned to modern culture than other forms of psychology. While Russell Jacoby[36] and others have argued repeatedly that Freud seemed more interested in theory than therapy, Freud could not, in any ultimate sense, have split the two. For him, the aim of analytic theory was to discover the truth, which was itself therapeutic. Rank's shift from theory to therapy thus indicated both his distrust of thinking about our past and his rejection of the search for and therapeutic value of truth itself.

Even though Freud insisted that psychoanalysis was a "science," the possibility of ever empirically validating many of the poetically derived truths of his science remained problematic. When Freud gave up the search, in his patients' histories, to determine what actually happened, and instead accepted their childhood fantasies as reality, he was closer to Rank's position than either man would care to admit. Nevertheless, Freud believed that universal patterns existed in the unconscious which he had discovered and which others, through his method of free association, could come to understand. On the other hand, Rank believed that *all* was illusion, and as such the search for truth itself was an illusion.

Rank repeatedly argued that Freudian psychoanalysis was ideologically laden by its search for universal patterns, while his own dynamic psychology was concerned with the individual in an assumedly less ideological way.[37] Although many of his patients reported his concern for the individual, his involvement in the therapeutic process reflected clear ideological assumptions. For example, when Rank helped Anais Nin discover the creative "woman within,"[38] she did so by moving rather quickly through his three conceptual categories of people: the lowest kind, the average person, whom he held in low esteem—they comprised the herd that lived and thrived on illusions as reality; the next highest was the neurotic type, who feared life or saw too much truth and had difficulty living with those illusions because of a negative inverted will; and lastly, the highest type was the creative artist, who made use of his or her conscious will to be creative. With Rank's help Anais Nin discovered that she was no ordinary woman—she was a creative artist.

Rank categorized people according to their consciousness: "The average man has reality consciousness more strongly developed, the creative type will consciousness, the neurotic individual self consciousness. Reality consciousness comes from adaptation of will, the creative phantasy consciousness from will affirmation, the neurotic self consciousness from will denial."[39] To him these were nonideological descriptions of types of people existing within civilization as social givens. Self-destructive neurotics were necessary as a kind of fertilizer of civilization.

> I think it is the type which we today designate as neurotic which the New Testament characterizes as "christian" and which Nietzsche in the ideology of earlier times has described as the slave type. These humans who constantly kill themselves, perhaps to escape being sacrificed, need at all events not to be killed any more in order to be utilized as fertilizers of civilization (Kulturdunger, an expression used by Freud who applied it in another connection). In offering themselves up as it were in a Christian sense, they make it not too hard for the others who slay, the lordly natures, the men of will.[40]

What, then, is to be done with these types of people? Are they to be cured of their neuroses so that they, too, might become creative artists like Rank,[41] or are they to be constructively adapted to the "patient docile Philistine" life which is the "usual lot of mankind"? Rank went on to say: "In view of the difficulties of the therapy one must ask whether it is not a vain therapeutic ambition to want to transform this sacrificial type into god-men, and even if this were successful, where shall be forthcoming the necessary hecatombs for the creative type."[42] The social order that Rank postulated in 1929 was one of "sacrificial types" and "god-men" or "creative types" who required sacrificial types for the slaughter. This view was ominously close to that of the fascists, who a few years later were stoking the crematoriums.

Rank concluded his discussion of will therapy on a note of adjustment to the inevitable neurotic splits in life, themselves a part of the creative process of life. Just as Schopenhauer had insisted that a person's character may not change, Rank insisted that,

> The patient must learn to live, to live with his split, his conflict, his ambivalence, which no therapy can take away, for if it could, it would take with it the actual spring of life. . . . If he only understands how to live in harmony with the inevitable, that is, with the inevitable in himself, not outside, then he will also be able to accept reality as it is. This is no fatalistic and passive acceptance, but rather an active constructive utilization. . . . In the last analysis therapy can only strive for a new attitude towards the self, a new valuation of it in relation to the past, and a new balancing in relation to and by means of, present reality.[43]

Rank's nonideological view of the social reality toward which adjustment was necessary was the clear recognition that the average individual "needs the external compulsion" and the neurotic needs to defend against too much external as well as internal compulsion. Only the artist, as the creative type, can "overcome compulsion through freedom" and use the positive will to create "for itself against the compulsion a reality of its own which makes it independent, but at the same time enables it to live in reality without falling into conflict with it."[44] While accepting themselves and their inner ideal formation, artists seek to adjust their environment and others to themselves. Sometimes this is done violently, as in the case of thoughtless people of action, but it reaches

> its highest level when the individual creates from himself and his own idealized will power, a world for himself, as the artist or the philosopher does, without wanting to force it on others. Certainly this peculiarly creative type also strives for recognition but it cannot as with the therapeutic reformative personality, be through force or violence, but rather must be the expression of a spontaneous movement of the individual who finds in the creator something related to himself.[45]

In the end, Rank saw himself as moving *Beyond Psychology* (1941), leaving behind all ideologically oriented psychology and insisting that ultimately there were no logical patterns within the human soul other than the highly individualized and nonideological ones he had described in *Will Therapy*. He came to the conclusion that his lifelong search "beyond" individual psychology led him not to a social psychology but to the "irrational basis of human nature which lies beyond any psychology, individual or collective."[46]

Rank's will therapy clearly was not free of ideological assumptions and commitments. His belief in the irrational basis of human nature and the social order, along with his rejection of the Socratic search for truth and his faith in the therapeutic uses of illusions, derived from a social perspective that accepted the injustice and suffering of humanity as necessarily realistic and saw the mass of people in terms of "Pharisees" or slaves, leaving only the creative elite free of compulsion. Perhaps it was Rank's social ideology which made his ideas about reality and illusion appear so relevant to psychiatric social workers in America. His exact impact on the field of social work is difficult to determine, however. Erich Fromm's suggestive hypothesis—that the effect of Rank's will therapy on social work is to place the problematic blame on the client rather than on social conditions and the economic structure[47]—requires further research and cannot be fully explored here. A cursory look at the evidence, however, suggests that Fromm might have been correct, especially if Almena Dawley, chief social worker for the Philadelphia Child Guidance Clinic, was accurate when she suggested, in her sympathetic eulogy of Rank, that the effect of his client-centered will therapy was to help the social worker see the need for emphasizing the "will" of the client rather than the content of the "worker's ideology."[48]

The question of Rank's influence on social workers in this country is complicated by many factors, not the least of which is how he is interpreted by those who use his therapeutic insights in social work. Some, such as Fay B. Karpf, interpret Rank's "therapeutic approach and general thought" as nonauthoritarian and client-centered. What authoritarian characteristics Karpf finds in Rank she attributes to his years of association with Freud and "other Freudians." In his post-Freudian years, she believes, he was nonauthoritarian because he argued for "the equal right of every individual to become and be himself, which actually means to accept his own differences and have it accepted by others."[49] While it is clear that the authoritarian characteristics implicit in Rank's philosophy and psychology predate and postdate his experiences with Freud, it is equally clear that the "client-centered" therapy espoused and used by Rank was highly authoritarian.

Unshackled by any authoritative concern for truth, the will therapist simply could help the client adjust to whatever illusions seemed to work. This gave the illusion of being nonauthoritarian. However, once the client entered into the therapeutic process, he or she would be categorized as one of Rank's three character types, and the corresponding problematic illusory world would be readily interpreted. Rank's short-cut therapy, as described by Anais Nin, was, in effect, highly authoritative.[50]

Was Rank an ideological fascist, as Fromm claimed, or was he, as he saw himself, *Der Kunstler*, someone who neurotically had seen too much reality but, through the power of his own creative will, had fashioned his way *Beyond Psychology* to freedom for himself and his patients? Rank had drunk deeply from that wellspring of nineteenth-century neo-romantic consciousness which, amid the growing crisis of the middle class in the twentieth century, had become a raging torrent of irrationalism, finding expression in modern art, music, literature, religion, and politics. In this sense, fascism was not an unfortunate accident of the twentieth century, dismissed once and for all by the Allied victory in 1945; rather, it was a political expression of a deeper cultural stream of consciousness that was not readily reversed by the force of arms. While much of the ideology upon which Rank based his dynamic psychology was similar to, if not the same as, many fascist ideologies in the twentieth century, he clearly stopped short of those who advocated the use of force and violence. If anything, his was a nonviolent, if not a "friendly," fascism. Yet the very conceptual structure of his thought inclined him to think in terms of a large segment of humanity as providing "the necessary hecatombs for the creative type." If Fromm was correct when he claimed that much of the philosophy that undergirded Rank's psychology was fascist, what can we make of Fromm's suggestion that such a philosophy may be nurtured under different symbols and terms?

Were fascism to be conceived of as the political by-product of a deeper cultural and ideological consciousness, whose psychosocial origins were transactionally related to the crisis of the middle class and the corporate structure sustaining that class, then it is clear that the underlying stream of irrationalism from which that fascism sprang not only persists but continues to find increasing expression in virtually every aspect of modern corporate culture, even though many of the specific historical circumstances that seem to have triggered some Western nations into the political fascism of the 1920s and the 1930s may no longer exist. The failure of society to develop a more humane political economy, one that lends to young and old alike a sense of worth, dignity, and purpose, underlies the decadence of our times. In this age, some frantically search for their "roots" to overcome an alienated existence; others turn off to life with drugs, alcohol, contemplation, and gurus; still others seek escape in the violence of punk rock, the absurdities of Chris Burden's "performance art," the psychic-enslavement in Synanon- and Moonie-type religious cults, the comforts of the plastic-packaged-middle-class-Praise-the-Lord phenomena, or the ultimate sickness unto death of the Jim Jones "religious" experience. Today, our art, music, literature, religion, philosophy, and psychology profoundly reflect the deeper malaise of the false consciousness emanating from our existentially alienated existence. With Rank, we therapeutically embrace this world of consciousness. Under the circumstances, it is understandable why such modern literary artists as Anais Nin and Henry Miller found Rank's sense of reality so appealing.

While the exact impact of Rank's thought on the field of psychiatric social work remains in doubt, the relevance of his ideas as a psychological reflection of the state of much of modern consciousness seems less doubtful. In retrospect, we might ask to what extent his subjective, relativistic view of reality and knowledge, his view of truth seeking as not only impossible but destructive, his elitist view of the social order, and his therapeutic uses of illusions more accurately reflect the course of Western culture than either Marx's or Freud's search for truth. The answer might give us some clue as to how far modern culture has not only adopted a fascist philosophy under different symbols and terms, but how far modern culture itself has abandoned the Enlightenment vision of both its past and future, and in so doing has destroyed the rational foundation of its own thought.

Notes

1. Erich Fromm, "The Social Philosophy of Will Therapy," *Psychiatry* 2(May 1939): 229–37.

2. In his article, Fromm recognized some reservations and indicated that there were certain contradictory elements in Rank's thinking that ran against his analysis. On the whole, however, he insisted that Rank held a fascist social philosophy. See ibid., p. 237.

3. Quoted in Jessie Taft, *Otto Rank* (New York: Julian Press, 1958), p. 258.

4. For an extended analysis of the complicated variety of ways fascism can be viewed, see Walter Laqueur, *Fascism: A Reader's Guide* (Berkeley: University of California Press, 1976).

5. Quoted in Martin Kitchen, "Ernst Nolte and the Phenomenology of Fascism," *Science and Society* 38(Summer 1974): 131.

6. See ibid. It should also be noted that Ernst Nolte was a student of Heidegger in Freiburg during the Third Reich. Heidegger, during those years, was a fascist himself. See Henry Pachter, "Heidegger and Hitler: The Incompatibility of Geist and Politics," *Boston University Journal* 24(3, 1976): 47.

7. For example, see William Raymond Manchester, *The Arms of Krupp* (Boston: Little Brown, 1968), and Joseph Borkin, *The Crime and Punishment of I. G. Farben* (New York: Macmillan Co., 1978).

8. There are, for example, some very interesting unexplored similarities over a period of time within this structure. When monopoly capitalism was being consolidated on a national scale at the turn of the century in America, and the American liberal state emerged as part of the political-social infrastructure, the National Civic Federation was formed to serve the interests of big labor, banking, corporations, and government by smoothing out their differences so that the overall system might work more effectively. See Gabriel Kolko, *The Triumph of Conservatism* (London: Free Press/Macmillan, 1963); James Weinstein, *The Corporate Ideal in the Liberal State: 1900–1918* (Boston: Beacon Press, 1968); and Robert H. Wiebe, *The Search for Order* (New York: Hill and Wang, 1967). In a strikingly similar way, today's liberals have attempted to pull together the interests of big labor, banking, multinational corporations, and government in the form of the Tri-Lateral Commission, which includes Japan, Western Europe, and America, in an attempt to iron out differences between the three major producing regions of the Western world. The purpose of the Tri-Lateral Commission is similar to that of the National Civic Federation; the difference, of course, is that NCF was national and TLC is international. See Michael J. Crozier, Samuel P. Huntington, and Joji Watanuki, *The Crisis of Democracy* (New York: New York University Press, 1975).

9. Fyodor Dostoyevski, *The Brothers Karamazov* (New York: Macmillan Co., 1912), p. 269.

10. Quoted in Taft, *Otto Rank*, p. 20.

11. See Ernest Jones, *The Life and Work of Sigmund Freud*, 3 vols. (New York: Basic Books, 1953, 1955, 1957), 2:160. See also Taft, *Otto Rank*, pp. 3–58.

12. Taft, *Otto Rank*, p. 22.

13. Ibid., p. 15.

14. Ibid., pp. 51, 52.

15. Sigmund Freud, *Collected Papers* (London: Hogarth Press, 1953), 1:307.

16. Gunther Stuhlmann, ed., *The Diary of Anais Nin*, 7 vols. (New York: Harcourt Brace and World, 1966), 1:279.

17. At the time Rank moved into the circle, it included Ferenczi, Abraham, Jones, Sachs, and Eitingon.

18. Otto Rank, *Truth and Reality* (1929; New York: W. W. Norton, 1978), p. 18.

19. For a critical treatment of Rank's behavior during this period (1923–26) see Ernest Jones, *Sigmund Freud: Life and Work*, vol. 3 (London: Hogarth Press, 1927); for a sympathetic account, see Taft, *Otto Rank*; for a more balanced treatment, see Paul Roazen, *Freud and His Followers* (New York: Alfred A. Knopf, 1975).

20. See Roazen, *Freud and His Followers*, p. 407.

21. See Jones, *Sigmund Freud: Life and Work*, 3:59–127.

22. Quoted in Roazen, *Freud and His Followers*, pp. 417–18. Roazen also reports that shortly before Freud died, Hans Sachs confirmed the fact that Freud had Rank in mind when writing this statement.

23. Ibid., pp. 408–18.

24. Taft, *Otto Rank*, p. 120.

25. Marcel Proust's *Remembrance of Things Past* comes immediately to mind.

26. For a discussion of these points see Arnold Hauser, *The Philosophy of Art History* (New York: World Publishing Co., 1963), p. 62.

27. It is essentially for these reasons that Marxists such as Arnold Hauser (ibid., p. 69) and others from the Frankfurt School could attempt to reinterpret Freud within an overall Marxist view of the social order. See Martin Jay, *The Dialectical Imagination* (Boston: Little Brown, 1973).

28. T. B. Bottomore, ed., *Karl Marx* (New York: McGraw Hill Book Co., 1956), p. 27.

29. Sigmund Freud, *The Future of an Illusion* (New York: Anchor Books, 1964), p. 92.

30. Note that Ludwig Wittgenstein, another twentieth-century philosopher who was deeply influenced by Schopenhauer, ended his thought with a similar pessimistic conclusion. For Schopenhauer's influence on Wittgenstein, see G. E. M. Anscombe, *Notebook 1914–1916* (Oxford: Oxford University Press, 1961).

31. Rank, *Truth and Reality*, p. 39.

32. Ibid., p. 42.

33. See Otto Rank, *Will Therapy* (New York: W. W. Norton and Co., 1978), p. 172.

34. Rank, *Truth and Reality*, p. 42.

35. Quoted in Jones, *Sigmund Freud: Life and Work*, 3:81.

36. See Russell Jacoby, *Social Amnesia* (Boston: Beacon Press, 1975).

37. See Rank, *Will Therapy*, pp. 106–7.

38. Stuhlmann, *Diary of Anais Nin*, p. 276.

39. Rank, *Truth and Reality*, p. 43.

40. Rank, *Will Therapy*, p. 200.

41. Rank literally conceived of himself as a creative artist, one who therapeutically created people.

42. Rank, *Will Therapy*, p. 200.

43. Ibid., p. 206.

44. Rank, *Truth and Reality*, p. 58.

45. Ibid.

46. Otto Rank, *Beyond Psychology* (Camden, N.J.: Haddon Craftsmen, 1941), p. 12.

47. See Erich Fromm, "The Social Philosophy of Will Therapy," *Psychiatry* 2(May 1939): 237. Christine M. Shea has begun such an exploration in "Otto Rank, Jessie Taft, and Functional Casework: A Case Study of the University of Pennsylvania School of Social Work," *Psychiatric Forum* 13(2, Winter 1984).

48. See Almena Dawley, "Otto Rank's Contribution to Social Work," *Social Work Today* (Jan. 1940): 19.

49. Fay B. Karpf, *The Psychology and Psychotherapy of Otto Rank* (New York: Philosophical Library, 1953), p. 16.

50. Stuhlmann, *Diary of Anais Nin*, 1:269–310.

Epilogue

In Otto Rank's will therapy we can sense the ultimate destruction of reason and the end of the Enlightenment quest for scientific understanding of mind. Rank's philosophical mentor, Arthur Schopenhauer, cast a long dark shadow across much of twentieth-century thought. Both he and Ludwig Wittgenstein came to the conclusion that ultimately "philosophy ends in silence," and in so doing gave way to a growing world of nihilistic value that reflected the kind of philosophical and cultural alienation crucial to creating the social reality on which many fascist minds were nurtured in the twentieth century.

Their conclusion clearly reflects the overall path that philosophy as a field of human discourse has taken in this century. From the early 1900s, philosophy as a discipline has become narrower in its concerns and increasingly divorced from the human condition, in spite of some valiant attempts by John Dewey and others to redirect it. A critical point in that narrowing and separating came at the turn of the century, when psychology separated from philosophy. That separation occurred in part as a consequence of the development of science and the increasing secularization of culture. We have witnessed an astounding expansion of scientific knowledge, and with it the secularization of the mind. Virtually all founders of modern psychology saw themselves as scientists of the mind—and thus secularizers of the human condition. As each one set out to cultivate his or her own science, each made unique, but inevitable, philosophical and religious assumptions regarding human nature.

On the wings of science, for better or worse, psychology

separated from philosophy as a discrete discipline. Philosophy, the parent discipline, traditionally had served as the reasoned linkage between what functioned as psychology and the much larger field of religion. Now, both fields moved away from religion. During the end of the nineteenth century, religious credibility suffered a serious decline as a consequence of a growing belief in Darwinian evolution, an increased respect for science, and a developing secularization of culture. As psychology separated from philosophy, and both turned away from religion, the theological society of the nineteenth century made way for the psychological society of the twentieth century.

William James served as midwife at the birth of the psychological society and reflected on its development in *The Varieties of Religious Experience*, which was most appropriately subtitled "A Study in Human Nature." His reconstruction of the ontological existence of God, from its embattled traditional Judeo-Christian moorings in the First Commandment to its serving a personal therapeutic psychological function, was crucial in building the intellectual bridge over which many modern people would pass from the theological society of their childhood to the psychological society of their adult lives. With James, that first and most important commandment undergirding the theological society, "I am the Lord thy God, thou shalt not have strange Gods before me," gave way to a belief in God based solely on pragmatic, therapeutic consequences. In a very real sense, James built a halfway house, designed to give shelter to those not yet ready to walk into the godless world of secularized twentieth-century culture.

As founders of modern American psychology, James and his students—George Herbert Mead, Edward L. Thorndike, G. Stanley Hall, and others—busily redefined human nature along more secular "scientific" lines. A founder of social psychology, Mead greatly influenced the social sciences, while Thorndike influenced educational psychology, and Hall significantly influenced the areas of child psychology and the development of adolescent psychology. As they forged their own particular psychological movement and developed their own peculiar science of the mind, each uniquely reflected the personal psychological problems with which they struggled and, more importantly, their own particular philosophical and religious assumptions regarding human nature. Each major movement of modern psychology was literally constructed out of these competing assumptions. In many respects these early assumptions have remained implicit, often unexamined, and continue to mark the ideological structural difference between competing psychologies throughout this century.

As noted in the Introduction, the theological society did not disappear with the rise of the psychological society—the two coexisted, each serving large groups of people. While many continued to trust in the religious construction of human nature and its explanation for human behavior, others put their trust in modern psychology. Just as religious clerics described the conditions of the "soul," psychologists described the conditions of the "mind"; if the former seemed to have trouble describing the existence of the "soul," so did the latter find it difficult to explain the "unconscious mind." While clerics spoke of "human character" as central to their concerns, psychologists spoke of "personality." To heal socially inflicted wounds, the religious community had developed both public and private confession; analogously, the psychological community developed the therapy session. Clerics spoke of conscience and sin, while psychologists spoke of a super ego and sickness.

Although Karl Marx found the reason for the existence of religious belief in the sentiment of a heartless world and the "soul of soulless conditions," and William James found it in the "help" that it offered a suffering humanity, the psychological society found its reason for existence in large part in its healing function. While Marx, in the nineteenth century, found religion to be an "opiate of the people," many people found psychology to have become such an opiate in the twentieth century. At the heart of the oppressed condition within the religious community was the issue of human deviation and the problem of "sin." At the center of the oppressed condition and human deviation within the psychological community was "sickness." Both communities developed their own mechanism for handling specific problems of guilt and aggression. Older, traditional religious communities had, over the centuries, developed rational checks on the use of these mechanisms; the newer religious cults, such as the Moonies and the Jim Jones cults, have not. As a consequence, the latter strike us as bizarre, indeed dangerous, because they have not yet developed the rationalized infrastructure that serves to check the use of such social control techniques. The techniques themselves, whether employed by the old church, the new church, or the psychological society, are all essentially the same techniques of human control.

While the religious community was concerned with "sin" and saving souls for eternal life, the psychological community was concerned with the sick soul and healing it for this life. In probing his own unconscious, Freud believed he had discovered the psychic terrain wherein the two worlds met, where "evil" was transformed into "sickness." Where the great religious traditions had analyzed the structure of evil, the modern psychological community claimed to analyze scientifically the structure of mental illness. Just as the religious community divided into competing cults to explain human nature, so too did the psychological community. Both communities vied for credibility; and both dealt with the same human subject, often making similar religious or philosophical assumptions. As the two fields became separated from what should have been their natural critic—i.e., philosophy— their basic assumptions respecting human nature tended to go unexamined. Philosophy had less and less a role to play, as it fell silent on the issue of critical human relationships. The individual who faced serious personal problems with respect to his or her soul or mind might turn to a religious cleric or to a psychologist for "help"; few, however, would turn to a philosopher. Philosophy had long ago vacated the field of such human relationships.

The need for critical philosophical analysis nevertheless remains. Under the present circumstances it is not difficult—or surprising—to find modern therapists in clinical practice often making unexamined philosophical and religious assumptions in the name of a science of mind. Recall that virtually all the major intellectual founders of the science of mind carried with them a large set of philosophical and religious assumptions which they retained from childhood, often in the name of science itself. For example, we can see in Freud's theories the ancient Hebraic doctrine of original sin, just as we can sense in George Herbert Mead's the reformist Christian ministry which placed the virtue of "cooperation" at the center of the community. Mead clearly transformed the Christian concept of the golden rule of loving thy neighbor as thyself, as reflected in Matt. 7:12, into his vision of the social self within the functioning moral community. Equally clear is the fact that to a considerable extent the stimulus-response psychology of the founder of behaviorist psychology was rooted in the meaning of reward and punishment, as reflected in his Baptist childhood. While Carl Jung found the faith of his father inadequate and reached back to the ancient world for the gnostic beliefs so necessary to his interpretation of the world, G. Stanley Hall drew on a variety of modern and ancient primitive cults to give shape to his evolutionary conception of "Mansoul." The faith that Alfred Adler described in terms of "social interest," in the end, was not far removed from that of Norman Vincent Peale. Thus, in shaping their own psychology, each of these figures fashioned his or her unique view of human nature and implicitly incorporated his or her religious and philosophical dimensions of life. Mead's social psychology, Thorndike's educational psychology, Hall's child psychology, Watson's behaviorism, and the therapies of Freud, Adler, Jung, Naumberg, and Rank all carried with them the largely unexamined religious and philosophical views of their founders.

Built into these psychological conceptions were also the peculiar psychological problems each individual had struggled to overcome. The two major movements that have dominated American psychology, behaviorism and psychoanalysis, were both nurtured in the crucible of the neuroses of their founders. Watson's fear of the dark and Freud's travel phobia were both clearly related to each man's scientific discoveries of mind. While Freud sought and thought he had found the laws governing both the conscious and unconscious mind, he was, it seems, still a nineteenth-century figure who embraced the rationalistic scientific principles of the Enlightenment. Watson, on the other hand, was more clearly a twentieth-century figure. His espousal of a "mindless" conception of human nature, which reduced his scientific behaviorism to mere technique, was highly relevant in manipulating masses of people in the modern world. His rejection of any philosophical or religious values governing the human mind, the existence of which he denied altogether, was highly significant. Scientific psychology predicated on the purely technical principle of prediction and control of human behavior could and readily did serve any master. Watson's stimulus-response behaviorism, unencumbered as it was by religious or philosophical ethics, could be used by anyone for whatever social purpose they desired. It is perfectly clear that Watson felt free to propagate whatever personal prejudice satisfied his childhood needs and whims, all under the guise of a scientific psychology. The perniciousness of separating means from ends, as John Dewey so often warned, perhaps is nowhere clearer than in Watson's case; and he did, of course, fully admit that he never really understood either Mead or Dewey.

The problem of separation of means from ends continues to

plague modern psychology and has only magnified since Dewey's time. Academic philosophers have tended to avoid discussing this very difficult problem. However, B. F. Skinner and other behavioral psychologists have postulated, in the name of science, that they treat the human being as an empty organism. In practice, that organism is virtually always filled with the ends and values of the "scientific" psychologist, who usually turns out to be simply representing the most socially, economically, and politically powerful. A scientific psychology of means could not determine the ends toward which humankind *ought* to strive. On the other hand, means could be highly significant in the determination of the end toward which humankind has striven. Means, reduced to the control and prediction of rat and dog behavior, projected onto human behavior, reduced human behavior to that of rat and dog behavior—therein exists the modern dilemma of the separation of modern psychology from both philosophy and religion behind the mantle of science. William James was quite correct when he warned psychologists that by their conception of human nature they can exalt human life or just as easily debase it. It is regrettable that so few psychologists have heeded his warning.

While the intellectual founders of modern psychology carried with them their own religious and/or philosophical assumptions regarding human nature, they often behaved as if they were creating alternative religious sects for the secular mind of the twentieth century. Freud's identification with Moses and Hall's identification with Jesus and Buddha are striking examples. Clearly, the young followers of Freud, Hall, Jung, Watson, Adler, and others appeared to be joining something more than a scientific movement in search of truth. The leader was most often treated as a lawgiver and a purveyor of what was and what was not acceptable dogma. In addition, in all of the lives examined here, except perhaps that of George Herbert Mead, we can find lurking an authoritarian figure. Authoritarianism was expressed in a variety of ways, each person hammering out a profession of scientific psychology and the particular niche carved for himself or herself. While we may be struck by the extent to which the authoritarian character repeatedly emerged, we must realize that without that strong-willed personality, confident in his or her authority, the movement might not have been founded at all.

As these men and women fashioned the structural foundations of the secular psychological society of the twentieth century, some began to reflect on what became, for many, a major rejection of the Enlightenment faith in the principles of science, reason, freedom, and rational understanding. The winds of nihilism, which swept up many European intellectuals at the turn of the century and helped generate the intellectual reality out of which many fascist minds were later to emerge, were also reflected in some of the ideas of the founders of modern psychology. Clearly, Hall's views on freedom and his discussion of "Mansoul" came very close to what later transpired in Germany. He was sensitive to some of the major currents of his time, which in the following decades revealed themselves as powerful fascist torrents. Just as clearly, Jung's gnostic groping not only embraced a reactionary past but, more importantly, it anesthetized the soul of the "apolitical scientist" from the barbarism of the fascist world. Rank obviously drank deeply from the neo-romantic well of nihilistic values and in the end denied the Enlightenment faith in human nature and its potential for human understanding. Fromm's charge that Rank's will therapy carried with it the intellectual ingredients and basic philosophical assumption of fascism appears, in retrospect, quite accurate. Although none of these men would be pleased to have their thought associated with fascism, each in his own conception of human nature sensitively reflected some of the major currents of the twentieth century that eventually emerged in full force as a fascist conception of mind and society. Unfortunately, the nihilism of value and the intellectual fascist milieu that grew out of such thought survived the war against fascism, much as Fromm feared it would.

As modern psychology continued to develop and become institutionalized, finding growing acceptance in both the medical and educational professions, it gradually became accepted in popular culture as well. In the face of a rising tide of scientific secularism, religion retreated, although it has managed to survive. By the third quarter of the twentieth century it was clear that Nietzsche's nineteenth-century death-of-God announcement had been premature. A large number of people have maintained their faith in spite of the growing secularization of our society. Some have had difficulty accepting the traditional view of God and have adopted the Jamesian justification of faith. They continue to believe in God because it satisfies their psychological need for something "more" in the universe.

Religious clerics and psychologists such as the Emmanuelists and Adlerians have insisted that there is no need for conflict between the two societies; others more in tune with Freud and

Hall point to the inevitable conflict. Nowhere are these differences more sharply focused than in an evaluation of human behavior in the courtrooms of this nation. As the psychological explanation for human behavior gradually replaced what was traditionally a religious explanation and found acceptance in the professions of education and medicine, it also became accepted, to a certain extent, by the legal profession. Its increasing use in the courtroom has tested the credibility of not only the psychologist but the field itself. Is the behavior of the defendant sinful or sick? If judged sinful, one kind of treatment ensues, usually involving some form of punishment; if judged sick, some form of mental health treatment is in order. The difficulty, of course, is that virtually all deviant behavior can be classified under either category, depending largely on which society one adheres to. Skinner, for example, argued that all behavior was conditioned and that a full application of a science of human behavior would do away with the constructs of freedom and responsibility, thus making the courts an anachronistic institution to be replaced by mental institutions.

Long ago, Goethe expressed fear that in the therapeutic world of the future, everyone would become everyone else's nurse. Although the world Skinner embraced and Goethe feared has not yet arrived, many of us worry about the increasing jural use of mental illness as an explanation for aberrant human behavior. Others worry about the similar ways in which both the United States and the Soviet Union increasingly define crimes against the state as a sickness requiring commitment to hospitals for prescribed scientific psychological treatment. Fundamental issues of freedom and responsibility are at stake with every insanity plea. While the courts hear a wide variety of such pleas, the tendency seems to be to classify the most extreme sort of behavior as "sick" and therefore requiring treatment. The implication is that one cannot be extremely "sinful"—and thus the more heinous the creme, the greater the chance the deed will go unpunished.

If the courts appeared troubled in determining where the traditional Judeo-Christian code of behavior left off and where the newer scientific psychological explanation took over, so too did the general population. Increasingly, in ordinary discourse, unwelcome behavior on the part of one's neighbors was as readily classified as neurotic or sick as it was classified sinful. The courts, the schools, the medical profession, the public media, and the family unit—all reflected this theological-psychological dichotomy. As people came to live in both worlds, they accepted a large share of unexamined philosophical and religious assumptions regarding human nature and the human condition. James, it seems, was correct in suggesting that when the Galileo of psychology arrived, he or she would, by virtue of the very nature of the subject, be a metaphysician. Clearly, such a person has not yet arrived.

Index

Abraham, Karl: and Otto Rank, 319
Abraxas, 264
Adams, Henry, 7
Adler, Alfred (1870–1937): and ahistorical thinking, 240; career changes, 232, 241; as "Citizen of Vienna" (1930), 243; at Columbia University (1929–31), 243; and communal value of the individual, 245; as competitor of psychoanalytic movement, 234; and cooperative social interest, 229, 242, 247, 339; and cooperative vs. competitive word, 251; and crossing cultural lines, 229; and educational reforms, 243; and experimental schools (Vienna), 243; on faculty at Long Island Medical College (1932), 244; as family physician to Otto Rank, 317; and fictitious history vs. current fictions, 240; and guesses, 237; and holistic psychology, 241; ideas permeate therapeutic community, 251; and the individual as shaper of the environment, 240; and individual psychology, 239, 245; and inferiority, 7; and inferiority complex, 211, 230; as lecturer at Institute of Pedagogical Studies (Vienna), 243; and liberal social reform, 233; as "malicious paranoic," 227; married

Raissa Timofeyevna Epstein (1897), 232; and National Socialists in Vienna (1934), 244; and neurosis as correctable error, 236; and Oedipus complex as masculine protest, 241; and problems of life, 244; as pupil of Sigmund Freud, 226; and repressed role of women, 233; as revenant, 227; and skepticism, 231; terror of dying, 229; and "third-force" psychology, 9; at University of Vienna Medical School, 231, 241; and Vienna Psychoanalytic Society, 226. Works include: *A Health Book for the Tailoring Trade*, 232; *Religion and Individual Psychologie* (with Ernest Jahn, 1933), 245; *Social Interest: A Challenge to Mankind* (1936), 245; *Studies of Organ Inferiority* (1907), 230, 234; *Understanding Human Nature* (1927), 245; *What Life Should Mean to You* (1931), 245
Adlerian groups, in America (1926–34), 243
Adolescence: conceptualized by G. Stanley Hall, 162; as distinct discipline of psychology, 161
Aesthetic revolution, 285
Agassiz, Louis: to Brazil with William James, 31

345

211; religion as, 17; and science, 323; therapeutic use of, 331

Imago, 318

Impressionism: attraction for younger artists, 285; as self-centered search for reality, 288; and spatial sense of reality, 288; as urban art form, 285

Individual existence, 316

Individualism: and laissez-faire political economy, 45; and William James, 49

Individual psychology: academics not acceptant of, 23; and Alfred Adler, 236, 239; and common deity with universal faith of humans, 233; defined, 248; and holistic faith, 249; and liberal reform, 242; as a movement, 241; and neuroses, 235; as part metaphysics, 248; reception in America, 244

Inferiority complex: 228; and Alfred Adler, 230, 251; universalized, 234

Instrumentalism: vs. social psychology, 75

Intelligence tests, 95

Introvert/extrovert, 276

Jacoby, Russell: and Otto Rank, 326

James, William (1842–1910): belief as therapy, 12; and the birth of the psychological society, 29, 161, 169, 336; and classical liberal tradition, 16, 46; degree in medicine (1869), 33; and Edward L. Thorndike, 90; education monitored by his father, 33; and the emerging secular culture, 28; emotional crisis in adolescence, 59; evolutionary position of, 17; and "faith ladder," 40; as father of American psychology, 14, 27, 29; and G. Stanley Hall, 163; and George Herbert Mead, 27, 69; and habit, 16; and human-centered universe of future, 21, 36; and identity crisis, 81; impact on education, through students, 15; and individualism, 93; as instructor at Harvard University (1873), 33; life history of "freedom," 26; lifelong neuras-

thenia, 33; link among psychology, philosophy, and religion, 15; and mysticism, 37; and nineteenth-century romanticism, 45; and Philadelphia School of Social Work, 19; as popularizer of pragmatism, 39, 60; and psychical research, 43; rejection of business world vs. acceptance of class status and values, 27; and secularized mind, 27; as social behaviorist, 76; "stream of consciousness," 306; studied for the ministry, at Princeton University, 30; as teacher, 43; and the therapeutic society, 44; and transition between psychological and theological societies, 12; as undisciplined, intellectual dilettante, 31. Works include: *Principles of Psychology* (1890), 1, 93; *Psychology, the Briefer Course*, 27; *The Varieties of Religious Experience* (1902), 12, 26, 28, 37, 38, 40, 41–42, 59, 129, 172

Jensen, Arthur: and Carl G. Jung's racial psychology, 272

Jones, Ernest: and Alfred Adler, 238; and Sigmund Freud, 210, 319

Jones, Jim: in Guyana, 11

Journal of Applied Psychology, 160

Juenger, Ernst: *Thunder of Steel* (1919), 257

Jung, Carl G. (1875–1961), 17, 227, 264, 290; and Alfred Adler, 210; and capitalist society as sick society, 277; direct religious experience as youth, 260; as "doctor of the soul," 274; and gnosticism, 19, 211, 260–62; and mystical faith, 212; and the psychoanalytic movement, 197; reality vs. Sigmund Freud's illusions, 259; as Sigmund Freud's prodigy, 209, 211; stereotyped view of Jews, 270; and "third-force" psychology, 9; and *Zentralblatt* (1934), 270, 275

Jungian process of individuation: in *Demian*, 257, 263

Jungian theory: and expressionist literature, 292

Justification of belief, 12

Index

vs. James B. Watson's environment, 96; and efficiency movement in education, 101; and egalitarianism, 100; as elitist, 98; and empirical psychology, 94; and eugenics, 99–100; as evolutionist, 95; faith in empirical science, 90; and heredity, 99, 100; impact on American education, 91, 101; and individual differences, 92; as individualist, 93; institutionalized bias of, 102; "knowledge is power," 90; and measurable behavioral objectives, 97; and meritocratic order/system, 46, 92; and moral education, 90; and new liberalism, 93; and new naturalistic faith, 90; and objective quantitative measurement, 96; and parents, Abbie Ladd and Edward Robert Thorndike, 89; and positivistic science, 90, 91; and predestination of the elect, 96; program for social progress, 99; and quantitative science of education, 97; and religion as irrational, 91; and scientific management, 94, 101; and segregation of superior intellects, 98; and social class system, 94; views on men and women, 97; at Wesleyan, Harvard, and Columbia universities, 90–91; and William James, 17, 46–47, 47–48; work with teachers, 93. Works include: *Animal Intelligence*, 118; *Educational Psychology: Briefer Course* (1914), 94; *Individuality*, 48; *Introduction to the Theory of Mental and Social Measurements* (1904), 95; *The Measurement of Intelligence* (1926), 95; *The Miracle* (a morality play), 89
Titchener, Edward: attacked by Edward L. Thorndike, 129; at Cornell University, 127
Toynbee, Arnold, 261
Transcendentalism, New England, 167
Transcendental meditation, 11
Transference, 207
Trotsky, Leon: *The Struggle Against Fascism in Germany*, 314

Twentieth-century movements: capitalism, 45, 50, 314; consciousness, 321; new bohemianism, 286; psychoanalysis, 259; scientific investigation, 259; secular psychological society, 340; totalitarianism, 185

Unconscious mind, 337; depth of, 303

Valéry, Paul, 258
Varhinger, H., *The Philosophy of "As If,"* 240
Vastation (Swedenborgian), 32; and William James's father, 42
Vienna Psychological Society, 210

Wagner, Richard, 178; creative artistry, 316, 321
Walden School (1914): 294
Wallace, Alfred: debt to Thomas Malthus, 5
Ward, Lester Frank: *Applied Sociology*, 6; attacked by Edward L. Thorndike, 100
Wasserman, Isidor, 237
Watson, John B. (1878–1958): and the AAAS, 131; as advertising vice-president, 134; and Albert B., 131; and animal psychology, 118, 119, 129; and associative learning in rats, 123; attacks Flechsig's "centers of association" theory, 122; basis for behaviorist revolution, 120; and "Batesburg Institute," 117; and "brave new world," 147; charisma of, 129; and Charles Darwin's *The Descent of Man*, 128; as child development expert, 112; college and vocations, 116; compulsion to work, 112; and conditioned reflex, 108; and consumer consciousness, 150; and consumer-oriented society, 136, 137; and depression, 145, 147; dialogue with Will Durant, 143; dogma of exclusive salvation, 109, 149; as environmentalist/determinist, 143; and experiments on children, 131; as expert in animal behavior, 127; fairness, humility of, 108; fear as a conditioned reflex,